W9-DGM-269

ROBIN MOORE

— THE —

GREEN BERETS

BALLANTINE BOOKS • NEW YORK

Library of Congress Catalog Card Number: 65-15849

ISBN   0-345-30747-X

Manufactured in the United States of America

First Ballantine Books Edition: January 1983

U.S. Army Photo by Ron Staszcuk

Two people made it possible for me to write this book, and to them, my parents, it is fondly and gratefully dedicated.

ACKNOWLEDGMENTS

Many interested people helped make this book possible.

Lieutenant Colonel Robert Prentiss at the Magazine and Book Branch of the office of the Chief of Information of the Department of the Army was first assigned to shepherd me through the mysterious corridors of Department of Defense procedure, and his successor, Lieutenant Colonel Charles W. Burtyk, Jr., has continued to give me much appreciated advice and cooperation. Major Barbara Jones at Office of the Chief of Information (OCINFO) gave generously of her time and interest in furthering the cause, and Lieutenant Sam Young, who has since left OCINFO to return to his old stand at Curtis Publishing Co., was of great assistance to me through the various crises which threatened my project as the moment of truth—i.e., my leaving for Vietnam—approached.

Major General William P. Yarborough, until recently Commanding General of the John F. Kennedy Special Warfare Center at Fort Bragg, certainly was one of the biggest influences on me during the entire research that went into writing this book. It was General Yarborough who made me understand the many intangible factors of irregular warfare—of which actual combat is only a part, albeit an important part—in Special Forces operations.

I feel a special place in my heart for the 7th Special Forces Group (Airborne) at Fort Bragg. I made my first night jump into the swamps with them on Swiftstrike III. The 7th gave me special equipment when I needed it, and sergeants of the 7th instructed me in the fine art of rappelling.

Colonel Theodore Leonard, Commanding Officer, U.S. Army Special Forces, Vietnam, (USASFV) made it possible for me to see the war at first hand all over the country. Lieutenant Colonel Joseph Font, Executive Officer, USASFV, somehow managed to keep track of me, and it was reassuring to know someone knew where I was at all times. And there was Sergeant Larry Throneburg, Colonel Leonard's secretary, an eighteen-month veteran of the war in Vietnam, who accompanied me on my first visit to an A team—and drew combat pay that month.

I must thank Special Forces veteran "Hare in the Eye," who was so helpful to me on the more covert and clandestine side of operations in Indo-China.

Major Irwin Nye, the very professional public information officer at the John F. Kennedy Special Warfare Center, at Fort Bragg, N.C., followed this project through from its inception and gave aid and comfort in a hundred different ways.

Major General George (Bud) Underwood, Chief of Information, U.S. Army, personally put in a great deal of time and effort clearing the way for much of the personal research I did.

I will always be grateful to Lieutenant Edward Charles Smith of Cleveland, Ohio, who took me in hand when I arrived, apprehensive and unknowledgeable, at Fort Benning to go through the Airborne School. And a word of commendation for such skilled instructors as Sergeant Garrison, who caught me just before I jumped from the 34-foot tower with a maladjusted harness.

During the final days of writing *The Green Berets*, Brigadier General Joseph W. Stilwell, new Commanding General of the John F. Kennedy Special Warfare Center, carried on General Yarborough's spirit of cooperation and encouragement which made this book on irregular warfare possible.

Throughout my tour in Vietnam, I lived with many Special Forces A and B detachments. Every man I met contributed in one way or another to the content and characterizations in the following stories. It is to these men that I owe the greatest debt of gratitude, and I sincerely hope they will feel that this book is a true portrayal of them and their activities in Vietnam and around the world.

Many people and institutions gave me assistance while I wrote this book, and for their help I thank the Sheraton Hotels in New York, San Francisco, and Washington, D.C.; Barbara Norton; Audrey Wertheim; Phyllis Fairbanks, lyricist and publisher of *The Green Beret*, official song of Special Forces, and Chet Gierlach, co-publisher. Also my brother, John Moore, biggest helper of all.

ROBIN MOORE

CONTENTS

BADGE OF
COURAGE

The Green Berets is a book of truth. I planned and researched it originally to be an account presenting, through a series of actual incidents, an inside informed view of the almost unknown marvelous undercover work of our Special Forces in Vietnam and countries around the world. It was to be a factual book based on personal experience, first-hand knowledge and observation, naming persons and places. But it turned out that there were major obstacles and disadvantages in this straight reportorial method. And so, for the variety of reasons mentioned below, I decided I could present the truth better and more accurately in the form of fiction.

You will find in these pages many things that you will find hard to believe. Believe them. They happened this way. I changed details and names, but I did not change the basic truth. I could not tell the basic truth without changing the details and the names. Here's why.

Many of the stories incorporate a number of events which if reported merely in isolation would fail to give the full meaning and background of the war in Vietnam. Saigon's elite press corps, and such excellent feature writers as Jim Lucas of Scripps-Howard, Jack Langguth of *The New York Times*, and Dickey Chappell of *The Reader's Digest* have reported the detailed incidents in the war. I felt that my job in this book was to give the broad overall picture of how Special Forces men operate, so each story basically is representative of a different facet of Special Forces action in wars like the one in Vietnam.

1

Also, as will be seen, Special Forces operations are, at times, highly unconventional. To report such occurrences factually, giving names, dates, and locations, could only embarrass U.S. planners in Vietnam and might even jeopardize the careers of invaluable officers. Time and again, I promised harried and heroic Special Forces men that their confidences were "off the record." To show the kind of men they are, to present an honest, comprehensive, and informed picture of their activities, one must get to know them as no writer could who was bound to report exactly what he saw and heard.

Moreover, I was in the unique—and enviable—position of having official aid and assistance without being bound by official restrictions. Even though I always made it clear I was in Vietnam in an unofficial capacity, under these auspices much was shown and told to me. I did not want to pull punches; at the same time I felt it wasn't right to abuse these special privileges and confidences by doing a straight reporting job.

The civic action portion of Special Forces operations can and should be reported factually. However, this book is more concerned with special missions, and I saw too many things that weren't for my eyes—or any eyes other than the participants' themselves—and assisted in too much imaginative circumvention of constricting ground rules merely to report what I saw under a thin disguise. The same blend of fact and "fiction" will be found in the locations in the book, many of which can be found on any map, while others are purely the author's invention.

So for these reasons *The Green Berets* is presented as a work of fiction.

It would have been impossible for me to write this book if I myself had not had Special Forces training and the proper letters of accreditation from the Department of Defense.

For, truly to understand and appreciate Special Forces operations, one really has to know the nature and the details of Special Forces training. . . .

It was early in the spring of 1963 and I was in Washington anxiously waiting for the Special Forces officer to show up at the Pentagon meeting. Various information officers had discussed my project, but now it needed the approval of a representative from the Special Warfare Center at Fort Bragg, North Carolina.

A lean, rugged-looking major entered the room. His weathered face, hard eyes, and erect carriage were exactly what I had expected of a man who wore the green beret. We shook hands and he regarded me with an appraising, unwavering stare. My eager smile he returned with a bleak one of his own.

"I understand you want to write a book about us."

"I'd like to, Major," I replied.

The information officers then outlined my proposal.

"So you want to come down and see what we do," he said, when they were finished. "Good, we'll be happy to have you."

My smile of satisfaction spread from jowl to jowl.

The Fort Bragg emissary gave a sidewise look at my slightly protuberant belly—and politely dropped a smoking white-phosphorus grenade in my lap.

"First, of course, you'll have to go to the airborne school at Fort Benning. Then, when you're jump-qualified, there's the three-month guerrilla warfare course—you'll make night jumps, live out in the swamps on exercises, run a couple of miles a day, get in some hand-to-hand combat training."

"But I'm thirty-seven, almost thirty-eight," I blurted. "If I could just get in with the guys. I'm a very good listener," I suggested hopefully.

"We don't have any short cuts in this business," the major said impassively. "If you really want to understand us, you should be able to go through our training. Then you'll begin to see what this green beanie means."

A twitch of amusement played at the corners of his lips. "So let's take it by the numbers. First jump school. If you get through that we'll discuss putting you through the guerrilla course. If you graduate from the Special Warfare School, you'll begin to understand Special Forces. Then, maybe, you'll be qualified to write about the green berets. . . ."

One month after the Pentagon meeting, I turned up at Fort Benning, Georgia, to become enrolled in the airborne school. I was issued jump boots and fatigues, and before I could say something appropriate, like "Geronimo," I found myself up at 5:00 every morning for muscle-tearing PT, followed by a brisk three- or four-mile run around the training areas.

As we ran, we sang (gasped):

"Airborne, airborne have you heard?
We're going to jump from the big-ass birds."

Jump school was the most physically punishing three weeks of my life. The weather was oppressively torrid at Fort Benning during June of 1963; years of good living poured from my body, and every morning I knew for a fact I wouldn't make it through the day. After two weeks on tortuous devices simulating parachute jumps and landings, I faced the moment of truth. The class was ready to go up in an airplane and jump out.

From my position halfway down the stick of jumpers, I looked from the open door down to the ground 1,200 feet below.

"Get ready!" the jump master cried.

My stomach knotted.

"Hook up!"

The blood drained from my fingertips as I hooked my static line into the cable running the length of the roof of the fuselage.

"Stand in the door!"

A reserve colonel, even older than I, took his place in the door.

"Go!"

They're kidding, I thought, as the prop blast sent me hurtling through the air. . . .

What in God's name was I doing here anyway?

What I was doing there all started in August of 1962 when I met the then Vice President of the United States, Lyndon B. Johnson. I was living at the time in Jamaica in the West Indies, and he had come down to represent the United States at that Caribbean country's independence celebrations. I had a chance to meet the Vice President and his military aide, Colonel William Jackson, and to give them copies of my book on guerrilla warfare in the Caribbean, *The Devil to Pay*.

I told Colonel Jackson I wanted to write my next book about Special Forces. A close look at this exciting young unit of the Army—distinguished by its green beret headgear—had never been encouraged. Special Forces operated mostly in secret; in those days few people not directly involved knew anything about it. Certainly there was little or nothing definitive in print about this highly trained unit of guerrilla-warfare experts fighting in the jungles of Southeast Asia.

The good offices of the then Vice President and Colonel Jackson had been responsible for the Pentagon meeting with that hard-bitten Special Forces major. And this had been responsible for the fact that a C-119 was sweeping past above me as, at a terrific rate of speed, I plummeted to earth.

Fortunately I made it down in one piece, and after five jumps (they gave us more equipment to carry on each jump, which, added to the stepped-up training, wiped out about one fourth of the class) the commandant of the school awarded me the first pair of silver jump wings won at the school by a civilian.

The next stop was Spartanburg, South Carolina, where the biggest war games ever to include guerrilla teams, Swiftstrike III, were going on. There I met the originator of the rugged schedule I was to follow if I wanted to write *The Green Berets*.

Major General William P. Yarborough, then commanding general of the Special Warfare Center, is a young-looking man to be wearing two stars; he is as lean and mean as his men. By this time I was pretty lean too.

The general had a surprise. He had scheduled me for a night jump into the swamps of South Carolina where a Special Forces team would take me to their snake-infested swamp headquarters.

"Night jump?" I murmured uneasily. "Snakes?"

After a week of assorted "assassinations," "kidnappings," "ambushes," "bridge and equipment destruction," and "raids," I was exfiltrated by a heliocourier or U-10, as this tough, short-takeoff and -landing airplane is known to the military, and a few days later I started the murderous guerrilla course at the Special Warfare Center.

My classmates, including Cuban exiles and Vietnamese, were officers from twenty-two different friendly nations. They ranged in age and grade from 1st lieutenants in their mid-twenties to lieutenant colonels in their mid-forties.

Three separate courses are given at what is now known as

the John F. Kennedy Special Warfare Center. Counter-insurgency, Psychological Warfare, and Unconventional (guerrilla) Warfare—for "tigers" like me! I had no choice; the guerrilla course produced wearers of the green beret.

The qualifications for officers who entered the Unconventional Warfare Course were awesome. All of them had to be airborne. All required top-security clearance. Most of them were Ranger qualified. Intensive psychological testing and examination of service records went into determining which officers would make good unconventional fighting men.

All that had been learned since the beginning of World War II about guerrilla warfare was taught at the School. I was fascinated at the vast number of weapons with which we were required to be familiar. Whether it was a Russian AK submachine gun, or a Swedish, Czech, East German or French weapon, Special Forces men learned to fire and fieldstrip it blindfolded. We were trained on the crossbow, the longbow, and the garrotte (for instant strangulation).

One of the most intricate portions of the course concerned advanced demolition techniques—all important to guerrillas behind enemy lines. We were schooled in chilling stratagems, such as mining a ditch beside the killing zone of an ambush to wipe out any troops still alive who try to take cover—a trap I saw sprung with deadly effectiveness a few months later in Vietnam.

In the techniques of hand-to-hand combat we learned to make our kill in the first thirty seconds—or stand a slim chance of living to do it at all.

Such new developments as Sky Hook were taught, in which a man can be jerked out of the jungle by airplane and winched to safety up in the sky. There are elaborate blends of many skills, as in the precision operation of a HALO-SCUBA infiltration. Fifteen to twenty thousand feet over the water—high enough to be invisible from the ground—a plane drops an infiltrator near the enemy coastline. The jumper freefalls, moving horizontally as well as vertically, and at fifteen hundred feet or less he opens his 'chute, hits the water and keeps going down, disengaging the parachute which sinks to the bottom. Using a breathing apparatus he then continues his infiltration underwater.

The course was also concerned with peaceful applications

of Special Forces training. Special Forces isn't all fighting; many missions are designed to prevent a guerrilla war from ever starting. Civic action projects, such as digging wells for villagers, establishing schools and hospitals, and even helping remote peoples improve their economic standards, were especially stressed.

By the time my classmates had completed the course and had been fully briefed on what they could expect in Vietnam and other trouble spots of the world, they were hard-eyed, serious men. As the instructors pointed out—and it proved to be all too tragically true—many friends we made during the rough days and nights of training would be lost in the coming year. One of my classmates, a tall, rugged captain—Roger Hugh Donlon—would sustain four wounds and win the Congressional Medal of Honor in Vietnam seven months later.

But I made it. I had graduated from the Special Warfare Center and really thought I was some kind of a guerrilla. Now, I said to the authorities, I did it your way. How about it? I want to go to Vietnam and see this training translated into action.

It was pathetic how much I still had to learn in the vicious, no-quarter jungle war in Indo-China.

Letters of accreditation were prepared. The Department of Defense sent out a teletype message to Military Assistance Command, Vietnam and to Colonel Theodore Leonard, commanding officer of U.S. Army Special Forces Vietnam, requesting I be given full cooperation. If the experienced combat officers of the Special Forces detachments who all received copies of the teletype setting forth my qualifications realized that perhaps I was far from the trained guerrilla fighter I at first considered myself, they were patient with me. Most important, because I was a graduate of jump school and the Special Warfare Center, these Special Forces men for the first time accepted an outsider—and a civilian at that—as one of their own.

On 6 January 1964, I arrived in Vietnam for a six-month tour. I was fortunate—at least from the standpoint of writing an authentic book—to be allowed to go into combat all over the country just as though I were a Special Forces trooper. In spite of the fact that correspondents traditionally are never armed, I never made a move without an automatic rifle—which accounts for the fact that I made it home to write this

7

book. Toward the end of the tour, A detachments began paying me the supreme compliment of sending me in place of another sergeant as the second American with an all-Vietnamese or montagnard patrol.

Special Forces, formed in 1952, traces its lineage back to the guerrilla operating teams of the Office of Strategic Services (OSS) (predecessor of the Central Intelligence Agency or CIA) and to such World War II-born units as the Rangers, the British and Canadian Commandos, Merrill's Marauders of Burma, and especially the Airborne Infantry or paratroopers.

Originally part of the Psychological Warfare Center which was moved from Fort Reilly, Kansas, to Fort Bragg, North Carolina, Special Forces was the brainchild of Colonel Aaron Bank, an OSS operator who had been preaching the need for a trained guerrilla unit within the Army for several years. With the outbreak of the Korean War, the need for behind-enemy-lines guerrilla units became apparent.

As part of a guerrilla group known as UNPIK (United Nations Partisan Infantry Korea), Special Forces men first saw action behind Communist lines late in 1952 and in 1953. A few years after the war, the original 77th Special Forces Group (Airborne) at Fort Bragg expanded to become the 7th Special Forces Group (Airborne) at Bragg and the 10th Special Forces Group (Airborne) at Bad Tölz, Germany. Today there are eight Special Forces groups stationed around the world.

Some means were sought to give the elite Special Forces man a distinctive type of insignia, and the green beret was adopted. The original crest on the beret was a silver Trojan horse worn on the left side above the ear. Now the flash denoting the wearer's group is worn directly above the left eye.

Conventional Army generals disliked the jaunty headgear and outlawed it. But the late President John F. Kennedy, recognizing the value of Special Forces, threw his full support behind the unit and restored the green beret in a message that exhorted the men to "wear the beret proudly, it will be a mark of distinction and a badge of courage in the difficult days ahead."

A green beret was returned to President Kennedy under the most tragic of circumstances two years later. Special Forces men formed the honor guard at the President's burial in

Arlington National Cemetery. At the ceremony's end Sergeant Major Francis Ruddy sorrowfully took the beret from his head and placed it on his commander-in-chief's grave. It (that is, its replacement) is still there, along with the hats of the Army, Navy, and Air Force. Special Forces men insure that a fresh green beret will always lie above the President, who so loved and respected his tough, highly competent guerrilla fighters.

The basic unit of a Special Forces group is the 12-man A detachment or A team.

The A team is commanded by a captain, the CO. The Executive Officer (XO) is a 1st lieutenant (there are no 2nd lieutenants in Special Forces). There are ten intensively trained and experienced enlisted men on the A team, most of them senior sergeants. These are undoubtedly the most multiskilled enlisted men in the armed forces today.

The team sergeant is a master sergeant and—the officers will be the first to confirm—runs the detachment. One of the primary jobs of the sergeant specialists is to train their officers in the skills they have spent many years perfecting. Only after an officer graduates from the Special Warfare Center and forms his team does his training really begin.

The second-ranking enlisted man on an A team is usually the intelligence sergeant who keeps track of what the enemy is doing and recruits and trains agents—particularly tricky in Asia for an American.

There are two medical specialists on the A team, skilled in the exotic diseases to be found in the remote areas to which teams are sent. Much of their training is in war wounds. Two communications experts, who could probably make radios out of sea shells should the need arise, keep the A teams in touch with each other and with the B and C teams which are field headquarters for the operational A detachments.

Two demolition-engineer specialists can do everything from building bridges to blowing them up. Demolition men receive a richly deserved extra $50 a month in hazardous-duty pay. One light and one heavy-weapons specialist complete the team. These two men have to be good teachers since they must instruct native or indigenous troops in the use of the latest weapons. Many of the local people have never seen anything more modern than a crossbow before a Special Forces A detachment comes to their area.

Besides their specialties, the men on a Special Forces team have further capabilities.

Every man on an A team speaks a second language, some several tongues. On any given A team all the languages in use in the area are spoken, including those of the enemy. Every man is cross-trained in at least two other basic team skills. A medic, say, can not only efficiently patch up the wounded and care for the sick, but knows how to lay down a deadly accurate mortar barrage and blow up the enemy's rail lines and bridges.

In hand-to-hand combat the men of Special Forces have no superiors, blending judo, karate, wrestling, and boxing techniques into their own lethal brand of barehanded, close-in fighting.

All Special Forces men are expert parachutists.

The Special Forces role is twofold. In a hot war situation the A detachment infiltrates enemy territory by parachuting in, or coming in by sea either in boats or with underwater apparatus, or across land routes. The job of the team is to build up, equip, train, and direct a guerrilla force of indigenous people. Special Forces men are carefully trained in all aspects of psychological warfare to both fan the flames of anti-Communist feeling among their civilian irregular troops and the citizens of the enemy country they are subverting, and keep the enemy government frightened and off-balance at all times.

In the type of counterinsurgency operations the United States had been backing in South Vietnam, the Special Forces teams train and equip the civilian irregular defense group troops, known as a strike force when organized in a Special Forces camp, as opposed to the conventional U.S. Army advisers in Vietnam who are assigned to the Army of the Republic of Vietnam regular troops. The strikers, as strike-force men are called, sign a contract to fight in a Special Forces-advised strike-force battalion for periods ranging from six months to two years. Basically, the A teams in Vietnam are training civilians to fight the Communist Viet Cong guerrillas as anti-guerrillas—much the same as killer submarines go after enemy subs.

In direct command of a strike-force camp is the captain of

the Vietnamese Special Forces team, which is modeled on the American Special Forces plan. The Americans' role is to advise the Vietnamese Special Forces (known by their Vietnamese name, Luc-Luong Dac-Biet, or LLDB) in training and leading its civilian irregular defense group troops in combat. Thus, each U.S. Special Forces adviser has his Vietnamese LLDB counterpart at every camp.

The headquarters of a Special Forces group in action against the enemy is known as the Special Forces Operating Base (SFOB). It performs all the basic functions of a regular unit headquarters—personnel, intelligence, operations, and supply. It also has a staff of Area Specialist Officers, each of whom is intimately acquainted with the area of operations in which he specializes. In South Vietnam there is one B detachment to each corps area, and four corps areas from IV Corps (the Mekong Delta) to I Corps (called "eye" Corps) in the northernmost mountain region bordering the 17th Parallel, which divides Communist North from free South Vietnam. Thus, there are four Area Specialist Officers at the Special Forces Operating Base (HQ) in Saigon.

The B team acts as a higher headquarters for approximately ten A teams. The B team is not an operational detachment, but supplies, administers and coordinates the activities of the A teams.

The Green Berets shows Special Forces in both its guerrilla and anti-guerrilla roles against the background of the Vietnam war in 1964.

It may help the reader's understanding to review, for a moment, the political background this book covers.

In January of 1964 South Vietnam was being run by a military junta headed by General Duong Van ("Big") Minh that had overthrown the dictatorship of President Ngo Dinh Diem. President Diem came to power in 1955 after Vietnam was divided into two separate states—North Vietnam and South Vietnam.

Under Diem important cabinet and civil service jobs were self-perpetuating, acquired through heredity, wealth, and connections with the Roman Catholic Ngo family. The Army was no exception to this so-called Mandarin system. Competency, bravery, and training had little or no bearing on promotions or the assignment of commands and desirable posts. Advancement in Diem's burgeoning U.S.-advised and -financed Army depended upon an officer's closeness to the President, his brother Ngo Dinh Nhu, and Madame Nhu: thus the phenomena of so many colonels and generals in their twenties and thirties, and lieutenants and captains in their late thirties and forties.

On January 30th "Big" Minh's junta was toppled after exactly three months in power by General Nguyen Khanh, an aggressive, businesslike young officer. Both Minh and Khanh were seriously hampered by incompetent holdovers from the Diem regime who had become too powerful to depose or jail.

President Diem and his brother Nhu had used the politically well-connected LLDB officers as palace guards and terrorist police—Buddhists were a prime target. In order to procure them the finest hardware, Diem and Nhu aligned the LLDB with the U.S. Special Forces, even to the point of calling them the Vietnamese 77th Special Forces Group after the first U.S. Special Forces Group to be activated.

When U.S. Special Forces teams began setting up camps on a large scale, their job of fighting Communist guerrillas was made far more difficult and dangerous because Diem saddled them with the untrained, combat-shy, and—by U.S. standards—corrupt LLDB as counterparts.

The elaborate systems of kickbacks, payroll juggling, and misappropriation of equipment—all considered standard operating procedure by so many Vietnamese officers—are shown in some detail in this book.

Obviously, strife and ferment often resulted from such diametrically opposed philosophies—especially when highly trained and dedicated Special Forces men were thrown together with the LLDB in isolated outposts. The Americans could only advise and hand out money and supplies. The LLDB officers were in command, and all too often many of them seemed allergic to firefights, considering themselves members of an elite unit.

That there was occasional bitterness between the men of the U.S. Special Forces and many of their LLDB counterparts should be understandable. At the same time, it is important to understand that Special Forces men do not comment on their counterparts to the outside world. Only after I had become one of them did they talk freely to me.

Since this book is an honest attempt to give the reader a vivid picture of the problems faced by the green berets, and since the relationship between the American advisers and their Vietnamese counterparts is as basic to these stories as the combat tactics described, I decided not to dodge this ticklish issue. The ability of an American to get along with his Vietnamese counterpart and persuade him to accept advice frequently is a matter of life or death to Americans and Vietnamese alike.

There are, of course, many honest and heroic Vietnamese officers, and with General Khanh's appointment of the experienced Colonel Lam Son to head up LLDB in mid-1964 the quality of the unit began to improve. However, Colonel Lam Son faced a long and frustrating struggle, still far from won, to make LLDB the true Vietnamese equivalent of the United States Army Special Forces.

The yo-yo that is Vietnamese politics isn't much help in establishing permanent improvements. In September General Khanh was replaced by a civilian government headed by Tran Van Huong which early in 1965 relinquished control to the self-same General Khanh. Then, shortly thereafter, Khanh resigned. No one can tell how long these power shifts will continue.

The Green Berets tells the story of Special Forces fighting Communism in Indo-China in 1964, but it could well have been written about the wearers of the green beret in many other countries in which they find themselves throughout the world.

In essence, these stories will be true of the political problems and combat situations Special Forces men are facing in 1965, or for that matter 1975, wherever Americans must fight to keep the perimeter of the free world from shrinking further.

Political and geographical considerations may vary from month to month and year to year; but in the global stalemate created by nuclear power, the wars the Communists call ''wars of liberation'' will be fought by dedicated soldiers like the men of Special Forces under conditions similar to those described in this book.

*   *   *

13

In the course of my narrative I have used a number of terms and abbreviations which are standard in Special Forces. Most of these will be familiar to most readers, but to avoid confusion I have listed them here for ready reference.

Acbat—a typical code name for an infiltration team. This is an A team, as Batcat is a B team.

Agency, The—No one ever refers to the CIA. They say "The Agency," or in Southeast Asia they use the name of the CIA's operating entity known as CSG (Combined Studies Group).

Ar-15—New high-powered light automatic rifle used by Special Forces. Officially designated the M-16 by the Army.

ARVN—Army of the Republic of Vietnam (South Vietnam).

ASO—Area Specialist Officer.

Asset—An individual, not a member of a Special Forces team, who has first-hand knowledge of the people and geography of a Special Forces operating area and works with the team.

BAR—Browning automatic rifle.

CIDG—Civilian irregular defense group.

Concertina—Barbed wire in rolls placed about the perimeter of fortified areas.

Country Team—When the United States gives military and economic aid to a country such as, Vietnam, it is administered by what is known as the Country Team. The Country Team is made up of five individuals: the U.S. ambassador, who nominally heads the team; the commanding general of Military Assistance Command; the head of USOM; the head of the United States Information Service in the country; and the station chief of the CIA in that country.

DA—Department of the Army.

Dai-uy—(Pronounced Di-wee) The Vietnamese word for captain.

DoD—Department of Defense.

DRVN—Democratic Republic of Vietnam (North Vietnam).

DZ—Drop zone for parachuted supplies or personnel.

Flash—The patch on the green beret which by color designates the group to which a Special Forces man is attached.

FOB—Forward operating base.

GWOA—Guerrilla Warfare Operating Area.

KIA—Killed in action.

KKK—Slang for Cambodian bandits.

Leg, or Straight Leg—A soldier who is not a parachute jumper.

LLDB—Luc-Luong Dac-Biet (Vietnamese Special Forces).

LZ—Landing zone for an airplane or helicopter.

MAAG—Military Assistance Advisory Group. MAAG is, in effect, the operational arm of MAC-V. MAAG is in charge of training and operations, and it is to MAAG that American officers and men working directly with ARVN as advisers are attached. Originally Special Forces was independent of MAAG, reporting directly to the Commanding General of MAC-V and certain unconventional warfare boards in Southeast Asia and Washington D.C. Then on May 1, 1964, some of the conventional generals in Saigon and Washington decided that in the interest of "streamlining," Special Forces should be put under MAAG.

MAC-V—Military Assistance Command Vietnam. This is the advisory and decision-making command in Vietnam that reports to the Joint Chiefs of Staff and the President of the United States.

NCO—Non-commissioned officer.

Okie—Okinawa, also known as "The Rock"; home of the 1st Special Forces Group.

Piastre—Vietnamese money; one p. is worth $.01 U.S. currency.

Province chief—Vietnam is divided into forty-two provinces and each province is ruled over by a military governor or province chief, usually a major or lieutenant colonel. The American adviser to the province chief, usually a major, is known as a sector adviser and provinces are referred to as sectors.

Short—When a soldier is "short" he has almost finished his tour of duty and is ready to ship.

SFOB—Special Forces Operating Base.

STRAC—Officially standing for Strategic Army Command, the word has come to mean neat, shipshape, in order.

USASFV—United States Army Special Forces, Vietnam.

USOM—United States Operations Mission. This is the overseas operating arm of AID (Agency for International Development). It is a civilian agency which supervises spending money and giving assistance to the people of a country. Everything from overhauling the police system to providing healthy pigs comes under USOM.

VC—Viet Cong.

XO—Executive Officer.

Yard—American abbreviation of montagnard, a hill tribesman.

1

A GREEN BERET—
ALL THE WAY

The headquarters of Special Forces Detachment B-520 in one of Vietnam's most active war zones looks exactly like a fort out of the old West. Although the B detachments are strictly support and administrative units for the Special Forces A teams fighting the Communist Viet Cong guerrillas in the jungles and rice paddies, this headquarters had been attacked twice in the last year by Viet Cong and both times had sustained casualties.

I was finally keeping my promise to visit the headquarters of Major (since his arrival in Vietnam, Lieutenant Colonel) Train. I deposited my combat pack in the orderly room and strode through the open door into the CO's office.

"Congratulations, Colonel."

Lieutenant Colonel Train, looking both youthful and weathered, smiled self-assuredly, blew a long stream of cigar smoke across his desk, and motioned for me to sit down.

Major Fenz, the operations officer, walked into the office abruptly. "Sorry to interrupt, sir. We just received word that another patrol out of Phan Chau ran into an ambush. We lost four friendlies KIA."

I sat up straight. "Old Kornie is getting himself some action."

Train frowned thoughtfully. "Third time in a week he's taken casualties." He drummed his fingertips on the top of his desk. "Any enemy KIA, or captured weapons?"

"No weapons captured. They think they killed several VC from blood found on the foliage. No bodies."

"I worry about Kornie," Train said, with a trace of petulance. "He's somehow managed to get two Vietnamese camp commanders relieved in the four months he's been here. The new one is just what he wants, pliable. Kornie runs the camp as he pleases."

"Kornie has killed more VC than any other A team in the three weeks since we've taken over here," Fenz pointed out.

"Kornie is too damned independent and unorthodox," Train said.

"That's what they taught us at Bragg, Colonel," I put in. "Or did I spend three months misunderstanding the message?"

"There are limits. I don't agree with all the School teaches."

"By the way, Colonel," I said before we could disagree openly, "one reason I came down here was to get out to Phan Chau and watch Kornie in action."

Train stared at me a moment. Then he said, "Let's have a cup of coffee. Join us, Fenz?"

We walked out of the administration offices, across the parade ground and volleyball court of the B-team headquarters, and entered the club which served as morning coffeehouse, reading and relaxing room, and evening bar. Train called to the pretty Vietnamese waitress to bring us coffee.

There were a number of Special Forces officers and sergeants lounging around. It was to the B team that the A-team field men came on their way to a rest and rehabilitation leave in Saigon. Later they returned to the B team to await flights back to their A teams deep in Viet Cong territory.

Lieutenant Colonel Train had been an enigma to me ever since I first met him as a major taking the guerrilla course at Fort Bragg. His background was Regular Army. In World War II he had seen two years of combat duty in the Infantry, rising to the rank of staff sergeant when the war ended. Since his high-school record had been outstanding and his Army service flawless, he received an appointment to West Point. From the Point to Japan to Korea, Train had served with distinction as an Infantry officer, and in 1954 he applied for jump school at Fort Benning and became a paratrooper.

Almost nine years later, in line with Train's interest in new developments, he had indicated that he would accept an assignment with Special Forces. I met him at Fort Bragg just after he had moved down Gruber Avenue from the 82nd

Airborne Division to Smoke Bomb Hill, the Special Warfare Center.

It was obvious to those close to Train that he did not accept wholeheartedly the doctrines of unconventional warfare. But President Kennedy's awareness of the importance of this facet of the military had made unconventional or special warfare experience a must for any officer who wanted to advance to top echelons.

As Train and I chatted and drank our coffee my interest grew in whether this dedicated officer was going to change and how he would operate in the guerrilla war in Vietnam.

"So you want to go to Phan Chau?" Train asked.

"I'd like to see Kornie in action," I said. "Remember him at Bragg? He was the guerrilla chief in the big maneuvers."

"Kornie has been one of the Army's characters for ten years," Train said sternly. "Of course I remember him. I'm afraid you'll get yourself in trouble if you go to Phan Chau."

"What do you mean by trouble?"

"I don't want the first civilian writer killed in Vietnam to get it with my command."

As I expected, Train was going to be a problem. "You think I stand a better chance of cashing in with Kornie than with some of the other A teams?"

Train took a long sip of coffee before answering. "He does damned dangerous things. I don't think he reports everything he does even to me."

"You've been here three weeks, Colonel. The last B team had him four months. What did Major Grunner say about him?"

Fenz, a Special Forces officer for six years, concentrated on his coffee. Train gave me a wry smile. "The last B team was pretty unorthodox even by Special Forces standards. Major Grunner is a fine officer; I'm not saying anything against him or the way he operated this B detachment." Train looked at me steadily. "But he let his A teams do things I won't permit. And of course he and Kornie were old friends from the 10th Special Forces Group in Germany." Train shook his head. "And that's the wildest-thinking bunch I ever came across in my military career."

Neither Fenz nor I made any reply. We sipped our coffee in silence. Train was one of the new breed of Special Forces officers. Unconventional warfare specialists had proven their

19

ability to cope with the burgeoning Communist brand of limited or guerrilla wars so conclusively that Special Forces had been authorized an increase in strength. Several new groups were being added to the old 1st in Okinawa, 10th in Bad Tölz, Germany, and the 5th and 7th at Fort Bragg.

New officers were picked from among the most outstanding men in airborne and conventional units. Since every Special Forces officer and enlisted man is a paratrooper, it was occasionally necessary to send some "straight-leg" officers to jump school at Fort Benning, Georgia, before they could attend the Special Warfare School at Fort Bragg prior to being assigned to a Special Forces group.

This new group of basically conventional officers in Special Forces were already beginning to make their influence felt early in 1964. Lieutenant Colonel Train was clearly going to be a hard man to develop into a "Green Beret—All the Way!"

I broke the silence, directing a question at Major Fenz. "When can you get me out to Phan Chau?"

Fenz looked to Train for guidance. Train smiled at me wryly. "We've got to let you go if you want to. But do us all a favor will you? Don't get yourself killed. I thought you'd had it on that night jump in Uwarrie . . ."

He turned to Fenz and told him the story. "They dropped our teams together on the ten-day field training exercise."

Fenz nodded; the ten-day field training exercise was a bond shared by all Special Warfare School graduates.

"The School picked us a drop zone in Uwarrie National Forest near Pisgah—that was something else. It was a terrible night," Train recalled. "Cold. And the wind came up before we reached the DZ. An equipment bundle got stuck in the door for six seconds so we had to make two passes. Our friend here was held at the door by the jump master and was first man out on the second pass. We were blown into the trees over a mile from the DZ. I got hung up, had to open my emergency chute and climb down the shroud lines to get on the ground. We had three broken legs and several other injuries on that DZ."

Train looked at me and smiled. "Our civilian, of course, came out best. Landed in a field the size of the volleyball court, threw his air items in the bag and helped pull his team together."

I looked out the window across the rice paddies where every peasant could be and probably was a Viet Cong. "At least they didn't have shit-dipped pungi stakes waiting for us in North Carolina," I said.

Train frowned briefly at my language. "I guess you and Kornie will get along fine, at that. As I remember, you pulled a few tricks on that exercise that weren't even in the books."

Fenz took this as his cue to volunteer the information that there was an Otter flying down to Phan Chau that afternoon with an interpreter to replace the one killed a few days before on patrol.

"You might as well take it," Train said. "How long do you want to stay?"

"Can't I just play it by ear, Colonel?"

"Certainly. If it looks like there's going to be serious trouble I'll get you evacuated."

"Negative! Please?"

Train stared at me; I met the look. Train gave a shrug. "OK, I'll go along with you, but I still don't—"

"No sweat. I don't want to get myself greased any more than you do."

"OK, get your gear together. Got your own weapon?"

"If you could lend me a folding-stock carbine and a few banana clips, that's all I need."

"Fenz, can you fix him up?"

"Yes, sir. The Otter takes off at 1300 hours."

"One thing," Train cautioned, "Kornie is upset because we transferred two companies of Hoa Hao troops from his camp on orders from the Vietnamese division commander, General Co. You know about the Hoa Hao?"

"They're supposed to be fierce fighters, aren't they?"

"That's right. They're a religious sect in the Mekong Delta with slightly different ethnic origins from the Vietnamese. General Co didn't like having two companies of Hoa Hao fighting together."

"You mean with coup fever raging, he was afraid the Hoa Hao might get together and make a deal with one of his rival generals?"

"We try to keep out of politics," Train said testily. "General Co's reasoning is not my concern."

"But it would concern Kornie to find himself on the Cambodian border in the middle of VC territory suddenly minus two companies of his best fighting men."

Train snorted in exasperation. "Just don't take Kornie's opinions on Vietnamese politics too seriously."

"I'll use discretion in anything I say," I promised.

"I hope so." It sounded like a threat.

Looking down at the sere-brown rice paddies, I felt a sense of quickening excitement as the little eight-place single-engine plane closed on Phan Chau in a hilly section along the Cambodian border. Across from me sat the thin, ascetic-looking young Vietnamese interpreter.

I thought of Steve Kornie. His first name was Sven actually. He was, at forty-four, a captain, as compared to Train, who was a lieutenant colonel at thirty-nine.

Kornie, originally a Finn, fought the Russians when they invaded his native land. Later he had joined the German Army and miraculously survived two years of fighting the Russians on the eastern front. After the war came a period in his life he never talked about. His career was re-entered on the record book when, under the Lodge Act of the early fifties, which permitted foreign nationals who joined the United States Army in Europe to become eligible for U.S. citizenship after five years service, Kornie enlisted.

In a barroom brawl in Germany in 1955, Kornie and some of his more obstreperous GI companions had committed the usually disastrous error of tangling with several soldiers wearing green berets with silver Trojan horse insignias on them. The blue-eyed Nordic giant, after decking twice his weight in berets, finally agreed to a truce.

Suspiciously he allowed these soldiers, who in spite of their alien headdress proclaimed themselves Americans, to buy him a drink. In his career with several armies he had never fought such tough barehanded fighters. As the several victims of Kornie's fists and flathanded chops came to, shook their heads, found their berets and replaced them on their heads, it became clear to Kornie that they were asking him to join their group. To his surprise and horror he discovered that one man he had knocked over the bar was a major.

Before the evening was over Kornie discovered the existence of the 10th Special Forces Group at Bad Tölz, had given the major his name, rank and serial number, and had been promised that he would soon be transferred to the elite, highly trained, virtually secret unit of the U.S. Army to which these men in green berets so proudly belonged.

When Special Forces realized the extent of Sven Kornie's combat experience and language capabilities, the commanding officer at Bad Tölz believed his claim that he had gone to the military college for almost three years in Finland, although his academic records had been lost in the war and he could not prove his educational qualifications. Kornie was sent to Officer Candidate School, and Special Forces was waiting to reclaim him immediately upon graduation. He performed many covert as well as overt missions in Europe as a Special Forces officer, several times on loan to the CIA, and finally, having reached the grade of captain, he was shipped to the 5th Special Forces Group at the Special Warfare Center, Fort Bragg.

In his early forties he knew his chances of ever making field grade were slim. For one thing, while in uniform he had killed a German civilian he knew to be a Russian agent with a single punch. Extenuating circumstances had won him an acquittal at his court-martial; nevertheless the affair was distasteful, particularly to conservative old line officers on promotion boards. There was also Kornie's inability to prove any higher education.

Sven Kornie was the ideal Special Forces officer. Special Forces was his life; fighting, especially unorthodox warfare, was what he lived for. He had no career to sacrifice; he had no desire to rise from operational to supervisory levels. And not the least of his assets, he was unmarried and had no attachments to anyone or anything in the world beyond Special Forces.

My thoughts of Kornie and speculations as to what fascinating mischief he would be up to were interrupted by the interpreter.

"Are you posted to Phan Chau?"

I shook my head, but he had an explanation coming. I wore the complete Special Forces uniform, the lightweight jungle fatigues and my highly prized green beret which an A team had given me after a combat mission.

"I will visit Phan Chau for maybe a week. I am a writer. A journalist. You understand?"

The interpreter's face lit up. "Ah, journalist. Yes. What

journal you write for?'' Hopefully: ''*Time* magazine? Maybe *Newsweek? Life?*''

He couldn't disguise his disappointment when he learned what a free-lance writer was.

We were getting close to Phan Chau. I recognized the area from several parachute supply drops I had flown to familiarize myself with the terrain.

The little Otter began circling. Only a few miles off I could look into Cambodia, the border running down the middle of the rough, rocky terrain. A dirt landing strip appeared below and in moments the plane was bumping along it.

I threw my combat pack out on the ground, and when the small plane had come to a complete stop jumped out after it. I saw a green beret among the camouflage-capped Vietnamese strike-force troopers milling around, and went up to the American sergeant and told him who I was. He recognized my name and mission, but I was surprised to hear Kornie wasn't expecting me.

''Sometimes we can't read the B team for half a day,'' the sergeant explained. ''The old man will be glad to see you. He's been wondering when you were coming.''

''I guess I missed some action this morning.''

''Yeah, it was a tough one. Four strikers KIA. We usually don't get ambushed so close to camp.'' The sergeant introduced himself to me as Borst, the radio operator. He was a well-set young man, his cropped hair below the green beret yellow, and his blue eyes fierce. I wondered if Kornie had collected an all-Viking A team. Anything unusual, with flair and color, would be typical Kornie.

''The old man is working out some big deal with Sergeant Bergholtz, he's our team sergeant, and Sergeant Falk, intelligence.''

''Where's Lieutenant Schmelzer?'' I asked. ''I knew him at Bragg last year while you were all in mission training.''

''He's still out with the patrol that was ambushed. They sent back the bodies and the wounded, and then kept going.''

Sergeant Borst picked up my combat pack, carried it to the truck, and threw it in back with the strikers and the new interpreter. He motioned me into the front seat, looked behind to make sure the mounted .30-caliber machine gun was manned, and drove off as soon as the Otter was airborne.

The low, white buildings with dark roofs which rose above

24

the mud walls of Phan Chau, and the tall steel fire-control tower were visible from the airstrip. Beyond them, directly west, loomed the rocky foothills which spilled along both sides of the Vietnam-Cambodia border. There were more hills and a scrub-brush jungle north of Phan Chau. To the south the land was open and bare. The airstrip was only a mile east of the camp.

"This the new camp?"

"Yes, sir," Borst answered. "The old one next to the town of Phan Chau was something else. Hills on all sides. We called it little Dien Bien Phu. Here at least we've got some open fields of fire and the VC can't drop mortar fire on us from above."

"From what I hear, you're out of that old French camp just in time."

"That's what we figure. They'd clobber us there. When this one is finished we'll be able to hold off about anything they can throw at us."

As we drove into the square fort, with sandbagged mud walls studded with machine-gun emplacements and surrounded with barbed wire, I could see men working on the walls and putting out more barbed wire. "Do you still have much work to do?"

"Quite a bit, sir. We're sure hoping we don't get hit in the next few days. The camp isn't secure yet."

Borst stopped before the Vietnamese Special Forces headquarters to let off the strikers and the new interpreter, and then drove me another twenty feet to a cement-block building with a wooden roof. He pulled to a stop and jumped out. Borst beat me inside and I heard him announce me.

It took a moment for my eyes to get used to the cool interior grayness after the hot, bright sunlight. The big form of Sven Kornie came toward me. He had a large grin on his lean, pleasant face and his blue eyes snapped. His huge hand enveloped mine as he welcomed me to Phan Chau. He introduced me to Sergeant Bergholtz, and I sensed my guess was correct that a Germanic-Viking crew had indeed been transported intact to the Vietnam-Cambodia border.

"Well, well," Kornie boomed cheerfully. "You come here at a dangerous time."

"What's happening?"

"By God damn! Those Vietnamese generals—stupid! Dan-

25

gerous stupid. Two hundred fifty my best men that sneak-eyed yellow-skin bastard corps commander take out of here yesterday—and our big American generals? Politics they play while this camp gets zapped."

"What are you talking about, Steve?"

"Two hundred fifty Hoa Hao fighting men I had. The best. Now General Co decides he don't want any Hoa Hao companies fighting together because maybe they get together under their colonel and pull another coup. So he breaks up the best fighting units in the Mekong Delta. God damn fool! And Phan Chau, what happens? We get more Vietnamese strikers we don't know if they fight for us or VC. You better go back to the B team," he finished lugubriously.

"Too late now," I said. "What action have you got going?"

"Two actions. The VC got one action and we got one. Tell him, Bergholtz."

The team sergeant began his briefing. "The VC have been making ladders for a couple of weeks now in all their villages. They're also making caskets. That means they figure on hitting us sometime soon. The ladders they use to throw across the barbed wire and the mine fields and later as stretchers to carry away the dead and wounded. The VC fight better when they know they're going to get a funeral and a nice wood box if they're killed. They see the coffins, it makes their morale go up."

"We are not ready for attack," Kornie said, "so it probably comes soon."

"What's Schmelzer's patrol doing?"

Kornie's deep laugh boomed out. "Schmelzer is looking for KKK."

"KKK? I thought we were in South Vietnam, not South Carolina."

"The KKK are Cambodian bandits. They fight only for money. They are very bad boys. Tell him, Bergholtz."

"Yes, sir." The team sergeant turned his rugged face to me. "The KKK—that's what everyone calls them—live around these hills. They even attack our patrols for the weapons if they are strong enough. We figure the ambush today may have been KKK. Last week four Buddhist monks went through here to Cambodia to buy gold leaf for their temple. All the local Buddhists kicked in to buy the stuff. You can't buy gold in Vietnam." Bergholtz paused. "We told the monks they'd better stay home but they said Buddha would protect them."

Kornie finished the story. "Three days ago I was leading a patrol in KKK area. We find the monks. They are lying on the trail, each has his head under his left arm. The KKK got them and their gold."

"And Schmelzer is going to get the KKK?" I asked.

"He is only trying to locate them. Maybe they will be useful to us on the operation we plan."

I gave him full attention, unslinging my carbine and leaning it against the wall.

"We get tired of the VC hitting us and running across the border to Cambodia where we can't get them," Kornie said. "This team of mine, we got only one month left before we go back to Fort Bragg. Garrison duty," Kornie growled. "Two cowardly Vietnamese camp commanders in a row we get. Sometimes is a week between good VC contact."

"But this time I hear you have a good counterpart."

"This one *is* good," Kornie conceded. "He maybe don't like patrols himself, but if the Americans want to kill themselves and only a reasonable number of strikers, that's our business by him. Come, follow me. I will show you what we are going to do." He led me out of the teamhouse, down the mud road and on past several cement barracks with wood and thatch roofs. We stopped at one and a guard saluted. His dark skin and imprecise features marked the striker in the tiger-stripe camouflage as a Cambodian. Kornie returned the salute and walked inside. There must have been about 50 men in the barracks. They were cleaning their rifles, making up packs, and apparently readying themselves to go out on a combat operation.

"These Cambodes good boys," Kornie boomed. "Loyal to the Americans who pay them and feed them. Not like the KKK."

The Cambodes evidently liked the captain, for Kornie lustily shouted some indistinguishable words and got back an enthusiastic response. "I ask them if they are ready to kill Communists anywhere, even in Cambodia. They are ready." He gave them a cheerful wave and we left.

"Let's go to the radio room and see what we hear from Schmelzer."

Borst was at the radio, earphones on, scribbling on a sheet of paper in front of him. He looked up as Kornie came in.

"Sir, Lieutenant Schmelzer is standing by on voice."

"Good!" Kornie exclaimed, taking the mike. "Handy, Handy," he called. "This is Grant, Grant. Come in Handy."

"Grant, this is Handy," came back over the receiver. "Made contact with bandits at BP 236581." On the map above the radio Kornie located the position of his executive officer from the coordinates. It was eight miles north of Phan Chau, almost straddling the border.

Schmelzer continued. "Our assets now have friendly talk with bandits. Believe you can go ahead with operation. That is all. Handy out."

"Grant out," Kornie said putting down the mike. He turned to me. "Our plans are coming along well. Now if the Viet Cong give us tonight without attacking, we will buy another few days to finish the camp's defenses. Then"—Kornie grinned—"they can throw a regiment at us and we kill them all."

Kornie led the way back to the operations room where Sergeant Bergholtz was waiting for him. As we walked in the sergeant said, "Falk just got another agent report. There are about 100 VC hiding in Chau Lu, resting and getting food. Less than half live there, the rest must be hard-core just come over from Cambodia."

"That is good, that is good," Kornie said, nodding. "Now, I will explain everything. Here." He pointed to the map. "You see the border running north and south? Our camp is three miles east from Cambodia. Four miles north of us is this nasty little village of Chau Lu right on the border near which we were ambushed this morning. Four more miles north of Chau Lu, still on the border, is where Schmelzer is right now, talking to the KKK."

"I'm with you so far," I said.

"Good. Now, in Cambodia, exactly opposite Chau Lu, ten miles in is a big VC camp. They got a hospital, barracks, all the comforts of a major installation. The attack on us will be launched from this big Communist camp. The VC will cross the border and build up in Chau Lu, like they do now. When they're ready, they hit us. If we try to hit their buildup on our side of the border they only got to run a hundred meters and they're back in Cambodia where we can't kill them. Even if we go over after them they pull back to their big camp where we get zapped and cause big international incident."

Kornie watched me intently for a reaction. I began to get a vague idea of what he had in mind. "Keep talking, Steve. I've always wanted to go inside Cambodia."

The big Viking laughed hugely. "Tonight, my Cambodes, 100 of them, cross the border and take up blocking positions two miles inside Cambodia between Chau Lu and the big VC camp. There is a river parallel to the border in there. My Cambodes put their backs to the river and ambush the VC who are running from Chau Lu, which we attack just before sunrise tomorrow morning. At the river my boys can see and kill any VC from the main camp who try to cross it and get behind them."

I had to laugh, the thinking was so typically Kornie, and just what Lieutenant Colonel Train, who was so scrupulous about international politics, was afraid of.

Kornie continued. "If the VC are suddenly cut to little pieces right where they think they are safe, in Cambodia, they will be careful for a while. Maybe they think they get attacked again in this sanctuary our politicians give them."

"They'll know you did it, Steve," I said soberly. "And then they'll raise international hell."

"Yes, they know we do it," Kornie agreed. "This will scare them. But international incident? No. They don't prove we have anything to do with it."

"Well, somebody had to ambush those VC," I pointed out. "If there's a bunch of shot-up bodies nobody's going to believe Cambodian-government troops did it to their Communist friends."

Kornie's blue eyes sparkled with humor and excitement. "Oh yes. But we got what you call, fall guys. Come, let's go back to the radio room."

Just after dark I accompanied Kornie and Sergeant Bergholtz as they led the company of cocky, spoiling-for-action Cambodians to the border where a rally point was established with a squad guarding it. This was the point at which the Cambodians would cross back to the Vietnam side of the border after their mission. Kornie wanted Bergholtz and every one of his Cambodians to be familiar with the place. It was at the base of one of the many hills along this section of the border. For positive identification Kornie sent another squad to the top of the hill. There they would start firing flares a few minutes after the shooting started and keep it up until all the Cambodians had found their way back to the rally point and were accounted for.

With the return point on the border clearly defined, Kornie, Bergholtz, I, and the company of Cambodians stealthily moved northward on the Vietnam side of the border. We carefully gave the Viet Cong village of Chau Lu a wide berth an hour later and kept pushing north two more miles. Halfway between Chau Lu and the KKK camp we stopped.

Kornie shook Bergholtz by the hand and silently clapped him on the back. Bergholtz made a sign to the Cambodian leader and they started due west across the ill-defined border into Cambodia. Kornie watched them until they melted into the dark, rugged terrain. In two and a half miles they would come to the river and follow it back south until they were squarely between Chau Lu and the Viet Cong camp. They would straddle the east-west road and bridge connecting the two Communist bases and set up blocking positions.

Kornie and I and a security squad walked the six miles back to camp, arriving about 3:00 A.M. We made straight for the radio room and Kornie called Schmelzer.

Schmelzer was handling his operation well. Fifty KKK bandits were already crossing into Cambodia. They would penetrate a mile and staying that far inside Cambodia walk south until they were opposite Chau Lu. Here, according to instructions, they would stop until sunrise. Then they would proceed another mile south. At the point where a needle of rock projected skyward they would cross back into Vietnam and report all they had observed to the Americans.

The KKK leader realized that the Americans had to know what the Viet Cong were doing. He also knew they couldn't send patrols across the border to find out. He was glad to mount an easy reconnaissance patrol in return for the equivalent of $10 a man plus five rifles and five automatic weapons.

Half the agreed-upon money and weapons Schmelzer had already presented to the KKK leader at the time his men began crossing the border. The balance would be forthcoming the moment the men crossed back into Vietnam at the needle-shaped rock and gave their reports.

In the radio room Kornie chortled as his operation began to tighten. "Schmelzer is good boy," he said. "Takes guts to deal with KKK. If they think for a minute they can take Schmelzer and his men, they do it.''

"Aren't you afraid they'll use those automatic weapons against you some day?" I asked.

Kornie shrugged. "Most of those KKK and their weapons will never get back from this mission."

He looked at his watch. It was 4:00 A.M. Kornie smiled at me and patted my shoulder. "Now is the time to start out for Chau Lu. We will drive the VC straight into the KKK at 0545, and Bergholtz and the Cambodes will cut both the KKK and VC to pieces and be out of there by 0600 hours." His laugh resounded in the radio shack. "Give me just a few more days and a regiment couldn't overrun Phan Chau."

There was a snapping of static and then the radio emitted Schmelzer's voice. "Grant, Grant, this is Handy. Come in, Grant."

Kornie picked up the mike. "This is Grant. Go ahead, Handy."

"Last of the bandits across. We are ready to carry out phase two. Is 0545 hours still correct?"

"Affirmative, Handy. But wait for us to start our little party off."

"Roger, Grant. We will be in position. When you open up we'll let go too. Leaving now. Handy out."

"Grant out," Kornie said into the mike and put it down. He walked out of the radio room, and on the parade ground we could sense more than see the company of Vietnamese strikers. Two Vietnamese Special Forces officers, the camp commander, Captain Lan, and his executive officer were standing in front of the company of civilian irregulars waiting for Kornie. They saluted him as he stood in the light flooding from the door of the radio room.

Kornie saluted back. "Are you ready to go, Captain Lan?"

"The men are ready," the Vietnamese commander said. "Lieutenant Cau and Sergeant Tuyet will lead them. I must stay in camp. Maybe B team need talk to me."

"Very good thinking, Captain," Kornie complimented his counterpart. "Yes, since I go out, very good you guard camp."

Pleased, Captain Lan turned his men over to Kornie and departed. "Lieutenant Cau, let's get these men on the move," Kornie urged. "You know the objective."

"Yes, sir. Chau Lu." In the dim light from the radio shack Kornie and I could just make out the broad grin on Cau's face. "We will clobber them, sir," he said, proud of his English slang.

Kornie nodded happily. "Right. We massacre them." To me he said, "Cau here is one of the tigers. If they had a few hundred more like him we could go home. He went through Bragg last year. Class before yours, I think."

For the second time that night we started north toward Chau Lu. Kornie seemed to be an inexhaustible tower of energy. Walking at the head of the column he kept up a brisk pace, but we had to stop frequently to let the short-legged Vietnamese catch up. It took exactly the estimated hour and a half to cover the almost five miles to the positions we took up south and east of the VC village. At 5:45 A.M. two companies of strikers were in place ready to attack Chau Lu. Schmelzer's men were ready to hit from the north.

Lieutenant Cau glanced from his wrist watch to the walls of the village one hundred yards away. He raised his carbine, looked at Kornie who nodded vigorously, and blasted away on full automatic. Instantly from all around the village the strike force began firing. Lieutenant Cau shrilled his whistle and his men moved forward. Fire spurted back at us from the village, incoming rounds whining. Instinctively I wanted to throw myself down on the ground but Cau and his men advanced into the fire from the village shouting and shooting. From the north Schmelzer's company charged in on the village also. Within moments the volume of return fire from the Viet Cong village faded to nothing.

"They're on their way now, escaping to their privileged sanctuary," Kornie yelled. "Cease fire, Lieutenant Cau."

After repeated blasts on the whistle the company gradually, reluctantly, stopped shooting. Schmelzer's people had also stopped and there was a startling silence.

The two companies entered the village and routed the civilians out of the protective shelters dug in the dirt floors of their houses.

Kornie looked at Lieutenant Cau in the pale light of dawn. Disappointment was clearly written on his face as his men herded civilians into the center of town. Cau had not been told about the rest of this operation. After a few minutes of preliminary questioning Cau came to Kornie.

"The people say no men in this village. All drafted into the Army. Just old men, women, and children."

Kornie glanced at his watch. 5:53. His infectious grin puzzled the Vietnamese officer. "Lieutenant Cau, you tell the people that in just a few minutes they'll know exactly where their men are."

Cau looked at Kornie, still puzzled. "They run across into Cambodia." He pointed across the town toward the border. "I would like to take my men after them." He smiled sadly. "But I think maybe I do my country more good if I am not in jail."

"You're so right, Cau. Now search the town. See if you can find any hidden arms."

"We are searching sir, but why would the VC hide guns here when just two hundred meters away they can keep them in complete safety."

Before Kornie could answer, a sudden, steadily increasing crackling of gunfire resounded through the crisp air of dawn. Kornie cocked an ear happily. The noise became louder and more scattered. Automatic weapons, the bang of grenades, sharp rifle reports and then the whooshing of hot air followed by the shattering explosions of recoilless-rifle rounds echoed up and down the border.

"Bergholtz is giving them hell," Kornie shouted gleefully, thumping me on the back. I tried to get out from under his powerful arms. "My God! I wish I was with Bergholtz and the Cambodes." A sharp burping of rounds which suddenly terminated with the explosion of a grenade caused Kornie to yell at Schmelzer, who was approaching us.

"Hey, Schmelzer. That was one of those Chinese machine guns we gave the KKK. Did you hear it jam?"

"I heard a grenade get it," Schmelzer answered.

The faces of the old men, women, and children were masks of sudden fear, confusion, and panic. They stole looks at we three Americans and a slow comprehension began to show in their eyes. Then their features twisted into sheer hatred.

The fire-fight raged for fifteen minutes as the sun was rising. To the south a steady series of flares spurted from the top of the hill, marking the rally point where Bergholtz and his Cambodians would cross back into Vietnam.

Kornie took a last look around the village. "OK, Schmelzer, let's go pay off the KKK. Give the ones that come back a

33

nice bonus. If they complain about being attacked by their good friends the VC, tell them"—Kornie grinned—"we're sorry about that."

He gave his executive officer a hearty slap on the back that would have sent a smaller man tumbling. "Be sure that your whole company has weapons at the ready," Kornie cautioned. "They might think we slipped it to them on purpose and do something naughty." Kornie was thoughtful for a moment. "Maybe I take a platoon of Lieutenant Cau's men and go with you. If we meet no trouble I'll go on south, find Bergholtz, and see how he did."

Leaving Lieutenant Cau the dreary task of searching the village and questioning the inhabitants, we started south. It was only a mile walk to the needle of rock, and a band of about 15 KKK were already there. Schmelzer, well covered by a platoon of his best riflemen, approached the KKK leader who was dressed in khaki pants and a black pajama shirt—two bandoleers of ammunition crossing his shoulders. An interpreter walked beside Schmelzer, and Kornie and I edged forward, being careful not to get between our riflemen and the KKK. Both Schmelzer and Kornie gave the thoroughly mean- and suspicious-looking bandit leader friendly smiles. Schmelzer reached inside his coat and produced a thick wallet. The sight of the money seemed to have a slightly calming effect on the KKK chief.

"When all your men are back I give you the other 25,000 piastres," Schmelzer said, counting the money.

The translator came back with the chief's retort. "Maybe my men do not all come back. Who they fight over there?"

"The VC of course," Schmelzer answered innocently. "Your men are friends of the Americans and Vietnamese aren't they?"

The KKK chief scowled, but he did not take his eyes off the money as Schmelzer counted it out. There was an uncomfortably long wait in a highly hostile atmosphere until the rest of the KKK started to arrive at needle rock from across the border.

Kornie and Schmelzer impassively watched the wounded, bloody men straggling in. Those who couldn't walk were helped by others. One or two carried shattered bodies.

"Remember how those monks looked with their heads under the arms?" Kornie asked Schmelzer, who nodded grimly.

Of the 50 KKK who had gone out, 30 were alive, only 10 unwounded. They brought back only six bodies.

The KKK chief, regarding his broken force, turned toward Kornie, his hand twitching at the trigger guard of the Chinese submachine gun Schmelzer had given him.

There was no doubt that the KKK knew they had been tricked by the Americans. Still, Kornie and Schmelzer played the game, expressing condolences at the number of KKK killed and wounded.

"Tell the chief," Schmelzer said, "we will pay a bounty of 500 piastres for each VC killed."

The chief's visage grew blacker as he talked to the survivors. The interpreter listened, turning his head sidewise to the KKK leader.

"He says," came the translation, "that his men were attacked from two directions at once. He says that first the shooting came from inside Cambodia and then from the VC running from the attack we made on Chau Lu. His men fired in both directions but killed mostly the men running from Chau Lu because they were easier to see. He says he wants to be paid for killing 100 VC. His men had no time to take ears or hands for proof. He says we tricked him, we did not tell him about Chau Lu."

"Tell him it was a very unfortunate misinterpretation of orders," Kornie said. "We'll pay him 500 piastres each for 25 VC dead, and we'll give him a 1,000 piastres for each of the men he lost KIA."

Schmelzer's company of Vietnamese irregulars sensed the hatred of the KKK for us and shifted their weapons uneasily; but the chief was in no position to instigate violence. His eyes glowed malevolently as he estimated our strength and then accepted the deal.

"Why do you pay him anything?" I asked. "He's going to try and get you anyway first chance that comes along."

Kornie grinned. "If a battle across the border is reported I think Saigon would accept the proposition that I paid a bunch of Cambodian bandits to break up the VC in Cambodia long enough to make my camp secure." To Schmelzer he said, "Get receipts from the leader for the money and get photographs of him accepting it."

The interpreter called to Kornie as he and I were about to

leave with a security platoon. "Sir, KKK chief say he lose three automatic weapons and two rifles. He want them replaced."

"You tell him I'm sorry about that. We gave him the guns. If he can't hold on to them, that's his fault." Kornie waited until his words had been translated. He stood facing the chief, staring down bleakly at the sinister little brown bandit. The KKK chief realized he had been accorded all the concessions he could expect and avoided Kornie's steady gaze. Schmelzer and his sergeant continued counting out the money for the Cambodian bandits.

The groans of the wounded men attracted Kornie's attention. He walked over to where they were sitting or lying in the dirt. After examining some of the more seriously wounded he straightened up.

"Schmelzer, before you go, ask the Vietnamese medics to help these men. They may be bandits fighting us tomorrow, looting merchants and monks the next day, but they do us a big service today—even though they do not mean to.

"And when you finish here go directly back to Phan Chau. And keep an alert rear guard all the time." Kornie grinned goodnaturedly at the scowling group around the KKK leader. "Those boys have big case of the ass with us."

Kornie and I and his platoon left the needle-rock rendezvous and walked south for two miles to our Cambodians' rally point, covering the distance in less than an hour.

Sergeant Falk and his security squad were just welcoming the returning Cambodians as we arrived. Sergeant Ebberson, the medic, had the tools of his trade spread out and ready. Stretchers and bearers were waiting.

Bergholtz, grinning from ear to ear, was waiting for us. "How goes, Bergholtz?" Kornie called, striding toward his big sergeant.

"We greased the shit out of them, sir," Bergholtz cried joyfully. "These Cambodes never had so much fun in their lives." The little dark men in tiger-striped suits bounced around happily, chattering to each other and displaying bloody ears, proof of the operation's success.

"How many VC killed in action?"

"Things were pretty confused, sir. From Chau Lu the VC walked right into us and the KKK. There was a lot of shooting going on in front of us. I think they killed as many of each other as we did in. Then the KKK and the VC both concentrated on us and our Cambodes flat-ass massacred everything that lived in front of us. If there aren't 60 dead VC lying out there I'll extend another six months. We lost a few dead and maybe 8 or 10 wounded but we didn't leave a body behind, sir.''

Kornie's eyes glistened with pride. ''By God damn, Bergholtz. We got the best camp in Vietnam. I volunteer us all to stay another six months. What you say?''

''Well, sir, we still have one more month left of our tour to burn the asses off the VC. This operation we made it out just in time. When we moved the VC were barreling down the road from the big camp, shooting like mad.''

Kornie watched as two Cambodians deposited the gore-smeared body of a comrade on the ground beside two other bodies. Sergeant Ebberson was working on the wounded as they were dragged and assisted in. Even the wounded were in good spirits. They had won a victory and the fact that it had been won by going illegally across the border only made the triumph more satisfying.

Kornie threw a massive arm around my shoulder, another around Bergholtz, and started us in the direction of Phan Chau. ''Let's go back, men. Maybe the VC call Phnom Penh and the Cambodian government will be screaming border violation. We must get immediate report to Colonel Train.''

We walked at the head of the security platoon for a few minutes and then Kornie said to me, ''You are friend of Colonel Train. How much of what happened today can I tell him? If the VC attack us tonight we might not be able to hold. But they won't hit us now.''

''I guess he'd understand that, Steve. Wouldn't look good for him to lose a camp. But he's still not really an unconventional warfare man.''

Kornie nodded in dour agreement.

''Too bad he couldn't spend a week with you,'' I went on. ''That would make a Sneaky Pete out of him if anything ever could.''

''He would court-martial me out of the Army after a week with me,'' Kornie declared. I tended to agree.

2.

It startled me to look at my watch as we marched into Phan Chau and see it was not quite 9:00 A.M. With all the action I thought it must be later. Kornie went into the operations room in the longhouse to prepare an after-action report. About noon, Falk completed his assessment of the interrogation's at Chau Lu and the account Bergholtz had given him. Kornie called a meeting to which he invited me.

It was the considered opinion of the Americans that there was little danger of the Viet Cong attacking Phan Chau for a few days at least. Kornie called for Sergeant Rodriguez. I was surprised to see the olive-complected Rodriguez in this camp of Viking types. Kornie's booming laugh when I stared at the Latin showed he had read my mind.

"Let me tell you, there is nothing more important than a good demolitions man in the kind of work we do. It takes a special devious mind to be a great demo man in the guerrilla game." Kornie gave Rodriguez a fond hug. "My teutonic knights miss that Latin demon in the spirit for explosives and detonating systems that makes Rodriguez the best demo man I know in ten years at this business." Without further explanation Kornie led the short, slight and swarthy sergeant, almost invisible in his commander's bear hug, toward a corner machine-gun bunker.

I considered taking a nap, but if Kornie, five years older than I, could look fresh and combat-ready, then I resolved not to sleep either. Instead I walked into the combined chow and recreation room, pulled up a chair and started making notes on what I'd seen that day.

About 3:30 there was a great commotion on the parade ground. I ran out at once. Lieutenant Cau, his pistol in the back of the neck of a striker, was herding a Vietnamese irregular toward the cage. This is a wire-mesh structure for punishment confinement common to all camps I had visited. It was impossible either to sit down or stand up in it, and during the day the sun broiled the occupant. Captured Viet Cong usually talked after two days without water in the cage.

A Vietnamese Special Forces sergeant opened the cage and the striker was crammed inside, the wire-mesh door locked behind him. Kornie and Rodriguez, who had been somewhere deep inside one of the fortress-camp's bunkers, crossed the parade ground and arrived at the cage as Lieutenant Cau finished a savage dressing-down of the prisoner.

"What's the flap, Cau?" Kornie asked.

"We discover this man cutting some barbed wire his work detail placing along west wall."

Kornie's face became grave. He turned to Rodriguez. "Finish that job even if you have to work all night."

"Yes, sir." Rodriguez left on the double.

Kornie stared thoughtfully at the prisoner. "Have you questioned him yet?"

"No, sir," Lieutenant Cau answered. "But I have put my best men along the walls and given orders that nobody leave Phan Chau. No man from here give VC any new information."

"Very good, Cau. So we do have VC infiltrators in the strike force. I expect it. I advise you and the camp commander to start interrogating this one now."

"Sir, Captain Lan took a convoy into town this afternoon." The lieutenant winked openly. "He may not be back until late tonight."

"That makes you acting camp commander, Cau. What are you going to do?"

Instantly Cau barked orders and two Vietnamese sergeants dragged the squirming striker out of the cage. "You should take this in," Kornie suggested to me, as the prisoner was hustled off. "Sergeant Ngoc, our Vietnamese Special Forces intelligence sergeant is an expert interrogator. He learned the trade with the Viet Minh before deciding he was not a Communist. I will introduce you to him, then I go back to work. I am worrying how much time we really did buy with our little operation this morning."

Kornie led me to the Vietnamese headquarters building. Newly constructed out of concrete with a wood roof, it already had the unkempt look and mouldering smell of Vietnamese military quarters.

Kornie led me along the dank corridor to a square cement room at the rear of the building. Slits at the top of the walls served as windows. A naked, glowing bulb hanging from the ceiling supplemented the light that seeped through the slits. A sallow-complexioned, almost cross-eyed Vietnamese Non-commissioned officer stood behind a crude wooden table surveying the trembling striker who had been brought in. I was introduced to Sergeant Ngoc and after he had milked my hand I rubbed it hard on my fatigue pants.

I stood in a far corner of the room and watched the proceedings. Ngoc ambled around the table toward the prisoner, seemingly paying him no attention. Suddenly Ngoc's right hand, palm cupped, swung out and with a hollow pop walloped the right ear of the captive, whose face contorted as he let out a whining yelp. Almost instantly Ngoc repeated the blow with his left hand to the left ear. The Viet Cong suspect desperately massaged under his ears and behind his jaw line. Ngoc asked him a question, but the answer did not satisfy him. A chop at the neck dropped the striker sagging to his knees. Ngoc gestured toward the table and two Vietnamese Special Forces enlisted men, acting as guards, dumped their charge into the chair.

Ngoc snatched at his victim's left hand and drew it toward him, turning it fingers up, forcing the wrist down on a leather strap nailed to the table. One of the guards fastened the strap tightly around the prisoner's wrist. Ngoc drew a bayonet from his belt and stabbed it into the table beside him. The prisoner flinched. From under the lapel of his camouflage uniform Ngoc pulled a long heavy pin with a purple globe for a head. In one swift movement he grabbed the striker's thumb with his left hand and with his right forced the pin under the thumbnail deep into the quick.

The suspect screamed. Ngoc pushed his face across the table and asked a question. The answer was unsatisfactory. Slowly, staring impassively at his victim, Ngoc worked the bayonet out of the table. Conversationally, he asked the prisoner a few questions and then, with emphasis, another. He waited. No answer. With the flat of the bayonet blade he tapped the head of the pin. The Viet Cong suspect let out another scream. Perspiration flowed from his face. One of the guards held the prisoner's right arm in a painful hammerlock.

Calmly, Ngoc replaced the bayonet on the table, reached into an inner pocket, and pulled out a notebook and ball-point pen. He laid them near at hand. Then he took up the ball-point pen in his right hand and poised it above the notebook while he quietly asked questions. The suspect blurted out words. Ngoc shook his head chidingly and carefully placed the pen back on the table. He picked up the bayonet and with a click tapped the needle almost to the depth of the quick. A tortured shriek was torn from the prisoner and tears rolled from his eyes.

Patiently, Ngoc exchanged the bayonet for the pen and waited expectantly. The prisoner was shaking and mumbling, but still he refused to divulge the information Ngoc was seeking. Ngoc waited for half a minute in silence, sighed, put down the pen and picked up the bayonet again. The prisoner's eyes followed each move Ngoc made. Ngoc held the flat of the blade above the purple pinhead, looked questioningly at the prisoner, and with slow, measured taps drove the needle down into the thumb-joint itself. The screeches extracted with each tap seemed to come not from conscious vocal mechanisms but from the suspect's inner being. Ngoc dropped his pose of patience and cried out savagely. The prisoner was obviously weakening, his brown face now red and sweat-soaked, his wet eyes glittering hysterically as he watched the flat of the bayonet hover above the head of the pin and then descend with a sharp clack which drove the needle all the way through the bent thumb-joint.

Lungs busily sucking in the dank air feeding the suspect's nerve-shattering screams, his whole body twitched and shuddered. It seemed that Ngoc had succeeded in breaking this man. When the echoes subsided, Ngoc began asking questions again. Perhaps the suspect regained control again or maybe the excruciating pain had parched his vocal cords. At any rate, a moment's relapse into apparent defiance angered Ngoc, who grabbed the head of the imbedded pin and shook it.

It took all the strength of the two guards to hold the screeching, thrashing body. Finally the prisoner slumped in exhaustion, gasping "Nuc," the Vietnamese word for water. Ngoc took up his pen again as the prisoner tried to talk, but the words whistled dryly from his throat. At a wave of Ngoc's hand a guard picked up a bucket of water and dashed it into the suspect's openmouthed face.

The water revived him sufficiently to talk. At once Ngoc began making notes. Whenever the prisoner seemed on the verge of cutting off the flow of information, Ngoc needed only to move a thumb and forefinger toward the head of the pin protruding from under the victim's thumbnail and his speech picked up speed.

After ten minutes of questioning Ngoc was satisfied. He said a few, almost gentle words to the prisoner—and then, a fast, deft move, and suddenly the needle, dripping blood, was in his fingers. The Viet Cong, for such he had finally admitted to being, moaned and slumped semi-conscious onto the table. Ngoc wiped the needle off in his victim's hair and thrust it back into the underside of his lapel. He turned to me with a satisfied look. Picking up his notebook and pen he motioned me to follow him.

Moments later we were out in the bright sunlight. I stood a moment breathing deeply but Ngoc hurried to Kornie's operations room.

An interpreter translated as Ngoc, consulting his notebook, delivered to Kornie, Bergholtz, Schmelzer, Falk and Lieutenant Cau the information he had extorted from the Viet Cong who had infiltrated the ranks of the Phan Chau strike force.

Ngoc now had the names of five other Viet Cong in the camp. It was possible there were more, but the five on Ngoc's list were the only ones the captured Viet Cong knew for sure. Furthermore, Ngoc reported, the attack had indeed been planned for tonight. The prisoner of course had no way of knowing how long it might be delayed now. He hadn't been among the strikers that raided Chau Lu.

Lieutenant Cau left to arrest the five men. Kornie looked at his wrist watch. "Too late now for the B-team intelligence boys with a polygraph crew to get here and question them." He shrugged. "Ngoc's methods work on some of these people, but I do not like torture. We do not even know if the five men our VC infiltrator named are really Communists. With Ngoc I find his victims say anything they think he wants to hear. The lie detector is best."

Kornie turned to Bergholtz. "Tell Borst to radio a report of this to the B team and ask for the polygraph crew tomorrow."

"Right, sir."

Kornie looked at me. "What do you think of our interrogation procedure?"

"It's always grim," I answered. "But I've been around some damned crude sessions. Ngoc is more refined than most."

Kornie nodded. "We have had a long, hard day. What say a little schnapps before supper. Hey? Schmelzer? Falk?" Kornie yelled down to the kitchen for ice, went to a cabinet, and took out a bottle of vodka. "Not like the schnapps we drink at my house in Fayetteville, eh?"

"That old aqua vitae was it, Steve."

"Yeah. It is too bad. The PX in Saigon don't carry schnapps." The ice arrived and Kornie poured us all a slug of vodka on the rocks. He held his glass up. "Well, even if we only buy another twenty-four hours, the operation was a success."

Kornie downed the rest of his drink. "Schmelzer, we keep 50 per cent alert tonight. Now I am going out to the corner bunkers."

Before he could leave, Bergholtz returned. "Borst got through to the B detachment," the team sergeant reported. "Captain Farnham and Sergeant Stitch will be out with the polygraph tomorrow afternoon at 1330 hours. Colonel Train is coming with them."

3.

The following morning there was feverish activity in camp. The concertina, barbed wire so named because it was put out in big cylindrical rolls shaped like an extended squeezebox, had been anchored to metal pickets around the entire outer perimeter of the camp. Beyond the concertina, tanglefoot barbed wire had been stretched out in the high grass. The inner perimeter was lined with sandbagged heavy log walls, with more barbed wire at their base and sharp bamboo pungi stakes pointing outwards. There was a third innermost defense position, the heavily sandbagged command bunker which could withstand even direct hits by mortar shells. On top of it was a protected observation post. The camp was pockmarked with round, sandbagged mortar emplacements. Phan Chau seemed all but impregnable to me, but Kornie, an experienced man at both assault and defense, was obviously concerned.

At noon I saw him inspecting the inner defenses and the bunkers for the fourth time that morning. I walked over to him. "Looks like it would take a Panzer division to move you out of here."

Kornie shook his head. "We don't even put out mines and booby traps yet. If they throw two battalions at us they might overrun the camp. It depends on how good the strike force fights. By God damn those politicians in Saigon should not have taken away my Hoa Hao troops." He studied the outer defense perimeter, a worried look on his ordinarily jovial face. "My Cambodes will stand up good. But when the attack comes the VC ultimately get through the outer barbed wire and we must fight them hand to hand between the perimeters."

"You're pretty sure it will come?"

"They got to attack. The VC been telling the people in all the hamlets around here they will take Phan Chau and then destroy every hamlet loyal to Saigon. They lose face they don't hit us. The VC know we get stronger every day."

Kornie strode toward the teamhouse. "I am going to tell Colonel Train the whole story," he said decisively. "Special Forces is going to have him for three years, maybe even six if he extends. He needs bad the education you don't get at the School. He may relieve me from command but before he goes from Vietnam he will know I am right."

Right on schedule at 1:30 P.M. the Huey landed outside camp. Kornie, Schmelzer, Captain Lan, who had returned from town, and Lieutenant Cau were out to meet Lieutenant Colonel Train and his men from the B team. The colonel alighted from the helicopter and shook hands all around. He asked me if I was finding things interesting enough. Following the colonel out of the chopper came Captain Farnham, the intelligence officer, and his sergeant carrying a large black case.

We walked through the two gates into camp and Kornie asked if anyone wanted a cold drink. Train shook his head. "Let's get on with the job."

"Right," agreed Kornie. "Sergeant Ngoc and Sergeant Falk are the intelligence NCO's here. They'll show Captain Farnham to the interrogation room and he can run the whole show from there."

Train nodded. "Now, Kornie, you and I have to talk some place secure. High command and the embassy have been asking some very strange questions about your operations out here."

"We can go to the operations room, sir."

Train took the cigar out of his mouth and gave me an apologetic smile. "You'll have to excuse us for an hour. Take a look at the polygraph in operation."

Sergeant Stitch had set up his machine on the table. With its dials, electrodes, and batteries it was a formidable-looking instrument. The interpreter, Ngoc, and Lieutenant Cau stared at the lie detector with great interest.

"OK," Captain Farnham said, "bring in the prisoners one by one." He asked Falk what he wanted to get out of them.

"Sir, we want to know if they are VC infiltrators. If they are we want to know the names of other VC sympathizers in the camp. We'd like to know more about the attack on Phan Chau. We think it was planned for last night. Fortunately, we headed it off temporarily."

Farnham gave the intelligence sergeant a sharp look. "That's what Colonel Train wants to find out about. What the hell did you do? Go right into Cambodia after them?"

"Sir, I guess Captain Kornie will be discussing that with the colonel."

"Good enough." Farnham turned to his sergeant. "Stitch here is an expert with the polygraph. If anybody can find the answers for you he's the man."

Lieutenant Cau opened the door and three guards shoved a tiger-suited striker into the room. He looked around fearfully and then saw the ominous-looking equipment on the table and recoiled. He was shoved roughly into the chair.

Stitch walked over to the frightened striker and said a few words in Vietnamese. The prisoner looked up, swallowed, and nodded. Farnham leaned toward me. "The only Vietnamese Stitch knows is how to say, 'We want to ask you some questions. If you tell the truth you won't be hurt.' "

The intelligence officer chuckled. "But the Vietnamese think he understands every word they say even though he uses an interpreter."

The reassuring words did little to erase the fear written on the suspect's face, and when Stitch started attaching the electrodes to the striker's wrists and then wrapped the blood-pressure tubes around his biceps and started to inflate them, terror shone from his eyes.

Stitch flicked a switch and made some adjustments on the machine. A needle began to oscillate. Then, through the interpreter, Stitch began to ask questions. Ngoc was fascinated with the machine and stared at the needle. It quivered as the interrogation proceeded, and then even before the translator put the question into Vietnamese it vibrated noticeably. Stitch had said "VC."

The prisoner denied he was a VC. The needle jumped.

Ngoc grasped the significance of the box at once and in an instant was on the prisoner, cuffing him sharply on the ears. The prisoner let out a startled yelp and gave Stitch a betrayed look.

"Tell him I said he won't get hurt if he tells the truth," Stitch said. "Tell him every time he lies this box tells me." Stitch went back to casual questions, forming a pattern of needle oscillation when the striker told the truth. Ngoc watched the needle intently.

"Do you know of any other VC who have infiltrated the strike force?" Stitch asked. The question was translated. The striker shook his head and said no.

The needle jumped and once again Ngoc was upon the prisoner, backhanding him across the temples.

Stitch waved Ngoc away. He turned dials and a humming noise came from the box. He pumped more air into the rubber tubes around the prisoner's biceps. "Now," Stitch said to the interpreter, "you tell this man that if he lies to me again this machine will blow his arm off."

From the look of terror on the striker's face there was no doubt he believed the infernal machine was quite capable of blowing his arm off or perpetrating any other form of fiendishness.

Stitch had the names of the other four strikers implicated by the Viet Cong Ngoc had questioned the day before. The translator asked by individual name if the other prisoners were Viet Cong infiltrators. The suspect, staring aghast at the machine, answered yes four times. The polygraph indicated he was telling the truth.

Ngoc was delighted. Through the interpreter he said, "This is truly a fine machine. Now we don't waste time. We know exactly who to torture."

Stitch shook his head. "When you learn to use this machine you don't need to use torture. I can find out whatever you want to know through the polygraph."

Ngoc listened to the translation and asked, "What if they refuse to say a word?"

"They're probably hard-core VC," Stitch replied. "Chances are you won't even torture the truth out of them."

"If they are truly the enemy they should be tortured anyway," Ngoc retorted.

"Now we get the Oriental mind at work," Stitch said

wearily to the Americans in the room. "If we stay here for twenty years we won't change them, and God save us from getting like them." To the translator, Stitch said, "Put this Communist in a solitary cell and let me work on another one."

While Sergeant Stitch demonstrated the effectiveness of the polygraph, Lieutenant Colonel Train and Captain Kornie were in heated discussion. Much later, Kornie gave me a detailed description of the interview.

"Look, Kornie," Train began, the moment he and Kornie had seated themselves in the operations room, facing the large map of the local terrain. "I know your record. You're a hell of a fighter. But whatever you did yesterday morning has got the ambassador and our generals in a serious flap. The Cambodian government complained that American-led Vietnamese troops violated the border and killed or wounded 25 Cambodian civilians. They named Phan Chau as the originating point of this aggression."

Kornie did not reply immediately to his superior, five years younger and vastly less experienced in unorthodox warfare. Train puffed on his cigar and Kornie tapped a cigarette out of his pack, lit it, and sat back waiting.

"I don't really believe you'd violate the border without telling us, Kornie," Train primed. "Apparently the Cambodian complaint was informal. They didn't make it public nor are they going to SEATO or the United Nations. But they said that if the United States and Vietnam do not remove the irresponsible officers who have no regard for the sovereignty of Cambodia, then Cambodia will ask for help from wherever they can get it to protect their citizens from American-inspired marauders." Train looked at Kornie sharply. "That means inviting in North Vietnam and Red China. Now what *did* happen?"

Kornie stood up and walked to the map. "In the first place, sir, if my camp had been attacked last night on schedule we would have been overrun. When we let the Vietnamese corps commander take away my 250 Hoa Hao strikers, they took the only troops I had besides the Cambodes that I could be certain were not infiltrated by Viet Cong sympathizers."

"Kornie," Train began, "you know what General Co said."

Kornie nodded. "He was afraid that Hoa Hao colonel

47

might unite his men in a power play. So he broke up all Hoa Hao units. But out here, with a damned VC regiment sitting safely across the border building up to hit me, I could count on the Hoa Hao to fight the Communists and be loyal to me.''

Train growled something inaudible and studied the burning end of his cigar. "Sir," Kornie continued, "when I lose the Hoa Hao I got only a company of Cambodes besides the Vietnamese strikers. I got a camp to defend that is half finished. We are vulnerable. We don't get the concertina until the day before yesterday. Even now we got no mines, no booby traps outside our wire. Phan Chau is supposed to be the most important border surveillance camp in this sector. We are the biggest deterrent to the Communists trying to get into the Mekong Delta through these hills." Kornie rapped the map with a big fist.

"The Viet Cong want us out of here, sir. If we finish the camp's defenses they cannot take Phan Chau. But if they hit us now, when we are weak, while they got infiltrators in our strike force, they stand a damned good chance of overrunning us and destroying Phan Chau.''

Kornie stopped talking for a moment, then continued. "Between the Hoa Haos and the Cambodes, even with the defenses not done, we could fight off two, maybe three battalions of VC. But because of Vietnamese politics I lose my real fighting force. Phan Chau is going to be attacked, sir," Kornie said forcefully. "Every day agent reports say we are in for it. Yesterday we catch a striker cutting barbed wire. He tells us the attack was planned for last night. And only Christ, maybe in this case Buddha, knows how many strikers in this camp are VC." He watched Train intently to see if the words were making an impression. Train puffed his cigar.

"Do you agree, sir," Kornie continued, "that I had to do something to head off this attack?"

Train took the cigar out of his mouth. "Perhaps, Kornie. But did you have to violate the border and cause an incident?''

"Sir, I did what I had to do to save my camp!''

"All right, Kornie," Train said. "Tell me everything. Don't leave out a single detail.''

"Right, sir.'' Kornie sat down again and for twenty minutes explained the operation. Train sucked hard on his cigar as he concentrated on Kornie's story. When it was over the colonel leaned back, an expression somewhere between pain and disbelief on his face. He ground out his cigar viciously.

"Captain, that is the most audacious, unorthodox, and irresponsible operation that any man in any command of mine has ever pulled. My God, Kornie, you are playing with already-inflamed politics."

"But, sir, it worked," Kornie argued. "Not only we hurt the VC and the KKK bandits, we stall off the attack. Even we get hit tonight, in the last twenty-four hours we doubled our defensive capabilities. We got claymore mines out at least, and one or two other little tricks for the Communists when they come. My men, the demo sergeant most of all, been working without sleep twenty-four hours."

"Kornie, you know you can't go off attacking across borders, hiring bandits, acting like"—he sputtered—"like the CIA. We're part of the United States Army." He picked up the green beret on the table beside him. "Do you think this hat gives you some kind of special license to go off on your own, conduct operations that may endanger the peace of the world?"

"Sir, I've been in Special Forces almost ten years. All that time we were trained to get special jobs done any way we can. And I was on loan to the Agency for a year. I know what I can and what I cannot do to get the job done."

Then, after a short pause: "It takes time to be a Special Forces officer. You will see, sir."

Nonplussed, Train pulled another cigar out of the pocket of his jungle fatigues, bit the end off, and lit up. Slowly he exhaled a puff of smoke, trying to decide just what to do about this difficult subordinate. "Kornie," he said finally, "I have to go to Saigon tomorrow and I'd like you to come with me."

"But, sir, we expect attack any day or night. I must be here, at least until the attack is over." He thought a minute. "We are both in trouble if I am away from my post when it is overrun."

Train considered the situation. Before he could answer there was a knock at the door. "See who it is," Train snapped.

Kornie opened to a worried Lieutenant Schmelzer, followed

by Lieutenant Cau. "Excuse me, sir," Schmelzer said to Train, "but this may be important."

"Go ahead, Lieutenant."

"Right, sir. We were interrogating the prisoners when a Vietnamese sergeant came in saying that two strikers on barbed-wire detail deserted. He had their names and Sergeant Stitch asked the man he was interrogating with the polygraph if they were VC sympathizers. The answer was yes."

Kornie turned to Train. "You understand what this maybe is, sir? If the deserters tell the VC we are grabbing infiltrators, they might attack tonight while they still got people on the inside."

"Sir!" Schmelzer interjected. "One of the strikers we questioned said he thought the attack *would* come tonight. They all said it was planned for last night."

Kornie shot a look at Train and then ordered Schmelzer to forget the interrogation. "Get as many more claymore mines out as you can. Tell Rodriguez all his systems must be working before dark. I want a 50 per cent alert until midnight, full alert for the rest of the night. Let the men who have the least sleep go to bed after supper."

Schmelzer and Cau left the operations room.

"Colonel," Kornie said, "let me stay here until the attack comes or we get our defenses so good the VC don't try to take the camp. We are in trouble now."

"Why did you let yourself get into this bind, Kornie?"

The captain struggled to keep his patience. "Sir, my Hoa Haos were taken away on a day's notice. If you check my requests you see that for last two days I am begging for two companies of Vietnamese Marines, Rangers, or paratroopers to help us hold until the camp is completed."

"All right, Kornie, you stay until the camp is secure. But make sure the job takes no more than a week. You and I have a date in Saigon."

"Thank you, sir."

"Now, let's put the intelligence section on the chopper and get them back to the B detachment."

"And you, sir?"

"I'll stay overnight."

"Sir," Kornie protested, "even after what we did yesterday, we expect an attack tonight."

"Yes, Captain. I suspect the VC have all the reinforcements they need right in Cambodia." And with finality he said, "I will be here if they do hit Phan Chau tonight."

4.

Lieutenant Colonel Train and I had a few brief words at 5:00 P.M. The Huey was waiting to take off with the intelligence section and the Viet Cong infiltrators, who were tied with wire and lying face down on the floor of the helicopter.

Lieutenant Colonel Train wanted me deported from the potential battle scene, and I had to remind him we had put in three months together at Fort Bragg and that he knew I was trained for this sort of thing. "Also," I said as a clincher, "I'm here with permission from the commander of Special Forces. If I get myself zapped that's tough, but it's my job to chance it."

Train, Kornie, and I saw the chopper off, then returned to the camp. At the outer perimeter of the concertina Kornie supervised the closing of the barbed-wire barricade as we went through. He repeated the process again at the inner gate.

There was a faint coolness between Train and Kornie at supper, but the B-team CO was every inch the commander who loved and admired his troops and was happiest when in the field. He could be personal with them without encouraging undue familiarity.

After supper the weapons sergeant brought Train a pistol belt and harness hung solidly with ammunition pouches. "There's four hundred rounds of AR-15 ammo on the belt, sir, and more in the mortar bunkers."

Kornie, the inexhaustible Viking, finally admitted that he hadn't slept in almost two days and asked Train's permission to be excused until midnight. So Train and I accompanied Lieutenant Schmelzer on his round of inspections along the walls.

"You graduated from the Point?" Train asked the lieutenant.

"Yes, sir. 'Fifty-eight."

"I thought I saw it on your record. I was class of 'forty-eight. Had three years enlisted service during the war." Train smiled at the young lieutenant. "You're about ready to make captain. I suppose you'll be going to a more conventional Infantry unit when you finish the Special Forces assignment?"

"I wouldn't go in any straight-leg outfit if I could help it, sir. I'm going to try and keep extending in Special Forces."

Train shook his head. "You're young, Schmelzer. You have the makings of a fine career. But none of us can afford to do more than two tours at most in Special Forces. After six years your thinking gets unorthodox. After nine years you're typed. You'll be lucky to retire a bird colonel."

"I know staying in Special Forces has slowed up a lot of careers, but I believe in it, sir. My wife believes in it, too. She's with me all the way," Schmelzer added proudly. "My father was Regular Army and he feels the same way you do, but wars are changing. We'll either be fighting against guerrillas like we are here, or we'll be guerrillas—maybe in Cuba or Eastern Europe, probably pretty soon now in North Vietnam." Schmelzer excused himself and mounted the key northwest bunker.

"Fine young officer," Train observed. "He'll work out well after his Special Forces service is behind him."

We waited for him to come down. "How is it, Lieutenant?"

"They're up there, sir, wide awake on that machine gun. I just hope they're ours."

"Why wouldn't they be?" Train asked sharply. "Major Tri—my counterpart at the B team—has full confidence in his men here and the strike-force personnel under them."

"Yes, sir," Schmelzer replied dutifully, but doubt showed in his voice.

Suddenly I felt tired. "If you fellows will excuse me, I think I'll grab a few hours sleep. I'll be ready at midnight, Lieutenant. You can put me anywhere you need an extra gun."

"We'll wake you up," Schmelzer promised. "Full alert for all Americans after midnight. Captain Lan won't agree to more than 50 per cent alert for the Vietnamese. I guess he's afraid he'll have to stay up all night too."

"Schmelzer, you should be more careful how you talk about your Vietnamese counterparts," Train said. "Major Tri tells me his officers are very sensitive about being deprecated by us."

"Yes, sir," I heard Schmelzer say as they walked off. "But you do have to watch them, sir."

Sergeant Bergholtz shook me awake after midnight and told me that the captain wanted me in the operations room. There I found Kornie, a tired but resolute Lieutenant Colonel Train, and Lieutenant Schmelzer looking as fresh and eager as though he'd just risen from a full night's sleep. "Looks like we maybe get hit," Kornie was saying when I came in. "There are lights we never seen all around us—fires, flashlights, signal flares. If they attack we radio the B team for Air Force flare ships to light up the area."

"Any place you want me?" I asked.

"You go with Bergholtz and Falk. They take over a 60-mm. mortar position and tell you what to do."

"Right."

"Ready to go, sir?" Bergholtz asked me.

"Any time."

They led me out of the operations room across the parade ground to a round sandbagged bunker between the American and Vietnamese headquarters. The mortar bunker was near the west wall—the wall facing the border from which the attack was expected. It had the least amount of open terrain, about three hundred yards from the outer defense perimeter to the scrub-brush and rocky base of the hills.

"Can you pull increments?" Bergholtz asked.

"Sure. Just tell me what charge you want."

"We'll probably be dropping them pretty close. Charge two. Your other job is to make damned sure none of our own strikers get near us if there's an attack. They might be VC and toss a grenade in with us."

"I'll keep my eyes open."

"Right. And if you hear anything heavy fall in here," Bergholtz said as we climbed over the sandbags, "yell grenade and we'll bail the hell out."

"Do we have any Vietnamese in this crew?"

"Yeah, they're still resting. But if the fireworks start they'll be in here. We'll identify them."

Falk indicated the wooden crates of mortar shells and we pulled two of them out of the depths of the heavily sandbagged ammunition section of the bunker and began opening cardboard tubes. On each shell we pulled the increments—little pouches of powder—from the tail fins, leaving just two, which would give the shell almost minimum-range propulsion. The other box was left with its rounds on full charge for longer-range shelling.

Captain Kornie, closely attended by Lieutenant Colonel Train, stopped by the bunker on one of his constant inspection rounds. When he left, Bergholtz and Falk discussed in low tones the possibilities of an attack that night. Falk, as intelligence sergeant, said all evidence pointed to the Viet Cong hitting. Bergholtz countered that the Viet Cong simulate preparations to hit camps all over Vietnam just to keep the Americans shaken up.

"I'll bet you 1,000 piastres to 500 we don't get hit tonight," Bergholtz said.

Falk looked up from a mortar round with interest. He was about to answer when an angry rattle shook the air overhead. Before Falk could answer Bergholtz cried, "You took too long, Babe. Bet's off."

The yell of "mortars" passed across the bunkers. I threw myself down next to the bunker wall. There was a violent explosion just behind us, followed by several more as a barrage of shells crashed eastwards across the camp.

"WP!" Falk cried. The flames from the white phosphorus rounds started setting fire to the buildings. Confused shouts came from the strike-force barracks to our rear. To our left, near the American longhouse, stood one of the Cambodians' barracks. In the flickering light of the fires I saw the Cambodes throwing combat harnesses over their shoulders as they rushed out and split into two sections: one went to the north wall, the other to the south.

"Goddamned good bunch," Bergholtz said. "They were ready."

Toward the rear of the camp two of the Vietnamese strike-force barracks blazed. Agonized screams came from them.

Falk winced. "God! Some of those poor kids must have got burned up in their sacks."

The field telephone buzzed and Bergholtz picked it up. "Number four," he said. He listened and then another whirring in the air made us huddle down. "Yes," Bergholtz was saying. "Six hundred meters, 270 degrees." He put the receiver back on the hook just as another series of searing blasts tore across the camp. "Flash the light on the 270-degree aiming stake for me, Babe," he said. Falk complied. Bergholtz stared through the mortar sight and cranked the correct azimuth and elevation into the weapon. "OK, charge four, give 'em four rounds of WP."

In rapid succession Falk exploded four shells out of the mortar tube. We waited for half a minute as the camp was rocked by VC mortars. Then the phone rang. Bergholtz picked it up, called his position number, and listened.

"The tower says our WP's on target. Fire HE now." Falk reached for the high-explosive rounds and plopped four down the tube. The hollow reports of the camp's other mortars sounded around us. Two positions were continuously firing illuminating rounds which lit up the fields outside with a sickly pale-yellow light. I sensed men running toward the bunker and pointed my carbine at them.

"They're ours," Bergholtz called.

Immediately after our second group of rounds exploded the field phone rang and Bergholtz grabbed it. "Tower says we were right in them," he reported. "Keep throwing it to 'em."

As Bergholtz and Falk with their two newly arrived Vietnamese mortarmen started lobbing high-explosive shells, I cautiously poked my head up and looked around the camp. Several of the buildings were burning. WP and HE rounds were exploding all around the camp. The smell of powder and explosives was everywhere. On the walls the strikers were peering out, holding their fire until they could see something to shoot at. It was a mortar duel for the time being, the spotters in the tower trying to call down our barrages on the enemy weapons. Every unwounded man in camp was against the walls in the square sand-bagged positions, which protected them from shell fragments bursting inside the camp as well as outside.

The heat and smoke from the fires became intense and, as the WP shelling continued, the unmistakable and sickening smell of burning flesh wafted over the camp.

The field telephone rang. Bergholtz took it, listened, and shouted, "Charge three. They're moving in from the west and north." The Vietnamese and American mortar crews were working smoothly and the rounds were pouring out of the camp just as fast, or faster than the incoming rounds were pounding us.

Again the field phone rang. I became aware of the firing on

the walls now. "Charge two!" Bergholtz shouted. "They're getting up to our outer wire."

We could hear our own rounds exploding just beyond the outer perimeter. The heavy machine guns along the wall were pumping bullets into the enemy. The whoosh of the camp's 57-mm. recoilless rifles and rocket launchers came from the west and north walls.

The phone to his ear, Bergholtz yelled, "Charge one!" He made for the mortar tube, changed the elevation and went back to the phone. "They're on the concertina!" he yelled.

The eerie, ear-splitting noise of incoming rockets followed by shattering explosions told us that the Communists had both 57- and 75-mm. recoilless rifles. Phan Chau was in trouble. All the bravado I had felt when insisting that Lieutenant Colonel Train let me stay seeped out of me.

In the heavily sandbagged iorn-ringed observation stand above the command bunker, Kornie and Train watched the progress of the attack. The Vietnamese camp commander was below in the nearly impregnable bunker, taking field telephone reports. A Vietnamese and an American heavy-weapons sergeant were in the tower directing the mortar fire. Borst, in the communications section of the main bunker, was keeping the B team appraised of the situation. Already flare ships were on the way to light up the battle. Meanwhile, our mortars, firing illuminating rounds, clearly lighted the outer perimeter of the camp, and into the circle of light a wave of black-uniformed men moved steadily forward.

Many hours later Kornie told me how the battle had looked from his position. Enemy rocket shells crashed into the barbed wire, opening rents toward which the Viet Cong headed. The attack was now concentrated on the west and north walls. Machine-gun and rifle fire from our walls raked the first wave of Viet Cong, dropping them in the tangled maze of barbed wire. Another Communist section charged the outer perimeter. The mortars were firing at minimum range now but the Communists came forward, many carrying ladders which they threw over the wire.

Suddenly, incomprehensibly, the key northwest bunker machine guns began to rake our own west and north walls. Cambodes and Vietnamese preparing to charge out and meet the incoming Communists were falling from the walls in crumpled heaps, either back into the camp or out onto the pungi stakes in front, which impaled their bodies.

"Kornie!" Train shouted. "What are those insane bastards doing?"

"We got VC in the strike force! They're on that bunker," Kornie yelled back. He snatched his field telephone and cranked the handle shouting, "Schmelzer, get reinforcements ready to take the northwest bunker. The VC got it!"

Schmelzer's position in a mortar bunker next to the operations room enabled him to watch at close range the fighting on the west wall. With Schmelzer was Lieutenant Cau talking on his field phone to Captain Lan safely in the main bunker. Schmelzer pounded his courterpart to indicate he should get all the strikers he could to take back the northwest bunker. Cau and Schmelzer could both see the devastating fire from the bunker spewing death along the west wall in front of them.

Lieutenant Colonel Train was appalled at the speed with which Phan Chau was seemingly falling apart. Then suddenly, shockingly, the northeast bunker started firing down the north wall, catching the hundred or more defenders in a murderous crossfire. Train turned to Kornie. "We'll have to evacuate to the southeast. Borst can call for gun ships to pick us up."

"Colonel," Kornie cried over the explosive din of the battle, "you are going to see how crazy and unconventional I really am."

He reached down to the floor of the observation post, kicked aside a sand bag and pulled out a box streaming insulated wires. In the light of the illuminating flares he studied the switches a moment. He threw one, then another.

Instantly, first the northwest and then the northeast bunker exploded, their treacherous machine gunners silenced. Over the field phone Kornie yelled, "Schmelzer, take the two bunkers."

The first wave of Viet Cong were well through the outer barbed-wire entanglements, not more than thirty yards from the walls. Kornie threw another knife switch on his detonating box. No less than a dozen simultaneous explosions rang out from the north wall, and the pressing mass of black-clad enemy crumpled beneath a lethal hail of jagged metal.

"Claymores!" Kornie yelled above the renewed firing. "Very good!"

Schmelzer and Lieutenant Cau had commandeered reinforcements from the south wall and were making for the two smoking bunkers. Jumping into the northwest bunker Schmelzer riddled the wounded Viet Cong with his AR-15, and the strikers behind him, Cambodes and Vietnamese, righted the overturned machine gun, dug ammunition belts out of the debris, pitched bodies over the wall and were set up and firing just as the next wave of Viet Cong broke through the outer defenses to threaten the walls once more.

During all this time the Viet Cong mortar fire never ceased, killing and wounding strikers everywhere within the camp. A round dropped onto the main bunker, its concussion flinging Kornie and Train to the bottom of the observation post. The sandbagging saved them from being shredded by the blast of steel fragments.

Kornie pulled himself up and looked out over the battle. By now an Air Force plane was circling overhead, dropping high intensity flares, and turning the battlefield into high noon. The mortars, relieved of the necessity of firing illuminating rounds, kept a steady rain of high-explosive rounds dropping on the attacking Viet Cong ranks.

When Kornie and Train recovered from the blast they saw that the enemy seemed slightly slowed down. With both bunkers in action again and the north wall spitting a solid sheet of death, the first Communist bid for a fast victory was gone. The Viet Cong rocket launchers kept up a steady fire, though many of the missiles were flying high over the camp in an effort to knock out the tower. It presented a small target, but if hit it would destroy the effectiveness of Phan Chau's mortar fire, since it acted as observation post.

The bunkers were under incessant recoilless-rifle fire, which was furiously returned. Abruptly from the west came the sound of bugles. Out of the blackness of the foothills and scrub-brush a few hundred yards away and into the bright light of the flares appeared over two hundred Viet Cong advancing on foot.

At the same moment the Viet Cong were pressing in from the direction of the Cambodian border, the attack from the north was launched anew. In a vicious salvo of rocket fire, mortar-shelling, and heavy machine-gunning the Viet Cong swept through the scattered outer-defense barbed wire and charged the north wall.

Schmelzer in the damaged northwest bunker was now under fire from two sides. Thanks to the foresight of Rodriguez, who had laid his charges in all the bunkers the day before against just such a possibility, Schmelzer had both of the heavy machine guns in operation. Rodriguez had carefully placed the charges to do as little damage to equipment as possible, while killing or wounding every man in the position.

Kornie had one eye on the north and west walls, the other on the southeast and southwest bunkers to make sure they didn't fall victim to similar treachery. Train was firing his automatic rifle now at the Viet Cong advancing toward the inner perimeter. The Communists were within twenty yards of the north wall when Lieutenant Cau screamed orders from the bunker he had taken, jumped down outside the walls and headed straight for the Viet Cong. Over the walls clambered a platoon of screaming Cambodian and Vietnamese strikers with bayonets fixed and charged the Viet Cong. Bayonets ripped bodies, tore out throats, and after five minutes of vicious, bloody, hand-to-hand combat the Viet Cong advance was halted. Schmelzer now was able to turn both of his heavy machine guns on the Communists who were now breaching the western outer-defense perimeter.

Kornie, watching intently from the observation post, reached for his black box. Again he threw a knife switch and a dozen claymore mines, trained on the western outer perimeter, went off. Black-clad enemy fell screaming, but others still came on. Their rockets and mortars had mangled the concertina and tanglefoot barbed wire. In spite of the heavy fire streaking from the west wall the Communists advanced. Mortar shells fell with uncanny accuracy on our walls, knocking out sections of the inner defenses and killing or wounding the defenders.

Through the western outer perimeter the Viet Cong streamed. Strikers rushed from the south and east walls to meet the new attack. Rockets tore out sections of the wall and reached for the machine-gun bunkers. The northwest and southwest bunkers were subjected to heavy recoilless-rifle fire. Only the north wall, thanks to Lieutenant Cau's bloody countercharge, had successfully beaten back the Communist attackers.

Kornie turned to Train. "It's up to the men now," he

shouted above the firing. "We got no more claymores. I had no time to lay on my full dose of secret weapons. But I can still knock out the other two bunkers if VC get into them."

As Kornie watched the Viet Cong steadily advancing from the west through the barbed wire and withering fire, a rocket made a direct hit on the northeast bunker, blowing off the top machine-gun position. Kornie clutched the edge of his post and stared. The machine gun in the lower, heavily protected base kept up its deadly grazing fire about a foot above the ground. But the gunners and crew on top were blown into scattered pieces. Kornie knew Schmelzer had been helping direct the fighting from the vantage point of the top of that bunker.

The Viet Cong, perhaps 50 of them, had reached the west wall and were trying to climb it. Hand-to-hand fighting raged. Train had set his AR-15 on semi-automatic and was picking away at the enemy from the observation post. The entire attack was now centered on the west wall. The camp's mortar positions were still battering the Viet Cong at close range, helping to hold them back at the outer perimeter.

From our mortar position we could see the Viet Cong clambering over the walls. Twice, figures in black pajamas fought their way into the camp and sprayed the defenders from the inside with automatic weapons until they were themselves shot down.

Bergholtz and Falk saw more and more Viet Cong begin to breach the walls. The Vietnamese strikers seemed to be losing heart. "Hey, Babe!" Bergholtz cried to Falk, "let's give them a hand on the wall. The Viets can handle the mortar."

"You'd better stay in here," Bergholtz shouted to me needlessly, and firing his AR-15 as he went he headed for the wall. The two big bare-headed Vikings reached the walls and with savage yells plunged into the fighting. The unexpected appearance in the thick of the battle of the American giants, towering a foot above the combatants on both sides seemed to stiffen the resolve of the flagging defenders. The strikers flocked about the two Americans, and screaming curses their resistance became more ferocious than ever. Falk, firing his automatic rifle with his left hand, grabbed a bayonet-tipped carbine from a lunging Viet Cong, gave it a twirl and plunged it through a Communist's back with such force that it pinned him, squirming, to the mud wall.

Before my eyes the tide turned again. Shrieking and yelling, the strikers jumped from the walls, now cleared of live Viet Cong, and pursued the enemy into the area between the perimeters. Another American sergeant wearing his green beret jumped over the wall, rallying the strikers behind him. The impact of the fighting was irresistible; shouting like a combatant, I leaped out of the safety of the bunker and ran for the wall. Looking down at the savage fight below, I could scarcely control the near-unconquerable impulse to jump. On the walls wounded strikers still able to fire weapons kept up a blast at the new squads unendingly breaching the outer perimeter.

It seemed impossible that we could hold out against another determined wave of these ferocious, suicidal Communists. Slowly our forces cleared the area outside the west wall, and the VC, hauling as many of their dead and wounded as they could with them, retreated beyond the outer perimeter. The strikers and the three American sergeants likewise retired behind their own walls again as renewed Communist mortar fire started falling.

I heard the incoming rounds and plastered myself to the wet red earth. A series of rounds plowed up the ground around us. When I pulled myself up I saw that Kornie had left his post and was standing behind the wall, assessing the damage. Bergholtz, his left arm gushing blood, and Falk, miraculously unwounded, rallied around him. The other sergeant who had gone out also came back wounded. I recognized the slight figure of the demolitions sergeant, Rodriguez. His fatigues were blood-soaked around his chest and he staggered, both hands held above his right breast.

"Where's Schmelzer?" Kornie asked. There was no answer. Kornie yelled the name of his executive officer into the strange lull in the fighting. There was no answer.

"Our orders," Kornie said hoarsely, "are for all Americans to exfiltrate the camp if we see it's going to be overrun. We're missing Schmelzer and maybe others. Falk, right now, find every American. Tell them to report to the control bunker. If anyone is dead try to drag the bodies in. I'll make the decision what we do then. Move!"

Falk took off to search the positions assigned to members of the American team. Screams and begging cries of the wounded arose from all sections of the camp. Kornie looked at me and shook his head. "We cannot hold against more than another company, two maybe. If they got another battalion they overrun us."

"How's Train?" I asked.

"He's in the commo bunker with Borst trying to get help over the radio. He's been talking to the flare ships about getting fighter support. The God damn Vietnamese Air Force don't fly at night and our nearest American fighters are at Soc Trang. That's more than a hundred and fifty miles."

From out in the foothills, beyond the area which the faithful Air Force C-47's were lighting up with flares, came the sharp, stinging notes of a bugle. It was joined by others. The bugles blasted fear into the hearts of the strike force who had regrouped on the walls. Sergeant Ebberson, the medic, appeared.

"Sir," he said to Kornie, "I've got three Vietnamese medics, two nurses and Sergeant Heimer working on the wounded. The dispensary's been hit twice but we put out the fires. If we pull out of Phan Chau, sir, a lot of wounded are going to die. Bergholtz and Rodriguez are both pretty bad. They couldn't walk far."

Kornie nodded in comprehension. "You heard those bugles, Ebberson? Maybe they are bluffing or maybe they really got another battalion. We'll soon find out. But we got to be ready to evacuate through the southeast gate if we're going to be overrun. Those are orders."

"Yes sir," Ebberson answered. "I'll get the medical section ready."

"Have you seen Schmelzer?" Kornie asked wearily.

"No, sir." Ebberson headed back for his dispensary.

The bugles sounded louder now, as though they were closer. "Stay with me," Kornie said to me, and headed away from the walls.

In the open parade ground he checked the fire arrow that indicated the direction of enemy strength. It was locked pointing due west at the attacking Viet Cong. Cans of sand, heavy oil and gasoline in them burning steadily, outlined the big wooden arrow. From the air, if help came, the pilots would know from the arrow where to strafe and drop their bombs. Kornie and I went up to his command post above the main bunker. The A team, except for Schmelzer, Train, Borst on the radio, Bergholtz, Rodriguez and the medics, gathered outside the main bunker.

"Get inside," Kornie commanded. "If I call down, head for the southeast gate. Borst will radio flare ships to illuminate only west of the camp. When we get out we head due east into the hills. And let us pray we do not run into our old friends, the KKK!"

The telltale whirring of incoming 60-mm. mortar rounds cut off further talk. The men scrambled into the security of the deep main bunker, Kornie and I remaining on top.

"Oh, my God," Kornie groaned. "Look."

The whole western approach to the camp, illuminated up to the hills, suddenly filled with black-uniformed enemy. Once again mortars smashed into camp. The shrill sounds of their bugles carried clearly to us. Lieutenant Cau, wounded in the face, arm, and leg in the slashing counterattack, came up to Kornie's post.

"Sir," the Vietnamese lieutenant reported, "I put almost every good man left in camp on west wall but a few men on other walls. What more advice you give me?"

"You and your men have fought well and bravely, Lieutenant. Where is Captain Lan?"

"Still in bunker." Cau indicated below where we were standing.

"My advice is give the VC bloody hell to the end, and you might say a few words to Buddha while you're at it."

"I am a Catholic, sir."

"Well try Jesus," Kornie said, meaning no irreverence. "You know, Lieutenant, the Americans have orders to evacuate—get out if they're getting overrun."

"Yes, sir. We'll cover you. I leave southeast bunker full staff to cover you."

"Thanks, Cau. If we get out of this, Lieutenant Colonel Train and I are going to see you make captain."

"Thank you, sir. Do not let them put me at desk in Saigon." Cau saluted and in spite of his wounds limped to the west wall to command the final defense of Phan Chau.

Kornie's eyes were moist. "My God. When you meet one like Cau, you hate your guts for all the bad things you say about the Vietnamese."

Our mortars, still directed by the Vietnamese sergeant in the tower, which so far had proved impossible for the Communists to destroy, poured accurate destruction into the advancing ranks of the fresh Viet Cong battalion.

"They want this place God damn bad," Kornie muttered. "They had two battalions broken and now they'll lose most of a third to get us." The strike force opened up with their 57-mm. recoilless rifles and rocket launchers, but the black horde kept coming, fanning out as though they would hit the north and south walls as well as the west. The machine-gun tracers stabbed out at them, but they moved inexorably toward us.

"This has to be it," Kornie said.

The remaining machine guns stuttered defiance as Viet Cong mortars continued to plow up the western section of the camp.

Suddenly, the loud snarls from the sky we had all been desperately hoping to hear split the air. A flight of six T-28 fighter planes came out of nowhere, whipped low over our beleaguered camp and opened up with their .50-caliber machine guns. Instantly, channels of broken, disintegrating bodies appeared in the ranks of the enemy battalion. At the same moment, brilliant white-hot pools of fire spread among the Communists as napalm bombs tumbled from the planes.

Black-uniformed bodies burst into flame, moved a step or two, and were incinerated. Human torches screamed out their last. The napalm bombs had crippled the attack. The T-28's banked sharply, circled and came in for another murderous run.

Still the Viet Cong wouldn't accept defeat. Every black-clad Communist still alive in front of us changed his direction of fire, and the sky became a pattern of crossing lines of tracer fire and bullets from automatic weapons. Into this near solid wall of crossfire the pilots dove their planes.

And then one of the low-flying T-28's burst into flames. It streaked for the low hills, crashed, and the hills burst into an inferno of red flames. The other planes, as though in retaliation, came back for yet another run, shattering the fleeing remnants of the third Communist battalion with .50-caliber machine-gun bullets.

The men on the walls screamed joyous cheers, jumping up and down, pounding each other. Kornie shouted his exhilaration at the sky. We watched the ragged Communist lines break and the skyward fire cease as the planes strafed and bombed the battalion to annihilation.

Phan Chau was saved. But the T-28's didn't let up, strafing the Viet Cong in pass after pass until there could not be a live Communist on the Vietnam side of the border. Finally the T-28 pilots made a last pass over the fiercely burning pyre of their comrade, pulled up into a barrel roll over Phan Chau and flew away.

Train, in high spirits, appeared from the bunker where he had been talking on the radio to the pilots. "I asked them why they took so long," he cried. "You know what those hot shots said? They radioed back that Special Forces usually didn't require fighter assistance. They complained we usually beat off the VC before the planes could reach their objective and join the fight."

Soberly, Kornie gazed across at the fiery beacon on the hillside that had been a T-28. Train followed his stare. "Yes," the lieutenant colonel said, "I feel very badly about that. They saved us."

"If we'd had those 250 Hoa Haos that the politicians with stars on their collars took away from us," Kornie couldn't help saying, "we could have destroyed that third battalion ourselves."

"In any case, Captain, I've never seen such heroic resistance."

"One thing, Colonel. You saw, I hope, that we would have been wiped out long before the air cover came if the VC had attacked one day sooner. Only in the last twenty-four hours we put in those little tricks that saved us."

"Yes, Captain," Train answered sternly. "I meant to ask you, isn't it a little unorthodox to mine your allies' bunkers? I don't suppose you told your counterpart? What do I tell Major Tri? What do I tell Saigon? That we place charges under our allies and don't tell them?"

"My God!" Kornie blurted out. "Tell the Vietnamese? Every striker would know in a day's time. Why the hell not send a radio message to Hanoi that at Phan Chau they'd better not jump our bunkers because—"

Train burst out laughing for the first time since I'd known him. He pounded Kornie's shoulder. "Kornie, relax. I agree. I am grateful to you for helping me understand this special unit of ours."

Then, looking around the carnage inside and outside the

walls of the camp he said quietly, "Let's see what we can do to help. Are all the Americans accounted for?"

Kornie shook his head sadly. "Schmelzer is missing." He pointed toward the demolished northwest bunker. "That's where he was last time I saw him, just before the VC 57 made a direct hit."

"Right," Train said. "Let's go see what we can do. And Kornie, next time you plan an operation like the one in Cambodia, will you invite me along? It will make it easier for me to invent"—Train smiled—"plausible deviations from the truth when necessary."

2

THE IMMORTAL
SERGEANT HANKS

One hundred and forty miles north of Saigon, on one of Vietnam's most beautiful stretches of seacoast, is the resort city of Nha Trang. Presently it is home to the Vietnam Air Force academy, the Army of the Republic of Vietnam NCO school, and the largest U.S. Army field hospital north of Saigon.

For a year Nha Trang served as headquarters of U.S. Army Special Forces; its central location made its large airfield an ideal logistical base for supplying the Special Forces A teams all over the country. By mid-1964 the Special Forces headquarters (known as the SFOB) was split, logistical control remaining in Nha Trang while the commanding officer of Special Forces and his intelligence and operations sections were moved to Saigon—where Military Assistance Command-Vietnam and Military Assistance Advisory Group could keep closer reins on their unconventional activities.

This story begins before the Special Forces Headquarters was split, during the time Special Forces enjoyed the autonomy which made many of its successful if occasionally unorthodox forays against the Communist Viet Cong possible. The Special Forces Headquarters was dominated by five huge white warehouses that dwarfed the complex of one-story barracks and offices; in them were stored the supplies for the 40 A detachments.

At one end of the rows of barracks was the PCOD (Personnel Coming Off Duty) lounge known as the Playboy Club. Special Forces officers and enlisted men gathered and drank there together.

At 5:00 one Saturday afternoon Captain Tim Pickins, one of the Area Specialist Officers at the Special Forces Headquarters, and I were having a few drinks. The area specialists were my closest link to activities around the country, and Pickins and I had particularly good rapport. We were talking about where I should go to get the best crack at a really good operation.

"You gonna run out of luck you keep hanging around with A teams," Pickins predicted solemnly.

"What about you?"

"You think I'm gonna cash in now? When I had an A team last year, maybe I could have got it. But now I only go out just enough to draw combat pay."

"Which is just enough to buy the six-by-two farm," I commented.

"I ought to send you to Muc Tan. They're pretty secure there. Least I wouldn't be worried about you getting greased."

I was protesting I didn't want to go where they're secure, when the door to the club burst open and in walked a tall whip of a captain and a lean, grim-faced master sergeant.

The men removed their green berets and came over to the bar. Pickins swiveled on his seat.

"Hey, Hillman, I never figured on seeing you in tonight. Now that your replacements are here, and with things so nice down in Saigon—all those girls and bars. . . ."

"It's our PCOD," said the captain. "We all got our blood tests and those as needed shots got them. Everyone's ready to go home to his wife or girl nice and clean."

The master sergeant grinned. "Of course some of the team stayed in Saigon. They fixed themselves up with an APCOD." At Pickins' questioning look the sergeant explained, "That's '*adjusted* pussy cut-off date.' "

"Yeah," Hillman added, "and that young stud of an XO of mine, he's staying down to Tuesday, worked himself out an AAPCOD with the doc. 'Absolute adjusted pussy cut-off date!' "

We all laughed, and Pickins introduced me to Sergeant Rucker and Captain Hillman. "Where's that poor sonofabitch who's going to replace me?" Hillman asked.

"Captain Farley's still over at the three shop getting briefed," Pickins replied. "He and his team will probably be in here pretty soon."

"Good. I want plenty of time to tell him personally what a mess he's getting into at Muc Tan."

"I heard things were reasonably pacified there," I said.

"With the VC, maybe. Christ, if all we had to do was fight the VC this war would be won damned soon. Our problem is the Viets right in our own camp. You've heard of LLDB?"

"I've been here a few months," I said stiffly.

Disgustedly, Hillman turned to his sergeant. "Tell the man what LLDB stands for."

" 'Lousy little dirty bug-outs,' " Rucker recited.

"I've seen some sorry LLDB types," I agreed. "But I've also seen LLDB officers and men who'd stand up number one in any army in the world."

"That may be," Rucker allowed. "I guess it just happened that in my three tours in Vietnam I never drew a good LLDB team."

"Wait'll you come back," I said confidently. "The new CO of LLDB is doing his damnedest to straighten his command out."

"I'll believe it when I see it," Rucker growled.

"As you may gather, Captain Hillman's team has been having some problems with their counterparts," Pickins explained drily.

Hillman glared at the area specialist. "If the colonel doesn't relieve that camp commander, Lieutenant Chi, we might as well close up the goddamn camp. The VC don't need to bother us with Chi on their side. Yes," said Hillman, ordering a second can of beer, "my replacement is in for trouble. Who is this Captain Farley? Does he know anything about Vietnam?"

"He's from the 5th at Bragg," Pickins answered. "He's never been here before. He's a good man though—spent three years with the 10th. Just graduated from the Special Warfare School."

"Zack Farley?" I asked. "He was in my class. I'll have to go down and see him."

"You'll see a man in trouble," Hillman promised. "Sonofa-bitch, just once we got ambushed by the VC, and a LLDB sergeant with a greasegun wouldn't get up and charge. Know what I did? I kicked his ass so hard he jumped up and his men followed him and we wiped out the ambush. And Lieutenant

Chi? He sends my name to Saigon for abusing Vietnamese NCO's.''

"Who's the team sergeant of the new detachment, sir?" Rucker asked Pickins.

"Sergeant Hanks.''

"Ed Hanks. Damned good man. We were in Laos working for the Agency together in '62. He'll keep the team ready and ship-shape.''

"I hope he's got some other men with Vietnam experience," Hillman said. "Those guys who come over from Bragg are usually first-timers here. Now take the 1st at Okie. I don't think there's a man who hasn't got at least two tours in Laos, Vietnam, or—'' He gave me a look and cut himself off, ending, "or some of the other places around here.''

"If this war keeps going the way it is," Pickins said, "every man in Special Forces will have one hell of a lot of Vietnam experience behind him.''

The door opened and into the Playboy Club strolled Captain Zack Farley and his entire team. He spotted me and I jumped up and shook my old classmate's hand. He offered a few good-natured insults about civilians, and Pickins introduced him to the man he was replacing.

Hanks and Rucker greeted each other happily and beers were ordered all around. "What the hell kind of morgue are they running here?" Hanks asked boisterously after his first drink. "Every lousy barrack has a big sign on front and is named after some guy I know was killed over here. Jesus. Everhardt, Goodman, Cordell—I served under Captain Cordell, one of the finest officers in the United States Army—Brock, all of them. Damned near came loose just walking down here.''

Rucker nodded. "I felt the same way.''

Hanks pushed a beer at his captain. "Captain Farley, sir," he said, "there's one thing I want. And maybe Captain Pickins can do something about it too. If they grease me on this tour"—he paused, and then went on—"I just want one thing. Name the shit house after me.''

Someone laughed, but Hanks shook his head. "No shit, sir, I mean it. If my name's going up on one of these buildings, make it one everybody uses. All those guys coming through here thinking of me for a few minutes each day. It would be like immortal.''

Farley raised his beer. "If the time ever comes, I promise to do my best."

"Thank you, sir," said Hanks, and ordered more beers all around.

The rest of the evening, except for a brief chow break, Hillman and Sergeant Rucker gave the new A team a profane, often obscene, and always derogatory toward the LLDB, briefing on what they could expect at Muc Tan. Before we broke up I promised Zack Farley that I would visit him at Muc Tan before the month was out.

As it happened, two months passed before I had a chance to make it to Muc Tan. Remembering all the warnings of Captain Hillman and Sergeant Rucker, I was curious to see how Zack was doing.

The dominating feature of Muc Tan is an enormous rubber plantation, along the north edge of which the Special Forces camp is situated. Occasional areas under cultivation are cleared from the surrounding thick scrub-brush and there are a few villages around the camp. The province capital is ten miles due east of the camp. The chief job of the Special Forces team at Muc Tan is border surveillance. The Cambodian border is ten miles to the west. The camp itself is only fifty miles from Saigon, to which daily convoys proceed. There is also the daily Air Force milk run between the province capital and Saigon.

Muc Tan is considered almost a showpiece Special Forces camp by Military Assistance Command-Vietnam, and it is here that visiting dignitaries are taken. There is always new construction work going on, the latrines are the newest and cleanest, the defenses are set-piece perfection and the Vietnamese strike force is one of the country's best disciplined. The area around Muc Tan, while not free of Viet Cong guerrillas, is at least so well patrolled that very few Communist raids on villages or ambushes occur. This last was the reason I had delayed so long in turning up. I might have put off the trip even longer had not Captain Pickins mentioned that a certain village near Muc Tan was suspected of being an important way station for Viet Cong infiltrators from Cambodia. Captain Farley wanted to raid the village, but Pickins and Lieutenant Colonel Train thought up a more unconventional plan. They would quietly surround the village, throw up barbed wire during the night, and then march in, hold every man and woman under arrest, and use the polygraph to interrogate them. Train felt that much more information could be derived this way. I decided to visit the camp in time to spend a couple of days with Farley before the operation.

No one at the A team was expecting me when I arrived at the airstrip via the milk run from Saigon. The radio message that I was on my way got to Farley after I'd been there about a day. However, I spotted a Special Forces sergeant sitting in a three-quarter ton truck. He watched me approach with some curiosity. Although I wore the Special Forces jungle fatigues with a name tape on my right breast and my jump wings sewed on my left, I wore no insignia on my collar, of course, nor any on my green bush hat. On my back was a standard lightweight combat pack. My folding-stock carbine was comfortably slung over my left shoulder.

Suddenly the medic from Farley's A team, Sergeant Menzes, recognized me and jumped from the truck, telling me Captain Farley had been looking for me for over a month. Apologetically, he said we'd have to wait a few minutes until he had picked up some supplies and mail. Along with several American advisers from various commands in the province and two American civilians, undoubtedly United States Operations Mission people, I watched crates, boxes, trunks, and spare machine parts slid and lifted down the Caribou's tail ramp.

Sergeant Menzes finally found his deliveries and, slinging the packages in back, where four grinning Vietnamese strikers were sitting, he reverently placed the precious orange mailsack on the front seat between us and drove off.

The roads to Muc Tan weren't at all bad. The strikers listlessly watched the sides of the road for ambushes, and from force of habit I snapped out the stock on my carbine, chambered a round, and held it pointed directly up the road for instant employment. "Guess you've been on some of them bad roads," Menzes said with a chuckle. "The only trouble we've got around here is with our so-called allies."

"I recall Captain Hillman and Sergeant Rucker telling you a few things about that," I replied. "Didn't appear to me you all really took them seriously."

"We sure found they was right, sir," Menzes said ruefully. "In fact, if anything things is worse. But I guess Captain Farley will tell you all that. He's pretty disgusted."

The medic concentrated on his driving. "Nice road," I said, "smooth, plenty of open space on both sides."

"Sure. This is the main road to the rubber plantation. Very important to them Frenchies. We never have any trouble on it because the plantation pays off the VC to leave them alone."

Soon the entire south side of the east-west road was deep in rubber trees. We drove for three miles before reaching the camp. True to what I had heard, this was the neatest Special Forces camp, the most perfectly laid out, I had ever seen. All the barracks were correctly aligned snow-white cement-block structures with attractive, pitched-shingle roofs. The camp's outer walls were straight, clean concrete embankments with perfect half-circle cement machine-gun emplacements all along them. At the entrance to the concertina, which stretched around the entire perimeter, two strikers in starched fatigues brought themselves up to attention and saluted smartly. We drove twenty yards inside the barbed-wire perimeter along the walls to the gate into the main fort. Again two immaculate guards came to attention and saluted as we drove through.

I whistled appreciatively at the orderly, military interior. "Nothing wrong with this camp."

Menzes shrugged in reply and brought his truck up in front of the long, tree-shaded sparkling-white headquarters building. Immediately, Sergeant Hanks emerged. "Mail come?"

The medic tossed him the orange mailbag, and just as Hanks was turning to go back into his office with it he noticed me. He welcomed me profusely and took me along the row of doors to one over which the sign COMMANDING OFFICER U.S. ARMY SPECIAL FORCES DETACHMENT A—799 shone out in gold letters on a blue background, perfectly matching the colors of the Special Forces shoulder patch. Captain Farley, seated at a metal desk, contemplating a sheaf of correspondence, looked up and came around to shake my hand.

"Hiya, Zack," I said. "If I knew what a nice camp you had I'd have come here before on R and R. Where's the swimming pool?"

Farley smiled wanly and showed me to a chair.

"The mail came in, sir," Hanks said. "I'll sort it and bring yours in. Where shall I put our guest's ruck, sir—in the guest room?"

"There's an extra sack in my room. He can bunk in there.

If we get attacked I'll be able to watch him." Both he and the sergeant guffawed loudly at this highly unlikely possibility.

"You picked a good time to come," Farley said when Hanks had left.

"Pickins told me about the operation and I thought it might be interesting."

"I'm not talking about that. It's the last day of the month. Pay day for the strikers and construction workers. You'll have a chance to see Lieutenant Chi in his best form."

"Hillman's favorite counterpart?"

"Even Hillman hadn't caught up with this larcenous little genius." He looked at his watch. "Come on, I'll show you something. You remember my Executive Officer, Lieutenant Cooke? Well, he and Sergeant Reilly are supervising paying the strike force. You wouldn't believe it, I suppose, but we have one hell of a high desertion rate at this camp."

I showed my surprise. "Damned right," Farley said grimly. "That smart, conniving, cheating, politicking camp commander Chi has everything all figured out."

We started to cross the cement parade ground toward a building outside of which stood a long line of Vietnamese strike-force troopers. I stared at them—so unusual was it to see civilian irregulars looking so crisp and military.

Farley laughed bitterly. "Oh they look good, all right. Christ, you'd think we were back in garrison instead of out on the Cambodian border. That's how Chi keeps his embezzling going so successfully. This is the best-looking camp in Vietnam. We get inspected about three times a week. Any time a wheel wants to see a Special Forces camp, this is where they come. But Chi is so rough on his strikers, he's such a damned stickler, that these civilian kids can't take it. About the middle of the month he starts shoving them in jail for five days if they have a shoelace untied. And the jail is something we don't show visitors. It's a pit where Chi throws the strikers for punishment. At least twice since I've been here cobras have fallen in and bitten prisoners. Just the threat of the pit scares these strikers into deserting. But the Viet top brass think Chi is some military mastermind and any little disciplinary action he sees fit to carry out is fine with them so long as the visiting VIP's are impressed."

Farley balefully watched the line of men move into the headquarters building to receive their pay. "In the last eight or ten days Chi has scared at least fifty men, maybe more, into deserting. Then what he does is collect their pay for himself. He even stuck my interpreter into the pit for telling me how many men deserted last week. We got him out; my men took him out by force before he'd been in more than a couple of hours. Chi sent a radio message to the Vietnamese LLDB major at the B team that I was interfering with his discipline. But Colonel Train knows the score now and told me to forget it."

We walked into the building, past the line of cleanly dressed, subdued strikers, and up to the table where two LLDB sergeants were sitting. The two Americans, Lieutenant Cooke and Sergeant Reilly, were passing them neatly stacked piastre notes, which they in turn passed to the strikers as they signed the paybook. Lieutenant Chi, a sullen-faced Vietnamese in the camouflage fatigues and beret of the LLDB, was standing behind the table watching the proceedings.

"How many of them have you seen come through twice so far?" Farley asked, not bothering to lower his voice for the benefit of the Viet paymasters.

"I've challenged about four of them, sir," Sergeant Reilly answered. "But Lieutenant Chi and these swinging dicks"—he indicated the two LLDB pay-clerks with a jerk of his thumb—"started giving me a hard time and swearing the strikers I called were coming through legally. What are you going to do?"

"Why don't you make them dip their hands in indelible ink each time they're paid," I suggested.

Wearily, three sets of American eyes stared at me. Then Farley said, "We already tried it, but Chi sent word to Saigon that the Americans were insulting the integrity of the Vietnamese. That ended that."

A striker came through, looking nervously at the four men behind the stacks of money on the table. He glanced for a moment at Lieutenant Chi and then took up the pen to sign the paybook.

"Hold it," Lieutenant Cooke said.

The striker paused with raised pen, looking up uncertainly.

"I know goddamned well this one's been through before," the Executive Officer said. "What do you think, Ramsey?"

"I'd say you're right, sir. Goddamn it though, it's sure hard to tell."

Lieutenant Chi approached the table. He said something to one of the Vietnamese at the table who repeated the camp commander's words in Vietnamese to Cooke. "Lieutenant Chi says he has been watching carefully and this man has not been through before."

"We could search him to see if he has any money," Cooke said, more in explanation to me than making a serious suggestion, "but he'd be clean. Chi's men take the money the minute these guys go through the line. If he's a repeater, the only way he'll get his own pay is if we give it to him now. If we don't, there's an investigation, Chi raises hell with the B-team commander, and we're in for about twenty-five pounds of paper work and this poor guy doesn't get paid. Shit!" Cooke glanced back at Captain Farley. "We'll pay, I just don't like that little crook to think we're absolute dickheads."

The money was paid, and the line progressed under the eyes of Lieutenant Chi. Cooke shook his head, his face grim with disgust. "These thieves give me such a case of the ass I don't feel right for a goddamned week."

"Have you paid off the construction workers yet?" Farley asked.

"No sir. They come next."

"When you've finished with them, come to my office and we'll start tightening the old noose," Farley said. "Reilly, I'm sure glad you were a bookkeeper before you got into the Army."

"Yes, sir," Reilly said enthusiastically.

We left the LLDB headquarters, Farley and Chi exchanging correct, grim nods. Back in the office we said nothing for a few moments and then Farley spoke out. "Chi's LLDB team right this minute is down at the contractor's office on the north side of the camp. We always have a hell of a lot of construction work going on. They like this camp so much in Saigon that anything we want in new construction gets the OK. And Chi, as camp commander, picks the contractor. He takes a piece from the contract or on his profits, and he's got another trick. His LLDB team picks the workers from the villages around here. Every one of them kicks back a percentage of their pay check. The Americans get the blame for this because Chi's men tell them that they kick back to us. The whole thing is a stinking business. And try and get Chi to go out on a combat patrol to the border!"

"So, Zack old man, what are you going to do for the next four months of your tour?"

"We're going to establish a Forward Operating Base on the Cambodian border and fight the VC. The hell with Lieutenant Chi's garrison duty."

"And just how do you intend doing this?"

"Sergeant Reilly is my secret weapon," Farley answered, smiling. "He should be an FBI accountant. We have two Vietnamese interpreters on our side. The one we took out of the pit and one other. They've been able to quietly get the names of all the deserters this month. It cost us some bribe money but it was worth it. Reilly can show on paper exactly how much Chi took this month on deserters.

"We also have one of the contractor's supervisors on our side. The interpreters even found out that Chi has been gambling in town. In the past two months he's lost and owes the equivalent of $300. That's a hell of a lot of money for a lieutenant in the Vietnamese Army. We got a statement from his gambling friends that he is not only $300 in the hole but that he lost another $300 in cash.

"It's cost money but we've built up a hell of a case. Just as soon as Reilly gets his figures laid out, I'm taking the whole dirty mess to the B team. That's as far as I can go. Then it's up to Colonel Train. He said that up to now we didn't have real proof and accusations would only drive a wedge between us and the Vietnamese."

"Isn't Colonel Train coming over for this operation?"

"Right. And his counterpart Major Tri too. But I don't think this is the place to clobber Chi. We'll do it at B-team headquarters. Oh, we've got a lot of other little surprises. Chi's medics are stealing our antibiotics and selling them in town, and of course that stuff goes right to the VC. We've tried to put a stop to that, but Chi complains that the Americans refuse to give them enough penicillin for their wounded. And that's a goddamned laugh because we get so damned few wounded."

Farley stood up and paced his small office in frustration. He stopped at the map on his wall and hit it with his fist. "If we'd go up here on the border where we're supposed to be maybe we would have a few dead and wounded, but we'd stop the VC from coming in through our area." He looked at his watch. "There isn't a damned thing more I can do today. I need a little nerve tonic."

"I have some Jim Beam in my ruck. I'm with you, Zack."

Half an hour later we were sitting in the teamroom drinking a bourbon and water when Reilly walked in, an angry expression on his face.

"Sir, Ho Vang Minh is missing."

Farley jumped up. "What do you mean, missing? We haven't been out on any operations with Minh."

"He's missing right out of this camp."

"How can that be? Minh would never go AWOL." Farley turned to me. "Minh is our second interpreter. He's been Reilly's number one helper on this report we're making."

"I think Lieutenant Chi knows what you're doing, sir. Maybe he grabbed Minh. Lieutenant Cooke and Hanks and I went down to the pit but he wasn't there. None of the LLDB are talking, you can bet the rest of that bottle of Beam on that."

Farley looked worried. "Well, have a shot while we try and figure out what happened. Where's Lieutenant Cooke?"

"He's trying to make the LLDB tell him where Minh is."

"I hope he doesn't try so hard he gets us all in trouble," Farley muttered. "Cooke has a way of getting physical when he gets the ass with our counterparts." The captain took a long drink and set the glass down. "What could Lieutenant Chi find out from Ho Vang Minh if he had him over in one of their barracks now and was working him over?"

"If Minh talked, Chi would know that you have him by the nuts, sir, and are just waiting for the right time to squeeze."

"Minh is a good man," Farley said grimly. "He almost makes up for the Chis. Minh's the kind this country needs if it's ever going to become a modern nation. Christ, I hope he's all right."

The bourbon had calmed Reilly down a bit. "Sir, Sergeant Hanks and Lieutenant Cooke both figure that if Lieutenant Chi has been talking to Minh, he thinks you're going to hit him with everything you got while Colonel Train and Major Tri are here tomorrow or the next day. Maybe he's panicked. No telling what he might do."

"I just hope they don't torture or kill him," said Farley tightly.

*   *   *

The next afternoon Lieutenant Colonel Train, Major Tri and Captain Pickins arrived at Muc Tan, and with them an American intelligence sergeant who carried a polygraph. A general briefing was held in the operations room.

Lieutenant Chi was clearly suspicious of the whole mission. It had not been his idea. Captain Farley had requested permission from the B team and Train had taken to the plan and pushed it onto Tri. Even though his own man at Muc Tan had neither originated nor approved the mission, Tri decided he had better give his approval. The use of the lie detector on the spot so intrigued him he had come out to see the results for himself.

In the briefing room Chi eyed the lie detector with an expression of mistrust and fear. By this time I had learned to understand the deviousness of the Vietnamese mind and I knew exactly what Chi must be thinking. The mission was a coverup for an investigation into his activities, and the lie detector was to be used on him and his men. The new government in Saigon had made sweeping statements about ending graft and shooting any Vietnamese officer who embezzled more than 100,000 piastres, about $10,000. The first test case had yet to be made, and misappropriation of funds and equipment was so prevalent that the new premier would lose a significant percentage of his officer corps if he tried to carry out this threat. Still, Lieutenant Chi was concerned; the government might be forced into action if presented with a good enough case.

Lieutenant Chi played the game all the way. As camp commander it was his prerogative to conduct the briefing for this operation he had not initiated, did not want to carry out, and believed to be merely a diversionary scheme of the Americans anyway. He now did so:

The mission would start out at midnight, he began. Two platoons would leave camp. The first, advised by Sergeant Hanks, would start ten minutes earlier than the second, advised by Captain Farley. Both platoons would follow a course of 225 degrees, or southwest, through the rubber plantation. Four miles on this course would bring the platoons out of the plantation onto a north-south road along the western edge of the rubber trees. From this point on the road Hanks' platoon would follow the road south two miles until he reached the objective village. His platoon would block the north and west sides of the village. Farley's platoon, ten minutes behind, would block the east and south sides of the village. Then the headquarters section, using bull horns, would tell the people their village was surrounded and no one would be shot unless the villagers fired first. Sergeant Hanks, firing flare rounds from the M-79 grenade launcher, would keep the village illuminated until dawn, as the headquarters and search sections moved in and started interrogating the villagers. It was hoped that an important key to the infiltration route of Viet Cong through this province would be discovered.

Lieutenant Chi was careful to point out on the map that he had set up an ambush opposite a rubber-workers' village which lay about a mile east of the road onto which the two platoons would emerge from the trees. Following their course of 225 degrees the platoons would, during the course of their march, pass less than a mile from this village. Since it was suspected that not only the French owners of the plantation but most of the rubber workers were Viet Cong sympathizers, the ambush was a precaution against a possible Viet Cong attack on the column from this village.

Major Tri congratulated Lieutenant Chi for devising a fine plan of attack. He said that a thorough search and questioning of the villagers of the objective town should be of great value to intelligence at the B team as well as at Muc Tan, which was doing such an excellent job of border surveillance.

During the evening Captain Farley conducted a meeting of the Americans who would be going on the mission. Sergeant Reilly, saying that after all the paperwork he'd been doing he thought he deserved a change of pace, was assigned to Sergeant Hanks. When Lieutenant Colonel Train asked about the paperwork Reilly had referred to, Captain Farley said it was something he'd like to take up with the B-team company commander the next day. Train agreed.

Sergeant Hanks stared at the acetate overlay on which positions and routes had been drawn in black and red grease pencil. Clearly he was bothered by the mission. Farley invited his team sergeant to speak out.

"I don't feel good about tonight, sir," Hanks growled. "I don't like that ambush Chi set up, without asking us about it, over by the rubber-workers' village."

"His point was well taken though, sergeant," Lieutenant

Colonel Train interjected. "If there are VC sympathizers in the village they might try attack."

"Sir," Hanks said slowly. "I'm as security-conscious as a man can be, but there ain't no hard-core VC fighters in that rubber village. Maybe a few of them have hidden some weapons they'd dig up and use to shoot a lone American or one of our strikers if they got the chance. But they'd never attack a squad, much less a platoon. You gotta remember, them Frenchies running that plantation don't want no trouble. We know they pay off both the VC and Saigon to leave them alone."

"Good point, Hanks," Farley said. "What do you think?"

Hanks looked uneasily at Train and then back at his captain. "I don't know exactly, sir. I just don't like it, is all."

"What do you want to say, Hanks?" Captain Pickins prodded. "You think those strikers Lieutenant Chi put out in the trees might be there to ambush *us*?"

Hanks grinned sheepishly. "Not after Chi told us where they were and gave us passwords in case we came too close to them. It's just a feeling I got."

"You want to stay back, Hanks?" Captain Farley asked. Then added, giving Hanks an honorable out: "You still got a touch of dysentery, maybe you'd better."

"No, sir. I want to go."

"I'll walk the first platoon with you, Hanks," Pickins said.

"If you want to, sir. I don't trust these strikers on compass reading. I'll be up at the point."

Exactly at midnight, Hanks, Pickins, and Reilly headed out with the first platoon of 50 strikers. Hanks walked directly behind the point man, Pickins positioned himself a few men behind Hanks, and Reilly took up the rear to prevent the inevitable stragglers getting separated from the platoon. The vague glow from the starlit sky clearly outlined the platoon in the darkness. The Americans loomed tall shadows, a head or more above the smaller strike-force troops. We watched the platoon disappear into the rubber trees on the other side of the road.

Ten minutes later Farley led out his platoon, walking behind the point. I took my position several men behind the captain. At the rear of the platoon, Lieutenant Colonel Train, Major Tri, Lieutenant Chi, the intelligence sergeant with his polygraph and Menzes, the medic, walked in a group, their special security squad behind them.

It occurred to me that Lieutenant Chi should be up here with the point man. I whispered this to Farley, who shrugged.

"For one thing I don't want him up here, for another he said he needed to be with Major Tri in case any questions came up. We've got to keep noise discipline," he added significantly.

We snaked through the rows of rubber trees. The point man, leading the way, kept his compass in his right hand. After the entire platoon was in the trees I saw Farley pull out his own compass, take a reading, and slip it back in the pocket of his fatigues. I was glad to be up front. Train had wanted me to stay back with the headquarters group, but I liked walking as close to the point as possible.

More than an hour went by, and I noticed that Farley, who had been constantly looking off to our left, seemed more relaxed now. As nearly as I could calculate we should have passed the ambush Lieutenant Chi had put out about fifteen minutes earlier. It had become a habit with me on night marches to keep a constant check on direction by watching the North Star, but in the dense rubber plantation it was almost impossible to get a look at the stars. We kept moving ahead; we wanted to get out of the rubber trees and onto the road before taking the first rest.

I calculated we were fifteen minutes from the road when Farley held up a hand and stopped the column. He reached into his pocket, pulled out his compass, and checked our direction. I saw him stiffen and tap the point man on the shoulder and show him his compass. There was a whispered discussion, through the interpreter, between Farley and the point man. I moved forward and heard Farley whispering angrily, urgently to his interpreter. A striker was dispatched to the rear of the column.

"Watch out," Farley whispered to me. "We're in some kind of trouble."

"What happened?"

"The point man has been going on a course of 15 degrees right of the one Chi gave us at briefing. Instead of being on an azimuth of 225 degrees we're choggying along on 240 degrees. That means we're closer to the road than we thought, and north of where we had planned to come out. I should have checked my compass sooner."

"Then all we have to do is walk south on the road until we hook up with Hanks."

"That's what we'll do. But the point man just told me that a couple of minutes before we left Muc Tan, Lieutenant Chi told him to follow 240 degrees ten minutes after we were out. I just sent back for Chi. If that sonofabitch is pulling something——"

The sudden crackling of riflefire broke out only a short distance ahead.

"Get moving forward!" Farley yelled, leading the way toward the firing. "Hanks must be getting it." The interpreter relayed the command, and the strikers followed Farley as he raced through the trees. Flares were illuminating the area ahead. I could see the end of the tree line fifty yards ahead. The firing continued and more illuminating rounds lit the air. We could hear yelling ahead. Then, abruptly, all fire ceased. Minutes later we came across the first platoon, milling about at the edge of the road. Reilly was yelling and thrusting his AR-15 belligerently at an enemy I could not see on the other side of the road.

I heard Pickins' voice from somewhere, weak but commanding, repeating the same phrase: "Don't shoot them, don't shoot them, men." Another illuminating flare burst above us as Farley and I reached the road. "Hanks! Hanks!" I heard Farley cry. "What happened?"

The flare revealed the sickening sight. Sergeant Hanks was lying beside the road, the back of his head a broken red mess. Near him lay Pickins, still crying, "Don't shoot them."

Farley, keeping his automatic rifle pointing at the west side of the road, stooped over Pickins. "What happened, Babe?"

"Stupid fucking ambush in the wrong place. Our own strike force got us."

"You hurt bad?"

"No, I'll be all right." His voice caught and became a sob. "But Sergeant Hanks. He—"

Slowly, Farley's platoon advanced across the road, weapons ready to fire, Reilly on the verge of letting go at any moment.

"Put that weapon down, Reilly," Farley cried sharply.

Slowly, Reilly obeyed. The strikers in the ambush party slowly came out of their positions. Through an interpreter Farley commanded them to drop their weapons. They did so and walked out onto the road. Another illuminating round went up.

"Menzes," Farley said. "Help Captain Pickins."

I squatted beside Pickins, waiting for the medic. He looked up at me, the yellow light of the flares giving his drawn face, lined with pain, a ghostly look. "Told you you'd get greased you keep going around with A teams," he said, with difficulty.

"Don't talk, sir," Menzes said, kneeling beside the Air Specialist Officer.

"You know"—it sounded as though Pickins was laughing, a grating, groaning laugh—"Hanks took it for Farley. Maybe you too."

Menzes opened his kit. "Don't bother with me, Doc," Pickins said. "Do what you can for the sergeant."

Menzes didn't answer. He gave Pickins a shot of morphine.

I stood up and found Farley talking with Lieutenant Colonel Train and Major Tri. Lieutenant Chi had disappeared with a squad of his men into the trees when the shooting had started and couldn't be located. Major Tri, who could speak good English when he wanted to, was saying that Lieutenant Chi must have tried to cut off the VC from escaping.

"It wasn't VC that ambushed us, Major," Farley insisted. "It was the ambush party that Lieutenant Chi sent out, only they were a mile and a half away from where they were supposed to be. Thanks to the bearing of 240 degrees Lieutenant Chi gave his point man on our platoon without telling us we would have walked right into it."

"Lieutenant Chi come back after catch VC," Major Tri insisted.

"VC!" Farley yelled in exasperation. "That little crook deliberately ambushed Sergeant Hanks. I'll kill the bastard personally."

Tri gave his counterpart an injured appeal.

"Farley!" Train commanded. "Get hold of yourself!"

"Yes sir. Here's Sergeant Reilly. Will you listen to him? Tell the colonel what happened."

"Well, sir," Reilly said, "we was following the azimuth

given at the briefing—225 degrees. We checked it every ten minutes. No mistakes.''

Farley looked down at the ground and grimaced. He knew he hadn't checked his point man frequently enough.

''Well, sir, we got about maybe four, five hundred meters from where Lieutenant Chi said he'd set out his ambush and Sergeant Hanks changed direction from southwest to due west to make sure we'd give that ambush a wide berth. He said all the time he didn't trust Lieutenant Chi and figured he'd try and get us.''

Major Tri began loud remonstrances but Train held up his hand for silence. ''Just the facts, Reilly.''

''Yes, sir. So we turned due west and headed for the road, figuring when we hit it we'd turn south and meet you.''

''What happened,'' Farley broke in, ''they hit the road where we would have, following the course Lieutenant Chi gave our point man. They just hit it a few minutes ahead of us and ran into the ambush set out for us.''

''That's jumping to conclusions, Captain,'' Train said sternly.

''They got Hanks, but Chi wanted me.''

''Why would your counterpart do a thing like that?'' Train asked in genuine surprise.

''Because I could prove how much he's been stealing at Muc Tan.''

Major Tri's multilingual protest was silenced by the arrival of Sergeant Menzes.

''Sir,'' he said to Farley, ''I fixed up a litter for Captain Pickins. Can we go now?''

''You're damned right we can, Sergeant,'' Colonel Train boomed out. ''Let's get out of here.''

Due to good radio work, a helicopter was waiting at Muc Tan to evacuate Pickins when we arrived back. His wounds weren't serious, but they wanted to get him to the naval hospital in Saigon as quickly as possible. The chopper also took out the body of Sergeant Hanks. At dawn the next morning there was still no sign of Lieutenant Chi. Major Tri, insisting that he must get back to the B team immediately, said that he knew Lieutenant Chi would come back as soon as he had finished chasing the Viet Cong.

''What are you going to do about Lieutenant Chi, sir?'' Farley asked Train.

"I don't know," Train answered wearily. "I'll lay all the evidence before the Vietnamese authorities. I don't see how there can be any doubt that he planned to ambush and kill you, but for God's sake don't anyone talk about the incident." He looked hard at me. "We've got enough problems over here now. I'm sure the Vietnamese authorities will take care of Lieutenant Chi once and for all. Captain, don't do anything stupid when and if Chi comes back to this camp. You know what I mean?"

"Yes, sir, though after what happened it's asking one inhuman damned lot."

Train nodded. "That's why Special Forces have these jobs, Captain. We've got a sonofabitch job over here. I'm sorry, Zack. If you think of anything I can do for you before my chopper comes let me know."

"I'll meet you in the teamroom, sir."

I accompanied Farley to his room where, wordlessly, he pulled out the bottle of bourbon and took a long pull. He offered it to me and I did the same, then passed it back. Farley took a long last one and tucked the nearly empty bottle away.

The sun had risen as I walked across the parade ground into the A-team longhouse. I sat down beside Train, who was meditatively sipping coffee. There wasn't much for us to say. We just drank coffee until Farley came in. He took a seat opposite Train and after swallowing half a cup of coffee said, "Colonel, I just thought of one thing you could do for the team, for Sergeant Hanks."

Train replied almost eagerly. "I'll do my best." He took a deep drink of his coffee.

In quiet tones, Zack told him about Hanks' request back at the Special Forces Operating Base.

Train sputtered and put the cup down, staring at Farley to see whether the captain was gulling him.

"It's true, sir," I said. "I was there and heard him. Hanks really meant it."

Train thought a moment. "I'll see what I can do, Farley. I promise you I will."

Two weeks later, in Saigon, I went to the naval hospital to see how Captain Pickins was coming along. His wounds were draining and he looked reasonably comfortable.

"By the way," he said, giving me a wan smile, "whatever happened to that sonofabitch, Chi?"

"You really want to know? I don't want you to have a relapse."

"Say no more. They transferred him to another A team in another corps area."

I nodded. "My buddies in personnel at the B team report he's camp commander of a new base in 'eye' corps. Lots of construction work going on there, they tell me. The Vietnamese told our B team up there that Chi had a lot of experience with contractors and workers."

Pickins stared wordlessly at the ceiling.

"But there's one thing," I said. "I was up in Nha Trang a couple of days ago. Had a touch of dysentery and spent some time in the enlisted men's latrine."

A slow smile began to spread across Pickins' face.

I nodded. "You can't miss it. A big sign freshly painted is right out there in front of it, big as life. It reads 'Hanks' Latrine.' "

3

THE CAO-DAI
PAGODA

Captain Dewart paused during the tour of his camp he was giving me to stare balefully at the decrepit hut, sandbagged nearly to its thatched roof. Hanging from the eaves was a faded blue board with a large human eye painted on it in white and green. Some Vietnamese words were lettered along the top.

"What is that thing?" I asked.

"That," he said disgustedly, "is the bane of my existence. Because of it, this camp of mine is unfinished—probably will *never* be finished."

"What do you mean?"

"Friend, I'll have you know what you're looking at is a pagoda. A genuine Cao-Dai pagoda that up to now was attended by one old lady, who couldn't have cared less if it fell apart."

"What happened," I asked. "She get religion?"

"Not her, but the local Cao-Dai Buddhists have suddenly decided this pagoda is very sacred to them. The Cao-Dai elders say we unenlightened Americans have desecrated their temple."

I was a bit confused, and said as much. "How did a pagoda find its way into the middle of your camp?"

Dewart laughed. "It didn't exactly find its way in. As a matter of fact, I built the camp around it. This happens to be the most strategic place in this district for an outpost. As you see, we have a river north of us, and the canal runs across the river at right angles to our west. South and east we have clear fields of fire except for that patch of jungle along part of the south wall which I've been trying to get the camp commander to clear out. It would take two battalions to overrun us."

"And this pagoda was standing right where you had to build the fort?"

"Correct. But first I talked to the old woman. She said she was the only Cao-Dai left who used the place and agreed to let me build her a new one somewhere else when the camp was finished. So we went ahead with the camp. The first thing I did was sandbag the pagoda and use it for an ammo dump." Dewart tugged off his green beret and stood bareheaded in the sun.

"I've never seen a Cao-Dai pagoda. Mind if I take a look?"

"Help yourself. There isn't much to see."

I walked across the open square past partially built buildings and entered the door under the sign. Ammunition cases were piled to the ceiling left of the door, taking up about half the interior. To the right was a large dark wooden table or altar, and above it, nailed to the wall, was a huge picture of a human eye—symbol of the Cao-Dai sect. All around the eye snakes and trees were painted giving the impression that the eye was staring out of some hideous jungle. There were some candles and tapers on the altar. More pictures of eyes adorned the other walls. Straight out of Salvador Dali, I thought.

Leaving the pagoda I found Captain Dewart in conversation with a burly middle-aged civilian. "This is Mr. Brucker from Research and Development at Fort Belvoir," Dewart said, introducing me as a writer friend from Fort Bragg.

"Mr. Brucker is trying out a new gimmick with us, a radio-detonated mine. We haven't had a chance to use it in combat yet, but I'm sure we will."

"I'd certainly like to know what you think of the device," Brucker said. "If you send your report to Saigon, I'll be in Vietnam for another two or three months."

Suddenly from above the river I heard a whirring, rattling noise in the air, and threw myself to the ground yelling, "Mortars!"

Dewart and Brucker remained standing above me, and I felt my face flush with embarrassment as I looked where

Dewart was pointing. A flock of birds following the edge of the river flapped their way over the camp.

"I see you're as fire shy as the rest of us," he said, grinning. "Been out here long?"

"Long enough," I answered, standing up and brushing the reddish clay dust off my combat fatigues.

"Did the same thing myself first time I heard them birds last evening," Brucker chuckled.

"I don't know what it is with 'em," Dewart said. "They come over every evening regular as taps in garrison, and they sure do sound like incoming 60 mm.'s."

"Well, Captain," Brucker said, "my chopper should be along pretty soon. If Sergeant Rutt is around I'd like to talk to him before I go."

Dewart looked off toward the entrance to the camp. "They found a VC mine planted outside the main gate. Rutt's using that radio bomb of yours to blow it. He's like a kid with a new toy. Never saw a happier demo sergeant."

A sharp blast rolled across the camp. "I guess it works," Dewart remarked.

"I'd better go see for myself," Brucker said, leaving Dewart in bitter contemplation of the pagoda.

Captain Dewart had briefed me on the whole incredible story of what had happened to his detachment since its arrival in Vietnam. Two months earlier his area had been pacified, so he split his detachment, leaving half his men to guard the old camp and finish turning it over to the Vietnamese. With two Civilian Irregular Defense Group companies his group marched through jungles and mucky rice paddies to reach a new location he had picked out by helicopter reconnaissance deep in the heart of hitherto unchallenged Viet Cong territory.

The first ambush was not unexpected. The Civilian Irregular Defense Group reacted well, charging into the ambushers and letting go with all their fire power. Two CIDG men had been killed and six wounded, but the two companies continued on toward the new campsite.

Two days later, almost within sight of the new location, the Viet Cong hit with another ambush, this time using a mortar. Discipline broke, Dewart's company fled, and he and Sergeant Rutt found themselves with only one Vietnamese sergeant who had vainly tried to rally his dispersing forces and organize for an attack.

Dewart led Rutt and the Vietnamese sergeant in a three-man charge on the Viet Cong ambush. Quickly they moved inside mortar range and Dewart killed three Viet Cong with his AR-15, the rounds from this lightweight powerful weapon destroying the Viet Cong bodies so thoroughly that the Communists had not even tried to carry them away. Rutt stepped into a pungi pit, but Dewart and the Vietnamese sergeant broke up the ambush and destroyed the mortar with a thermite grenade down the tube. Then Dewart pulled Rutt out of the trap. The sharp stakes had been unable to pierce the sheet metal in the soles of his boots, but the sergeant's knee had been painfully twisted.

It was the middle of the afternoon before Dewart, half carrying Rutt, finally rounded up the second CIDG company, which had been joined by his own "bug outs." They were several miles from the objective location. Radioing for a helicopter evacuation of the dead and wounded, Dewart urged the men on, and just before dark they reached the site of what would become the new permanent camp.

"As soon as the VC saw we had a strong fort going up right in the middle of their territory they attacked. We beat them off, killed eight and lost only one friendly. They haven't hit us again. Now"—he turned from the pagoda as though the sight pained him—"they're trying something else—seeing if they can knock us out without spilling a drop of blood. They're smart, the VC. Damned smart. They've been terrorizing the local Cao-Dai people hereabouts, making them complain all the way up to Saigon that the Americans are desecrating their sacred temple. They're saying the government should make us leave this camp. And you know how those generals running this country feel about religion, especially after the way Diem and Nhu persecuted the Buddhists."

"They wouldn't really make you move, would they?"

"They damned well might. Look around. The whole place is half-finished. No roof on the teamhouse. The dispensary not built. Bunkers unfinished on the walls. We have orders not to spend any more money until this Cao-Dai dispute is settled, and that won't be for almost a month. We can't get enough troops to secure this unfinished fort and still send out effective patrols in company size. No matter what happens, the VC have gained at least a month without harassment. Yesterday, a full colonel, American, came through and said there was a fifty-fifty chance we would have to relocate because Big Minh doesn't want to offend the Cao-Dai sect.''

"It's a damned shame, especially with so good a location.''

"Shame?'' Dewart sputtered. "It's a goddamned tragedy if we're going to let religion and politics lose us big hunks of this war.''

A Vietnamese interpreter approached and saluted smartly. Dewart returned the salute and clapped the beret back on his head.

"Dai-uy, Cao-Dai elders at the gate wish to visit the pagoda.''

"How many?'' Dewart asked.

"Maybe 20.''

"Twenty!'' he exclaimed looking at me. "The old woman said there hadn't been a dozen people in that pagoda since it was first thrown together.''

"They are here, Dai-uy. It is the time of the full moon.''

"All right, Lang. Let them in. But search them first.''

"Dai-uy,'' Lang protested, "I cannot search priests and elders.''

Dewart swore beneath his breath. "See what I mean? Saigon says we have to be careful not to hurt their sensitive feelings.'' He made an impatient beckoning gesture at the group of men standing around the gate and Lang went off to escort them to the pagoda.

Dewart watched carefully as the Cao-Dais, most of them in long white robes, filed past. He did not miss the way the eyes of many of the worshippers flickered about the inside of the camp, noting the mortar and machine-gun mounts.

"What kind of war are we supposed to be fighting when we invite the enemy in to look the plant over before they attack.''

"Those are elders, sir?''

Dewart turned to Sergeant Penny, his tall Negro medic. "That's what Lang says.'' He raised his voice. "Hey, Lang, come here.''

The interpreter turned up on the double. "I thought you said they were priests and elders. Most of those swingers aren't more than thirty.''

"Dai-uy,'' Lang explained, "they are ranked by their strong belief, not their age.''

Penny looked at him suspiciously. "Are you a Cao-Dai?''

"No," Lang replied. "But we are all Buddhists."

Dewart dourly watched the procession file past the sand-bagged entrance into the small pagoda. "At least when they see all that ammo they'll think twice about attacking us again."

Lang objected. "The Cao-Dai are loyal to the new government, Dai-uy, and they never fought beside the VC even though they hate Diem."

"How many of those studs that just passed do you think are really Cao-Dais?"

"They all say they Cao-Dai, Dai-uy."

"Sometimes I wonder whose side you're on, Lang." Dewart turned to Sergeant Penny. "Tell our guys not to take their eyes off these religious zealots for one second."

"Just look around you, sir," Penny replied.

Dewart did so. Except for Sergeant Rutt, earnestly engaged in conversation with Brucker, all the Americans were standing on the walls or in strategic locations, their AR-15's held in readiness, their eyes shifting from the Cao-Dais to the fields outside the walls and back to the Cao-Dais again.

Another flock of river birds whirred and rattled overhead. Many of the Cao-Dais reacted like soldiers—as I had—their eyes searching the area for cover until they realized these were not incoming mortar rounds.

Suddenly Dewart laughed aloud. "I've got the answer!"

I looked at him questioningly.

"You hang around, I'll show you how we're going to take care of those spook-sheeted dickheads."

Patiently he waited for the Cao-Dais to finish their supposed prayers in front of the grotesque paintings. Finally they filed out again and one of the leaders, a young man with a crafty glint in his eye, beckoned the interpreter and spoke to him in low tones. Lang returned to Dewart.

"Dai-uy, tomorrow is the night of the full moon, and the Cao-Dai wish to return to worship at their temple."

Dewart's decision was a tough one. The security of the camp depended upon his Civilian Irregular Defense Group strike force and their Vietnamese Special Forces or LLDB leaders—Buddhists to a man. Though they might well suspect the local Cao-Dais, one hundred and fifty miles from the sect's main strength in Tay Ninh province, were being terrorized into helping the Viet Cong, still the religious bond they

93

all shared was stronger than most Westerners could realize. This was particularly true since only a few months earlier Buddhists in Vietnam had been persecuted, jailed, and tortured by adherents of Catholicism, a predominantly Western religion.

"Let me talk to the Cao-Dai leader," Dewart said.

The interpreter returned with a delegation of three men. One, spare and truly old, clad in a loose white robe, a fibrous, forked white beard hanging from his chin, was introduced as the chief elder. The second was a cunning young Vietnamese, and the third, a young Oriental who wore his surly expression as a challenge and was dressed in the black pajamas common to Vietnamese peasants—and the Viet Cong.

Dewart addressed himself to the elder through Lang. "I am told you want to come into this camp tomorrow night."

The old man shifted his feet and then answered in a few mumbled words. "The Cao-Dai elder," Lang translated, "says it is the end of the lunar month, and traditional to pray at the pagoda."

"We are expecting a VC attack any night," Dewart said. "It would be most dangerous for you to be in the camp during such an attack, especially since the VC must know we have been storing our ammunition in the pagoda."

Dewart watched the derisive expression come to the faces of the two younger men. They began talking back to Lang, ignoring the old man. After a few moments Lang turned to Dewart.

"They say there are no VC here. They say even if VC were here the VC respect religious nights and pagodas." Lang paused, apparently embarrassed to go on.

"Keep talking, Lang. What else did they say?"

"They say VC have more respect for religion than Americans who helped ex-President Diem burn pagodas and who even now store the materials for war in a sacred Cao-Dai temple."

Dewart nodded gravely. "Tell them, Lang, that Americans respect all religions. And to prove it, tell them that tomorrow we will move our ammunition from their temple. We know the Cao-Dai priests are powerful and they have the ear of the generals in Saigon. Tell them we will permit them to come in tomorrow night for one hour during the full moon. We are sorry it cannot be longer, but because of the VC attack we do

94

not want civilians endangered. Ask them what hour they would like to come."

With triumphant smirks the young men replied to the translation. The elder remained impassive and silent.

"Dai-uy, they say again no VC will attack this post tonight or tomorrow night."

"How do they know that unless they are VC themselves?"

The dart translated brought a surprised look to the young men. They muttered to Lang.

"They say they will come into the camp at 11:00 tomorrow night. They say also that the Americans must move this camp away from the sacred Cao-Dai pagoda. It was built by one of the first Cao-Dai elders to come here from Tay Ninh. They do not want another pagoda somewhere else, only this one."

Dewart nodded at the men sympathetically. "I know we must help the Cao-Dai who are allied with the new government. They may come into camp tomorrow night at 11:00 for one hour."

Lang looked at the captain in surprise. "Dai-uy, do you think it is good to let them all in tomorrow night? Some of them might be VC."

Dewart professed shock. "Why, Lang, you were just telling me the Cao-Dai are loyal. And you didn't even want to search them. Tell you the truth, I thought you were on their side."

"I did not mean to seem that way to you, Dai-uy."

"You tell the Cao-Dais what I said. And then you find the LLDB camp commander and tell him I have agreed to cooperate with our Buddhist friends if he gives permission for them to come in and pray tomorrow night. You tell those Cao-Dais if they are not allowed in tomorrow night it is because one of their fellow Buddhists doesn't trust them, not the Americans.

"Come on," Dewart said to me and turned on his heel.

"OK, here it is," he announced as we reached the gate where Sergeant Rutt and the R and D man were happily discussing demolitions. "Brucker, I believe you are Heaven-sent, or should I say Nirvana-sent."

Dewart then explained his problem with Viet Cong-dominated local Cao-Dais.

"I don't think you should let them in tomorrow night, sir," Sergeant Rutt said.

"We won't have to, because you and Mr. Brucker are going to fix things up for me."

He and the R and D man went into a huddle. I heard something about getting Rutt squared away on a radio-controlled series of explosions.

That night I sat around with the team in the unfinished, unroofed teamhouse, all of us dressed in black Vietnamese pajamas. "I always wondered how the camp commander would react in case of an attack," Sergeant Rutt mused aloud.

"Looks like we'll find out," said Sergeant Penny. "You sure you got them claymore mines aimed high, Rutt?"

"I tipped them so they'd fire at a 40 degree angle. When they start spitting shrapnel it will sound as though the stuff is going past your ears. But don't sweat it, those pieces of metal will be flying fifty feet above the walls."

"Well, I hope so," Penny said. "I don't want no more medic work tonight. Near 100 people came down the canals in their sampans to my sick call today."

Captain Dewart finished the letter to his wife and sealed it in an envelope. "I'm about ready to get some sleep. It's 10:30. What say we get this VC attack started and over with."

"Anytime you say, sir." Rutt went over to a table on which was what appeared to be a small radio transmitter sprouting a three-foot antenna. There were two knobs for adjusting transmission frequency and band and a vertical row of toggle switches down one side. The only thing missing was a microphone.

Everyone stared in silence at the Research and Development trial device.

"OK, Rutt, no time like the present," Dewart said. "Let's have the first 'VC attack' from that patch of jungle near the south wall, the place I've been trying to get Captain Bao to clean up."

"Right, sir." Rutt picked up the radio detonator. "OK, you guys, everyone down behind the sandbags. Those claymores just might fire low."

The team crouched behind the sandbagged wall of the all-but-roofless teamhouse. "Here goes!" Rutt toggled a switch and a sudden, sharp explosion rent the night air. The nerve-jangling whine of shrapnel from the claymore mines screamed over the camp. Instantly, all the machine guns on the jungle side of the camp opened up with a vengeance. The loud, shrill tweeting of a police whistle attested to the fact that the camp commander was alert and rallying his troops.

"It's a good thing we got more ammo than we know what to do with," the weapons sergeant laughed. "Those swinging dicks on the wall won't quit shooting 'til they run out."

After more than five minutes with no incoming fire, the chatter of the machine guns died out to sporadic bursts.

"Guess we'd better goose them again from the jungle," Dewart said.

"One more VC wave coming in, sir," Rutt acknowledged. He toggled a switch. Another blast from outside the camp, followed by the whine of shrapnel. Savagely the machine guns chopped at the jungle again.

"OK, give it to them from out where the 'mortar rounds' are going to come from tomorrow," Dewart commanded. Rutt toggled twice. Two thunderous blasts from the rice fields to the east, and the corner bunker machine-gunner switched from the jungle and cut loose across the rice paddies. There was more whistle blowing and the troops moved to reinforce the east wall.

"That's enough," Dewart ordered. "Safety that radio detonator, Rutt."

Machine-gun and riflefire continued to cut through the night.

Bao, the camp commander, dashed to Dewart. "Dai-uy, VC attacking!"

The American shook his head. "Just a probe, I think, Dai-uy. Did your men see any VC?"

"Yes, many," Bao answered in excitement. "They come from jungle but we too-much shoot. Kill maybe five, maybe ten."

"How about from the east?"

"Yes, they come. But we too-much shoot. They go away. Maybe they come back with more men."

"Not tonight," Dewart replied with assurance. "They didn't lay any mortars on us. You have good alert men, Dai-uy. Congratulations. We Americans sleep well knowing our Vietnamese friends always ready for VC attack."

The LLDB captain smiled at such high praise from his American Special Forces counterpart.

The next morning Dewart suggested that Bao send out a patrol across the rice paddies to look for signs of a VC buildup. Reluctantly, the camp commander agreed to send two platoons. "Maybe too many VC in jungle past rice paddy to east," he protested. "Maybe our men be ambushed by too many VC."

"No, Dai-uy," Dewart reassured his counterpart. "Our men can handle the VC, and besides," he paused to give full significance to his next statement—"we can cover them with very accurate mortar fire from here. Good thing, too, because at that range a good VC mortarman can lay a round in your lap if he wants to."

Sergeant Rutt took the patrol out, and Dewart asked Bao to order a detail of his men to help transfer the ammunition from the Cao-Dai pagoda to temporary bunkers some distance from the Buddhist house of worship.

"The Cao-Dai should be pleased with our respect for their religion," Dewart said to Bao as the last of the heavy ammunition crates were wrestled from the shrine.

Bao agreed. "I am not Cao-Dai but we all Buddhists." After a moment he added, "I no like we leave this camp only because of pagoda."

Dewart shrugged. "Are you ready for a VC attack tonight?"

"We OK. I no like Cao-Dai come in camp tonight. Maybe VC come in too."

"Then tell them they can't come in," Dewart suggested.

"No," Bao replied positively. "In Saigon tell province chief, district chief we must"—Bao paused, searching for the words in English—"we must work with Cao-Dai. In Saigon they no think Cao-Dai here work with VC. We think maybe VC make Cao-Dai work with them. But we no tell Saigon. Saigon tell we."

Dewart turned to me with a grin. "You know, he's got a good point. It's the same in every army. What the general at the top says goes, no matter how far away and how wrong he is."

Late in the afternoon Sergeant Rutt and the two CIDG platoons returned.

"Dai-uy Bao," Rutt reported, "we see many signs of VC. They are watching us."

Bao nodded somberly. "VC all around. They no want us here."

"They need two, maybe three battalions to overrun us," Dewart speculated. "They will harass us; they will give us mortar rounds"—he paused, then went on—"but VC do not want three, four hundred men dead just to take this place."

Bao nodded thoughtfully.

"Are the Cao-Dai chiefs coming back this afternoon?" Dewart asked.

"Yes," Bao answered. "Old priest and other two. They come see Pagoda with no guns, no ammunition store in it—like you promise—so all is good for pray tonight."

"That's fine, Bao. Very good. Have Lang call me when they get to the gate."

Dewart led Sergeant Rutt and me into his thatched-over corner of the teamhouse. "How did you do, Rutt?"

"Fine, sir. I placed the three charges. They'll sound like mortar rounds being fired. What about the three charges in camp?"

"We put them in while the ammo was being moved. Check with Sergeant Lyons to make sure you have them set up in the right order on your radio detonator."

"Yes, sir. Say, this is a real precision operation," the demo sergeant said. "Mr. Brucker would sure like to have a written report on it."

"I don't need a court-martial this year, thank you. My wife's having a baby. Now get busy. I want to pull this off just right, while the old Cao-Dai and his two VC hoods are in camp."

"Yes, sir."

"And Rutt, watch me closely for the signals."

"No sweat, sir."

It was 5:00 when the Cao-Dai elder and his two hard-eyed advisers arrived at the gate. Lang, a gracious Captain Dewart, and a worried Captain Bao greeted them. The two young men sneered openly to see they had succeeded in forcing the Americans to remove their war supplies from the pagoda.

The Cao-Dai priest, white robes gathered around him, walked into the shrine and emerged moments later. He bowed to the American captain, and through Lang announced there would be many Cao-Dai in for prayer that night when the moon was full.

"How many Cao-Dai will come in tonight?"

The two youths flanking the old man snapped some words to Lang, who appeared concerned as he turned back to Captain Dewart. "They say 30 to 40 members of the sect have gathered for prayers tonight."

"Maybe 40 men," Bao repeated. "That is bad."

"Maybe you say no. Explain later to the district chief, province chief, and Saigon," Dewart suggested blandly.

Bao shook his head. "But we watch them hard all time," he said vehemently.

Dewart bowed slightly to the two defiant young Vietnamese and the captive Cao-Dai priest. "Lang, tell the Cao-Dai leaders that we will be expecting them tonight."

Lang translated. The Cao-Dai elder placed the palms of his hands together and held them toward the American, bowing his head slightly. His two companions stared sullenly. Then the three of them started to walk from the pagoda toward the gate.

Everything depended upon the river birds flying over at the regular time. Dewart looked up the river. I followed his glance. There they came, right on schedule, heading for the camp.

The white birds were about half a minute away when Dewart made a sign with his left hand. Rutt nodded and then a low, distant pop resounded to the east.

Dewart significantly cocked his head. A second bang rumbled across the rice paddies, then a third sharp pop. "You hear that, Bao?"

"VC fire mortar at us from east!" Bao cried. "Soon hit!"

The camp commander shouted a warning in Vietnamese at the Cao-Dai elder. The two Communist hoods turned back toward the invitingly-secure sandbagged pagoda, surprise and fear mirrored on their faces. The biggest lack in Viet Cong guerrilla war was communications. I restrained a laugh, reading the minds of the two young Communists. Someone hadn't given them the word, they were probably muttering to each other. Of all fool times to harass the American camp!

Out of the corner of my eyes I saw the birds. Then came the whirring rattle from above.

"Incoming!" Dewart yelled. Lang screamed the warning in Vietnamese. The old Cao-Dai priest was knocked to the ground in the sudden dash his two young advisers made for the safety of the heavily bunkered pagoda. Bao jumped to the aid of the old Cao-Dai priest, sheltering the holy man's body with his own.

Dewart slapped an armlock on Lang who had turned toward the pagoda and threw him to the ground. Gingerly, I lay down on a grassy spot.

When he saw the two Viet Cong had made it inside the pagoda, Dewart gave Rutt the signal. Three successive explosions swelled the ground under us, concussion waves knocking the breath out of me. This seemed overdoing realism.

Slowly Dewart regained his feet, pulling his frightened interpreter up beside him. Captain Bao helped up the shaken Cao-Dai priest and slapped some of the dust out of his robes. Dust and debris were sifting down into the middle of the camp. On the walls the BAR's had opened up, spraying the area east of the camp with heavy fire.

The first blast had torn out the sandbagging and the outer wall of the camp for a radius of three feet along the river. The second blast had walked back and exploded halfway to the center of camp, blasting a sizeable crater in an open area but doing no damage.

Shaking uncontrollably, Lang stared at the results of the third explosion—what had once been the Cao-Dai pagoda, the refuge he was seeking when Captain Dewart threw him to the ground: a huge cloud of settling dust, bits of building material and thatching hung above a smoking crater.

Bao stared incredulously at the wreckage. "Direct hit," he managed to say at last.

Dewart nodded. "Good thing we moved the ammo. I told you a good VC mortarman can land a round on your handkerchief from the edge of the paddies."

The old Cao-Dai priest gazed for some moments at the smoking ruin, and slowly comprehension seemed to get through to him. He turned, and the American captain saw relief, then satisfaction appear in the old man's eyes. There was no need for a translator.

Dewart placed his palms together and bowed solemnly. To Lang he said, "Tell the Cao-Dai priest that we will build him a new pagoda any place he directs, five kilometers or better from the camp." Dewart gestured toward the blasted sandbags. "Tell him no chance of finding any bodies for funeral. Tell him"—he paused—"I'm sorry about that."

Dewart turned from Bao and the priest, winked at me, and caught Rutt's huge grin as the demolitions sergeant peered over the sandbagged teamhouse. Sternly, Captain Dewart called out, "OK Rutt, police up the rest of the team, and start getting this camp cleaned up. Tomorrow we go to work finishing this fort. I want a damned roof over our heads by tomorrow night."

"Yes, sir. One tin roof coming up, sir!"

4

TWO BIRDS WITH
ONE STONE

I met Captain Brandy Martell a few weeks after General Nguyen Khanh took over direction of the South Vietnam government from "Big" Minh—a change American advisers welcomed as one for the better. Brandy's real name was François, but no one called him that. Originally from Belgium, an OSS agent during World War II, Brandy found his way into the American Army in the early fifties and became a U.S. citizen.

I was in Saigon with Captain Tim Pickins, now fully recovered from his wounds. Tim had commandeered a jeep and was giving me a guided tour of the town. At 11:00 in the morning we were passing a small open coffeehouse removed from the more Americanized center of town when he spotted Captain Martell. Brandy was seated at a table near the sidewalk dressed in dapper sports-clothes, reading a French newspaper.

Tim pulled the jeep to a halt. "Nobody knows what the hell Brandy does when he gets into town," he said. "He just becomes one of the Saigon frogs and we never see him. Personally, I think he's working part time for the Agency." Pickins grinned wickedly. "Wait'll he sees us. He hates to be seen with Americans."

"Maybe we should leave him alone."

"Better grab him while you can. You can't ever be sure of finding Captain Martell at Nam Luong—that's his camp. He does jobs even I don't know about. And I'm supposed to know everything that happens at the ten A teams in my area."

Brandy turned a long angular face up at us as we entered the coffeehouse, his deep-brown, almost liquid eyes regarding us mournfully. His hair was coal black, he wore it long in defiance of Army convention, and he looked incredibly young.

"Good morning, Brandy," Pickins said cheerfully.

Martell nodded but said nothing in return.

"All right if we sit down? I want to introduce someone who's been wanting to meet you."

Brandy regarded me a moment with what must be a permanently doleful expression, I thought. Then he turned and called over an old Vietnamese waiter. "Garçon? L'addition s'il vous plaît."

The waiter handed Brandy a check. He put down a few piastres and stood up. "Et maintenant, messieurs, si vous voulez, nous parlerons chez moi."

We followed Brandy out of the restaurant. "At that place," Brandy said in his rolling French accent, "they know me only as Robair, a French planter from Tay Ninh. They do not know that I even speak English. It is a very useful place. But they will wonder that I was talking to Americans."

Pickins chuckled. "Sorry if we blew your cover."

Brandy shrugged expressively, long lines accenting his long thin face. Then he turned to me and apologized for his rudeness.

"Nothing to forgive," I said. "But I'd sure like to hear about what you are doing over here."

"Eh bien, I am meeting my medical specialist and intelligence sergeant for lunch at The Peacock. You are welcome to join us."

With a wave, Pickins was off, and Brandy and I walked the two blocks to the restaurant, where we found Sergeant Ossidian, the dark, heavy-featured intelligence specialist, and Sergeant Targar, the medic.

Targar had a pronounced but pleasant accent, and he told me he had been born in Hungary but left in 1952 and joined the U.S. Army. His somewhat Oriental appearance I attributed to centuries of invasions and population movements in the Balkans.

The luncheon was lively and informative, and when it was over Captain Martell gave his men nearly a *carte blanche* to tell me about the team's mission. This they did over cool drinks at Caprice's, a favorite Special Forces hangout, where the girls were good to look at—and even touch if we felt so inclined.

The two biggest problems at Nam Luong, I learned, were recruiting strike-force troopers and good intelligence agents. Both problems had been handled with typical Special Forces ingenuity.

The sergeants took obvious relish in recounting how their captain had wangled a badly needed extra company of strike-force irregulars. From a previous mission, Martell was personally acquainted with the chief of police in Saigon under President Diem. Brandy knew what the Saigon jail was like, and he hit upon the idea of bailing out the juvenile delinquents, and giving them a chance to join his strike force and fight the Communists rather than rot in the ancient, festering prison cells. It took presidential approval but finally Martell acquired about 100 assorted thieves, rapists, muggers, dope pushers, pimps, homosexuals, and murderers. These last were released to Nam Luong because they had only murdered other delinquents, not useful citizens.

The chief of police promised the young hoods jail for life if they deserted Nam Luong, and in front of them gave Captain Martell and his then LLDB counterpart permission to shoot any of the jailbirds that gave trouble.

The company of Saigon irregulars proved to be a hard-fighting group, though given to various types of body mutilation after a battle. So terrified were they of a life in prison that unlike the other companies in the camp there were no desertions.

Unfortunately, after the fall of President Diem, his successor, "Big" Minh, currying popular favor, decreed a general amnesty and threw Diem's chief of police into jail. Most of the strike-force company of Saigon criminals deserted forthwith. Only a few stayed, converted by the reform efforts of the Americans.

But now with Viet Cong activity on the upswing around Nam Luong, and the aggressive General Khanh recently come to power, one of Captain Martell's missions on this trip was to replenish his strike force of hoods. Ossidian and Targar had the utmost confidence that "the old man" would somehow turn the trick.

Recruiting new agents was more of a problem, however, especially since Nam Luong was situated in a province of constantly increasing Viet Cong domination—indeed, it was believed to contain the headquarters of the Viet Cong command staff.

Until two weeks ago Ossidian had a prize agent, one Tang, a lieutenant in the Viet Cong stationed near the province capital, which was only five miles from the Special Forces camp. Well-educated, Tang spoke English, Vietnamese of course, French, and Chinese. As a Buddhist, he had been unable to reach the level of advancement he felt due him in the Diem Roman Catholic administration. The Viet Cong, or as they preferred to be known, "The National Liberation Front," spotted the low-level dissident government employee and recruited him.

Tang was not a bloodthirsty type, however, and he had been revolted at the Viet Cong terrorist tactics in which he had participated. The day he found himself dragging pregnant women into the town square where their stomachs were slit open and the foetuses pulled out, his sensibilities were so outraged he knew he could no longer be part of the Communist organization.

One of Ossidian's agents who came and went freely through the Viet Cong camps reported Tang's discontent and a meeting between Ossidian and Tang was arranged in a safe house in the province capital. Tang soon began accumulating wealth. His information was so good that the LLDB camp commander at Nam Luong persuaded his B-team commander to request, to insist in fact, that Captain Martell divulge to him his source of intelligence.

Martell obeyed the order only after a new B-team superior, Major Fanshaw, in the country for one week, took a chopper into Nam Luong to see personally that full disclosure of all intelligence sources was made to Captain Cam, Martell's counterpart.

Ossidian grunted in disgust. "It takes a good B-team commander a couple of months, sometimes more, sometimes never, to learn when not to go strictly by State and Defense Department policy."

Two weeks after Cam's face to face meeting with Tang, Ossidian, carrying an envelope heavy with piastres, had gone to meet his prize agent. At the safe house the intelligence sergeant found Tang, horribly tortured to death, propped up in a chair facing the door.

"Is Cam a VC sympathizer?" I asked.

"It's worse than that." Ossidian stared darkly at the glass of beer before him. "It's part of this Oriental face thing. Cam had to discredit our success with Tang. So he took off for corps headquarters to boast that he had recruited the VC lieutenant himself and should get credit for all the good intelligence coming out of Nam Luong. The spy system the VC have in all the ARVN corps headquarters is so good they zapped Tang even before Cam could get back to camp."

"What are you doing for replacement agents?"

"That is a good question," Ossidian replied, winking at Targar.

"The old man said to tell him whatever he wanted to know," Targar said. "It's a good story." He gestured toward his teammate. "Take it from me, Ossidian here is the dirtiest-thinking sonofabitch I've ever known in my life. I wouldn't talk to him back home on Okinawa, but here in Vietnam give me this sneaky Syrian on my team every time."

"I've been in intelligence ten years, advising in five different countries," Ossidian said, confirming the lefthanded compliment.

Together Ossidian and Targar told me how they had recruited their present star agent.

Ossidian had always wanted a pretty female agent to spy on the Viet Cong in his territory. But there was only one way to get a really good-looking, intelligent, dedicated female agent. You had to find a girl who hated the enemy with all her soul. She must desperately want revenge. How do you find such a girl? Ossidian figured it out.

Hardly a week went by that the Viet Cong didn't hit a government hamlet. These were villages built by the Saigon government and housed people who had been moved from Viet Cong threatened areas. They were protected by an armed civilian militia with ARVN troops near enough to help in case of a Viet Cong attack. However, the militia usually was unable to beat back night attacks, and ARVN troops wouldn't come out after dark. The first thing the Viet Cong did after such an attack was make an example of the village chief, his wife, and children if any.

Ossidian persuaded Captain Martell to request a helicopter to be available for one week on a few moments' notice. He kept the radio man on the alert twenty-four hours a day. On the third day of this alert the news he was waiting for came.

The Viet Cong had overrun an important government hamlet twenty-five miles to the north during the night.

Ossidian, Targar, and Captain Martell called for their chopper and were actually landing in the hamlet as the last of the Viet Cong guerrillas were running from the fast-approaching government troops. There was the usual weeping by new widows and as Targar, with his medical kit, started to do the best he could for the wounded lying on the ground, Ossidian, his camera at the ready, strode into the town square.

The grisly sight he had expected was there before him. Shocked and wailing townspeople were standing around, numbed at the horror they had been forced to witness.

Even Ossidian, hardened as he was, confessed to a touch of nausea as he went about the business of taking photographs of the hamlet chief and his young son, perhaps twelve years old. Both had been tied up by the thumbs and disemboweled. He took portrait shots of the old man's face turned to his boy, eyes open, pupils rolled back, the deep lines of agony still set. The youngster's gaping body was a tragic sight, head back, mouth open, tongue bitten through.

Standing back, Ossidian snapped several shots showing the intestines of the father and son hanging down in the dirt, flies buzzing in them. Then came a masterpiece of the grotesque.

A pig, snorting unconcernedly, rooted its way across the square, and as it came to the hanging entrails of the village chief noisily began to eat them. Ossidian managed to take the picture before Martell rushed upon the pig, kicking it squealing away. The wife of the chief hung jaggedly, tied between two upright stakes. Carefully Ossidian photographed the body in which every bone had been methodically broken. Again, he carefully focused on the broken but quite recognizable face for a closeup.

In his serviceable Vietnamese, Ossidian inquired politely where the home of the late village chief stood. A dazed old man led the intelligence sergeant across dirt paths to a substantial concrete-block house, painted blue and trimmed in red. Above the door the date it had been built, 1962, was indicated in raised numbers painted white. Probably then the hamlet chief had been a Catholic, using the Christian calendar instead of the Buddhist.

Inside, Ossidian, assisted by Captain Martell, found a desk, and above it the picture of a family of three daughters and two sons, one the boy hanging in the square. He took the picture down and then went through all the papers and envelopes. An hour and a half later, as the vanguard of the ARVN battalion entered the stricken town, Ossidian had found what he was looking for, and he and Martell were urging Targar, cleaning and dressing wounds, to hurry.

Back at the A team, Ossidian took a jeep and drove into town. At the photography shop he went into the darkroom with the proprietor and stayed with him while the films were developed and certain shots enlarged. The pictures made the darkroom technician sick and Ossidian had to help him get the prints completed.

The following morning Ossidian was on the milk run to Saigon from the province capital, the address of the butchered hamlet-chief's daughter and several of her letters to the family written in both French and Vietnamese in his plastic briefcase. Also, of course, he had complete photographic documentation of what the Viet Cong had done to her parents.

From the letters he had determined that Lin Son Binh, the daughter, was a teacher in a Catholic school for young girls being prepared to complete their education in France.

Ossidian worked on the premise that the Viet Cong always had an agent watching him even in Saigon, so at Special Forces headquarters he handed a letter addressed to Co Binh (Miss Binh) to be delivered to her personally through a Vietnamese courier who could not be recognized by anyone, Viet Cong or government, as an agent of the Americans.

The news of the attack on the hamlet had not yet been released in the Saigon newspapers. Ossidian would have to tell Co Binh of her parents' fate. He had wanted it this way.

At 4:00 in the afternoon, dressed in civilian clothes, Ossidian arrived at the Air Vietnam reservation offices. He had thought of asking her to meet him in a cafe, but proper Vietnamese girls didn't walk into such places alone. He walked inside the air-conditioned room and waited. He wasn't sure which of the daughters in the picture would be Co Binh. Ten minutes after he arrived, a nervous-looking Vietnamese girl in a white au-dai entered the office, looking about uncertainly.

Ossidian whistled softly to himself. This was a very beautiful girl, delicate and slim, with an air of hauteur that made a man want to break through and get to her. "Wouldn't some Viet Cong big shot like to take that," the intelligence sergeant had thought to himself, even as he approached her, a reassuring smile on his face.

"Co Binh?" he asked politely.

She looked up at Ossidian and nodded firmly.

"Do you speak English?" he asked. "Ou aimez-vous mieux que nous parlerons en français?"

Co Binh smiled for the first time. "I think maybe we speak English."

Ossidian smiled. He had no illusions about his French although he could get along in the language. "Good. Will you come with me so we can talk about your family?"

When the girl hesitated Ossidian drew the family picture from his briefcase and showed it to her. Co Binh gasped, looking at the framed photograph, hand-tinted, that she knew hung in her father's house. "You were at my father's house?"

Ossidian nodded and thought he detected a blush on Co Binh's face, a momentary sag in her proud carriage. "What did he tell you about me?" she demanded defensively.

Ossidian was both relieved and concerned: relieved because he suspected Co Binh had left home under some stigma, undoubtedly something to do with a man; concerned because she might no longer love her parents enough so that their horrible deaths would cause her to become an agent against the Viet Cong. However, surely her little brother's ghastly death would affect her violently.

"If you will come with me, I have some things to tell you about your father and mother."

"Maybe we can talk here?" she suggested.

Ossidian shook his head. "Please come with me. It is important."

Reluctantly, Co Binh allowed herself to be led to a tiny blue Saigon taxicab and put inside. Ossidian gave the driver an address on Minh Mang in Cholon, the Chinese section of Saigon. He did not want to tell Co Binh about her parents' death in the cab so he asked her about herself and the school where she taught French. Her father had been loyal to the Diem regime and part of his reward had been the excellent education Co Binh and her brothers and sisters had received.

Co Binh replied impatiently to Ossidian's questions. Finally, before they reached their destination, the intelligence sergeant said to Co Binh, "We are almost there. A Vietnamese doctor friend of mine will allow us to use his house to talk comfortably. Both he and his wife will be present.''

The cab pulled up in front of a doctor's office and Ossidian led Co Binh, still clearly showing her reluctance, to the front door. He hoped that she would not know that Doctor Hinh was one of the most noted abortionists in Saigon. If they were being watched, Ossidian thought wryly, there could be no doubt in anyone's mind why the American and the hesitant, nervous Vietnamese girl were entering Doctor Hinh's office.

The doctor, who had provided Ossidian with a safe house before, greeted them and led them to his sitting room, heavy with dark furniture and gaudy Buddhist religious symbols. He talked in Vietnamese for a few moments with Co Binh, pointed to an open door to another room where he and his wife were having tea, and then left Ossidian and Co Binh alone.

"Now," the girl demanded. "Why you bring me here?"

Ossidian gave her a look of deep sympathy and said, "I was at your father's hamlet yesterday just after he and your mother and brother were murdered by the Viet Cong."

Co Binh let out a sharp cry of anguish, her hands flying to her face. The reaction gratified Ossidian.

"When did you last see your family?" he asked.

"It has been almost a year. My father was angry when I brought to the village a boy who was a Buddhist to meet him. He . . ." Co Binh suddenly stiffened and gave Ossidian a sharp look. "Are you sure they are dead? How can I know? Why did not the government tell me?"

"They are dead, Co Binh."

"What happened to them?"

"You know what the Viet Cong do to hamlet chiefs?"

"Here in Saigon we do not feel there is really a war. I have never been hurt by the Viet Cong. They are bad because they are Communists and hate the Church but . . ."

Ossidian knew the moment for the necessary brutality had arrived. He took the long shots of Co Binh's father, mother and young brother from his briefcase and showed them to her.

She stared at them uncomprehendingly a moment and then the full impact hit her. She screamed. The wife of Doctor Hinh appeared at the door but Ossidian motioned her away.

One by one, Ossidian placed the other pictures in front of Co Binh, who stared at them, shocked, white-faced, shaking, and moaning softly. When Co Binh saw the picture of the pig rooting in her father's entrails she cried out and dug her fingers into her eyes.

"No. No. No more. Please," she cried.

"Do you see what the Viet Cong are?" Ossidian pursued. "Do you see what they do all over your country, every day?"

Co Binh, incapable of coherent talk, was now screaming hysterically. Ossidian put his arm on her shoulders to comfort her, but she shook it off. He stood up and motioned to Doctor Hinh who was standing just inside the sitting room.

The doctor went to her, a prepared hypodermic needle in his hand, and gave the convulsing girl a sedative.

Co Binh spent the night at the doctor's house and the next day, still in a partial state of shock, Ossidian began to talk to her of revenge and duty to Vietnam.

Two weeks later, as part of their civic action program, the Special Forces A team at Nam Luong fixed up a ramshackle old schoolbuilding in the province capital. Desks and chairs were bought, books and blackboards installed in the rooms, and the new school for refugee orphans of the province was ready by the time the new teacher from Saigon arrived. Co Binh became immediately popular with the children as well as the male adults of the town.

Ossidian carefully instructed Co Binh to become friendly with Mr. Hinh, a prominent lawyer and businessman working both sides of the war. Through past agents Ossidian knew that Hinh had close contacts with the highest officers in the National Liberation Front.

Hinh developed an immediate interest in Co Binh, who talked frequently about the Americans and their camp which she had been invited to visit several times. As Ossidian had foreseen, Hinh soon realized that Co Binh could be a useful tool in fostering his relations with the National Liberation Front commanders.

Hinh introduced her to Colonel Ling, the Viet Cong commander of the whole corps area, who was an occasional visitor to the Hinh establishment in the province capital. She convinced Ling that she was against the government and the Americans meddling in her country.

Ling invited her to visit his headquarters, a permanent, comfortable series of concrete and stone buildings in the thick jungle and scrub forest thirty miles northwest of the province capital. In spite of constant urging by the American advisers, no segment of the Vietnamese Army had ever dared go into this hill country near the Cambodian border.

Now Mr. Hinh and Colonel Ling were each trying to make Hinh's protégé his mistress, Ossidian told me proudly.

Targar shook his head. "I'm a humane fellow, a medic. If I wasn't too old to go back to college I'd become a doctor. This man, Ossidian, sometimes I am sick with him." Targar grinned at his teammate. Then to me he said, "So what is our intelligence sergeant doing in Saigon? Already he is looking for a new agent to replace Co Binh when she is caught."

"She's just about to be her most effective," Ossidian explained. "Unfortunately, maximum effectiveness is usually soon followed by compromise."

"But, my friend," Targar said, "she cannot reach max performance without the help of the medic."

"You see, Co Binh has been playing off Mr. Hinh against Colonel Ling just a little. And, the colonel has been out in the jungle without anything nice like Co Binh around for one hellofa long time. His Communist nuts are mighty hot for our girl; he wants her all to himself and told Hinh the Front would execute him if he attempted to seduce a loyal female agent."

The intelligence sergeant's laugh was deep. "For the last week Hinh has been pleading with Co Binh to spread for Ling. Old Hinh is one scared double-agent businessman."

Ossidian's problem now was that Co Binh's hatred was so intense for all National Liberation Front members that while she was willing to use her body to bring defeat to the Communists she had a terror of a Viet Cong-fathered child growing in her body. She knew she would kill such a child at the moment of its birth, before if possible; and this would be such a mortal sin—after her Catholic training—that she could never live with herself or face a priest the rest of her life.

To the surprise of Ossidian and Targar, Co Binh had absolutely no knowledge of contraceptives. The intelligence sergeant, however, was as resolved as the impassioned Colonel Ling that Co Binh and the Viet Cong commander should have frequent sexual congress, the earlier the better.

Thus, while Co Binh kept putting off an increasingly anxious and more irritable Colonel Ling, Ossidian asked Captain Martell to request through B-team channels that a female contraceptive kit be immediately flown into Nam Luong.

The order had arrived on Major Fanshaw's desk his first

week in command. The explosion was instantly radioed back to Captain Martell, who was summoned to the B team forthwith.

With his continental urbanity Brandy succeeded in making Fanshaw—carrying out his first Special Forces assignment—appear, even to himself, naive and inexperienced in intelligence matters. It was with enormous disinclination that Major Fanshaw took on the most distasteful chore of his career. He appealed to the chief naval surgeon in Saigon for a graduated set of contraceptive diaphragms from small to medium. He further requested the proper instrument to determine the correct-size article that should be issued. The remainder, he promised, would be returned.

The day following the request, as Ossidian and undoubtedly Colonel Ling grew increasingly restive, word came back from Fanshaw to Captain Martell that neither the Navy hospital nor any of its dispensaries carried such medical supplies. Martell, standing by the radio as his sergeant decoded the message, sent back in exasperation—"Make request for subject medical supplies to Central Intelligence Agency operating group at MAAG headquarters, Saigon. Will arrive Saigon tomorrow personally to accept issue."

Targar held up a handsome, leatherette kit. "And here is subject issue. Madame Nhu really had this country tied up. There still isn't any way a poor girl can have a little fun and keep out of trouble."

"Suppose she's a virgin," I said.

Ossidian shook his head. "I don't think she is. But if so—Targar, you know your duty. That girl's got to be able to use the thing immediately!"

The intelligence sergeant looked at his watch and then pushed his chair back. "Got to leave you for a while. I have another interview at the office of the good Doctor Hinh—no relation, by the way, to Mr. Hinh. I checked that out. I'll meet you and the old man at the Continental at 1730 hours. See you then." Ossidian hauled his bulky though disciplined and even agile body out of the chair and headed for the door.

"Another schoolteacher, this time?" I asked.

"Thank God, no," Targar replied. "This is a high-class whore whose family were killed, and her sisters raped. We're going to get into a new kind of civic action program. We're starting a high-class whorehouse in the province capital. Only the highest-ranking VC will get in."

At 5:30 Targar and I found Captain Martell sitting in the back of the Continental Palace terrace bar, looking out over the busy square. "Some day the VC are going to toss a bomb in here," I grumbled, sitting down.

"Never will that happen," Brandy assured me. "This is French-owned. They pay their taxes to the VC. This is the safest place in town. And nice. None of those steel-wire screens. What will you have?"

Targar and I drank beer as Brandy slowly sipped his vermouth. "Ossidian went to interview the young lady?"

Targar nodded. "Did you have any luck policing up strike-force recruits, sir?"

"Yes," Brandy said. "I wonder if you would mind going over to the prison with me tomorrow and giving our share of delinquents a physical examination. We have enough diseases out at Nam Luong without importing more from Saigon."

"*Our* share, sir?"

"Some of the other A-team captains in need of VC fodder heard of my idea. But I got first choice. You'll see a number of our old copains, Targar."

Brandy looked up, smiling. "Ah, here comes Lieutenant Vinh. He is the LLDB Executive Officer at Nam Luong," Brandy explained to me. "He has come in town with two of his best sergeants to personally escort our young warriors back to where their talents for mayhem and assassination can be put to work on behalf of national objectives." Martell gestured to the empty chair and Lieutenant Vinh sat down. We were introduced. "By the way," Martell asked me, "how about coming back to Nam Luong with us?"

"You couldn't keep me away."

"Good. We'll go out on the MAAG milk run tomorrow afternoon. Vinh will put our new contingent of hoods on a special morning flight as soon as Targar checks them over."

"How close do you want me to check, sir?"

"No leprosy, no chancres. I don't want any blood-spitters. If they have the clap, and I assume most of them will, we can stick them full of penicillin when they get to Nam Luong."

Brandy grinned at me. "The first time I came to Vietnam the Army had only two physical tests. A man must not uncontrollably spit blood when he talked. Then they had a ring about five inches in diameter for the pinhead test. If the top of the recruit's head protruded through the ring he was,

115

quite rightly, judged a cretin. He didn't have to serve. My first advice was to make the ring a bit larger. Too many troopers who could drool and make monkey-chatter were passing the physical. Of course"—Brandy gave a Gallic shrug—"most of them were shot for insubordination."

Captain Martell turned to Lieutenant Vinh. "May I buy you a drink?"

2.

The Army Caribou clattered to a halt on the perforated-steel strip runway, and Martell, Ossidian, Targar, and I disembarked.

A jeep pulled up to meet us, driven by a tall, open-faced, smiling first lieutenant, green beret low on his forehead. I was introduced to Bob Barton, Captain Martell's Executive Officer, and we piled into the jeep. It was about 1:00 in the afternoon when we arrived, and the drive to Nam Luong took another twenty minutes. Barton drove full tilt down the road and I held on tightly to my treasured jungle campaign hat.

Brandy laughed. "Too fast? We make it as hard as possible for the odd sniper to get one of us."

Finally Barton turned off the once-paved main road, now fast disintegrating to gravel, and took a right up to the outer barbed-wire perimeter around Nam Luong. Outside the perimeter were rows of wooden shacks.

"We've got about two hundred and fifty women and children dependents of the strike force living there," Brandy said.

Two tiger-suited strikers saluted and let us into the outer perimeter. We drove another fifty yards to the bamboo-spiked mud and stone walls. Again two guards saluted and let us past the corner machine-gun bunker. Behind us a barbed-wire barricade was slid back into place.

"Nice permanent cement-type buildings you have here," I remarked.

"Used to be a French fort. The Viet Minh took it for a while and then the French captured it again and really fixed it up."

The jeep stopped under a tree in the center of an L formed

by two cement longhouses. "Ahead of us is the American chow hall, the kitchen, and further down the operations and supply room." Brandy pointed at a long low building with a series of doors along it. "There's where we sack out. Bring your gear. There's an extra cot in my room." Brandy's accent was particularly noticeable when he used American slang.

After depositing my pack in the captain's quarters I was introduced to the other members of the team—all but two sergeants who were out on an operation. "Let's get some chow, now," Brandy suggested. "Then, you will see everything."

Barton and Ed Swiggert, the team sergeant, sat down with us. A Chinese girl came in with a pan of hot rice. "Ah, yes, there she is. Sweet Lips." Brandy called out, "Sweet Lips, you don't let any of these boys be naughty with you when I go away?"

Sweet Lips giggled and filled our bowls. Brandy turned to his Executive Officer. "Bob, I think we will see problems with this new bunch of criminals. They all arrived with Lieutenant Vinh?"

"Oh, yes. They're here, every one you bailed out of jail this morning is accounted for. What's the trouble besides we all have to get new pickproof locks on our doors?"

"We must keep them fighting all the time, always on operations, like before. Only now we have Captain Cam who tries to cut down on combat operations. But I think we are in for trouble with Major Fanshaw. He doesn't like our hoods."

"He isn't the only one, sir," said Master Sergeant Swiggert.

"He doesn't even like them being here," Martell added. "He is planning a big inspection this week. We must try to shape them up. Maybe we take the best of this new group, make an honor guard, give them special colored scarf or something. Give them little extra privileges. Then the others try to be better soldiers so they can be honor guard."

"Right, sir," said Barton.

"Good. Now, while Swiggert and I go over some things maybe you will show our guest here around the camp."

I followed Barton out into the hot sun and he began pointing out the various facilities of the camp. Near the strike-force barracks on the opposite side of the parade ground from the American quarters was a large, shrieking and laughing crowd of strikers.

"What gives?" I asked.

"That's the zoo." A sheepish grin came over Barton's wide, ruddy-complexioned face. "The strikers get a big jolt out of the monkeys." Seeing I was interested, he walked me in the direction of the noisy throng. "The boys have a funny sense of humor. Looks like some of the returnees from the Saigon jail checking up to see if their old monkey friends are still around."

As we strolled toward the monkey cage Barton told me about the camp's most popular pet, a gibbon. "We started out with a male and a female in the cage together. Trouble was the female was frigid. Our male turned out to be an oversexed little bastard. He had a miserable time. The goddamned female would bite him every time he came after her." Barton laughed. "Well, one of our hoods felt sorry for the poor sonofabitch and tossed a hen in with him."

"A hen?"

Barton laughed. "Come on." He shoved his way through the crowd around the cage, the strikers laughing and plucking at him. In front of the cage there was a mean-faced little Viet holding a clucking hen just outside the gibbon's reach. Both hairy arms were thrust through the chicken wire, bright eyes fixed on the nervous fowl. The striker would let the gibbon almost get to the hen and then pull it an inch out of the little beast's reach. Each time this happened the gibbon screamed in shrill frustration, ran around the cage several times, and banged his head. This was the signal to put the hen close to him again and the gibbon immediately made another lunge through the cage. The screams of laughter from the strikers drowned out the siren-like shrieks of the gibbon.

Seeing that the American officer and another American were present, the striker in charge of the entertainment decided to get down to the main attraction. The laughter and what could only be Vietnamese obscenities reached a crescendo as the door to the cage was opened a crack and the hen thrown inside.

The lusty cheers that went up as the gibbon chased a now thoroughly terrified hen around the cage and finally caught it, reminded me of the first appearance of the bull in a corrida.

In a businesslike, down-to-earth manner the gibbon turned the hen upside down and began to pluck out the screeching fowl's tail feathers. Expertly he divested the hen of every

118

feather about its tail and then ignoring the furious protestations, assaulted the rear of the squawking biddy.

That such a noise could come out of a small bird rocked me. Even the strikers, fighting each other for a better view of the proceedings and crying out encouragements to the camp mascot, couldn't drown out the reedy shrieks.

The gibbon was soon surfeited and threw the now limp and wounded hen aside, where it lay, flapping its wings. The show was over and the still noisy strikers began to disperse.

"Quite a matinee," I remarked.

"When they really want a spectacle they throw in a rooster." Barton chuckled grimly. "Oh yes, we do have a ball with our allies around here."

We walked back toward the chow hall and met Ossidian and Targar, who said Captain Martell suggested they take me downtown and show me their civic action project—the school.

"Watch out for these two," Barton warned with a grin. "They'll sure as hell get you in trouble."

Ossidian got behind the wheel of the jeep; Targar and two boxes of medical equipment took up the back. "It's sick call at the school today," Targar explained as the green-bereted sergeant drove off at a frightening pace. In town he wove through a tangle of streets and finally pulled up in a plesant, grassy yard with a brightly painted jungle gym, slides and swings.

"School," Ossidian announced.

A crowd of children surged out of the door and the freshly painted structure. They called out happily and surrounded the two sergeants as they stepped from the jeep. Recognizing me as an American, some of the kids grabbed me too.

Co Binh, wearing a white au-dai, emerged into the sunlight. Her pique at the children for summarily deserting her classroom made her delicate features all the more appealing.

"Ah, hello, Co Binh," Targar called to her cheerfully. "Your gynecologist is here!" Although his words obviously meant nothing to her, Co Binh blushed prettily. She had been expecting Targar for two days.

Ossidian nudged me. "What do you think of this place? Killing two birds with one stone. Civic action at its best and intelligence at its most effective. The taxpayers ought to be happy—two deals for the price of one."

Ossidian and Targar met each other's eyes for a moment.

"Oh, shit," Ossidian muttered. "What are you going to do? We're over here to win, aren't we?"

Targar, a medical kit slung over his shoulder, went over to Co Binh, said something, and then they walked toward the back of the school.

"Funny thing about old Victor Charlie," Ossidian mused. "He thinks Americans are dickheads for coming over here and trying to drill water wells and build schools and orphanages. The only time he respects us is when we're killing him."

The intelligence sergeant took a handful of candy from his pocket and started distributing it to the children. "You'd think it would be compromising Co Binh for all of us to be around the school this way—Targar going back there alone with her. But hell no. When we get on this do-good kick Victor Charlie just thinks we're nuts and laughs. It's funny to them. We finance a school and pay one of their agents because we want everyone to love us."

About fifteen minutes later Targar rejoined us out in the yard. He started getting the kids lined up for medical inspection.

"How'd it go?" Ossidian asked.

"No sweat. I've found my niche in life at last. I have just the right bedside manner to be a hellofa specialist in intimate female problems. That's where the money in medicine is, you know. Got her measured up, gave her the right size, showed her how to use it without Colonel Ling being any the wiser. And I do not embarrass her at all. She thinks I am great. I think she is falling in love with her gynecologist."

Targar grabbed a little boy by the arm. One eye was almost closed and full of pus. "My God. What is this? I got to get sick call going. Ossidian, she wants to see you—got big things to tell you. Now I got to take care of my kids." Targar looked up at me. "If you like to help . . . ?"

"Just tell me what to do."

For almost two hours Targar examined and treated the children's ills. He muttered in various of the languages he spoke as he worked. In English he asked aloud several times, "What are all you kids going to do when you lose Co Binh?"

Finally he was finished, and I helped him gather up his medical equipment and store it away in the olive-drab case. Ossidian appeared just as we were ready to leave. We all said good-bye to Co Binh, Targar had a few *sotto voce* last words of advice for her, and again we took to the jeep.

"Let's go to MAAG headquarters," Ossidian said to Targar who was driving. "Captain Martell wants us to meet him there."

We drove into the tree-shaded grounds of a large stucco house. There were several Army vehicles in the driveway. Targar found a patch of shade and parked.

Several pleasant American officers and sergeants in the main lounge of MAAG headquarters offered us cans of cold beer, and we took them to a garden table out under a tree to wait for Martell. "What did you find out?" Targar asked.

Ossidian stared at the blue sky thoughtfully. Finally he said, "I got the most frustrating job on the team. What good does it do to recruit agents and get them killed when you can't get action at the top on the intelligence you collect?"

Before Targar could answer, Captain Martell drove up in his jeep and waved at us to follow him inside. We hastily swallowed our beers.

Brandy herded us in to the MAAG intelligence officer where I was introduced to Captain Percy. "OK, Ossidian, let's give Captain Percy and MAAG the benefit of any intelligence you may have acquired today."

"Yes, sir," said Ossidian. Captain Percy, intense and young-looking, swung his swivel chair toward the map to which Ossidian had addressed himself.

The intelligence sergeant indicated a point about two miles from the Cambodian border. "You know this place, sir?" he asked Percy.

"Certainly. There are five model hamlets there. We trained the Civil Defense people there. The United States Operations Mission has spent over $150,000 on those hamlets to improve the economy. They have a large pig program going and agricultural experts have spent a couple of months helping those people learn new ways of fertilizing their fields."

"In other words, sir," Ossidian said, "those five hamlets, with a combined population of about 3,000 people, are a loyal government hold on a lot of real estate along the Cambodian border."

"We're all proud of our work out there, Sergeant. I suppose you are going to tell me that the Viet Cong plan to attack one or more of those hamlets?"

"Tonight, sir. They have the largest of the five already infiltrated. The doors will be open and the VC will walk in bloodlessly. They'll kill the hamlet chief, the security chief, and the information chief. Then they will occupy the other four hamlets with no sweat because they already have the strongest one."

"There is an ARVN battalion stationed only ten miles from those hamlets," Captain Percy said. "We'll get word to the commander and our adviser with that battalion, Captain Canham. He's a good, conscientious man. If that battalion will move right now, they should be able to save those hamlets."

"They won't move," Ossidian said resignedly. "You, I, and the VC know it. Even Captain Canham knows it."

"We can try," Percy argued. "We're beginning to establish good working relations now between advisers and Vietnamese commanders."

"I'm glad to hear that, sir"—Ossidian's tone was heavy with irony—"because there's a lot more to this than another hamlet attack. The Communists are going to challenge ARVN and Saigon to get them out in less than forty-eight hours. Then very solicitously they are going to tell all the people to get down into the holes they've dug in the floors of their houses. And then they're going to wait for a typical Vietnamese Army attack. They know there isn't a battalion commander in the ARVN that would take a chance on getting himself or his officers shot. They know the Viets will call in artillery, American 105's with American advisers. They know the Viets will call in air strikes, flown by American pilots because the Viet pilots prefer not to fly low enough to do any good. When the artillery and air strikes really get going good and clobber the place, the Viets will slip out of these hamlets and run across to Cambodia." Ossidian's black eyes burned.

"So what's the net result? All the work USOM and MAAG have done to build up those villages will be destroyed because the Viet battalion commanders won't fight like men and push the VC out of the village in man-to-man fighting. What do we do? We turn five hamlets of loyal peasants into VC sympathizers overnight. The VC won't be killing them and their cattle and destroying their houses—it will be the Americans."

Ossidian rapped the map with his knuckles and stepped away. "And that's straight from a reliable agent."

"Thank you, Sergeant. As usual your information is timely."

Martell had been listening soberly to Ossidian's briefing. "What are you going to do about it, Captain Percy?"

"I am on my way to discuss it right now with our senior sector adviser and the Vietnamese division commander."

Martell stood up. "If we can help we'll be standing by. If nothing else, we can send in our medical team when the attack is over."

That night at Nam Luong the Americans showed an epic western for the Vietnamese strike force, projecting it against the side of a whitewashed building. It was a Cinemascope production, but the camp's 16-mm. movie projector was not equipped with a Cinemascope lens so the cowboys, Indians and horses all were long and thin. However, the strikers loved the action and identified themselves with it. When the Indians appeared the strikers screamed "VC," and when the soldiers or cowboys came to the rescue the Nam Luong irregulars vied with each other in shouting out the number of their own strike-force companies.

We were sitting around the operations room after the movie when the radio started to sputter dots and dashes. The communications sergeant wrote furiously on his pad and then turned to Martell. "Sir, the VC have occupied those hamlets already. They say they will stay for forty-eight hours."

Two mornings later I went into the hamlets with Targar and his assistant medic Ritchie. Everything Ossidian had predicted had come true. Piteously wounded and burned children were dying everywhere, men, women and cattle lay dead, the stench abominable. The ARVN battalion, which occupied the hamlets after the Viet Cong had fled the Vietnamese-ordered American bombings and American-advised artillery barrages, suffered not a single casualty. Captain Canham had vainly tried to persuade the Vietnamese battalion commander to attack the Viet Cong on the hamlet walls in hand-to-hand combat; he was devastated with frustration.

Just before dark a chopper evacuated the Nam Luong medical team from the hamlet. Back at camp we learned that the next day Major Fanshaw would be in to inspect the camp.

Promptly at 10:00 Saturday morning an HU21b, the

executive-type chopper, settled down on its runners just outside Nam Luong. Twenty of the Saigon delinquents made up the honor guard dressed in starched tiger pattern fatigues, yellow scarfs around necks and red bands around their cloth fatigue caps. They held their big M1 Garand rifles at attention as the major walked between the facing ranks. Fanshaw, his Vietnamese counterpart, Major Xuan, Captain Martell and his counterpart, Captain Cam, walked together. The American major eyed the honor guard with approval and complimented Martell on the military discipline in his strike force.

As Fanshaw proceeded with the inspection, I tagged along at a discreet distance. He looked into every one of the rooms in the cement barracks building occupied by the Americans. Recently an order had come down from higher headquarters that Special Forces men would not post any pinup girls—since such displays might be offensive to our allies, the gibbon-taunting Vietnamese strikers!

Various aspects of the camp did distress Fanshaw—its smell of undrained sewage, for one thing. After the inspection he took his A team into their operations room and was closeted with them for an hour. Then he called in Major Xuan and Captain Cam for another half-hour conference.

Shortly after noon, declining to stay for lunch, Fanshaw walked out of the camp to reboard his chopper. He brightened at the double row of honor guard waiting to see him off. Walking between the immaculate, crisply uniformed Saigon delinquents, Fanshaw was so pleased that he paused before each and shook his hand. Then he and Major Xuan boarded their helicopter and were soon on their way back to the B team.

Captain Martell immediately ordered another meeting of his A team in the operations room. I was invited to sit in on this one. The atmosphere of disgruntlement was apparent.

Major Fanshaw had found much to criticize, Brandy said. The fact that the Americans could only advise and cajole their counterparts into keeping Nam Luong clean and keeping up sanitary maintenance had made small impression on their commander. He was particularly irked at a long list of complaints the Vietnamese camp commander, Captain Cam, had sent up to Major Xuan at the B team. Foremost on the list was rudeness on the part of the Americans toward their LLDB counterparts.

The radio sergeant shifted his attention to his receiver as a call started to come in on voice. He put on his earphones so Captain Martell would not be disturbed.

"Sir!" The commo sergeant's voice suddenly interrupted. "The pilot of Major Fanshaw's helicopter just called in. Major Fanshaw's black star-sapphire ring is missing off his right hand. He thinks one of the honor guard milked it off him when he was shaking hands."

"Sergeant Swiggert," Brandy's voice cut through the silence in the room. "Every man in the honor guard will stand a shakedown inspection—with Captain Cam's approval. Since I know we won't find anything, they will be assigned to the point squad on tomorrow night's operation."

Loud, appreciative laughter broke out. Brandy let the chortling continue until the atmosphere of depression was dispelled.

"OK men!" Brandy held up a hand. "Let's get this briefing finished. We're short. Less than a month to go before we leave Vietnam. I want to see us go out of here as heroes, an A detachment that will be remembered. Lieutenant Barton and Sergeant Swiggert have volunteered to deliberately walk into a VC ambush. I want every man in this detachment to get with the program. Let's end up big!

"Now, I am going to let Ossidian brief you on his intelligence operations and then Sergeant Swiggert will tell you about tomorrow night's patrol. Go ahead, Ossidian. You got the limelight."

A few goodnaturedly uncomplimentary noises met Ossidian as he took his place in front of the map of the surrounding terrain.

"First, you all know about our civic action project, the school for orphans. You've all seen Co Binh and I guess you know she's working for us in more ways than one. Well, on Wednesday Dr. Targar, the famous Hungarian pussy specialist"—Ossidian bowed to the medic amid raucous laughter—"made it possible for Co Binh to, shall we say, step up her relationship with Colonel Ling. Ling is a full colonel in both the Army of North Vietnam and the National Liberation Front here in South Vietnam."

Ossidian turned to the map and pointed to a hilly, jungle region close to the Cambodian border. "This is where Colonel Ling has his headquarters, about forty miles from the province capital. ARVN has never had the guts to conduct operations in that area; even the French never tried to hit it when it was a Viet Minh stronghold.

"Colonel Ling is the commander of all Viet Cong operations in this corps area. In other words, he coordinates all Communist guerrilla fighting for one quarter of South Vietnam. If we could capture him it would be one of the most important victories of the war." Ossidian let his words have an effect.

"Let me give you a little more background," he continued. "On Wednesday night, after Doctor Targar performed his invaluable services, our friend Mr. Hinh drove Co Binh out to visit Colonel Ling at his headquarters."

Ossidian flashed a lewd grin. "Talking to Co Binh this morning I found out that Ling has something in common with most of us studs in this room. He doesn't like a short time. When he has a woman he wants her for all night. Co Binh got out to Ling's headquarters in Mr. Hinh's car about 10:00 at night. After a nice, intimate talk she finally gave Ling what he'd been wanting so bad. But she made Hinh wait and drive her home."

The intelligence sergeant chuckled sardonically. "I guess Ling was still as horny as a bag of toads when Co Binh said good-bye, but she told him the Americans would be suspicious if she wasn't at school first thing in the morning. Then our girl told Ling that she would have some special information for him next time she saw him. This was when he told her about hitting those five hamlets."

"Well," said Ossidian, "it's toujours l'amour, tonight for sure for Colonel Ling. Co Binh is going out there. But—like last time—old Ling is only going to get a short time. Maybe let just a couple more toads out of the bag, is all. Co Binh runs a Sunday school and the Americans will be over. She can't compromise her usefulness by not getting back.

"Tonight she will show Ling how useful she can be to him. She's heard us talking. The Americans are going out on an operation Sunday night and just before dawn they are going to cross some river and attack a town called Phu Nhu."

Ossidian went to the map, pointed out a river that ran from west to east about twelve miles north of Nam Luong, and then to a spot on the map about a mile north of the river. "We know, and the VC know we know that they are building up an arms cache here. We've been wanting to hit it for three months, but the camp commander refuses to cross the river—too many VC, he says. We say yes, many VC, that's why we want to attack there.

"The reason Co Binh knows this is our plan, she tells Ling, is because we were all bad-mouthing our counterparts for being cowards and betting with each other that they won't cross the river this time either. She heard us say we're only taking one platoon because that's all we need for a surprise attack at dawn and any more would get in the way."

Ossidian prowled back and forth in front of us a few moments. "Before she leaves with Hinh tonight Co Binh is going to tell Ling that she hates a short time too. She is going to suggest that he come into town, stay at Mr. Hinh's house like he did the night they met, and then they can have all night together."

Ossidian stopped his pacing. "Here's where Ling may get just the tiniest bit suspicious. He'll probably wait and see if the Phu Nhu operation comes off. If it does and his VC hit us and inflict casualties he'll be feeling pretty good about Co Binh. Probably Tuesday or Wednesday night his Democratic Republic of Vietnam gonads will be in a mighty big uproar for more of Co Binh. Since he now knows she's a tried and true American-hating VC he'll come into town. And then"—Ossidian grinned at his audience—"somehow we'll snatch him."

Ossidian sat down and Captain Martell stood up in front of his detachment. "Ossidian, that was a charming and explicit briefing. I find it impossible to follow the act. So, I turn the briefing over to Sergeant Swiggert who will outline our plans for tomorrow night's operation."

3.

Three Americans went out with the first platoon of Delta (for delinquent) Company of the Nam Luong strike force. The patrol, clad in tiger suits, slipped from the security of the camp and moved out into the moonlight.

Lieutenant Barton's twisted grin would have worried Lieutenant Vinh had he looked back. Sergeant Ritchie, the medic, also wore a knowing smile; it was hard for him not to laugh aloud.

I was the third American on the patrol. Brandy had objected strenuously to letting me go on a patrol whose mission was to walk into an ambush. But finally he agreed to let me accompany the second platoon. This one, led by an LLDB sergeant and advised by Master Sergeant Swiggert, would leave Nam Luong twenty minutes after the first platoon. Swiggert's mission was to provide cover when the ambush was sprung on the first platoon. Of course none of the strikers or the LLDB team knew about the ambush. I held out for the first platoon and when we walked out of Nam Luong's gate Brandy wrung my hand as though he would never see me again.

One hour out of camp Lieutenant Vinh halted the platoon to rest the young hoods in his charge. Sergeant Hanh, known as Ho Chi Hanh to the Americans, walked up and down the file during the break, slapping a striker silently on the shoulder or chucking one under the chin. Hanh was a soldier in anyone's language and army, having fought the French for four years with the Viet Minh. But he was a lover of freedom and free enterprise and turned against the Communists after the French left Vietnam. The men loved Sergeant Hanh, who took them to the local whorehouse and let them take pictures of him hacking. Hanh kept a supply of pictures of himself in action with the two overworked prostitutes in town known as "Dracula" and "Witch Hazel" to pass out to his fans.

In ten minutes we were marching again on our course toward Phu Nhu. The strikers carrying BAR's were dwarfed by the heavy automatic rifles they proudly bore over their shoulders. The big BAR's were awarded to the most reliable strikers. The honor guard from Saturday's inspection were up front of the 50-man platoon.

The planning of our cover platoon, twenty minutes behind us, had made for an interesting discussion between Captain Martell, Lieutenant Barton, Swiggert, and Ossidian. Barton, with the first platoon, had requested that the second platoon be equipped with 60-mm. mortars. He knew what it was like to get hit by an ambush and he wanted something behind him that would quickly disperse it. Swiggert was in agreement. But Ossidian had vetoed the idea.

It would make it look as though we were expecting something to have not only a cover platoon but one equipped with mortars. Better for the overall plan for the first platoon to fight its way out as best it could. Martell, reluctantly, sided with Ossidian—so there were no mortars behind us.

On the second break Barton sat down beside me, fanning his face with his tattered lucky campaign hat. "Couple more hours and we'll be in the middle of them," he said in low tones. "Better drop fast, right in the trail when you hear it coming in."

"I know what to do, old man," I replied. In an ambush both sides of the trail would be mined, or at least planted with pungi stakes, which give agonizing death to anyone falling on them.

The rest period over, we started off again across the rice paddies, dry in this season of the year. The constant grinding and rattling of the wood cutters' oxcarts crawling back to town from the thick scrub forests indicated we were still paralleling the main road. Half an hour later the clatter of oxcarts became more distant and finally faded completely. Now we were heading directly at the North Star hanging low on the horizon.

We stalked along the edges of the rice paddies and fields, staying within the shadows of the bordering woods. Suddenly I saw dark forms ahead dart out of the patrol formation and become clearly silhouetted in the open field. They bent over, picked objects up and scurried back into the line of march. Barton cursed under his breath.

"You can't teach them," he snapped. "We go through a watermelon patch and they have to load up. If the VC are watching they'll know just where we are."

My carbine, sixty rounds belted to the folding stock and two banana clips taped butt to butt in the lock, began to be awkward to carry. Technically, I was a noncombatant, but the Viet Cong didn't know this, so the weapon was ready for instant employment.

Perhaps the strikers sensed approaching danger for they began observing excellent noise discipline, picking up their feet and placing them down softly. In alarm, I felt the tickling in my throat of a persistent cough which had latched onto me some months ago in a cold spell just before I left New York.

New York was the other side of the Milky Way now, but the cough wouldn't quit. A slight croak tore loose from my throat. Instantly Barton's cautioning hand was on my shoulder. I reached swiftly into the pocket of my loose jungle fatigues for the bottle of GI gin. A good slug of this 80 proof terpin hydrate elixir guarantees an hour free of coughing.

As we pushed on through the night, Barton glanced frequently at the luminous dial of his watch. Daylight was not far off, and neither, I judged, was the enemy, when the patrol halted. I followed Barton forward. Through the trees ahead the river shimmered in the bright starlight. The moon had set.

I watched as Barton and Lieutenant Vinh talked in inaudible whispers. Finally, Barton turned to me. "Lieutenant Vinh came up with a new one. He says we can't cross the river because there are too many alligators in it." Barton grinned. "This is the time I would have to make an excuse for not crossing. I'm glad he did it for me. The point section is going up as far as the river and wait for daylight. Vinh says, 'Maybe we go back to Nam Luong when daylight comes.' "

From the trees we watched as 20 strikers, led by Sergeant Hanh, made their way to the river's edge. The white, flat light of dawn was beginning to erase the stars and seep into the scrub forest. Sergeant Ritchie and Barton, their carbines ready, peered through the tangled growth in all directions.

Suddenly, from the other side of the river, shattering bursts of automatic-weapons fire ploughed into the point section. Hanh dropped to the ground, shouting orders, and the strikers began crawling back to rejoin the platoon.

Before the rest of the platoon could put up a heavy volume of fire to cover the retreating strikers, we were hit from our left flank. I threw myself to the trail and fired bursts from my carbine. Barton, Ritchie, and the irregulars around us were returning. I wondered how many of the honor guard would make it back to us. Our volume of fire built up as the BAR men began pumping heavy slugs back at the ambushers. The fire from across the river ceased. Probably all of the point section that were going to make it had scurried back from the river bank, leaving no more targets.

Barton looked back at me and then up and down the column lying in the trail. Finally he spotted Lieutenant Vinh. "Hey, Vinh," he shouted. "We get pinned down, all dead here we don't attack. Not big ambush now but more VC come from Phu Nhu soon."

Sergeant Hanh crawled up to us. He said something to the interpreter who stayed near to Lieutenant Barton. The interpreter cried, "Men on point back. Sergeant Hanh say we must go attack ambush. VC coming across the river now."

"Vinh!" Barton shouted, "You hear that? Let's go."

To my enormous surprise, Lieutenant Vinh suddenly shouted a string of commands and holding his carbine, stock pressed against his side with his right elbow, raised up into a crouching position and firing long bursts, started into the ambush. Sergeant Hanh, yelling commands was up and moving too, firing into the scrub ahead of us. The strikers, shouting Vietnamese curses, jumped up and moved into the ambush.

Barton turned to me. "You and Ritchie stay where you are, I'm going in." With that, his tall frame bent low, Barton moved up with the strikers. I watched him jerk a grenade off his combat harness, and lob it into the bush ahead of him. There was a sharp blast, followed by screams as Barton crashed on into the ambush.

As abruptly as it had started the Viet Cong ambush ceased firing and pulled back into the dry jungle. The strikers slowly ceased firing and orders were shouted. The platoon reassembled on the trail. Miraculously only three strikers had been wounded and one killed in breaking up the ambush. It was light now and Ritchie went to work on the wounded men who had been dragged back by their comrades.

"Very good," Lieutenant Barton complimented his counterpart, clapping him on the shoulder. Vinh smiled proudly. Hanh, patrolling the column now reassembled on the trail, came up to Vinh and reported. Barton's interpreter relayed Hanh's words.

"Sergeant Hanh say three men dead beside river, two more wounded. He go with strikers and bring them back. He say we must dee-dee quick. VC come again."

"Hanh knows the score," Barton said approvingly. "We've got to marry up with the second platoon fast." Hanh, with a squad of strikers, went back to the river and returned carrying dead and wounded.

Ritchie hurriedly did what he could for the wounded, giving the more seriously hurt shots of morphine, and then we started back to join the cover platoon. Between the dead and wounded and those men required to carry them, the first platoon was considerably less than 50 per cent operational. We made the best time back we could to rejoin Swiggert's platoon. Lieutenant Vinh, talking over his PRC-10 radio, motioned to Barton, who moved up the file to the Vietnamese officer and took the receiver from his hand. He talked a few moments, handed the radio back to Vinh, and waited for Ritchie and me to catch up.

"Swiggert is waiting for us, we'll be there in ten minutes. He said if he heard any more firing he'd come up and relieve us."

The wounded held us up as was to be expected, and Ritchie, checking his hastily applied dressings, moved from one to another. We were carrying five absolutely reformed Saigon delinquents. They were dead.

"Hey, Vinh," Barton called. "Maybe we put out flank security?" Vinh nodded wearily and called to Hanh who had tapped three men for the job when the scrub jungle to our right suddenly burst out with fire. It was broad daylight and we made clear targets. We pitched forward, most of the Viet Cong rounds going high. Fortunately the Viet Cong on this ambush were not hard-core North Vietnamese or their first fusillade would have been disastrous.

Strewn along the trail, dead and wounded men interspersed with strikers returning a withering fire of their own, the first platoon was a distressing sight. The Viet Cong incoming fire was so intense, if inaccurate, that Ritchie couldn't move to attend the wounds of those crying out. Vinh was lying next to Barton, Hanh was up ahead with the remnants of the point.

Barton shouted something into Vinh's ear and then rolled over to me. "We're going to stay down, we've lost too many men in this intelligence operation already," he cried above the noise of the fire-fight. "We can hold until the second platoon comes up and flanks them. Five minutes at the most."

Minutes later I had fired my entire basic load, and the diminishing volume of our return fire indicated that the entire platoon was running low on ammo. To our enormous relief a sudden massive swell of fire and grenade explosions split the air to the south. The second platoon had surprised our ambushers, who no doubt thought they were about to finish us off. Almost instantly the incoming rounds that had been whining over us stopped as the Viet Cong switched direction of fire. The second platoon was driving them out of their ambush positions now and we heard the fire-fight move northward and then cease altogether as the Communists broke contact and disappeared in the jungle.

Barton stood up and took a count of our casualties. We were lucky. Only two more dead and three wounded. The second platoon began to filter in around us. They were in high spirits, having suffered no casualties and killed several Viet Cong. Swiggert and Barton helped Lieutenant Vinh regroup the two platoons into one solid section. The seven dead and twelve immobile wounded were carried in the center. Flank security was put out, and we waited only for Ritchie to finish patching up the strikers hit in the second ambush before proceeding back to camp.

While we waited, a small squad of four delinquents-turned-strikers returned, grinning broadly. None of them were wounded but there was blood on the tiger suits of two. Swiggert eyed them sourly as they displayed wet, red things to envious fellow irregulars.

"Nasty little bastards," Swiggert growled. "Take a chance on getting themselves trapped out there to cut the hearts out of a few dead VC's."

Ossidian was delighted with the results of the patrol. Co Binh would now be Colonel Ling's valued and trusted agent and mistress. There was, moreover, another and unforeseen salutary byproduct of the operation: the hot-tempered miscreants of Delta Company were desperate to go out after the Viet Cong again and revenge their seven dead.

After he had been briefed on the entire operation by Lieutenant Barton, Ossidian drove into the school and told Co Binh she could report that Nam Luong had suffered a disastrous 20 dead and 35 wounded. The Viet Cong had probably exaggerated even further to their commanders, Ossidian knew, so the accounts would tally. As a result there would be no more operations going out of Nam Luong until more strikers could be recruited and the camp had recovered from this terrible blow to its morale.

On Monday night the Americans had a quiet celebration, drinking some of the bourbon I had brought with me, and talking about their wives or girl friends. It is always surprising to realize how deeply dependent on their wives and families most of these highly skilled and unusually sophisticated soldiers were. Ossidian alone had no wife or girl hoping he would safely get out of Vietnam.

Tuesday was a dull, restful day. With no operations going out, the entire team, except for the two medics who were always overworked, caught up on rest and letter writing. Tuesday evening Ossidian returned from town, excitement shining from his black eyes. Colonel Ling was coming into town Wednesday for an all-nighter with Co Binh. The tryst was set up at Mr. Hinh's house.

The moment of fulfillment for Ossidian was at hand. The Syrian, as I understood now, lived for those occasional great intelligence coups that come so infrequently to the professional and almost never to the amateur. All else to him was merely existing.

Martell, another intelligence professional, though far better rounded as a man and a soldier, understood Ossidian perfectly and gave over to him full details of planning even though it was Martell's entire career if anything went wrong and Vietnamese high officials found grounds for serious criticism.

The planning session ran most of Tuesday night and stirred hot debate among team members. But Ossidian, backed by Captain Martell, carried the meeting. The one thing Brandy insisted on, against Ossidian's wishes, was the composition of a special top secret message to Major Fanshaw. As Ossidian pointed out, this meant that Major Xuan, with his spy system deeply entrenched in the American B team, would probably read the message even before Fanshaw, and send word to the local province chief and ARVN division commander who received healthy kickbacks from Mr. Hinh. The whole mission would be compromised and another agent lost.

Captain Martell and Sergeant Ossidian wrote and rewrote the message to Major Fanshaw and finally it was sent as follows:

A-2 intelligence source [A-2 was almost as reliable as a source could be, the code graduating from A-1, most reliable agent positive of information, to E-5, habitual liar unsure of information] *informs us that Colonel Ling, VC commanding officer this corps area, entering province capital tomorrow night Wednesday. Request permission to capture him. Further request this information not go beyond Special Forces headquarters and detention of subject individual be left entirely to Detachment A-681. Please reply soonest. Martell.*

The message went out encoded to the B team sometime after midnight and the reply came in to a nervously waiting A team at 2:00 P.M. Permission was granted with the reservation that once Ling had been apprehended he must be turned over to the province chief.

"Not so bad," Ossidian commented. "We'll turn him over to the province chief—when we're ready."

4.

Mr. Hinh's house stood at the intersection of the main street of the capital and a lesser, unlighted street. A large stone and concrete building, it was set back from the road and even though Hinh was probably the safest human being in the province, the grounds of the house were surrounded by concertina wire. The main entrance was guarded by two soldiers at all times. Thus did the ARVN division commander accommodate the province's most important merchant and lawyer in this and many other ways.

At thirty minutes after midnight Captain Martell and Sergeant Ossidian drove up in the camp's jeep and parked it down the main street on the far side of the intersection from the Hinh residence. They could clearly see the lights at the entrance gate and the two ARVN guards listlessly lounging around the two sentry boxes. I sat in the back seat of the jeep where I could follow the action. At the same time Martell parked his jeep, Sergeant Swiggert drove up the side street to the rear of the barbed-wire perimeter surrounding Hinh's mansion, and parked. A few minutes later Sergeant Targar parked behind him in a closed ambulance, which he had borrowed from MAAG to transport some of his wounded out to a plane the next morning for evacuation to Saigon.

At 12:45 in the morning six black-clad carefully picked volunteers from Delta Company ("Saigon's finest second-story men," Swiggert had reported) slipped out of the truck Swiggert had driven. Two of them were carrying a ladder. Silently they laid it over the concertina wire and one after the other they scampered over the wire into Mr. Hinh's back yard. Two of the figures stole around to the front of the house, hugging the shadows until they had taken up their positions behind the guards. Each within an easy leap of silencing his man, they waited in the shadows cast by the two sentry boxes.

The other four members of the task force picked a likely part of the rough stone walls of the house and began to climb toward the second story of the large square building. One by one they gained a foothold along the second-floor ledge.

Co Binh lay stiffly staring at the ceiling next to the nude body of the man she hated. Although it was contrary to Vietnamese custom she had persuaded a stimulated and unargumentative Colonel Ling that she could sleep only with plenty of fresh air and had insisted that the barred window be open enough to admit the night breeze. Ling's mind was not on the window. Besides, for two years he had been staying at Hinh's house whenever he had come into the capital. Wasn't he being guarded by alert government troops?

At exactly 12:55—Co Binh was wearing a luminous-dial watch Ossidian had given her—she stirred, and despising what she had to do slowly slid the backs of her smooth legs over the colonel's so the rear of her thighs rested above Ling's groin. It was a friendly custom for Vietnamese girls to sleep like this with their lovers and had a sensuous effect on both partners. The colonel stirred. Knowing this was the last time she would have to give herself to the man who had ordered the death by horrifying torture of her father, mother, brother and thousands of others, Co Binh gently moved her thighs in a massaging motion.

Ling woke up stimulated and passionate. Greedily he reached out. He twisted around, forced her thighs apart and with lust, long unappeased by anything so exquisite, brutally possessed her.

Now, as she had been coached by Ossidian from the time he first asked her to do this with the hated Viet Cong colonel, she cried out in mock throes of ecstasy, her cries becoming louder as the fervid Ling used her body with increasing ferocity. Her throaty outbursts of passion, so unusual in the usually discreet and passive well-bred Vietnamese woman, only whetted Ling's appetite, and his animal grunts carried well beyond the open window.

Four black forms converged, quickly pulled the window open, and jumped into the room. After a few seconds of what they considered well-deserved voyeurism, they savagely clobbered Ling on the back of his neck and head with blackjacks provided by Ossidian.

Ossidian had anticipated perfectly the reaction of his little thugs as they pulled Ling off Co Binh's naked young body. For a moment each of them almost lost his sense of the mission as he stared down lasciviously. Then they remembered Ossidian's dire threats. They also thought of the promised week in Saigon with 5,000 piastres each to spend if the operation were a success. As Co Binh snatched the sheet around her and sat upright, temptation was quickly overcome. One of the task force remained behind to help Co Binh get out while the other three, after tying a rope around the inert Ling's waist, lowered him to the ground below.

The two strike-force members chosen for sentry elimination watched the minute hand on their watches turn to 1:05. Then each, with a foot and a half length of soft nylon cord held at the ends, jumped his target, throwing the garrotte around the guard's neck, pulling it tight enough to shut off all sound. The guards stared up at the black-pajamaed men and knew they were dead. Three other black-clad phantoms carrying a naked man rushed through the gates. The guards did not see the familiar ambulance drive up and the three intruders with their victim jump into it even as the truck sped away.

Hanging between life and death, staring straight up, the luckless sentries could only wonder why it took so long before the fatal twist of the rope. They didn't see the last of the invaders, half dragging, half carrying a partially dressed woman, run past them through the gate and jump into the cab of a three-quarter ton truck which pulled up at the gate.

Then the garrottes were tightened and the guards died a little. When they came back to life there was no sign of any disturbance and no sounds from the home of Mr. Hinh. Since they were alive and unharmed and neither had a bruise on his neck they decided to follow their superiors' example and not bring unpleasant matters to official attention. Instead they continued to patrol the entrance to Mr. Hinh's home, perhaps with more vigilance than before.

The rendezvous point was Co Binh's quarters behind the school. Targar entered, personally carrying the comparatively diminutive Ling. The colonel was thrown naked on the floor and a light bulb turned on him. His three abductors stared down at him. Ossidian, Martell, and I had arrived first, driving off in the jeep as soon as we saw the operation had come off successfully. A few moments later, Swiggert, Co

Binh and the other three members of our special task force arrived.

Colonel Ling began to moan and Targar motioned to the three strikers who had kidnapped the prisoner. Immediately they jumped him and held him down while Targar got a needle into the vein in the bend of his arm and injected sodium pentathol into the Communist's blood stream.

Then Ling was hoisted onto a cot and Ossidian's great moment came. Through an interpreter he had been training for two months, he interrogated the Viet Cong leader, now full of the so-called truth serum, for almost three hours. The entire interrogation was recorded on tape.

Meanwhile, Brandy helped Co Binh calm down, talking to her in French, which was like her native language. He helped her pack those things she wanted to keep, gave her 10,000 piastres, and warned her that even though Mr. Hinh had been collaborating with the Viet Cong there was nothing the local authorities would do to him. He gave them all too much money.

Therefore, Brandy warned, she had better go quietly back to the Catholic school and ask for her job back. She had enough money to live comfortably and anonymously for a year or two, and by then the Viet Cong would no longer be looking for her, if, indeed, they ever did.

Brandy and I drove Co Binh out to the province capital airstrip. It was almost 5:00 A.M. now. The guards saluted as we drove in. Brandy stopped the jeep, jumped out, licked a finger to test the wind direction, and drove to the far end of the strip and parked the jeep heading downwind.

He and Co Binh talked in French for a few moments. Co Binh said she was happy and she was sure the Church would forgive her for what she had done to help us capture the Communist leader.

The buzz of a plane sounded overhead and Brandy snapped on the lights of the jeep. Five minutes later a cantilevered high-wing, single engine heliocourier, or U-10, landed and pulled up in front of the jeep.

Only Combined Studies Group, the operating arm of the CIA, flew heliocouriers in Vietnam. Brandy led Co Binh from her jeep to the civilian pilot of the plane who helped her in.

"Take good care of this girl," Brandy said. "She's given much to keep this war from getting completely out of control."

"Will do, Captain," the pilot acknowledged cheerfully. Making sure Co Binh was safely strapped in, he hopped up into the plane beside her and in moments the engine was turning over and the plane was airborne.

Brandy watched the trim little airship take off in under fifty feet, and then we got back into the jeep and headed for town.

"You know," Brandy said musingly, "this is the first woman agent I ever got out alive? And she was the one I most hoped would be permitted to live.

"Ossidian had a big argument about this operation with me," he said drolly. "He thought the girl could have made Hinh think she had nothing to do with our little job tonight and gone on being an agent for us."

We started back toward the school and Brandy's delight bubbled over. "Well, now we get the whorehouse going and a new female agent working. With the money we make operating the whorehouse we can pay maybe two teachers to keep the school going. And still we do what Ossidian likes so much, we kill two birds with one stone."

5

COUP DE GRÂCE

The city of Saigon is the rest and rehabilitation center for every fighting man in South Vietnam with an abundance of piastres in his pockets—including, as I was shortly to discover, off-duty Viet Cong guerrillas.

Almost all Americans get to "the Paris of the Orient" at least once during a tour of duty. They can eat excellent meals at the many restaurants and enjoy some of the world's most exotic and available women. Religious demonstrations notwithstanding, Saigon manifests few indications of the vicious guerrilla war festering throughout the rest of the country.

Since my work was with Special Forces in the boondocks, I tried to keep out of Saigon as much as possible but Major Fritz Scharne had his office there. Scharne was on loan from Special Forces to direct the training of the Vietnamese Rangers, the elite assault troops of the ARVN. Born in Germany, he had been a member of the Hitler Youth. In 1939, at the age of fifteen, he left Germany when his father came to the United States to take over a deceased brother's prosperous business in Milwaukee.

Fritz made the adjustment from militant German youth to militant American youth, and was a valuable asset to the United States from D-Day until the end of the war. He was a natural warrior, and after finishing college and trying business for a few years he applied for a commission in the Army. Wounded twice in Korea, he discovered Special Forces in 1953, shortly after the unit had been activated; he had stuck with it ever since. He was a Special Forces legend. While serving with the 10th Special Forces Group in Bad Tölz he had been so popular that the Bavarians tried to elect him mayor. Scharne had to decline. The Army had a rule against moonlighting, to say nothing of the State Department's stringent ban on citizens running for elective offices in foreign countries.

Major Scharne was one of the first in Special Forces to fight the Pathet Lao Communists in Laos and had completed two tours of duty in Vietnam. Wherever I went I heard stories about Fritzie, and finally I had arranged an introduction.

I couldn't have picked a less opportune moment to come to Saigon. South Vietnam's capital was about due for its second snowstorm of the year—the arrival of a jetload of high U.S. administration officials from Washington. Prior to their visit, blanket requests were issued for optimistic progress reports—which were then neatly transcribed to little white cards for easy referral at the briefing sessions. This was always a discouraging and frustrating time for field officers who were close to the unpleasant truths of daily fighting in Vietnam.

I met Major Scharne in his office at the MAAG compound, and that evening we had drinks on the roof of his hotel. We had many friends in common, including the late Captain Andy Bellman who had been killed on a Ranger operation shortly after being transferred from a Special Forces group at Fort Bragg to serve as Scharne's assistant. Soon Scharne and I were conversing like old friends, discussing the coming top-level briefings. Acidly he told me how he had spent the last two days supplying his share of favorable after-action reports for the white-card snow job; the unpalatable truths he would have liked to pass on to the Washington decision-makers were rejected out of hand.

"I have never, in my career, seen so many panic-hit colonels and generals," Scharne stated in his curious high-pitched voice. "I was at the embassy, even, for a lecture. Everybody is afraid that somebody will be rocking the boat. So it goes in an election year." He stared across the rooftops of Saigon's Chinese community thoughtfully. "All of us who have been known to talk too loud at the wrong time, they are sending out of Saigon."

Then Fritz smiled at me. "But I must say one thing to you—our government of the United States may not be the best possible government, but it is still the best government the world has ever known in its history."

He drained his beer. "Well, they want me out of Saigon when the Secretary and his party come in next week. So I will take the graduating class of Rangers out on an operation against the Viet Cong. I like to watch them train on stand-up-shoot-back targets."

I said I'd like to go out on an operation like that.

"Don't be too eager," he said. "It was on the last one that Andy Bellman was murdered."

"Murdered!"

"Yes murdered," Scharne repeated harshly. "We were hit by a hard-core VC battalion and Andy was wounded in both legs. We had to fall back or lose the whole class. When the VC finally disappeared into the jungle, we returned and found Andy had been shot through the head with a pistol at a range of about six inches. Traditional coup de grâce."

"But that doesn't sound like the VC—"

"Certain things about the operation are classified," Scharne said.

I knew a wave-off when I heard one. "I've got to stick around Saigon for a day or so," I said. "I might catch a story. But I won't be able to stand Saigon very long, particularly with all the wheels arriving. How about it? Will you take me on the next operation?"

"Tomorrow is Sunday," Scharne replied. "Come to the Cercle Racquette as my guest tomorrow. We'll talk about the operation then."

"Sounds pretty fancy."

"I joined a couple of months ago. Tennis courts, a big swimming pool, lots of pretty French girls. . . . Of course they all dislike Americans." Scharne laughed. "Now I know how my cousins from the fatherland felt when they were occupying Paris during the war."

"They couldn't hate us too much if they let Americans join their club." I pointed out.

"Sheer economic necessity. The Cercle costs a lot to keep up, and there are not so many rich Frenchmen around Saigon now. Incidentally, I always talk French there. That way it isn't so obvious we're Americans."

"You've got a guest—French speaking," I added.

"Good. I'll pick you up in my jeep tomorrow morning."

Promptly at 11:00 Scharne arrived at the Continental Palace. He was wearing white duck slacks and a white sport shirt. I remarked how stylish he looked as we set off in his jeep.

It was about a fifteen-minute drive to the Cercle Racquette—an oasis in the middle of the torrid city. Black wood and brass doors in the high white wall led to manicured lawns lined with clipped box hedges. Scharne took me downstairs in the spacious colonial-style clubhouse where we changed. Sitting at the pool we ordered Pernod and water and talking in French—English for technical phrases—we sunbathed and swam.

"How about a game of tennis before lunch?" he asked.

"OK, if you have an extra racket."

He went back to the locker room, got two rackets, and we walked over to the courts. Suddenly Scharne recoiled, his eyes fixed on the tennis court where a mixed doubles game was in progress. The girls were both very pretty, one of them streaming long blonde hair as she went for the ball, but it was her partner who drew the major's intense stare.

"It's the cowboy!" Scharne said, his voice shrill with surprise, his eyes fixed on the dark, well-built man in a net shirt who was serving.

"Cowboy?" I asked.

"Let's sit down a minute." I followed him to a table under the nearby shade tree.

"What's the flap, Fritz?" I asked settling in a wicker chair.

Scharne didn't answer for a few moments and then, reluctantly, he turned from the tennis court. "I told you the whole thing is classified. Well, you knew Bellman." He glanced at the tennis court again and back to me. "That stud who just won his serve leads the VC battalion that hit our last operation. He was the one who murdered Andy."

"But he's a Caucasian!"

"Look, this is all highly classified. It would be my career if the thing gets out and is blown up into a big international flap."

"You can trust me to keep quiet, Fritz. What happened?"

Scharne was staring at the tennis player. "We call him the cowboy. He wears a Stetson, fights bare-chested with a whistle dangling from his neck, always has on a pair of Levis and Western boots. He's a Frenchman, of course.''

"So there is truth in the rumor that the VC have French advisers.''

"They're not just advisers, they have operational control. They're more realistic than we are,'' Scharne added bitterly.

I looked over at the tennis court. "That's the man who killed Andy Bellman?''

"Affirmative. With a .45 slug through the head. I saw him myself through a pair of field glasses, although I never knew before who he was. Oh, that's the cowboy, all right. Other Ranger and paratroop companies have been hit by his battalion. He singles out a company or two of the best we have to offer, and whips them bad, killing all the wounded. He particularly likes to get Americans.''

"Sounds like the cowboy is doing a real job on morale.''

"You have to hand it to him. Just when we were beginning to give the so-called elite ARVN units confidence in themselves and in us, he knocks it to hell. They're going to think American advisers aren't as good as the cowboy and the other frogs working with the Communists.''

"Are American advisers the best?'' I asked, hoping to provoke a reaction.

Scharne gave me a sharp look. "Makes a big difference in a fight when you can give direct orders. If I had operational control of a Vietnamese Ranger battalion—one I had trained myself—I could tear up anything the VC had. I'd go after a VC regiment. But you know what it is to advise, wait for your counterpart to make up his mind how much, if any, of your advice he's going to accept, and only then begin to act.''

Sitting in his swim trunks, a towel draped around his neck, Scharne's eyes never strayed from the man on the tennis court. "Just because the damned frogs couldn't win their own war over here, and got kicked out of their richest colony, they can't stand to see us win now.

"The French have the funny notion they can do business with the Communists. If these people''—he waved, taking in the whole anachronistic group of French colonials—"and France, can persuade the United States to sit down at the bargaining table and neutralize South Vietnam, they think the Commies will let them keep their rich properties instead of having to sell control of them to the Vietnamese according to the agreements signed in Geneva after they were licked at Dien Bien Phu.''

Scharne shrugged. ''And the way our hands are tied in this war we'll end up doing just that. But by me the French are a mean, money-grabbing, spiteful—''

''I seem to detect a somewhat Germanic outlook,'' I couldn't help saying.

''Whatever it is, that bastard killed Andy. Now that I know who he is, he's got to be greased!''

''This I want to see.''

The tennis match ended, the cowboy and his pretty partner apparently the winners. There was a short conversation at the net and then the couple walked toward us and took the adjoining table under the shade tree. A Vietnamese waiter materialized beside them, took their order and left.

''The French get all the service around here,'' Scharne mock-grumbled in English when he returned a few minutes later with their order. Scharne spoke to the waiter loudly, in poor but comprehensible French. ''I have been trying to make the best fighting men in Vietnam out of your Rangers and when I come back here to relax I can't get service.''

The waiter might have remarked that he had been very attentive to the American officer's needs in the past hour and a half. He might even have expressed surprise at the sudden deterioration of the new member's French. However, stony-faced, he took Scharne's order for two more Bamuiba beers.

The Frenchman at the next table had not missed a word, even turning slightly in his chair to have a direct look at Scharne. In English Scharne continued his harangue at me.

''I sometimes wonder if we Americans are welcome at this club. I've been a member for two months and no one but other Americans talk to me.'' Then shifting into French again, ''Je parle français tout le temps, mais malgré de cela, les Françaises ne parlent jamais à moi. Peut-être ils n'aiment pas les Américains.''

''Peut-être,'' I agreed.

Scharne had made his point. The Frenchman at the next table cleared his throat and said in fair English, ''Pardon, monsieur. I could not help hearing what you say. May I be permitted to introduce myself to you and tell you personally that we are most happy to have you and the other Americans as members of our club?''

Scharne swiveled his body to face the smiling Frenchman. "Thank you, monsieur. You are the first member to offer to introduce himself to me. I am Major Fritz Scharne."

"Henri Huyot," the Frenchman replied. He made a courtly gesture toward the pretty, suntanned blonde. "May I have the honor to present Mademoiselle Denise Lefevre?"

Scharne stood up and bowed to the French girl. "Enchanté, Mademoiselle," he said enthusiastically. After a long moment of unabashed admiration of the girl, whose tennis shorts and halter top showed her off to striking advantage, he introduced me.

"Enchanté," I said, standing and bowing slightly.

"But please, Major," Huyot said, "won't you and your friend join us?"

"It is very kind of you, but I'm afraid we would be intruding."

"Mais non, monsieur." The girl looked up at Scharne, her eyes wide, smiling at his frank appraisal of her face and figure. "We will be most—how you say?—disappointed, if you do not join us."

Scharne needed no more encouragement. In a travesty of the foreign conception of an American soldier confronted with a beautiful girl, he uprooted his chair and swung it down beside Mlle. Lefevre, placing himself between her and Huyot. I moved my chair to the other side of the table.

"You are in Saigon on leave?" Huyot asked Scharne in French. "Or perhaps you are stationed here permanently."

"I have an office in Saigon but my real work is out in the field." Scharne's heavy American accent caused a fleeting smile to cross Mlle. Lefevre's lips.

"But you must do very interesting work," she said, trying to draw him out.

Both the girl and Huyot professed tremendous interest in the work Americans were doing in Vietnam. Huyot even went so far as to say, "We couldn't win over here, but perhaps you Americans will be successful where we failed."

"We are not fighting, Huyot," Scharne said quickly. "We are merely advising the Vietnamese in their fight. This isn't an American war."

"It is an American war," Huyot stated positively. And then, with sincerity and a trace of bitterness: "We could have won our war here instead of losing it in 1954. But our

146

generals and colonels were all conventional soldiers, unsuited to this war in Vietnam. Our St. Cyr War Academy leaders refused to accept this war as different from what they were taught. They knew little of guerrilla tactics and had no concept of how the jungle fighter thinks. So two hundred thousand Frenchmen were killed and wounded by the time we finally lost Dien Bien Phu. I fought out here. I know.''

Denise reached a sun-gold arm across the table and took Huyot's hand in hers. "Henri, please don't upset yourself." She turned to Scharne. "Henri's family were among the first to settle in Vietnam. They own one of the largest rubber estates in the country, which Henri runs until he can get somewhere near what it's worth. We must sell control of all our interests to the Vietnamese, you know.''

Scharne nodded sympathetically, but Henri could not forgo a final outburst. "I said the Americans could win.'' He laughed derisively. "Oui, but you are making our mistakes all over again in some ways. And to cap the climax you do not even have control of the fighting troops.'' Huyot winked. "Your straight-leg colonels and generals will be your downfall here too.''

Scharne was genuinely impressed. Here he was hearing his own words come back at him from the man whose death he planned to contrive.

"You know something about us, Huyot, I see.'' Scharne's French was becoming revealingly fluent and accentless, and I worried that he might give himself away. "You even know our term for the conventional soldiers who do not jump from airplanes.''

"I was a paratrooper,'' Huyot said proudly. "My battalion was among the last to try and relieve Dien Bien Phu, but it was too late. Our conventional Paris generals had already lost the war and officers like me were disgusted with an army that refused to let men who knew fighting in Vietnam have any influence on our operations.''

Scharne seemed immersed in this discussion with his enemy. "If the legs had their way they'd get Special Forces out of Vietnam entirely.''

"Mistrust of the different, the unorthodox, is universal in military thinking,'' Huyot commented bleakly.

The Frenchman insisted on buying us another round of

drinks; he and Scharne appeared on the way to establishing a mutual basis of understanding.

"Where is your plantation?" Scharne asked.

"The big rubber plantation is in Tay Ninh province."

"Henri's family have many properties in Vietnam," Denise added.

Huyot smiled fondly at the girl. "She has come all the way out here from France to live and marry. She loves the country and the properties so much I sometimes wonder if it is me or the estates she is marrying."

Scharne and I had both noticed the large diamond shimmering on the appropriate finger. "Vietnam is beautiful," I said. "I've never seen such varied scenery and climate in the tropics before."

"Oh, I pray we can always live here," Denise said enthusiastically. The glad expression clouded a moment as she caught Huyot's eye. "We will be able to stay, Henri? Always? And visit France every other year?"

Her fiancé laughed mirthlessly. "But of course, my dear. I'm sure the Viets will give me a job on one of the plantations when they finally take all our property. We could always hire out as a couple. The Viets are getting so disgustingly rich stealing from the Americans they can afford French servants now."

Denise shook her head slightly and subsided back in her chair. Huyot turned to Scharne. "Enough of our problems. I am interested in how you Americans propose to train the Viets to win this war. Didn't I hear you say you're training the Vietnamese Rangers?"

"I'm up at Duc Phung supervising training," Scharne acknowledged. "We're turning out some good classes. I'd put my Rangers, assuming good leadership, against the best the Viet Cong have to offer."

Casually Huyot reached for his drink. "Have you observed your students in actual combat?"

"Every few weeks we take the graduating class on an exercise against what we hope will be an inferior number of Communists. Unfortunately, two weeks ago we suffered serious losses, and one American killed, another wounded." Scharne's accent was poor again, I was relieved to see, as he eased back into his role.

"You ran into something bigger than you expected?" Huyot prodded.

"We sure did. I had 300 men out, the best officers in the camp commanding. We started out to track down what we thought was a company of VC and found we were up against a battalion. We Americans tried to help the Vietnamese officers direct their men, but our advice didn't get through and the VC had surprisingly good leadership." Scharne shook his head. "I can't understand it. The VC were shooting low, they deployed themselves around us like a veteran battle group. Intelligence gave us no warning of a hard-core battalion in the area."

I sneaked a look at Huyot; there was no mistaking his smugness.

"After such a defeat you will of course give up such training exercises?"

"The Vietnamese officers in charge of the school are thinking of dropping them. Typical Vietnamese reaction to a defeat. I advised them to try it again and reluctantly they agreed to one more operation. The new class, unfortunately, is smaller than the last one and the quality of the men is somewhat inferior too. A little combat will stiffen them, though."

"You'll take them the same place?" Huyot asked, his eyebrows lifting in surprise. "After the experience you had?"

Scharne gave a knowing smile. "I'll take them somewhere and do it next week instead of the following one, which is our regular schedule as I'm sure the VC know. By the time we're in the jungle a week from tomorrow it will be too late for the VC to pinpoint us."

"That is very clever," Huyot said.

"We'll just flush out a few VC without taking any casualties. The worst thing that could happen to the whole Ranger training program would be another defeat. That would end subsequent field exercises against a real enemy—the most important part of the course."

"It is hard to work with the Viet colonels and generals, no?"

"Usually. Sometimes I wonder why we bother at all. Let them find out what would happen without us."

"Precisely," Huyot replied. "Why do you Americans risk your lives twelve thousand miles from home for these people

149

who steal most of what you give them and are afraid to fight for their own country?"

I was curious to hear how Fritz would respond to this near echo of his own words—now uttered by an adversary.

Scharne thought a few moments. "Two reasons, both you should be able to understand. First, I am a professional soldier and I take orders and do what I'm told. Second, I don't want my children fighting the Communists at home."

Huyot nodded. "Good answers." He glanced at his watch and then at Denise. "My dear, we do not have much time if we are going to get ready."

To Scharne, he said, "It was a pleasure to have met you, Major. I will be in Saigon most of this week. I hope I will see you again. I come to the club every day for lunch. I am fascinated to hear how you train the Viets. I tried to make paratroopers out of them during our war here. Perhaps we could trade experiences."

"Your experience would be most valuable to me," Scharne replied.

Huyot and Denise Lefevre stood up, Scharne and I stood also and shaking hands all around we bid them adieu.

"A most attractive couple," Fritz said. "It is too bad—this whole mess of a situation here. I wonder if she will stay on in Vietnam if her fiancé is killed."

2.

The ensuing week was as depressing as I expected. I went out with the press corps to watch the familiar blue and white United States government jet come into Tan Son Nhut, Saigon's international airport. The pattern never varied. A long flat-bed truck had been rolled up beside the honor guard lining the short walk from the bottom of the jet's steps to the entrance of the VIP section of the airport. The truck was crowded with photographers.

We watched an impressive array of Washington officials disembark from the plane. "Must have been quite a junket," one reporter remarked. The usual complement of intense newly important young men from various government agencies and departments brought up the end of the procession.

The speeches at the airport were identical to those we in Saigon had all heard before on such occasions, and then black limousines whirled the government toppers away. Correspondents looked at each other and shrugged, perspiring heavily in the heat outside the air-conditioned VIP lounge. I hopped a ride in one of the major news-magazine cars and rode back to Saigon.

"No hard news is coming out of this visit," a journalist who had been sent down from the Hong Kong bureau grumbled.

"Does it ever?" the Saigon man asked.

The next day a helicopter inspection trip of some of the government's strategic hamlets and a recent battle site had been scheduled. I went out to Tan Son Nhut to see the official picnic party off. Two Special Forces officers, one the Area Specialist of the corps which the officials would visit that day, watched the proceedings.

"I can think of six priority missions in my corps for those choppers today," the Area Specialist Officer said longingly, as they took off. "Do you think there's any chance that the Secretary or someone he listens to will go out where we really have things tough. There are a hellofa lot of guys who could tell him the truth about what's going on, and they're hoping he'll get to them."

I handed the captain a press advisory. "Here's part of his schedule. You figure out what he has time to do."

"They'd better do something—the whole war has been called off while they're in the country."

In Saigon a general atmosphere of frenzy prevailed. Every staff officer seemed to have only two things in mind: Where and for whom the next briefing was being held, and whether they would have freshly starched fatigues in case of an unexpected briefing. Officers were begging, borrowing and otherwise acquiring crisp fatigues, changing two and three times a day as the searing heat and humidity reduced uniforms to soggy shapelessness. Hotel maids and valets grew rich constantly laundering and pressing fatigues.

Finally I could stand the Saigon merry-go-round no longer. I managed to hop a flight to the Ranger Training Center and spent a few days watching the training and getting outfitted to go on the operation scheduled to start Monday morning. Scharne made a desultory attempt to talk me out of going, but I knew he was pleased to have someone, particularly a writer

151

who would respect classified information until the full story could be told, see his whole plan evolve.

On the preceding Tuesday Scharne had again met the cowboy at the Cercle Raquette. Over a few friendly drinks he divulged the date of the patrol and the fact that he was worried because this was the worst class he had trained to date. Huyot had questioned him casually about the operational area but Scharne told him this was secret information.

On Sunday evening Scharne outlined his plan to get the cowboy to me and the two replacement officers, Lieutenant Dant and Captain Paul, who had replaced Bellman. He would take 200 men, two companies, on this patrol.

"We'll tell the Vietnamese officers to get their men out of camp and into the jungle before sunrise tomorrow morning," Scharne was saying in the briefing room. "Paul, you and Dant let them do things their own way, which means they'll be marching out of here long after daylight. Huyot's spies will see exactly which way we're going—due north. We've only got a couple of hundred student Rangers, so the VC will be over-confident. I figure they'll let us march all day and hit us late tomorrow afternoon. What a deal this will look like to the cowboy! Killing three Americans and massacring the graduating class of the Ranger Training School."

I regarded the map thoughtfully. "I must say, old man, that's just the way it looks to me. Except that our French friend will be getting four Americans."

On the acetate overlay Scharne drew a red line from the training camp north through the surrounding hills. "By 1400 hours we'll be marching through this valley and by about 1530 we'll be in this open plain surrounded by hills."

He drew a red circle around the plain. "This would be the perfect place to hit us. There's not a chance we could get back into the jungle and escape. We'd just have to fight it out in open terrain and the Viet Cong battalion would wipe us out to the last man. A terrible disaster for American advisers and Vietnamese Rangers. It would set the Ranger program back a year—in fact it would probably finish it."

Scharne flashed me a wise look as I stared at the mournful story spelled out on the map. Taking up a blue pencil he continued. "However, it will be Huyot and his battalion that will be destroyed—just at the moment they see themselves making Viet Cong history."

152

To the east and west of the red line demarking our next day's line of march, Scharne drew four round circles in blue. "Each of these circles represents a full strike-force company from the two Special Forces camps in this province. Two companies will be to the east of us and two to the west. Each company is under the operational control of two American Special Forces sergeants. They are out there right now, and all day tomorrow they'll be covering our flanks. They are the real guerrillas in this operation. The cowboy and his VC's will never know they're there until it's too late."

"We're the bait for the trap," I said.

"Right. We'll be in for some heavy fighting. When Huyot springs his attack, we'll have to hold out until the strike-force companies can hit them from behind. The strikers will never be more than fifteen minutes away, actually they should be closer. We'll be in radio communication with them all the time."

"The last time I heard that, the radio batteries went dead," I commented.

"I am personally going to watch fresh batteries put in the radios the last thing before I go to bed," Scharne retorted.

"Sounds like a good plan," I acknowledged. "I hope we'll be in position to see Huyot's face when he's hit by surprise just as he's figuring to give us the coup de grâce."

"I, too, want to see Monsieur Huyot out there," Scharne said grimly.

I continued studying the map. Scharne's plan looked lethal if the cowboy attacked us in the strength he was estimated to be carrying. Two companies of well-trained and heavily armed strikers five kilometers out on both flanks, one always abreast of us, the other always two clicks ahead, should certainly be able to zap any attacking battalion.

Scharne's assumption also seemed valid that the cowboy would hit us in the big, open plain south of the large tea plantation that dominated the northern section of the fertile plain.

The main east-west road ran through the tea plantation and on into the province capital. The population of the capital was loyal to the government because a division of the Army of the Republic of Vietnam kept the whole area safe from Viet Cong attack. Yet if less than ten miles away near the main road two companies of the crack Vietnamese Rangers were slaughtered, a couple of hundred corpses left to rot where the populace and government officials of this important province could view the massacre, the damage to civilian and military morale would be incalculable.

"Very slick, Fritz," I complimented him. "I see only one problem."

"Oh?"

"Well, you've got two Special Forces camps involved, right?"

"Right. Captain De Grasso to the west on our left and Captain O'Malley on our right."

"There must have been quite a planning operation. Special Forces is due to come under MAAG control any week now. Surely your friends at MAAG were consulted, as well as the province chief and the ARVN division commander. A lot of Vietnamese officers had to approve?"

A crafty smile crossed Scharne's face. "Yes, I see what's worrying you. I keep forgetting you've been around this war for a while. You are right, of course. I know personally of one Vietnamese captain in division headquarters who's a VC sympathizer. There are others I'm sure. So this time we do things different," he said. "We did not clear this operation with my colleagues at MAAG whose duty it would be to give the province chief and division four days to approve the operation."

Scharne turned to the map. "No, this time we are very lucky. I don't expect I'll ever see such a combination of circumstances again. Special Forces has a bit more time before they lose their autonomy and set up the perfect leak to the Viet Cong and Monsieur Huyot."

"You answered my question, Fritz. If the cowboy plays it anything like the way you figure, it should be an outstanding operation tomorrow."

"He'll hit us tomorrow. If not, the next day. My spies at the Cercle Racquette tell me he left Saigon right after he saw me Tuesday. Now why would a man, particularly a Frenchman, leave such a beautiful and undoubtedly passionate young woman as Denise except for an even greater passion?"

Scharne's blue eyes snapped ominously. "Such as killing American advisers and wiping out my graduating class of Rangers."

154

3.

Lieutenant Dant was adviser to the first company of Rangers and Captain Paul advised the second company. Major Scharne and I walked between the two companies, at the tail end of A Company and the head of B Company. A radio man, his PRC-10 strapped to his back, preceded us. Beside Scharne was his counterpart, Major Lim, commander of the Vietnamese Ranger Training Center at Duc Phung. In theory, by the time Scharne had completed his year's tour, Major Lim would have absorbed his American adviser's years of experience gained in combat in World War II, Korea, Laos, and Vietnam.

The student Rangers marched out of their camp, heading north. The sun, just risen, silhouetted the men and their shouldered weapons to any observers who might be in the hills watching the training camp. Scharne, a wry smile on his face, glanced up at the hills ahead of us through which we would soon be marching. It would be bright daylight before the last of B Company, clearly telegraphing the direction of march, entered the protective cover of the jungle.

"It is too bad your officers couldn't get the men into the jungle earlier," Scharne remarked to Major Lim.

Lim made no answer. It was rude of the American officer to so pointedly refer to a simple error in timing. As the march toward the hills ahead progressed, men kept falling out of ranks to defecate, their friends holding up the column to wait for them.

"If this was an American column I'd make them shit in their pants and walk in it all day," Scharne growled loudly. He looked at the rising run. "Not even the point man in Company A made it into the jungle before daylight." Then he glanced at me and shrugged.

The sun was just beginning to glare in my eyes uncomfortably when we entered the green jungle cover. To our left we could hear a river burbling, occasionally catching glimpses of its shimmering surface as the path took us closer to its banks.

Hills rose to our left and right. Although there was no indication of them, it was reassuring to know that on both

sides of us there was a company of Special Forces-trained and
-led guerrilla fighters paralleling our course along the ridge
lines above. The Ranger companies put out flank security to
the right and left to guard against an ambush, and the main
column walked along on the jungle floor, following the trail
due north.

Every hour we stopped for a ten-minute break that length-
ened to fifteen and twenty minutes by noontime. We all wore
the same jungle camouflage fatigues and soft caps and carried
combat packs with three-days' rations and two canteens. It
was hot in the jungle and a man needed plenty of drinking
water to keep going. We took salt pills about every two
hours.

Scharne carried his favorite jungle weapon, a folding-stock
automatic carbine. Major Lim had his pack carried by a
Ranger. His only encumbrances were two canteens and a
pistol on his web belt. The Americans, officers as well as
enlisted men, carried all their own equipment.

During the noon break for chow, Scharne had the radio
man follow him to the river where there was a clearing. He
called De Grasso and O'Malley, giving them the coordinates
of our position. This was unnecessary, the Special Forces
men radioed back; they had us under observation most of the
time. Besides, our noise discipline was so poor they could
follow us without having to see us. There was no reported
sighting of enemy forces. Scharne said he would make radio
contact again at 1500 hours, at which time we'd be on the
plain three kilometers south of the east-west road running
through the tea plantation.

The march continued, and the 200 men, shambling along,
spread out farther and farther until they became an elongated
line, the flankers crashing through the jungle about thirty
yards out on both sides.

Scharne shook his head. "This is the worst bunch of
dickheads I've seen yet. It's funny how some classes are
number one and others number ten thousand."

At 1500 hours we could see the end of the hills and knew
the plain was ahead. Major Scharne suggested to Major Lim
that the two companies hold at the edge of the jungle before
proceeding onto the plain. Lim agreed and on the radio
Scharne called Lieutenant Dant ahead of him and Captain Paul
behind, asking them to hold up and come to his position.

Then he contacted captains O'Malley and De Grasso. They were watching us, and once in the open we would be covered at all times with their 81-mm. mortars.

Dant and Paul arrived at Scharne's position. "Make your men stay together from now on," Scharne told his officers. "There's too damned much high bush between here and the tea plantation. A VC battalion could easily be lying in wait right now and we'd never know until we were hit."

Scharne turned to Captain Paul. "You're senior adviser if I get it. And Dant, if Paul is hit you take over. Just try to make them keep in a tight group and keep up a high rate of fire if we're attacked. Before you run out of ammo, and that's just what the VC will be waiting for you to do, four heavily armed strike companies will zap them."

"My counterpart doesn't want any advice, sir," Lieutenant Dant complained.

"He will when the shooting starts. You'll probably have to take over. We've got the worst officer students yet. It'll be a hairy one, I can promise you that." He turned from them with a sharp, "Let's go!"

The two companies slowly proceeded across the scrub-dotted plains, ignoring such teaching points as noise discipline and keeping weapons always at the ready. This is a tiring way to carry a rifle on a long march, but in enemy territory it is a must for fast reaction to an ambush or sudden attack. About three miles ahead the tall loft towers of the tea plantation could be seen clearly. The Rangers were obviously expecting nothing but an easy, combat-free patrol. They knew that this was Viet Cong-free territory and within the area protected by the ARVN division. Their obvious appearance of unpreparedness was just what Scharne wanted, however. He surveyed the fields around us tensely. The hill line was now about a mile and a half on either side, the long oval-shaped valley stretching out in front of the advancing Rangers.

Scharne paused, pulled a pair of field glasses from their case, and studied the French tea plantation. Here, he was convinced, was an outright Viet Cong sanctuary. If they could ever get permission to search the lofts they'd probably find a rich cache of Viet Cong weapons under the tea leaves. Both Captain De Grasso and Captain O'Malley were certain the Viet Cong had long-range radio equipment operating out of the plantation, and that hard-core Communist officers actually lived in the several square miles that made up the property.

As we approached the tea plantation, the valley widened until the hills were almost two miles away—putting us out of effective range of the strike-force 81-mm. mortars covering us from the edge of the jungle.

Scharne seemed to be having doubts. He had anticipated the attack before this. We were less than a mile from the tea plantation.

"Maybe Huyot decided to go back to Denise," I suggested facetiously.

Scharne didn't bother to reply. It wasn't necessary. The deep-throated static of BAR's pumping rounds into the column sounded ahead. Lieutenant Dant's A Company took the opening gambit of the attack. The enemy fire spewing out of the bush in front of them transformed these Vietnamese infantrymen who had volunteered to become Rangers into disciplined fighting men. They returned a heavy volume of fire, and in orderly fashion pulled back, the men on the point hurling grenades at the enemy automatic-rifle positions.

The first burst of fire killed or wounded several men, their comrades dragging them back as they retreated. The Rangers in A Company carrying elephant guns, as the M-79 grenade launchers had been dubbed, turned loose carefully aimed anti-personnel rounds on the clumps of scrub trees and bush from which spurted the enemy fire. These 40-mm. shells will kill anything within a radius of twenty-five yards of their impact point. The Viet Cong shooting dwindled as the grenades sailed in and burst among the Communists. With an effective range of well over two hundred yards the lead company could continue pulling back and still lay in grenades on the enemy.

Scharne grabbed the radio handset and talked urgently into it. As he talked B Company closed ranks, pushing in toward Scharne's position in the center, which was the command post now.

For a few moments all enemy fire ceased, and then came another, vastly unsettling, sound. The sharp, stinging notes of a bugle blared across the valley.

Responding immediately to the bugle call, black-clad men ran out of the central positions up ahead and moved down our flanks staying just out of easy range of our light weapons. As

158

we watched, the two Viet Cong sections, one on either side of our column, began a pincer movement on A Company, closing in from both flanks to snip the company in half.

A hundred men closed in on either side of A Company, attacking a small area of the column. The Rangers poured fire back at the Communists, and with grenades and automatic weapons desperately strove to keep the two points of the Viet Cong pincers from cutting off the forward section of the company. Even as the Rangers fought off the first encirclement, another two platoons of Viet Cong, again precisely on signal from the weird-sounding bugle, leaped up from the heavy underbrush on our flanks and started a second pincer movement, the two points aimed at Scharne's position. Incoming rounds screamed in on us and whined overhead.

The Viet Cong strategy was now, finally, apparent. A series of pincer attacks would cut up the two companies into about 40-man sections, which could be crushed one by one at will, permitting not a single man to escape annihilation.

"Dant!" Scharne cried into the radio. "Do you read?"

"Roger, sir."

"Hold up front. Don't pull back any further. Can you hold?"

"Yes, sir."

"OK. Hold and throw yellow smoke grenades into the main force in front of us. We'll move up on you."

Scharne paused, took a low crouching position, and holding the radio handset with one hand pointed his carbine out at the charging pincer point of the screaming, shooting Viet Cong coming directly into us. "Paul," he cried into the radio, "do you read?"

"Clear, sir."

"Move up tight and watch your flanks. We've got to hold this column together."

"Moving up, sir. We haven't been hit back here yet."

"You'll get it. Close up fast!"

Acrid cordite smoke rose from the rifles and machine guns as the Rangers stood off the closing pincer points. One Ranger stood up, carefully aimed his elephant gun, and fired. Eighty yards off our right flank there was an explosion and three men in black crumpled and fell. Other grenade launchers were turned on the attacking Viet Cong with devastating effect.

"Move forward," Scharne cried. "Close up to the front."
He repeated the command in Vietnamese.

We moved forward, and the men at the head of B Company behind us found themselves where we had been, fighting off the two Viet Cong fingers fanatically trying to slice the column.

Over the firing, the bugle sounded again and pincers began to spread open as the Viet Cong on the two points of the fingers pulled back just out of lethal firing range. The Viet Cong kept up their fire from a safe distance on our flanks.

"Keep moving forward on A Company," Scharne cried.

Major Lim, taking occasional ineffective shots with his pistol at the Viet Cong, seemed incapable of giving orders.

Ahead, yellow smoke was billowing up, marking the main enemy position still firing into the front of A Company.

Scharne watched the smoke curling up and grinned wickedly. In the slight lull he cried to me, "They think they have us. They don't want to get too many of their men killed when they can cut us up and finish us off at leisure as our ammo runs out."

With field glasses to his eyes Scharne searched the two edges of the valley and then grunted with satisfaction. "In about four more minutes Monsieur Huyot is going to get a surprise that will kill him."

Fire continued to rip into the column from all directions. Scharne was so absorbed in his strategy that he didn't seem to realize how close we all were to taking our death round through the hide.

From up ahead we heard the *crump, crump, crump* of Viet Cong mortar rounds. Then the clatter of incoming 60-mm. rounds overhead sent us burrowing into the earth. A shattering series of explosions straddled the column, and then the screams of a man in agony came from in front of us.

Slowly the wounded man's cries subsided. Scharne raised his head and then pulled himself to a crouching position looking to both sides of the column. There was another lull and then, off in the distance first to the east and then the west, came the distant reports of our covering 81-mm. mortar shells exploding out of the tubes. This was the most welcome sound we had heard all day.

A series of much-closer explosions let us know we were in for another shower of enemy shells.

"Those will be their last," Scharne called out exuberantly, before flattening himself into the valley floor. The bursting mortar rounds shook the ground. They were right on target. Shrapnel flew above us. Several of the Rangers were hit.

Ahead of A Company a tremendous string of explosions blasted the Viet Cong main positions so clearly marked with yellow smoke. The 81-mm. rounds from the Special Forces-led strike force were supporting us at last. Scharne jumped to his feet, looking north. He grabbed his radio handset from the carrier's back.

"Able, Able, this is Sierra," Scharne called. "How close did our mortars come to the target?"

"Sierra, this is Able. Tell them to keep it up. They're right on target."

Scharne reached for the radio pack, changed frequencies, and contacted the strike-force leaders, calling for continued mortar fire. The Communists' 60-mm. mortars hadn't spoken since the blast.

Scharne turned his field glasses toward the east and then the west. After a few moments he handed them to me and pointed eastwards. I could make out the two strike-force companies moving up through the brush behind the unsuspecting Viet Cong who were firing into the entire length of our column. The same happy sight greeted my eyes as I swung the glasses to the west.

Then, in the Communist positions ahead, whistles shrilled and bugles blew. The black pajama-clad Viet Cong guerrillas on our flanks started moving in on us again. With our unexpected mortar support the cowboy probably decided to finish us off and get away.

The Rangers, back to back, fired everything they had, as once again the Viet Cong sought to cut the column with pincer attacks on both flanks at once.

Suddenly heavy automatic-rifle and machine-gun fire raked the advancing black-uniformed men from the rear. The Rangers cheered as the Communists fell, torn and bloody, to the ground. They were catching intense fire from both sides and we stayed low so as not to get hit by friendly rounds.

In front of us the Communist main positions were shaken by new blasts of 81-mm. mortar rounds. All fire from the Viet Cong ahead ceased. A series of desperate bugle calls and shrill whistling sounded from the Communist Command Post.

In instant answer to these signals the Viet Cong on our flanks withdrew. But the strike-force companies were upon them before they could even start back for their main positions.

Demoralized, the Communists who minutes before thought they were about to destroy us were trapped between their intended victims and heavily-armed companies that had appeared from nowhere. Their only chance of escape was to the south, away from the remainder of their battalion. Turning in this direction and running, they were raked by fire from B Company. Few survivors of Scharne's carefully laid trap were left to escape into the mountainous jungles from which we had come that morning.

Scharne was holding the radio handset to his ear, listening intently, blocking the other ear against the noise of the skirmishing.

"Go after them!" I heard him call into the instrument. He jammed the handset into its place on the radio.

"Huyot and his VC's are making it to the north," Scharne said turning to me. "Now's the time to get him."

The Rangers of Company A, led by their lieutenant with Dant beside him, got into a low crouch and started toward the Communist positions ahead, spraying machine-gun fire and tossing grenades before them.

The sporadic answering fire showed how surprised, demoralized, and hurt the Viet Cong were. With the strike force battling the two companies of Viet Cong that had been on our flanks, the Rangers charged the Viet Cong positions that had first opened fire on us. Viet Cong bodies littering the ground testified to the hasty and disordered withdrawal of what was left of the battalion.

Less than a half a mile ahead of us another fire-fight broke out almost at the gates of the tea plantation. "That's O'Malley," Fritz cried. "He said he wanted to cover that French plantation."

Scharne and the Rangers ran toward the firing. More faltering bugle calls sounded. Then 80 to 100 Viet Cong who had been heading for sanctuary in the tea plantation wheeled away from O'Malley and his strikers ranged in front of it and headed east for the jungles and hills.

Scharne turned to the right on a course that would cut them off before they could escape. As we bore down on them, Scharne, now leading the two Ranger companies, pointed. At the head of the fleeing Communists was a tall, bare-chested Caucasian wearing a cowboy hat, levis, and boots, and carrying a light submachine gun. He was fast closing on the safety of the mountainous jungle.

The Rangers fired as they ran headlong after the frantic Viet Cong. Black pajamas were dropping in limp heaps as bullets from both the Rangers and O'Malley's pursuing strikers made hits.

As the Rangers chased the Communists, Scharne, looking around, suddenly reached out and collared a Ranger. Together they fell out of the pursuing column. I halted beside them.

The Ranger had been carrying an M-79 grenade launcher. Scharne snatched the elephant gun, which looks like a king-size single-barrel shotgun, and broke open the breech. He took a 40-mm. grenade shell from the Ranger and inserted it in the barrel. Snapping the weapon shut he adjusted the sights for maximum range. We were still close to three hundred yards away from the cowboy, who had nearly reached the jungle's edge. Scharne took careful aim and pressed the trigger. Without waiting to watch the trajectory of the shell, he took a second one, reloaded, aimed and fired. He kept on firing as fast as he could reload, and Ranger alertly slapping rounds into Scharne's outstretched hand.

The first round actually dropped beyond the cowboy and his men. The explosion turned the running Viet Cong away from it and toward us. The second and third grenades also dropped with astonishing accuracy, wounding more of the fleeing Communists. The fourth round landed squarely in front of the cowboy and stopped him as though he had run into an invisible wall. He was hurled backward to the ground.

Scharne handed the grenade launcher back to the Ranger and started toward the man he had brought down. I followed.

Huyot was still alive when I reached him, though almost unrecognizable. His handsome face had been torn badly by shrapnel, his nose lying on his cheek. Blood burbled from ugly rents in his bare chest. Wounds in his arms, groin, and legs bled profusely. His eyes were open, fixed on Scharne who stood looking down at him.

Huyot's lips moved but no words would come.

Other Rangers gathered to look at the formidable cowboy, barely identifiable as a Caucasian now except perhaps for his

163

great size. Scharne stared down at him impassively until finally with a grating moan Huyot gave in to his wounds and died.

Fritz turned from the dead Frenchman to me. "He knew who I was. He knew who it was got him."

To the Ranger officer beside him he said, "See what the medics can do for the wounded. Then we'll go back and search the tea plantation."

I was still staring at the appalling damage the elephant gun's shell had done to the lately big, strong body of Henri Huyot. Scharne looked back at the victim of the M-79. "You know," he said, "the poor, misguided sonofabitch thought he was fighting for the glory of France and the perpetuation of his family's estate in Vietnam. I'd have let him get away alive if it hadn't been for what he did to Andy Bellman."

Scharne shook his head. "I hope his girl has good friends out here. Maybe you could figure some way to break the news to her."

"I'll handle it, Fritz."

Scharne turned from the broken corpse. "Anyway," he said, "I can thank the frog for one thing. At last I finally have something favorable to report to the visiting brass: Huyot showed me that we've got a much finer graduating class of Vietnamese Rangers than I suspected before this little fight began today."

6

HOME TO NANETTE

Bernard Arklin and I were introduced for the first time just after the events in this story took place. He was a lean, almost cadaverous-looking man when I met him, just out of the Laos mountains. There was an unmistakably bitter twist at the corners of his mouth. The close-cropped hair around the spreading bald spot on top of his head was sandy-colored shot with gray.

Arklin regarded me with predictable suspicion that first evening at the Officers Club bar on the roof of the Rex Hotel in Saigon. I was, after all, a civilian; a writer in fact.

Mutual friends assured Arklin that although I might be a civilian I jumped from planes and went on patrols to cover the war. The beginnings of a friendship between myself and Arklin developed. By the time he had left Saigon for the United States ten days later, Bernie Arklin had told me the story of his life as a revered chief of the hard-fighting, squat, barrel-chested Meo tribesmen of Laos.

The United States officially withdrew its military assistance from Laos as a result of the Geneva accords which in theory neutralized the country in October of 1962. Fortunately, a few highly placed Americans were wise enough to realize that the Communists might not abide by the agreements they had signed and the Communist Pathet Lao with the assistance of their Uncle Ho in North Vietnam would again try to take over Laos.

With the Royal Laotian Army torn by political dissension and hardly a match for a determined Communist drive, attention turned to one group of fighting men who in the opinion of the U.S. Central Intelligence Agency, which was then in charge of Special Forces activities in Laos, would make the effort to stand up against the Pathet Lao and North Vietnamese Viet Cong troops, or Viet Minh as they are still called in Laos—the hardy Meo tribesmen. A product of different ethnic origins from the torpid Laotians, they would fight bravely for their mountaintop homes. They would also, when properly led and supplied, carry on guerrilla warfare against the Communists. Thus, it was Meos who were trained and armed by Special Forces teams to resist Communist aggression.

One of the most successful Special Forces officers to work with the Meo tribesmen had been Major Bernard Arklin. Operating under the control of the CIA, Arklin's Special Forces team equipped and trained a large group of Meo tribesmen who took a heavy toll of Pathet Lao lives and equipment in 1962, when the Communists pushed through the jungles toward Vientiane, the capital of Laos, unopposed by the fleeing Royal Laotian troops.

With the end of official military assistance, the Central Intelligence Agency decided that Arklin was one of the men they needed to covertly keep the Meos in readiness to resist any possible Communist attacks in violation of the Geneva convention.

Arklin had just become reacquainted with his wife and three children back at Fort Bragg and was beginning to develop a taste for normal home life when he received orders sending him on detached service with the CIA in Thailand.

In Bangkok, Arklin began to feel his first excitement—and a sense of impending accomplishment—over the opportunity of rejoining the Meo tribesmen at the eastern approaches to the strategic Plain of Jars. This time he would not be wearing a uniform, but would dress as did his charges—in camouflage suits, miscellaneous clothing and the native loincloth. The only thing that distressed Arklin was that he could neither send nor receive mail. Methuan, his CIA control, would typewrite inconsequential letters to Arklin's wife above the endearments and signatures previously signed by Arklin on a large number of blank pieces of stationery to keep her from wondering what had happened to him.

In mid-June of 1963 Major Arklin took off from a small airstrip in the north of Thailand on the Laos border. He was equipped with a powerful radio transmitter, a medical kit (Arklin had been crosstrained as a medic) and as many weapons and boxes of ammunition as could be crowded into the single-engine plane. It was Arklin's third trip from the control base in Thailand to his Meo headquarters. This time he would be staying.

Arklin's first flight had been made only a week after he arrived in Bangkok. CIA had carefully planned for Arklin to visit his old friend Pay Dang, chief of the Meo tribesmen in the mountains around the Plain of Jars. There was a small dirt airstrip only seven hundred feet long on a slanting field near the top of the mountain where Arklin and his Special Forces A team had, a year and a half before, first established their montagnard training camp.

The flight was made in an unmarked U-10, a single-engine airplane built to carry heavy loads into and out of short, rough fields.

Arklin's first landing was preceded by ten minutes of buzzing the Meo mountaintop camp. Looking down at the village he and his men had taught the montagnards to keep clean and trim the major felt a stab of disappointment. The huts were once again ramshackle; the bridge across the gully that surrounded the village looked as though it would collapse in a light breeze. Tribesmen looked up and, recognizing the type of plane the Americans had formerly used, waved vigorously. They could be seen starting for the airstrip.

Arklin and the pilot waited over an hour after landing for the Meos to come down from their camp. Finally the first of them arrived, wearing the ragged remnants of the combat fatigues the Americans had given them. Cautiously, they emerged from the heavy jungle around the overgrown landing strip on which only the incredibly rugged U-10 could have landed.

Arklin's throat lumped as he saw the crude collection of weapons they were carrying. Most of the men had crossbows and a few had ancient rifles, some of which were homemade by the montagnards, who had spent months boring out long iron cylinders with white-hot rods to make rifle barrels. When Arklin and his A team left the Meo village it had been their duty to disarm the tribesmen—a delicate task. The Meo men cherished the fine weapons the Americans had given them and taught them how to use effectively.

As Arklin realized at the time, the Meo chiefs were absolutely right to protest against disarmament. The chiefs didn't understand Geneva, United States policy and, most of all, neutralism. All they knew was that the Americans had come in, given them guns and helped them attack the hated Pathet Lao Communists. Now the Americans were taking away the guns, and no matter what the big men back in America said, the Meos knew that as soon as their arms were gone the Communists would attack them.

It was a tribute to the esteem in which they held Arklin and his Special Forces team that they finally give up their arms, or most of them. Even though it went against the treaty his government had signed, and was a court-martial offense, Arklin deliberately had failed to notice that his heavy-weapons sergeant had left behind two submachine guns and a large stock of ammunition. At least they would be able to hold off the Pathet Lao for a while.

From the group of tribesmen now warily approaching the plane one man, whose camouflage suit looked in better repair than the others', stepped forward. Arklin recognized Pay Dang and they reached out and clasped hands, left hands gripping right wrists in the montagnard two-handed shake.

They greeted each other in Meo, which Arklin had learned to speak fluently, and the first question Pay Dang asked was if the Americans were coming back. Arklin replied that he alone was returning.

"Do you bring guns?" the chief asked anxiously.

At Arklin's nod Pay Dang let out a shout, brandishing his crossbow, and relayed the news to his people who cheered and held up their crude weapons.

"Twice the Pathet have attacked us in small numbers," Pay Dang said. "Only because we were able to find the two machine guns you 'lost,' were we able to defeat the enemy. They will try again." His smile faded to almost a scowl. "Your big chief in America knows nothing about the Pathet Lao and Viet Minh. They lie to him and say they want peace. You believe them. You go and take back your guns. Now the Pathet Lao can come and kill the Meo!"

"I'm here to help again, Pay Dang. Tell your men to take the weapons from the airplane. More will come."

Pay Dang shouted instructions and the Meos, crying happily, dropped their crossbows and old rifles and made for the U-10. Quickly they unloaded the plane.

"I hold you responsible for those weapons, Pay Dang," Arklin said sternly. "I'll be back with more and we'll start training again. Is the old weapons shed still standing?"

Pay Dang shook his head. "The people took the wood planks from it for their houses."

"Well, I will be back to live with you soon. In the meanwhile I'll bring in more guns. From now on I want you to keep men out here on permanent guard."

"The field will be secure," the Meo promised. "Shall we take the bush off and make it as it was before?"

"No. It's good enough for this airplane the way it is. We do not wish to tell the Pathet Lao what we do." Major Arklin gave a last look around the mountain that would once again be his home. "I must go now, Pay Dang. The plane has been here too long already. After this you have only five minutes to unload. The plane will not stop its engine, so tell your men to stay away from the propeller."

"Yes, Major."

"And start bringing in the best men from the other villages, but be careful what you tell them. Americans not legal here now."

"We kill Pathet!" Pay Dang shouted.

"When I say so," Arklin said firmly. "But it must be a big secret I am here. You understand?"

"Big secret," agreed Pay Dang soberly.

Arklin climbed back into the U-10. The pilot taxied to one end of the grass strip, gunned the engine, and the plane was airborne in less than forty feet.

Back at the CIA operations base Arklin went over the program with Frank Methuan, and gave him a list of supplies that would have to be sent in. Methuan looked it over.

"That's a lot of stuff to take in by light plane under covert operating procedure."

"Don't you ever use choppers?"

"Sometimes. The Agency doesn't have one of its own here now. The U-10 does the job better anyway. It takes too much maintenance using helicopters, too many men in on the act. Remember, Bernie," Methuan said firmly, "this operation is top secret. Don't get yourself captured. All our good old play-it-straight-down-the-line government needs is to get caught violating the Geneva agreements. It's OK for the Commies to build up for a takeover and disregard the convention, but we have to live by the rules."

"I know what to do, Frank. I've been wearing the green beanie a long time—too long."

"Getting you down?"

"I've got a wife better than I deserve and three kids, two boys. You know how much I've seen them in the last four years?"

"Not much, I guess."

"Not much is right. Not that I'm unhappy with my work," Arklin added hastily. "But when you start closing on forty and you haven't been able to give the family as much of yourself as you wish—well . . ." He shrugged. "Anyway, you know what happens if you stay too long in Special Forces. They think there's something wrong with you up at DA. I'd like to get back into a conventional outfit some day, hang up the beret and be with the family. Won't be long before I'm coming up for the lieutenant colonel list."

He flashed an embarrassed smile at his control. "Sorry for sounding off. But the thing I'll hate most about this job is no mail. Pretty tough not to know for months at a time what your family is doing."

"If anything happens at the Arklin residence I'll give you a radio flash. And I'll take special care to make sure the letters I write will keep your wife happy."

Now, at last, after a month of preparation, Arklin was making his final trip to the Meo village. The pilot skillfully brought in the equipment-laden U-10, and rolled to a stop twenty-five feet from touchdown point in front of a big clump of bushes. Instantly montagnards in their camouflage fatigues, new ones now, materialized from around the field. Half the men were equipped with weapons. Their high morale showed in their gleaming dark eyes, sparkling white-toothed grins and quick gait as they trotted toward the plane. Those not encumbered with weapons quickly unloaded the U-10, and in a mere six minutes the plane was aloft again.

Arklin did not watch the plane take off, so intent was he on getting equipment and men back into the jungle. For the first time in eight months he would be spending the night back on the mountaintop. But now he was alone. All the skills and influence of the eleven highly trained A-team specialists who had been with him before were now concentrated in the single entity of their former Commanding Officer.

Pay Dang exuded the exuberance he and his men felt at Arklin's return. He also made it clear as they hiked up the rugged mountain path to the village that every Meo tribesman considered the American major his unquestioned leader. In the old days Pay Dang had been the commander; Arklin and his team were advisers, suppliers, and teachers. Pay Dang had been fiercely jealous of his authority as Meo chief, something the Americans encouraged, even as they gradually trained him and his lieutenants in the intricacies of modern warfare.

Gaily dressed women wearing blue and white turbans and heavy solid-silver necklaces, old men in loincloths or the tribal blue and white loose-fitting pantaloons and blouse, and curious children were lined up at the camp's inner gate when Arklin and the Meo men arrived at the bridge. Arklin watched the men walking catlike across the rotting, swaying structure his team had built almost a year ago over the gorge. The Meos were careful never to have two men on the bridge at the same time.

"The first thing we do is fix the bridge," Arklin said to Pay Dang. "You have the rope I sent?"

"Everything is here, Major." The last of the montagnards crossed into the village and then Pay Dang gestured for Arklin to precede him. Half expecting the bridge to disintegrate under the weight of a full-size American, Arklin crossed the decaying wood-slat structure, holding onto the frayed-rope handrail. He made it to the other side and the montagnards cheered.

"We go to your house first, Major," the Meo chief said and led him toward a thatched bamboo longhouse on stilts sitting about four feet above the ground. It was obvious that much recent work had been done, and just beside the door was a miniature of the house, also on stilts. The mountain tribesmen store their food outside their houses, and this little crib was well stocked with vegetables, rice, manioc, and other montagnard foodstuffs.

A notched log hung from the doorway to the ground and Pay Dang indicated that the major should climb up. Arklin unslung his pack and threw it up into the house and then, with his new AR-15 automatic rifle still slung, he mounted the

171

steps. The house was clean and he was touched to see that the tribesmen had remembered what American furniture was like. There was a crude but serviceable table and chair, and a square frame on the floor had been stuffed with fresh grass and palm fronds to make a bed. The montagnards themselves just threw a mat on the floor and slept on their backs. Arklin noticed there was a montagnard mat on the floor near his bed.

"Thank you, my old friend," he said to Pay Dang. "This is a good home and office. It will be our command post from now on. Tell the men carrying the radio to put it in here beside the table." Arklin walked around his new residence. It was about twenty feet long by ten feet wide—palatial accommodations in these mountains for one man.

"Longhouse not home yet," Pay Dang said with a wide, flashing grin. He went to the door, shouted at the group of women, and three girls came forward. Their swelling breasts strained for release from the open wraparound bodices; their dark-brown bodies were slim and their features regular. Their blue skirts were finely pleated and short, barely reaching their knees.

One of the girls was much lighter colored than the others, smaller breasted and more delicately boned. Pay Dang laughed when he saw Arklin eyeing her.

"She is half French," he explained. "Her father came to this mountain in the early days of the war against the Viet Minh for the same reason you are here now."

"I don't remember her from before," Arklin said. "If I'd ever seen her, or any of my men had, we would never forget her."

"She was at another village. And she was too young then. But now she is fifteen," Pay Dang said proudly. "She will take care of your house and cooking."

Pay Dang seemed worried over Arklin's hesitation. "We thought you would want her."

Arklin shook his head, looking down from the door of his new abode. "Pay Dang, you must remember when I was here before. The Americans do not take girls from the village to live with them."

"But this is not the same. You're one man alone. And you are our chief, Major. It is not the same," Pay Dang insisted. "My people will not understand if you will not have one of

172

their women for your house. You have come up here to be one of us and lead us against the Pathet Lao and Viet Minh."

"I cannot lead you, Pay Dang," Arklin said gently. "I will train you again, keep you supplied, tell you when to attack the Communists, and go with you on these attacks, but I am still only your adviser. America is not fighting this war, it is only helping its friends to win. You, Pay Dang, are the chief and leader."

"These are the words of politics," the Meo said, brushing aside Arklin's statement. "But the girl,"—his eyes took on a crafty gleam—"that is something real. The Meo will feel you are part of them if the girl is part of you. She will be your wife. She has never had a husband."

"I have a wife, Pay Dang."

"I have had many, three now," Pay Dang answered.

Arklin hesitated. Then— "All right. I will be honored if the daughter of a man who also came a long way to help your people would live in my house."

Pay Dang clapped Arklin on the shoulder and let out a shout. The girl Ha Ban, or Nanette as her father had called her, would be the wife of the new American military chief of the Meo.

Nanette looked shyly at the ground and the other two girls turned away, hardly concealing their disappointment. Pay Dang bounded down the precarious notched log, took the girl by the hand and led her back up to the house. The girl's silver necklace gleamed above her almost bare bosom; a toothbrush also hung from her neck. "Ha Ban is your wife!" Pay Dang declared happily. "Now we will have a sacrifice. Then, tomorrow you help us get ready to kill the Pathet and Viet Minh."

Arklin bowed to the inevitable. But still, discipline had to be maintained. "Pay Dang, as long as I am with you we will have regular guards at all times. No man on guard duty will be permitted to drink any Meo liquor. Is that understood? Otherwise there will be no sacrifice."

Pay Dang looked nonplussed a moment. Then he grinned and laughed loudly. "You are the chief, Major. We will have two sacrifices for you and Ha Ban. Half the men stay on guard tonight, the other half tomorrow night."

Arklin's long experience with many different tribes of

montagnards had taught him that it was useless to try to talk, order, plead, or threaten them out of a party or two.

"It will be as you say, Pay Dang," Arklin agreed. "Two sacrifices and a 50 per cent alert both nights."

Pay Dang bounded out the door again, happily saying he would go find a buffalo to beat to death—the traditional prelude to all montagnard parties.

"Vous parlez français, Nanette?" Arklin asked when they were alone.

"Mais certainement, monsieur. J'avais cinq ans quand les Viet Minh ont tué mon père. Ma mère parle français, aussi, et il y a beaucoup d'hommes ici qui ont été avec L'Armée Française."

"Bon, Nanette, we will speak in French then, you and I. Now, we are expected to live in this house together?"

"Oh yes, sir," Nanette answered, smiling happily.

"You mustn't worry about anything, Nanette. You will cook and sleep in this house, but I will not—" Arklin searched his French and Meo vocabularies for words to tell her that he did not intend to actually consummate their Meo nuptials, that she could go on being a happy, innocent young girl. But when he said them, a shadow crossed her delicately featured face. Arklin tried to avert his eyes from her upturned, firm yet demure breasts, so insecurely captive in her bodice.

"My own daughter is only two years younger than you, Nanette," he finished lamely. Nanette, he realized, was obviously far more Meo than European in attitude. To her mind it would probably be an insult and a disgrace if they lived together without his enjoying the connubial pleasure she was expecting to give him—and, he suspected, looking at her wide, sensual mouth and heavy lidded eyes, receive in return.

He gave her a friendly smile. "Nanette, we will talk about this later. Over a gourd of Meo liquor perhaps."

The girl immediately brightened and came toward him. She held her head up, and he rubbed the tip of her nose with his. She laughed happily.

"Now, Nanette, I've got to start bringing some discipline back to this village." He looked out the door at the sun hanging low in the western sky. "Not much time before it gets dark," he said, more to himself. "I'll need a secure weapons house, we'll have to start building ammo bunkers and machine-gun emplacements."

Arklin started down the notched log, making mental notes of all he must do to make the village secure against the inevitable Communist attacks, which would come whenever Peking and Hanoi and Pathet Lao headquarters decided the time had come to break the Geneva treaty.

2.

Arklin's resolutions to keep his relationship platonic proved no match for Nanette's efforts to make him treat her as the loving wife she knew herself to be. True, he had lasted through two wild wedding sacrifices without acceding to her wishes, and during this time she had become alternately sullen and melancholy.

Not only that, the reason for her ill humor was obvious to everyone in the village, and Arklin could feel the resentment against him pervade the montagnard community. He noticed that he was having difficulty in getting tasks completed. A secure weapons room was still unfinished after six days' desultory work.

Finally it took Pay Dang's not-so-subtle hint that perhaps the American thought he was too good for the Meos to make Arklin realize there was more to doing his duty than training mountain tribesmen.

In fact, Arklin was very much taken with this girl the Meos had picked for his bride. Her thoughtfulness, her desire to please, the way she personally took his fatigues, filthy from hard work in the constant heat, down to the stream and would let no one help her wash them—everything about her made him realize that he had a fine woman by any standards. And while Arklin had trained himself to suppress his natural desires, living with Nanette, or Ha Ban as he called her in front of the Meo people, her charms constantly and so tantalizingly bursting out at him, made it excruciatingly difficult to turn away from her at night and pretend to sleep.

On the sixth night following their second wedding party, a sacrifice was held to celebrate the return of a Meo tribesman who had been away from the village for several years. Out of desperation born of his inability to circumvent his morals and nearly inflexible sense of responsibility, Arklin drank three gourds of Meo liquor. The alcohol produced the release and Arklin consummated his "marriage" to Nanette. Once the breakthrough had been effected, Arklin so thoroughly pleased and satisfied his young bride that the Meos, seeing her the next day, knew at once that the American was finally one of them. They slapped his back wherever he went, calling rude suggestions that were approved by everyone.

Tasks were accomplished more quickly now. The weapons room was finished, and Arklin kept the key to it hanging around his neck. Sandbags were filled and molded into bunkers, and on the firing range the montagnards worked hard to improve their marksmanship. He managed to get the entire village back into the habit of purifying all the drinking water with iodine or halizone pills, reducing the prevalent dysentery almost to nil. Even the bridge was put back into safe, serviceable condition.

It was three months after Arklin first entered the Meo village that he had his first direct contact with control. All radio messages were sent to Bangkok in code and were kept to terse intelligence reports on Pathet Lao movements. It had been decided not to risk flights to the airstrip except when absolutely necessary. If Prince Souphanouvong, the Communist leader in the three-party Laotian government, got word that there was American-supported activity in the montagnard country it would be not only embarrassing, but might even cause such minimal U.S. precautionary activity as Arklin's mission to be rolled up.

Ammunition for the range was low when, in October of 1963, Arklin received the message that two U-10's, loaded with equipment and ammunition, would arrive on the 20th at 6:45 A.M. The message said further that control would be aboard one of the U-10's and that Arklin should be there to receive him.

Excitement and anticipation built up in Arklin as the day approached. Maybe they would bring him some letters from home. Young Bernard would have started high school, his daughter must be having all kinds of teen-age problems. A thirteen-year-old girl needs her Dad; he should be on hand to advise her. In his whole career he had never been so completely cut off from home and family. But he was a professional soldier—more to the point, a Special Forces officer; nevertheless, as he had told Methuan, he had made up his mind that when this assignment was ended he would take the tour of duty with a more conventional unit, which was long overdue him. He wanted to watch his family grow up and he certainly wanted to make lieutenant colonel and bird colonel, and there was no reason why he shouldn't make general officer before he retired.

Major Arklin smiled to himself as he looked around the village he was transforming into an orderly paramilitary operation. What would the brass at Military Assistance Command say if they could see him now. Hair long and unkempt, almost as dirty and messy as that of his montagnards—he had ordered barber scissors to be sent in. Razor blades were in such short supply that he seldom shaved. His camouflage suit was clean but far from the crisply starched fatigues he was accustomed to wearing. Most of all, he chuckled wryly, what would they say if they could see Nanette, all but bare-bosomed, proudly following him at a respectful two paces to the rear.

The chuckle became a sigh as he thought of his wife back in Fayetteville. Would it ever be possible for her to understand the wholly alien life he was living on this assignment?

Arklin and Pay Dang took a platoon from the 3rd Meo Strike Company to provide security for the aircraft reception party. By now, with almost 350 able-bodied Meos, and the number growing, Arklin had established three 120-man companies each with its designated captain, platoon leaders, and squad leaders.

Arklin had brought along a complete insignia kit, and every time a Meo was appointed an officer or sergeant the appropriate insignia was sewed on his camouflage suit and Arklin made a ceremony of the affair. To Pay Dang he had presented the three silver buttons designating the rank of colonel in many armies of Southeast Asia; Pay Dang wore them proudly.

With Nanette coaching the women, Arklin was able to re-establish certain sanitary practices, such as the use of the latrines he had ordered rebuilt. The pigs were now confined to central pens instead of wandering all around the village, messing as the urge hit them. All refuse was buried outside of camp instead of being allowed to collect in the putrefying piles Arklin had found on his arrival.

What had disturbed him most when he first came was that in the eight months since his American team had left, all these basic sanitary habits his men had introduced, they thought permanently, had been completely abandoned, and the Meos had reverted to their old casual and undisciplined way of life.

But then Arklin recalled hearing an American missionary explain the frustrations of trying to make the montagnards improve their lot. This man had been an evangelist and had lived with montagnards for thirty-five years. By giving them a true religion he had got them to observe clean habits, and give up such cherished traditions as torturing animals to death to appease evil spirits and cutting the upper teeth out of boys and girls on reaching puberty. The mountain tribesmen who had been converted to Christianity never went back to their old ways, or so the missionary said. To support this he cited many montagnards who had been sergeants and even commissioned officers in the French Army, leading the most civilized existence with clean uniforms and a respect for sanitation and discipline.

Yet when the French left and these men returned to their tribes, it was common knowledge that they had reverted all too quickly to loincloths and the same primitive existence of the tribesmen who had never been out of their home mountains.

Arklin and Pay Dang and their 40 armed men left the camp the afternoon before the two planes were due. Arklin watched with satisfaction as the months of retraining asserted itself. Every men carried his weapon properly at the alert. The platoon leader set out squads to walk in the bush on both sides of the main group as flank security against ambushes. When they stopped, the men alternately faced to the right and left of the trail.

Interspersed with the security platoon was an armed group of 20 men who could carry the supplies back. These were men whose marksmanship wasn't as accurate as it should have been, or who had proven difficult to discipline. Arklin made it clear that a man could always advance from the work force into the strike force by showing the proper attitude and improving in military skills. All in all Arklin was pleased with his little Meo battalion. With the new load of arms they would pick up, he would be able to arm two rifle companies properly.

They arrived at the ragged, overgrown airstrip just before dusk and Pay Dang personally took charge of setting out the security ring around the landing zone. He made sure the work force was camped at the side of the field ready to rush out and unload the planes the moment they landed at dawn. Then he spread out his poncho and blankets alongside Arklin. They sat talking into the night, the Meo leader smoking his pipe loaded with the tobacco the tribe grew and cured.

Right on time the next morning, two U-10's suddenly appeared from over the mountains and in the red glow of sunrise landed on the precarious mountainside field.

Both planes cut their engines as the 20 Meo carriers ran onto the field. Arklin, followed by Pay Dang, rapidly approached the two U-10's as the wide doors of the powerful single-engine planes swung open. Strong brown arms reached into the planes and began unloading the heavy boxes.

Frank Methuan stepped out of the first plane and shook Arklin's hand.

"You look in good shape, Bernie," he said. "For a minute there I thought you were a tall montagnard."

"I'm beginning to think I am," Arklin replied. "Did you bring me the razor blades and scissors?"

"Sure did. Where are you going to find a barber?"

"I'll cut this stuff off myself if I have to. Did you bring any mail?"

Methuan reached back into the plane and drew out an orange mailbag. "This should keep you busy for a while. I answered all the letters for you. Only you forgot to tell me you don't play tennis," he said sheepishly. "I had you playing with a bunch of VIP's and then Nancy wrote back and asked when you had found time to learn."

"What did I answer?"

"Oh, on one of your long trips out of Bangkok there was a court, and since you had plenty of time you began batting the ball around."

"Batting the ball around," Arklin snorted. "How would you like to spend a week batting the ball around with me here? What's happening in the outside world?"

"Things are pretty quiet in Laos except for the Viet Cong coming down their Ho Chi Minh trail along the Vietnam border. But so far it looks like Prince Souphanouvong and his Pathet Lao are behaving. Our people in Vientiane think someone's going to break things up before the end of the year or in '64 for sure. Your patrols report no Pathet activity?"

"None. But we're always set for trouble. Before it comes

you'd better get me more weapons. I have three companies and weapons for less than two."

"I brought you four 3.5-inch rocket launchers and 100 rounds. We'll get you more rockets before the end of the year. Oh, and we brought in a bunch of goodies. Even a few cases of C rations in case you're missing that good old American home cooking."

Arklin thought of the fall season at home and Thanksgiving and Christmas. "How long do you people want me to stay out here?"

"I know it's a rough one, Bernie," Methuan said sympathetically. "If it's too much, we'll get someone to relieve you."

"I'll stay. Nobody else could come in now and work with these people. At least not without a lot of preparation. They figure I'm one of them." He looked down at himself and ran a hand through his matted hair. "I guess I am."

"Got you a nice Meo girl to take care of you?"

Arklin looked at his control sharply. Methuan laughed. "You're not the only one out with these people. They all say if you don't have a Meo wife you can't work with them."

"They're about right," Arklin answered curtly. He noticed that the planes had been unloaded. "Well, I guess that does it."

"Right, Bernie. By the way, burn those letters as soon as you've read them. We don't want anything lying around that could identify you as an American."

Methuan clapped him on the shoulder. "Keep patrols and agents out watching the Pathet. They'll hit one day, no doubt about it, and the only thing that's going to slow them up when they start for Vientiane is the Meo tribesmen led by guys like you."

"How many of us are there out here?"

"That's top secret, need to know basis only. Just be sure that you make it tough on the Communists in your area when they do try to cut this country in half through the Plain of Jars. If you guys out here can give us a week or ten days before Laos falls completely, old Uncle Samuel will probably take action."

"We'll do our part," Arklin said. "Well, see you next trip."

"Right. Happy Thanksgiving and Merry Christmas."

"Wish my wife a Happy New Year for me too," Arklin answered dryly. "And don't forget to send some presents to the kids."

"The Agency has activated a fine Christmas shopping section for its boys in the field. And Bernie, you'll find a few trinkets for your Meo family in a box with your code number on it." With a raucous laugh he pulled the door shut. Immediately the pilots started up the engines, and Arklin and his Meos hastened from the field.

The platoon arrived back at the village by mid-day. Arklin saw that all the new weapons and equipment were stored in the arms room, and then took the mail sack and wood chest and went back to his house. Once inside he pried open the box.

He burst out laughing as he pulled out a pink Angora sweater and held it up to Nanette. One of the guys must have some sense of humor, he thought.

"Here." He handed it to her. "This will keep you warm these cold mornings."

"But I have you," Nanette protested.

"Try it on," Arklin urged. "I just hope it stretches good."

"If if will please you."

She took the sweater and pulled it on over her head. Arklin chuckled. "God, what a sweater girl. If they could see you back in the States the girls would all give up."

"This is good?" Nanette asked anxiously.

He nodded and looked into the box. "Let's see what else we've got." He pulled out a longhandled mirror, a comb and brush and gave them to Nanette. She looked at herself in the mirror with delight and began combing her hair.

Further down in the chest was a complete selection of contraceptive devices, for both male and female use. "Son of a bitch," he said aloud. "If that isn't locking the barn after the horse is out." He examined Nanette a few moments and made some rapid calculations. "Maybe not, though." He decided that he would start giving Nanette a little advanced training in certain intimate female matters.

"You keep looking through the box, Nanette. I've got some homework to do."

Going over to the door where the daylight streamed in, he sat on the floor and pulled out a large stack of letters.

Tenderly, envelope by envelope, he sorted the mail by date and then began to read in order. So absorbed was he in the news from home that he suddenly realized it was too dark to read. He looked up, for a second surprised to find himself where he was, and saw Nanette staring at him, a strange expression on her face. Her eyes went from his face to the pile of letters and back to his face. Wearing the Angora sweater she could have been a suntanned teenager; she had worked vigorously at her sleek black hair with the comb and brush.

"I wish I could write a letter," Nanette said. "Would you read them if I sent them to your other home when you go?"

"Of course."

"Your other wife won't mind? I will learn to write."

Arklin hesitated too long formulating an answer.

"Your other wife would hate me!" Nanette burst out.

"Perhaps not," Arklin said thoughtfully. "Not if she could understand this other world over here."

"What would she think if she knew about me?" Nanette pursued.

"Let's not talk about it," Arklin said quietly. "I'm here with you. We are living and working together. That's what is important now."

"But you will leave me for your American wife!" Nanette started to sob and Arklin went to her and held her in his arms. The sweater came between them, and impatiently she tore it off, her breasts exposed and pushing to her man now.

She fell back on the blankets, pulling Arklin to her, kissing him. One of her hands pulled at the belt to his fatigue pants. She slipped her hand inside.

Arklin groaned inwardly. He adored his Nanette, but right now, after reading the letters from his wife and children—

He pulled away from her gently. "Please, Nanette. I'm very tired. It's been a hard two days."

"You don't love me, you want your other wife," Nanette cried. "You will leave me and forget all about me just as soon as the Meo do what you want them to."

She stood up, her face an immobile mask of sullen anger. "You just use us, all of us, to get what you want. Then you leave us the way you did before." Holding her head high she walked out the door of the house and down the notched log into the darkness.

182

What she says is basically true, Arklin thought miserably.

Then he remembered Methuan's final warning. Gathering the letters in a thick bundle he stepped down to the ground and squatting in front of the nearest fire he sadly burned the letters one by one. How much it would have meant to be able to keep and reread them. But this was his duty.

Only after the last letter had become ash did he straighten up and start back to his house. Suddenly Nanette came rushing from the darkness and threw herself on him, kissing him, taking one of his hands and placing it high up between her strong thighs.

"You do love me and not her," Nanette cried. "You burned her letters."

Nanette half dragged Arklin back up to their house, happily crying, "You burned her letters, you love me."

But before they lay down together there was one thing he badly needed. He rummaged in the box until he found one of the bottles of good bourbon whisky.

3.

Peacefully 1964 crept into Laos. The Laotians paid no attention to the Viet Cong Communists from North Vietnam who openly used the country as a sanctuary for organizing their forces and infiltrating South Vietnam. The VC, after all, only caused trouble to the South Vietnamese. And most Western diplomatic missions in Vientiane enjoyed, to the full, the amenities the city offered, secure in the apparently peaceful intentions of the Pathet Lao.

But not a member of the Meo tribe doubted that the Communists would soon be on the march again. As a result, Arklin had no trouble convincing his charges that they must be constantly ready to meet and kill the Pathets. Pay Dang, in fact, frequently expressed the consensus of Meo opinion when he said they should launch a surprise attack on the Pathet with their new weapons. That way they might be able to kill more than 100 and lose few men themselves.

Arklin tried to explain the Geneva convention: How the Pathet, neutralists, and rightists had promised to live together in harmony, and all foreigners had promised to cease military aid to any of the three factions making up the government. How it was not the way of democratic countries to anticipate Communist aggressive designs and attack first. The entire concept of not attacking first was beyond the realistic Meos' comprehension.

As Arklin's patrols and agents reported a steady flow of Communist troops and equipment traveling south unmolested along a trail only thirty-five or forty miles away, it was difficult to resist Pay Dang's coaxing that they take a company and ambush a Communist column. The montagnards were getting anxious to kill their hated enemies. Arklin had to permit more frequent animal sacrifices and drinking parties to hold in check his tribesmen's blood lust, inflamed by the profusion of new weapons and their ability to use them well.

The Communists were quietly biding their time; Arklin wished they would attack and get it over with. He was constantly worried that some of the Meos might disobey his orders and stage a raid on a Pathet Lao village. Meanwhile U-10 flights kept him supplied and brought in more arms.

By March, 1964, the weapons room contained enough heavy and light weapons and ammunition for battalion operations. Arklin had more than 400 men. They were paid monthly in Laotian currency flown in to him. Morale was high and the men were honed to a keen fighting edge when the first signs of militancy on the part of the Pathets was reported by a patrol.

In April Communist military units were processing only twenty miles away to the North and then marching south to Pathet Lao headquarters at Khang Khay. Arklin radioed this information to control and requested permission to ambush the columns of Communists now moving along trails within striking range of the strongly fortified Meo village.

Permission was refused, pending the Pathet showing their hand more openly, but during the first week of May a message arrived that control would be at the airstrip the next morning. Arklin took an entire company with him to meet the plane.

Two U-10's landed and the Meo carriers ran across the field to unload. It was a less-than-jolly Frank Methuan who stepped from the ship. Arklin noticed his control's mood at once.

"What's the matter, Frank? I'm the one that should be looking like a six-week case of the ass."

"You look like the sorriest major I ever saw," the CIA man snapped.

Abashed, Arklin realized that unconsciously he may well have been letting himself go. In spite of all his precautions he had somehow contracted dysentery, which had taken its toll physically, to say nothing of reducing his desire to preserve military neatness at all times.

"I'm sorry, Frank. Guess I *have* been kind of careless lately. Not that it ever mattered to you before."

"Oh, Christ. I'm sorry, Bernie. I wish I was up here with you instead of fighting the Saigon-Bangkok-Pentagon-State Department war."

"What's it all about?"

"There's been a big flap between Military Assistance Command and the rest of the country team in Vietnam and Thailand."

"That sort of Olympian struggle never gets down to my level," Arklin said. "At least not when I'm out here with a bunch of restless montagnards."

"Well, it's getting down to you and your montagnards. For one thing all Special Forces in Vietnam now come directly under Military Assistance Command. They're trying to streamline things—they think. But what it comes down to is that a lot of Special Forces and our Combined Studies Group programs are being run by conventional army generals."

"This one too? In Laos?"

"They haven't gotten around to Laos yet. It may be a while, since the orthodox types running this crazy war don't like to admit to themselves that Americans are violating treaties—even though if we didn't the Commies would take this dinky little country that happens to be so strategically located any week they wanted."

"That's going to change a lot of things. From what you say, conventional officers sitting in comfortable offices will be writing the efficiency reports on Special Forces officers out in the field who are trying to outfight and outsmart the Viet Cong with their hands tied behind their backs."

"That's exactly what happened on May 1st."

"And my little operation? Are we going to piss all over the

185

Meos again, take their weapons away like we did before and leave them to be butchered by the Pathet Lao?''

"Not as long as the Agency is running the show."

"We'll keep running it. We're ready to go. We have been for six months."

"You'll be getting action, plenty of it, soon. There's been a half-assed *coup d'état* in Vientiane. Nothing much. A new right-wing general has taken over control of the government temporarily. But this is all it takes to give the Communists an excuse to start moving into Vientiane."

Methuan pointed across the entrance to the flat Plain of Jars below them to the east. "General Kong Le has a few thousand troops over there which are all that's standing between the Communists and his Headquarters at Vang Vieng. If the Pathet can roll into Vang Vieng they'll be fifty easy miles from Vientiane and taking over Laos. Your job is to do everything you can to harass and slow down the Pathets. We won't be able to give you direct orders. All we can do is tell you they're rolling. The rest is up to you."

"Fair enough."

"If it looks like you're going to get overrun we'll try and evacuate you by chopper. So I guess you'd better cut a chopper pad at the village." Methuan put his hand on Arklin's shoulder. "Your next control may be Military Assistance Command. By the way"—he handed Arklin the familiar orange bag of mail—"everything is smooth at home."

"Thanks," Arklin murmured. He reached into his pocket and pulled out a long letter. "Will you mail this to Nancy? There is nothing in it about what I'm doing, of course."

"Someone will have to look it over to make sure, Bernie," the CIA man said, "but I'll see it gets off to her." He climbed back into the plane. Before closing the door he called, "If the Pathet look like they're going to attack and you have to move, radio us before you do anything. And don't get yourself captured, Bernie!"

Arklin watched the two planes leap up into the air, and then began the familiar, exhausting trek up the side of the mountain. He poked the mailbag into his pack resolving this time to devise some way of keeping Nanette from seeing it. He was surprised to realize how much he looked forward to returning to the house on stilts and Nanette.

He was sitting with her outside their house next to the fire after eating a nostalgic American supper of fruit cocktail and beef stew when Pay Dang came up with a barefoot montagnard dressed in loincloth and blanket. Arklin motioned them to be seated and Pay Dang said that the newcomer was from a Meo village twenty miles to the northeast. It was mostly populated by old people and women and children who cultivated and milked opium poppies.

"Their men, some of them are with us," Pay Dang said, "are leaving the village because the Pathet Lao and Viet Minh are moving west and the Meo do not want to be forced to fight for them."

"Ask him how many Communists are moving toward us," Arklin said. "Try to get an accurate number from him, not just 'many, many Pathet come.' "

Pay Dang questioned the youth at length. Finally he turned back. "He says many hundred."

"OK, Pay Dang," Arklin said decisively. "Let this boy lead a platoon out to where the Pathet are moving. Be sure you send along a good scout who can count. Tell them to pick up any people they see and bring them back. If they can capture a Pathet prisoner, so much the better."

"Yes, Major." Pay Dang stood up. He flashed his big toothy grin. "Soon we kill Pathet and Viet Minh."

"If they don't get us first. Tell them to move fast and get back as soon as possible."

When they had gone Nanette turned to him fearfully. "Soon the war starts again?"

"Looks that way, Nanette."

"We had so little chance to be together."

"We've got plenty of time ahead of us," Arklin said with a heartiness that sounded false even to him.

Nanette said nothing, then stood up and started for the house. "I will wait for you inside. Always mail comes to you in the airplane."

Arklin watched her lithe figure, bare from the tightly knotted cloth skirt up, daintily mount the notched log and disappear into the dark bamboo house. He sighed and reached for the mailbag. . . .

For the next day and a half Arklin had every company commander check his men's equipment. Excitement was in the atmosphere. The Meo seemed to sense their enemy's proximity, but Arklin did not want to base an operation on the mystical feelings of his men.

From control, late in the afternoon, came a message that the Pathet Lao had attacked a government-controlled and -fortified village in the north near the Red Chinese border—the first overt breach of neutrality. Twenty-four hours later the reconnaissance platoon Arklin had sent to spy out Pathet positions returned. He hurried to the bridge to meet them. The two scouts he had trained so laboriously in map reading, compass work, and reconnaissance met around the fire, along with Pay Dang and the platoon leader. The chief scout, only a boy but exceptionally receptive to instruction, spread a map out on the ground and described the route the patrol had taken.

"On a bearing of 70 degrees from here, only twenty kilometers from where we now sit," the boy said—technical words in English, narrative in Meo—"we found camped last night a company of Pathet Lao. We hid until morning and watched them moving south. I saw maybe 50 Viet Minh in their brown uniforms with them. There were maybe 200 men walking along the trail."

So the Viet Minh were marching south with the Communist Laotians, Arklin thought. This was an unmistakable sign that the North Vietnamese Communists were egging on the Pathet Lao to make another attempt to take over Laos. When such a large force reached its destination a sudden attack on neutral Laotian forces would surely follow. If this Communist column could be stopped, there might be time for the pro-government Army to prepare for the onslaught.

Arklin studied the map for a while and turned to Pay Dang. "If we took the 3rd and 4th companies out tonight, heading southeast, we could cut them off above Pathet Lao headquarters at Khang Khay and ambush them." Arklin traced the route on the map as Pay Dang and the others watched intently. "Maybe we could kill half the company or more."

"We must go out now? At night?" Pay Dang asked.

The montagnards were still superstitious, even though Arklin had been training them in night patrolling for six months.

The American shrugged. "Someday maybe we'll have another chance to kill the Pathet." He started for his house.

"No!" Pay Dang cried, suddenly determined. "We are ready now. We go now. I give the orders." Then he looked

188

at Arklin for confirmation. "This will not hurt you with your big political men?"

"Only if we do not kill fast and run," Arklin answered. "I do not want any of our men captured alive. You understand? The Pathet Lao will make them talk. If one of your people tells them there is an American fighting with the Meo it will cause trouble."

"We will go," Pay Dang declared. "We leave as soon as moon comes up. It will help us find paths."

"Good. Bring the two company commanders and the platoon leaders to me."

Pay Dang ran off to get the two companies ready. Arklin beckoned a husky young Meo boy to follow and climbed the log into his stilt house. Nanette watched as the boy got on the seat of the radio's generator, and with both hands began turning the cranks over, making electricity for the "Angry 9" radio transmitter.

On his code pad, by flashlight, Arklin composed the message he would send to control station one hundred and fifty miles southwest across Laos in Thailand. From this forward base the message would be relayed back to Bangkok where it would be decided whether or not Arklin had done the right thing. The Agency would approve, he felt sure. His orders were to slow down the Pathet, and even though nobody else knew they were on the move again, he did. If he took no action the somnolent Laotian government might be defeated before it could prepare to fight off the Communists. There would be no time for the United States to come to the aid of Laos and protect its neutrality.

Arklin tapped out the message in his slow but adequate keying that only Methuan would be able to decode, then told the boy to stop cranking. The receiver worked by battery. He received an immediate confirmation that the message had been received and sat by the radio hoping for approval of his operation plan.

Pay Dang arrived at the house, combat-ready, his automatic rifle slung over his shoulder, and pouches of ammunition and hand grenades hung all over him.

"We are ready, Major. The men want to kill the Pathet and Viet Minh."

Arklin nodded and threw a hopeless glance at the silent radio. Strapping on his pistol belt and harness, and picking up his AR-15 automatic rifle, he rubbed noses with Nanette, kissed her in the warmth of her neck and followed the Meo chief out.

The two companies were drawn up in ranks ready to go. Arklin assembled the company commanders and platoon leaders, and on the ground, using his flashlight, gave them a thorough description of the mission and what was expected of them.

The ambush, which would extend about two hundred yards, would be set when they reached the road to Khang Khay at a point about twelve miles from the foot of their mountain. They would reach their objective before dawn, set up, wait, and when the Communists were in their killing zone let them have it with all the fire power at the strike force's command.

The two companies started off in high spirits. Arklin and Pay Dang walked between the lead and rear company, posting scouts ahead of the first company to make sure they followed the correct course to the objective. Arklin checked his watch and saw it was 9:30. He had slight trepidations about how the news would be received at higher headquarters that he and his montagnards might be firing the first shots in the new Communist campaign to take over neutralized Laos. He rationalized by considering the Agency's message reporting the Communist attack in the north as giving him open season on the Pathets in his area. In any case, if all went as planned and no one was captured or left behind, the Communists publicly could only blame the ambush on internal dissension within the country.

The march to the road into Khang Khay was almost entirely downhill. Arklin worried about the trip back with wounded and dead. It would be a tough one, even for his hardy Meos who had been walking up and down the mountains all their lives, since they would have to take evasive action and thus couldn't follow the trail.

Before dawn they came upon the road in virtually undisputed Pathet Lao territory. Though they were a scant ten miles from Pathet Lao headquarters in Khang Khay, there was no sign of guards or road security. Under Arklin's unobtrusive supervision Pay Dang and his two company commanders set out the ambush. Each company covered one hundred yards of road. At the beginning and end of the ambush, two L's of heavily armed men stretched fifty yards back into the jungle. These were secondary ambushes to stop Pathet Lao or Viet Minh troops who might rally their forces and try to flank the ambushers. Arklin was proud of the professional manner in which his so-called primitive tribesmen prepared to receive the Communists.

The two company commanders positioned themselves at the extremities of the ambush, each holding a radio handset transmitter. When the last of the enemy passed into the ambush, the company commander on the north would signal with his transmitter button. Pay Dang, standing on a rise in the middle of the ambush zone and able to view most of the road, also carried a handset. It would be he, guided by Arklin, who would give the signal to open up. If, by chance, the enemy column was longer than expected and the vanguard passed out of the killing zone to the south before the rear came through, Pay Dang and Arklin would decide when to start firing. Hopefully they could distribute the enemy free to flank the ambush evenly to north and south, where the L's on each end should be able to take care of them.

By the time daylight fully penetrated the jungle the Meos were in position, machine guns, automatic rifles and heavy M-1's leveled at the road. Each man had his grenades hanging loosely from his harness and belt for instant plucking. Every man in both companies knew his job and route of withdrawal.

As they waited for the enemy to walk into the ambush Arklin thought of all the things that could go wrong. What if the Pathet had already passed this point? This did not seem likely. More important, he knew he should not have come down here himself. Though he was personally outfitted entirely with sterile equipment—nothing he wore or carried could identify him as an American and none of his supplies had been manufactured in the United States—if he were captured or his body was found there could be no disguising the fact that a Caucasian was with the Meo tribesmen. It would give the Communists great propaganda capital and embarrass the U.S. government. Everything depended on the discipline the Meo maintained. This would be the test.

Arklin and Pay Dang stood tensely above the middle of the ambush, concealed by the thick jungle. The cool of dawn dissipated into the muggy heat of the tropical day. Arklin looked across the road at the mucky drainage ditch on the other side. It was an inviting depression, just what the surprised Communists would jump into. His eyes hardened, his lips twitched in a thin smile. . . .

Four slight clicks sounded from the radio handset. The Pathet column had been sighted. Pay Dang nudged Arklin excitedly. Arklin laid a restraining hand on the Meo's shoulder. They waited in absolute silence. Then the company commander to the north pressed his transmitter button three times and three clicks came over Pay Dang's set. The point of the enemy column had entered the ambush. Minutes later, off to their left, Arklin and Pay Dang saw the first of the Communists on their way to join the Pathet Lao battalions at Khang Khay for the drive across the Plain of Jars. They were wearing a conglomeration of uniforms—black pajamas, khakis, and combat fatigues. They were well armed and walked with precision, officers in khaki ranging up and down the column.

"Viet Minh!" Pay Dang whispered, as black-clad, flat-helmeted, machine-gun-carrying men began to appear, closely interspersed with the shabbier-looking Pathet Lao troops.

Arklin prayed the training and discipline he'd instilled in his men would hold up. The Laotian government soldiers were quelled by the mere mention of Viet Minh—they believed implicitly in their savagery and invincibility and were paralyzed with fear at the idea of fighting them—and it took only a small number of North Vietnamese to terrorize and set them to flight. Even the Meo, although they would not admit it, were afraid of the Viet Minh; but they hated the Communists even more, so they would fight.

Arklin was ready for the first sign of flagging courage on the part of his Meos should the Viet Minh be able to mount a determined counterattack into the ambush. From squad leaders all the way up to Pay Dang, the Meos knew they must force their men to stay and battle until the signal came to pull back, dragging all dead and wounded with them.

As the Pathet Lao and Viet Minh marched along the road in front of them, Arklin realized he was wise to have brought two full companies. Either his scouts had miscounted or more troops had been picked up since the patrol had sighted the column two days before and counted 200 men.

Two clicks sounded on the handset. The van of the column had passed the second Meo company commander to the south and was already out of the killing zone. Arklin waited for the single click which would tell him that the end of the column had entered the ambush.

Arklin looked up the tree in which a scout was posted. The scout gave him a vigorous shake of his clenched fist. To Pay Dang, Arklin whispered, "He sees the end of the column. We can't wait for it to get into the ambush. The point will get too far out. Shoot!"

Pay Dang needed no more encouragement. Sighting down the barrel of his automatic carbine he squeezed the trigger. In the burst, shattering the early-morning silence, two khaki-clad North Vietnamese dropped. Instantly the Meos opened up. Firing cracked and stuttered up and down the line as the shocked Communists, deep in the supposed safety of their own territory, froze in panic and surprise. The officers shouted at their men and began shooting even as rounds tore through them. Following their officers' orders the Communists sprayed back bursts of fire, but they could not see their targets. Fusillades of bullets and grenades ripped into the column. Those not killed or wounded in the first, intense blast from the ambush, fell and tumbled into the ditch on the opposite side of the road and began returning heavy fire.

To the south, the section that had walked through and out of the killing zone had turned back through the jungle in an effort to hit the ambush from behind. The same was happening on the north end of the ambush. Pay Dang screamed with joy as he poured fire into the Communists pinned down in the ditch. The exultant shouts of the Meo could be heard even over the heavy firing. Within minutes after the first burst of fire the ambush had become a stalemate. Those Communists left alive were either pinned down in the ditch and firing back or skirmishing to the north and south against the protective L's.

"Let's get out of here, Pay Dang," Arklin commanded. He pulled a flare gun from his pistol belt.

"We stay, kill more Pathet and Viet Minh," Pay Dang shouted.

Arklin grabbed the montagnard leader by the shoulder and swung him away from the firing. The American's eyes flashed. "We go now. Hit them again later."

Pay Dang regained his control. "We go, Major."

"But first—" Arklin handed the signal pistol to Pay Dang

and picked up a small hand detonator. He gave the handle a sharp twist and there was an ear-splitting explosion along the entire length of the ambush. Screams came from the ditch. Pieces of legs, arms, heads, and unidentifiable red meat blasted onto the road. The Meos shrieked with chilling glee at the mayhem wreaked on their hated enemy.

Arklin snatched the flare gun from a hypnotized Pay Dang staring raptly at the carnage below. He fired a red flare, reloaded and fired again, then a third time.

Immediately the Meo began pulling back from their positions. Crouched low they ran through the jungle, converging in an orderly, self-protecting formation on their rallying point half a mile behind the ambush site. Even as he ran Arklin couldn't help thinking that never had he seen detonating cord used with such devastating effect. It had only taken ten minutes to string the highly explosive half-inch cord the length of the ditch, giving the line a few extra swirls in likely places of refuge to increase the force of the blast. It had been a simple matter to stretch the thin electric wire across the road and conceal it in the dirt. Every Communist in the ditch must have been killed or badly wounded.

Well, Arklin thought, for once we hit first and hardest. Now the problem was to get his Meos back to the village without running into a Communist unit.

At the rally point the company commanders rapidly took count of their men. The ambush had been successful. Arklin estimated that two-thirds of the Communists had been killed or maimed. At final count only three Meo men had been killed in the heavy return fire and seven wounded. Each of the bodies was tied to poles slung on the shoulders of two men. Others took turns carrying them. The walking wounded were helped by their comrades. Three men were seriously hurt and had to be carried. Arklin stifled the groans of the badly wounded with shots of morphine.

Now began the long uphill march back to the village. At Arklin's insistence they followed a different route; Pay Dang, though he knew this was the most basic doctrine of guerrilla warfare, still tried to persuade Arklin to follow the easier, shorter path. Arklin refused.

It was a struggle through the jungle with the dead and wounded but the montagnards kept going. Arklin and Pay Dang moved up and down the long, twisting column encouraging the men. Once they came so close to the beaten, less-steep path they had followed down from the village that Arklin was afraid he would have another argument with Pay Dang. By late afternoon they were still six hours from camp because of the difficulty of forcing their way through trailless jungle. The men were exhausted. They found a small hilltop with a stream flowing by and Arklin let them camp, though maintaining a 50 per cent security guard.

When all the stragglers reached the hill, Arklin went searching for the wounded men to tend their wounds and administer more morphine. He pushed through the growth, stepping on men lying exhausted, but nowhere could he find the three litter cases and four walking wounded.

He returned to the command post he and Pay Dang had set up. The Meo chief was sitting on the ground, his back against a tree, puffing on his stubby pipe.

"Pay Dang," Arklin said sharply, "I can't find the wounded."

The Meo gave him a bland look, saying nothing.

"Do you know where they are?" Arklin insisted.

When there was still no answer Arklin knew. "Did the wounded and some of the men take the other trail home when we passed by?"

"I could not stop them," Pay Dang finally replied. "They are men. We do not stop men from doing what they must."

"But this is a military operation. You are in command. You take my advice and they must take your orders."

Pay Dang stubbornly continued to smoke his pipe. Arklin realized there was nothing he could do now. For a while, because things had gone well, he had deluded himself into believing he had created a real paramilitary organization. "I hope they get back all right, Pay Dang. Did they have any security?"

"Two squads, 20 men go with the wounded."

Arklin glanced at his watch. It was 4:00 in the afternoon. "They should be reaching camp in a few hours." He gave Pay Dang a steady look. "Pay Dang, this is very dangerous for all of us. Do you realize what will happen if they're caught? They'll be tortured. The wounded will tell the Pathet that two-thirds of the camp is out. Maybe they attack."

"They do not get ambushed or captured," Pay Dang said positively. "No Pathet around these hills."

"That's what the Pathet thought about us this morning when we ambushed them."

This gave Pay Dang a moment's searching thought. Finally he said, "I did not see my people go, a platoon leader told me. I do not tell you, make you feel bad after big win."

"Listen to me carefully," Arklin said forcefully. "I know the men are tired. I am more tired than any of them." Painfully he knew this to be true; at thirty-eight a man, no matter how strenuously he has trained, bounces back from extreme physical exertion slowly.

"We must start right now and keep going until we get back to camp." The Meo chief's eyes widened in surprise. "Don't you understand, Pay Dang, if those people who broke away from us are ambushed and caught, the village may be lost. The Pathet will find out that we are a long way from home. We have most of the weapons with us. The Pathet could take the camp."

The Meo chief began to get a glimmer of the seriousness of the situation. He stood up and stretched. "Meo people will do what you want, Major. But they say you make them train too hard. No Pathet near us now. Meo men happy they kill so many. They want to rest now."

"Pay Dang," Arklin said urgently, "tell your men, the company commanders, the platoon leaders and the squad sergeants, that I want them to follow me. Tell them we must keep going. We will be home before dawn. There's a good moon."

Arklin saw that he was making some headway, but a clincher was needed. Something to appeal to the human side of the Meos. He thought a minute and then, smiling, he walked to the pipe-puffing, still-unconvinced chief and put an arm around the small man's immense shoulders. Winking broadly Arklin said, "Tell the men I promised Ha Ban I'd give her the biggest loving she ever had before daylight tomorrow."

Arklin slapped his right bicep with his left hand, clenching his right fist at the end of a rigid forearm. The gesture was universally unmistakable. "If we don't get back, maybe she'll go to that big captain we left guarding the village."

In a roar of laughter Pay Dang spit the pipe out of his mouth, wheezing and coughing from the foul smoke of his home-grown tobacco. He bent over, convulsed, and weakly picked up his pipe and jammed it back in his mouth. "OK, we go," he said in English. "We go take Major to Ha Ban." Pay Dang went to find his officers and give orders to move out.

Arklin pulled out his map and studied it. Only two and a half hours of daylight, then blackness until the moon came up. He decided to change the route, bringing it closer to the direct one they had followed from camp, but still far enough to circumvent ambushes that the wily Pathet and their even more sophisticated mentors, the Viet Minh, might have set out.

Ten minutes later Pay Dang, still grinning, returned. The men would push on, he reported. In fact some of them were also worried about their women, especially since many of the men in the 5th Meo Strike Company, who had been left to guard the camp, had come from another village and did not have their own women.

The two companies pushed on again, with Arklin this time at the point to make sure they followed the new bearing. The jungle was thick, necessitating considerable slashing at vines and trees, but Arklin and his Meos fought their way onward.

It was almost dark when the thing he had feared, yet perversely had almost hoped for, happened.

To their north a sudden, nerve-jangling thunderclap of shooting broke out. The unmistakable clatter of light automatic weapons, the deep-throated stuttering of BAR's and then the loud bang of grenades echoed across the jungle. Arklin glanced at his watch. It was 6:35 P.M. The whole column stopped to listen as the furious fire-fight raged. In less than five minutes the last shots died away. An ominous silence pervaded the mountainous jungle as dusk and then darkness fell.

"Tell your men to move fast," Arklin whispered to Pay Dang. "It won't take the Pathet long to find out what they want to know."

Gone was the good-humored joking and chatter that had been the bane of Arklin's efforts to enforce noise discipline. The Meos pushed steadily, grimly on. It was all uphill. Arklin was almost sick with exhaustion but he kept pushing himself, occasionally pausing a few moments to suck water from his canteen. At the end of an hour he signalled a break and fell to the ground limply, gasping, his legs aching and threatening to give out. Shakily he reached for his first-aid pouch, and rummaged in it until he found what he wanted. He poured two special pep tablets into his mouth but he was so dry he could not swallow them. From his nearly empty canteen he took just enough water to get the pills down. One was supposed to give a man enough extra stamina to keep going in spite of acute fatigue. Arklin felt he'd be lucky if he made it back with two.

Lying absolutely limp for ten minutes Arklin felt the pills begin to take. After fifteen minutes he was able to start forward again.

Every twenty minutes the column halted and its leaders listened intently in the darkness. There was no need for talk about the firing they had heard. Every man in the column knew only too well that the Pathet had found the Meo path to the ambush site and had lain in wait for them to return. The moonlight helped the Meos follow in file, each man staying in sight of the man ahead. Pushing their way up the mountain they began to move with more spirit as they approached their camp on top.

The Meo men near Arklin, Pay Dang especially, watched him closely, responding to his slightest signal or whispered command. While he was certain that there would never again be a breach of discipline as long as he was leading these tribesmen, the price paid for absolute obedience had been too high—not only in men, but in irreplaceable weapons.

Upwards they climbed in the dark through the tangled jungle growth. Checking his compass and watch constantly, Arklin figured that the column was less than an hour from camp when he called a break. It was taking them longer to reach the village than he had first estimated. The pills, at least, had worked, and Arklin knew a strange sense of clarity and awareness, a sort of detachment from his exhausted body.

They would be in the village before dawn, and fatigued though they were their additional fire power should be enough to beat off any ordinary Communist attack. As his legs carried him upward Arklin had a moment of prescience. His mission here was a success. All his efforts, the months he had lived alone out here, were at last to count for something. The Communists would have to wipe out the little fortress he had created before they could call the Plain of Jars secure for their operations.

Ten days Methuan had asked for. Arklin would try to give

them to him. And then he could go home. He visualized his name on the promotion list to make lieutenant colonel. His thoughts went to the comfortable home in Fayetteville where a man could wake up in the morning, put on a clean uniform, and go to work like a normal person. . . .

Pay Dang, walking ahead of him, paused and pointed. On the mountaintop above them was reflected the glow of dying fires. Before long they should encounter the camp's listening posts and outer security guard.

Suddenly, in front of them, the flash of fire and eruption of automatic weapons burst forth. Arklin groaned. Already the Communists were hitting the village. Were his men too exhausted to fight?

"Pay Dang," Arklin shouted over the shooting. "Tell the men to spread out and hit the Pathet from the rear. Take one platoon to the bridge!"

Pay Dang shouted the orders and the Meos deployed. Only sporadic return fire emanated from the camp. A mortar round exploded from a tube somewhere in front of them; twenty seconds later there was a flash and explosion from inside the camp and a fierce fire started to burn.

"White phosphorous!" Arklin shouted. "Let's get that mortar." Pay Dang, Arklin, and a squad fought their way through the tangled growth. The flash of mortar rounds being fired clearly indicated the position of the weapon.

Twenty yards ahead of them they could actually see the mortar and its crew.

"Let's go!" Arklin yelled, crashing through the heavy foliage. He pulled a grenade off his belt, jerked the pin out, held the handle down until he had a clear pitch, and then let it go.

A deafening explosion and bright flash outlined the mortar tube tumbling in the air. The Meos fell upon the Communists, shooting at them and slicing at the living and dead with knives.

From all around the camp now the Communists had turned from the village and were firing into the darkness filled with enraged Meo men. Shrill whistle blasts and shouted commands told Arklin that the Communists were trying to escape through the encircling Meo tribesmen. Screams, gunfire and the blasts of grenades split the night.

Arklin aimed his flare gun high—and fired a green star

above the camp as the signal for the defenders to stop firing. Anything from inside now probably would kill more Meo than Communists.

"Pay Dang," Arklin shouted, "the Pathet are on the run. Tell our men to stop firing. They'll kill each other." Arklin fired two more green flares and Pay Dang yelled orders. Slowly the firing came to a halt.

"Let's get into camp, Pay Dang."

Arklin paused at the recent Communist mortar position. Two Meos were hacking at the Communists. One Pathet, barely alive and moaning, was minus ears and hands.

"Go to the village," Arklin cried in Meo. The tribesmen looked up from their grisly task and seeing it was Arklin obeyed instantly, carrying their bloody souvenirs with them.

Shouting the identifying password the Meos made their way to the bridge, crossed and entered their village, horrifyingly illuminated by the flickering fires caused by the Communist WP-mortar barrage.

Men rushed to their houses and shouts of anguish in the night bespoke the death of women and children. Arklin made for his stilt house and to his immense relief found it undamaged. He shouted for Ha Ban and found her huddled under the house. She threw herself into his arms, weeping.

"You must help me, Nanette," he said. "Remember all I taught you about bandaging wounds and treating burns?"

She nodded and pulled herself together. "I will get the medical box."

With sunrise Arklin was able to evaluate the damage done to the village. A cluster of houses had burned to the ground. Only the complete stillness of the air had prevented the entire village from going up in a holocaust. Ten blackened and unidentifiable bodies were laid out for burial. A hospital section had been set up, and Ha Ban and some of the other women were taking care of the burned and wounded men, women, and children.

Pay Dang followed Arklin on his inspection rounds, looking as grim as the Major, knowing, as did all the Meos, that all this was the result of not obeying their American leader's orders.

"They didn't get the weapons room," Arklin said in an effort at optimism.

Roll call showed 32 men missing. When the sun had risen

above the mountains Arklin took a detail outside camp. Most of the Communist bodies, including those mutilated by the Meo, had been dragged away by stealthily returning Pathet Lao. Most enemy weapons also had been retrieved.

The bodies of three Meos whom Arklin suspected had been shot by the defenders in error were pulled back into the village and laid beside the others for burial.

By mid-morning much of the evidence of the battle had been cleaned up. The bodies had been taken to the burial ground to lie in woven bamboo huts while commemorative wooden posts were carved. Then they would be buried and the posts placed above the graves.

The burned houses were already being rebuilt by a work detail, and the three company captains had taken accurate casualty counts and reorganized their commands.

Arklin was gray and shaking with exhaustion. The pills had worn off and he didn't dare sit down, knowing he would collapse into sleep. He ordered the entire 5th Meo Strike Company, which had stayed in camp during the ambush, to mount outer and inner security guard.

Pay Dang asked permission to send a platoon to see what had happened to the men ambushed on the trail. Arklin insisted the platoon take an extra section to walk flank security. Then with things reasonably under control he shuffled to his house, made it up the notched log and collapsed on the floor into a deep coma-like sleep.

The heat and the sun streaming through the door slowly awakened him. He opened his eyes to find his head cradled between Nanette's breasts, her familiar musky odor in his nostrils turning his mind to sensual thoughts. At once reality intruded. The Communist attack on the village could be repeated. He should report to control.

Nanette, seeing he was awake, stroked his forehead. Arklin sighed wearily and propped his head on one elbow. "There will be much fighting in the next week. The Pathet will attack this camp in force the next time. We will all have to leave here before then."

"If I am with you I do not care where we go."

"I can't promise you what will happen."

Nanette reached out and clutched Arklin's arms. Her hands were very strong for a woman's, he thought. She didn't say anything for a few moments and then, shoulders sagging, fingers opening, she fell against his shoulder. He put an arm around her and held her to him. It was all wrong, this thing with the half-French half-Meo girl. Yet down deep he knew much of his success with the Meo tribesmen was due to her. Much as he loved and missed his home and family, he had derived great comfort from Nanette. He was human and, goddamn it, Nanette had provided the few simple pleasures and the companionship that made it possible for him to live and work out here, almost a year now, in a state of comparative happiness.

Arklin realized he must soon talk to Nanette about the future. Seeing his expression, she raised her lips to him and drew him down on top of her again, stroking and caressing him. Still fatigued, he submitted, and then finally, reluctantly, he forced himself up. He must contact control.

Calling a boy to come grind the radio's generator, he sat behind the transmitting key, code pad in front of him, and composed a terse message.

"Ambush success, destroyed enemy company. Thirty friendly killed or captured."

Arklin listened carefully for an answer. His message was acknowledged and then the dots and dashes told him to stand by. He waited for twenty minutes before the considerately slow keying of the control operator began. Arklin wrote the incoming message down letter by letter on his code pad. When it was finished he quickly decoded the signal.

The message read, "Keep hitting at your discretion. Mark helicopter Landing Zone in your village immediately." The message was signed with Methuan's code.

Arklin left to look for a likely Landing Zone. A clear area, enlarged by the burned-out houses from the Communist mortar barrage, was the right size and he ordered the debris cleared away. On his return, Nanette told him excitedly that the radio receiver had been clicking. Hastily he summoned a boy to crank the generator and transmitted that he had not received the message and to please repeat. He listened intently and copied a long message from control on his code pad. Acknowledging receipt he proceeded to decode the new signal. Some of the words had been garbled and it took him a while to get the sense of the entire communication. It was from Methuan.

The message informed him that the Communists were already complaining about an American-inspired ground attack on their headquarters. Higher U.S. command was not as pleased as the Agency with the attack which, the Communists said, precluded negotiations. Control then said that agent reports indicated a Pathet buildup to regimental strength northwest of Khang Khay. It was reported that there were Chinese Communist officers advising the troops. Finally control suggested that if a Chinese Communist officer could be captured it would help give the United States cause in the eyes of the world to use whatever means necessary to halt further Communist military aggression in Laos.

4.

Coordinates of the Communist buildup had been given in the message and Arklin plotted the exact location on his map. While Khang Khay was almost due south of the village, the new Communist positions were southwest, close to the edge of the Plain of Jars, but still in jungle terrain. This apparently would be the jumping-off area for large-scale attacks that would spearhead the Communist movement across the last of the country's government-held territory.

Arklin took the map out to the gate, crossed the bridge and looked down the mountainside and across toward the Plain of Jars, directly west of the camp. Looking southward he could see, about ten miles away, the jungle-covered foothills in which the Pathet Lao, Viet Minh and apparently Chicoms too, were getting their troops ready to finish off Laos as a neutralist nation.

Arklin made his plans for the attack, the purpose of which would be to capture Chinese prisoners. He went to the weapons room, unlocked the door and made an inventory of the contents. There was a fine supply of ammunition for the four 3.5-inch rocket launchers, the most potent weapons at his disposal.

The rocket launchers, he decided, would be the key to his strategy.

Each of the three Meo companies had a weapons platoon, but their training in the rocket launcher had been minimal. Still, there were four two-man teams in each company with some experience on this bazooka: twelve teams in the camp. Arklin would have to determine the four best teams. Walking out of the shed he laughed at the idea forming in his head. He really was becoming a Meo.

Arklin would sponsor a shooting contest to determine which bazooka men were the best. Afterwards the winners would be feted at a drinking party and then accorded the honor of firing the deadly rockets into the Pathet Lao camp. Most important, after being guests of honor at the village revel the winners would die before they'd fail in their mission. Always, to get montagnards working and fighting at peak skill you had to devise tricks, games, contests, and other incentives. Also, he thought, a contest and party would take their minds off the unnecessary loss of life in the ambush and attack on the village.

Arklin had outlined the strategy in his mind when in the distance he heard a buffalo horn, the signal that friendly forces were approaching camp. He arrived at the main gate in time to see the vanguard of Pay Dang's relief column. Arklin grimly watched body after body being carried by the Meos, the corpses tied hands and feet to heavy poles or slung over the backs of the tribesmen.

There was absolute silence in the village. The Meos crossed the bridge, walked to the burial ground and deposited the corpses. When the mournful procession was completed there were 15 bodies laid out. Arklin couldn't repress a shudder. The Communists were no slouches at mutilating the dead either. Stoically, the villagers gazed down at the bodies. Some women, whose men were not among the bodies brought into camp, went anxiously to the gate to see whether more might be coming.

The last of the patrol entered the village with a wounded man on a bamboo litter and took him to the hospital area. His woman was already beside him, pulling at the clothing over his wound. Arklin gently pushed her aside, and cut the clothes away from a chest wound. The bullet had cut across the chest, searing a bloody path, but had not, fortunately, entered the lungs. Loss of blood had weakened the tribesman so that he could not walk. "This man run into jungle. Pathet try but cannot find him," Pay Dang explained.

Arklin hung a bottle of plasma from a post and introduced

a needle into the montagnard's artery. The woman moaned as he worked.

"Could he tell you anything?" Arklin asked Pay Dang.

"He said the shooting was sudden. He was at the end of the column and ran away. He hid in the jungle until the Pathet go away. They tortured and killed the wounded and then attacked the village."

"How many Pathet in the ambush?"

"He say many, many, a hundred, maybe 200."

"Probably a band of 30." Arklin finished cleaning the wound and bandaged it. As he walked away from the wounded man, Pay Dang anxiously trailed him.

"What do we do now, Major?"

Arklin shrugged his shoulders. "If your men will not obey the orders we give I cannot take them out again to kill the Pathet and Viet Minh. It is too bad. I have a fine plan to kill many Communists."

Pay Dang, his face pitiful with remorse, reached out and held Arklin. "Meos never again disobey your orders, Major. I make you blood pledge. I kill any Meo who does not do what you say."

They had reached Arklin's longhouse and the major gestured Pay Dang up the notched log and followed him. In the house Arklin pointed to the map on the wall. "All right, Pay Dang, we will try again to hit the Pathet and Viet Minh."

The Meo let out a happy cry.

"This is going to be a very hard operation. Every man must know his job perfectly. We will have only one day to practice the attack and then we go hit the Pathet at their new camp."

"Kill the Pathet!" Pay Dang cried.

Minutely, Arklin outlined his plan. An hour later, when Pay Dang understood it completely, he left Arklin's house to start operations moving.

The best four scouts in camp were sent to Arklin for briefing. "You'll wear your old Meo clothing," he told them. "Loincloth and blanket. You'll go barefoot." At this last they grimaced. Shoes, army boots, had come to be one of their chief status symbols, and even though uncomfortable on their wide splayfeet, the pride they took in owning them more than compensated for any discomfort they produced.

"You will carry no weapons but your own hunting crossbows.

Watch the Pathet camp and look for the Chinese. You understand?'' The four scouts nodded vigorously.

"You will travel tonight and watch all day tomorrow. Two of you will return tomorrow night and be here before sunrise the next day." Arklin designated which two by slapping their shoulders. "You other two will keep watching the camp, marking the place the Chinese stay. You two scouts who come back will lead us to the Pathet camp.''

Arklin spent another half-hour drilling his scouts, and then let them go to change into their Meo garb and start out. His next order was for a work party to clear the helicopter Landing Zone. Finally, just before dark, he called out the heavy-weapons men for a meeting.

Meanwhile the old people and women prepared for the mass funeral. The relatives of those whose bodies had been brought back to camp worked cheerfully at their tasks of carving wood monuments for the graves. The spirits of their men would be released from the home village, which was as it should be. The relatives of those whose bodies had not been returned were the ones who grieved and moaned fitfully. There could be no worse fate for a dead montagnard and his family than not having the body properly buried at home. The ghost would wander forever in the mountains.

The next morning, after the final rites for the dead had been completed and the ill effects of the funeral-drinking thrown off, Arklin took ten rocket-launcher teams about a mile from the village to a clearing in the jungle. At Arklin's bidding, the entire village including women were invited to watch, giving the teams even greater incentive to win the competition for accurate rocket fire. Everybody knew that the four winning teams would soon hit the Pathet Lao and Viet Minh with fiery death. The winners, Arklin had been careful to promise, would be heroes of the camp. He doubted if many of them would live through the job he required of them, but for the raid to be successful these rocket-launcher teams would have to do their jobs fearlessly.

The clearing overlooked another barren spot in the jungle about two hundred and fifty yards away and slightly lower on the mountainside. In the middle of this clearing a circle had been marked out with bamboo stakes. Each team had three practice rockets; the object was to get all three into the circle. Pay Dang and the three company commanders were the judges.

The two-man teams had to come sprinting from the jungle, fall, set up, and fire. They had one minute from the time they hit the ground to get off their three rounds.

Arklin, watching from the shade at the jungle's edge, did not really care who won, or how good the shooting was for that matter. They would be firing white-phosphorus rounds during the actual attack and it would be an area target, not a point target. But the excitement of the contest was contagious so that every man in the village was looking forward to being part of the carefully planned attack.

The first two-man team dashed out of the jungle, hit the ground, and one Meo tribesman held the launcher across his shoulder and aimed while the other pulled a nine-pound rocket out of the pouch he was carrying and fed it into the breech, instantly throwing himself out of the way. The gunner fired. Flame shot out the back of the tube and all eyes watched the circle in the field below. A few seconds later the practice rocket hit with a dull explosion and puff of smoke outside the circle. Even as the crowd laughed and jeered the second rocket was being fed and this time the rocket, when it hit, tore down a few of the bamboo poles marking the edge of the target. The third round, after the gunner had taken a little more time to aim, fell inside the circle. The three shots were off in less than a minute.

As the contest continued, generating huge excitement and much wagering, Arklin slipped away from the cheering Meos and for the next two hours personally checked out the guards posted about the village. As he suspected, they were trying to get close enough to watch the competition, and he had to order them back to their positions.

The sun had reached its zenith and was starting its descent when the Meo village population left the scene of the rocket-launching contest for the party. The drinking party, Arklin realized, was of the utmost necessity to the success of any venture involving montagnard participation. However, he had compromised by making it an afternoon and evening party, all liquor to be shut off at 9:00. The next day they would be starting out for the Pathet camp.

By mid-afternoon all but the guards had shed their camouflage uniforms and were attired in loin cloths, drinking and eating heartily of sacrificed buffalo and pig. The funeral and the dead were almost forgotten in the anticipation of the new adventure.

Arklin, in line with his established policy of being one with the Meo, had also shucked his fatigues and was wearing a Meo loincloth. His skin had been burned almost as dark as theirs and only the graying stubble of beard on his chin outwardly identified him as Caucasian. Gingerly he sipped a gourd of the biting, odoriferous native liquor through a bamboo straw. He was constantly on the alert, checking that the guards inside the village were ready for trouble at any moment.

All at once Arklin became aware of a distant chuffing in the air and suddenly realized that a helicopter was in the area. This was fantastic; with a Pathet Lao buildup forming only fifteen miles away it seemed incredible that a U.S. helicopter would be flying over. The Laotians had no choppers or pilots, and he had never heard of North Vietnam using them.

He shouted loudly, halting the reedy music and drums and chatter. There was quiet as he pointed skyward. The Meos listened and first heard and then saw the helicopter, which seemed to be settling toward the camp.

The Agency always seemed to know what it was doing, Arklin thought, and control had requested a chopper pad. Closely followed by Nanette, he picked up a smoke grenade from one of the little storage cribs on stilts near the cleared helicopter Landing Zone and watched as the chopper settled lower in the sky. To his surprise, Arklin saw the markings of U.S. Army Aviation. He pulled the pin on the grenade and tossed it into the center of the Landing Zone. It blossomed yellow smoke and immediately the helicopter slid in toward them.

The Meos ringed the Landing Zone, staring at the first helicopter many of them had ever seen. It hovered directly over the village and then descended into the Landing Zone. The helicopter's downdraft intensified as the chopper slowed its descent and a wild, swirling dust storm scattered the Meos. Arklin grabbed Nanette and turned her back to the blast until the chopper was on the ground.

From under the turbine-driven rotors, spinning themselves out with the power turned off, emerged a sergeant carrying an M-14 rifle. Behind him, dressed in the crisply starched fatigues Arklin had not seen in almost a year, came a full colonel, silver eagle resplendent on his block cap. The embroidered nametape on his bright breast proclaimed his name to be Williston. The colonel looked about impatiently as though expecting to be met by someone who wasn't there.

Arklin, suddenly and painfully conscious of his dirty body, matted hair and loin cloth, walked forward to meet the colonel. He saluted. "Sir, I am Major Arklin, assigned to training and advising the Meo tribesmen in this area."

The colonel looked at Arklin incredulously. Twice he started to say something and thought better of it. Finally, he merely returned the salute. Nanette, standing behind Arklin, regarded the newcomers with mixed fear and curiosity. The sergeant, shifting his rifle, gave Nanette a lewd grin as he stared at her bare, upturned breasts.

Slowly the Meos who had fled the blasts from the rotor blades returned to stare at the helicopter. Many of the inner-security guards, weapons at the ready, had surrounded the machine, watching Arklin for any signs that this might be a hostile craft. Still the colonel could find no words to say as he stared at the strange assemblage surrounding him. Arklin, who noticed the colonel and sergeant were wearing the shoulder patch of Military Assistance Command, finally broke the strained silence. "We are not too secure around here from groundfire, sir."

"You don't look very secure from anything around here," the colonel retorted. "What kind of a show are you running up on this mountain, Major?"

"I'm on detached service from Special Forces to the Agency, sir."

The colonel looked him up and down. Arklin noticed the colonel did not wear jump wings above his left breast pocket; a MAC straight leg, he said to himself. The colonel finally seemed to remember something, for he snapped out, "I'm Colonel Williston, Military Assistance Command. We're taking over direct control of Special Forces operations and a number of the Combined Studies Group projects—this one included."

"My control hasn't informed me of that yet, sir."

"I'm just looking things over today. It will be another week or two, maybe longer, before we actually take over some of these operations in Laos."

"As I mentioned, sir, this place is a little dangerous right now. We're surrounded by Pathet Lao and Viet Minh. Your helicopter just lets them know for sure we're planning an operation against them.''

The slight admonishment angered Williston. ''Major, it looks to me as though you would be in serious trouble if so much as a squad of Communists probed you.'' He walked up close to Arklin and then stopped, wrinkling his nose. ''It appears to me that you're running some kind of a drinking party here, Major. I never thought it was possible that I would see an officer, much less a field-grade officer, in such deplorable condition.''

''This isn't the usual-type military operation, sir. I'm trying to make these Meo tribesmen do a job for us. They are the only fighting men you can count on in Laos. But you have to handle them differently than a regular military unit.''

''But this,'' the colonel spread his arms and looked around, ''this is appalling, Major. Drinking in the middle of the afternoon. You, Major, drinking with them. And I suppose that,'' he pointed at Nanette, ''is your woman. I'm sure CIA couldn't know how you run things. Or more likely they do. This is the Agency's idea of a tight little clandestine operation.'' The colonel laughed mirthlessly. ''It appears to me that we should have taken over these operations much sooner. We've found the same problems in Vietnam. You Special Forces people always go native or something.''

''Sir,'' Arklin began, reining his temper, ''I think we proved our effectiveness yesterday morning. We ambushed more than a company of Pathet Lao and Viet Minh massing for an attack on the Plain of Jars, and killed or wounded at least two-thirds of them.''

''I heard about that, Major. You pulled that one off without telling anyone. There may be serious international complications. The ambassador is still trying to convince the coalition government in Vientiane that the U.S. is not involved.''

''I radioed my control, sir. I had standing orders from the Agency to hit the Communists at will.''

''But we're still trying to negotiate with them,'' Williston protested.

''The more cut-up they are the easier they'll be to negotiate with.''

''We should have been notified of the attack, Arklin,'' Williston said, trying to hold his voice level. ''That's why we are taking over all these covert little operations that are acting so independently.''

"Sir, the only way to fight the Communists out here in the jungle is the way we're doing it now.''

"Can't you at least look like an officer?'' was Williston's reply.

"I'm sorry I don't look like an officer, sir. I don't enjoy it out here. My job is to live with these people as one of them. When three well-trained rifle companies are suddenly needed to stop the Communists who aren't supposed to be here, my Meo tribesmen are ready.''

"I didn't come out here to argue with you, Major. I came after facts.'' Williston stared at Arklin with unconcealed distaste. "My God, and you are on the lieutenant colonels list.'' He shook his head. "Within the month I'll be writing your efficiency report.''

Arklin felt his heart sink. He knew how much chance he had now of ever making lieutenant colonel. All that he had looked forward to after this assignment was lost. The sad and ironic thing was that Arklin wanted to be just what Colonel Williston expected of him—but the colonel didn't understand living alone with the montagnards.

The Meos had gradually slipped away from the major and his visitor and were drinking again and munching on roasted buffalo. "Major, I should relieve you on the spot. This whole camp is a disgrace. Why aren't your men, to say nothing of yourself, dressed in fatigues?''

"You will notice, sir, that all the men on duty, one full company, are wearing their tiger suits.''

The colonel looked about, noted the ring of armed, correctly attired guards surrounding them and said nothing. Then, "And you, Major?''

"The men have just finished a firing contest on the range. We are having a little celebration before an operation tomorrow. The men who will be doing the hardest fighting are relaxing in loincloths. It makes them feel I am one of them, since I will be leading them tomorrow, if I appear to relax with them.''

"You're leading an attack tomorrow?'' Williston cried. "Under whose orders have you taken this upon yourself?''

"I'm still under the Agency, sir.'' His stomach knotted as he added, "Unless you have orders for me to the contrary.''

"I don't have them with me, Arklin. But they'll soon be cut."

Arklin breathed a sigh of relief. "Well, sir, in that case I'll follow my orders from the Agency which are to harass the Communists as I see fit and slow them up as they try to cut Laos in two."

"I can't leave you here, Arklin," the colonel said suddenly, decisively. "I believe you are dangerous to the objectives of the Military Assistance Command. I am relieving you now. Go get your gear, get out of those filthy native rags, put on your fatigues, and we'll fly out of here together. I'll send in an officer to manage these tribesmen tomorrow."

Arklin, dressed in his loin cloth, stared levelly at the elegantly combat-garbed Colonel Williston and watched his career and future shatter. Perhaps the colonel sensed Arklin's thoughts, for he said patronizingly, "The Agency shouldn't do to a man what it's done to you, Major. You come with me now. A week or two among your own people, clean new uniforms, decent eating and living conditions and you'll be ready for a real command. You come with me now and I give you my word I will do nothing that might cause you to be passed over for promotion."

Arklin believed Colonel Williston. He could still save his career. And he knew his chances of getting killed or wounded the next day were high. The colonel went on talking soothingly and Arklin began to wonder if perhaps he really had gone native and slightly mad. He looked down at himself. He was dark-skinned and filthy. From the rear, he knew he looked nude, the loincloth disappearing as it did in the fold between the buttocks. Nanette was staring at him anxiously. She couldn't understand what was being said, but instinctively she knew she was close to losing her man. It had to come some day; but not now, she fervently hoped. Pay Dang was also watching the Americans in alarm. The guards in their fatigues and the celebrants in loincloths began to press in close to the colonel and their major.

Arklin glanced around the circle of primitive though familiar faces. He fought off the feeling of unreality, of being unrelated to this aboriginal environment, which had assailed him as the cool, clean brisk colonel talked. Once again he was Major Arklin of the Meo people. He was proud of his tribesmen and what he had accomplished with them. He would stay. He knew that it was more important to him to do his job right here than to allow himself to be relieved and thus save his career.

"Colonel Williston, perhaps you weren't properly briefed on what we are doing here. I have to stay with the Meo people at least a few weeks longer. By that time, either real power will be thrown in here or Laos will be one more country lost to the free world. My job is to buy time and I'm staying here and doing it."

The colonel looked to his sergeant with the rifle; there was another armed man in the helicopter. Major Arklin saw what the colonel was thinking. "I will not be relieved, sir. My Meos will prevent it."

Sensing the situation, Pay Dang and the Meo guards shifted their weapons so they pointed at the helicopter and the armed sergeant. They pushed in closer around their American leader. Colonel Williston turned abruptly on his heel and headed for the helicopter. Just before boarding, he looked at Arklin. "You'd better get ready to leave here, Major, because this is going all the way up to the commanding general."

"I'm not leaving until my job is done, sir. And in a few days when the Pathet Lao start rolling over Laos, a few generals should be damned glad I'm here."

"You'll be through in a week and court-martialed. That's a promise, Major."

"Colonel, if that's so I guess I'm in the wrong Army, run by the wrong people, and I'll be just as well out."

Colonel Williston whirled away from Major Arklin and the pilot was already starting up the powerful turbines as the colonel strapped himself into his seat. Arklin watched the base of the rotor blades catch the blast of the turbines and start whirling. The Meo tribesmen ran from the downblast and the helicopter took off.

The Meos seemed to realize that a crisis had occurred in Arklin's life. They knew he had in some way taken their side against his own people, and they sensed that the angry man who went away in the helicopter was going to try and do their major some harm.

Pay Dang's solution was to hand Arklin a fresh gourd of raw liquor, which he took and drank down. Nanette came to him, smiling apprehensively, and Arklin dropped his arm over her shoulder, pulling her to him tightly in a way he

213

never had done before in sight of the Meos. They cheered him and the party started up again, the drums knocking and the stringed instruments and reedy flutes adding to the din of revelry.

Arklin pointed to his wrist watch. "Remember, we all stop at 9:00, Pay Dang."

5.

Early the next morning, as he expected, Arklin received a message from control. It was terse and heartwarming. "Keep hitting Pathet. Agency with you. Try capture Chicom."

With this signal Arklin felt as though he and his Meos could lick the entire Communist Army. His two scouts returned on schedule. They reported enemy strength as a battalion of about 500 men. The scouts had seen many Viet Minh and also some Chinese. In the dirt they drew a diagram of the Communist camp and the area where the Chinese and Viet Minh officers were living in hastily constructed bamboo houses. The Pathet Lao troops were all living in the open. Arklin told his scouts to sleep all day and be ready to go out before dark.

The remainder of the day Arklin spent drilling his Meos in tactics, actually rehearsing the movements they would employ in the pre-dawn raid the next morning. With bamboo sticks he built a model of the Communist camp from the diagrams and descriptions his scouts had given him so that his men would know the camp's layout perfectly.

Late the next afternoon Arklin's operation was underway. Earlier he had sent one platoon to secure the airstrip. He left an entire company to guard the camp, ordering the company commander to maintain a 50 per cent alert at all times.

Just before leaving camp he had tapped out a radio message to control telling him to have a U-10 at the airstrip as soon as there was enough light to land.

The Pathet Lao buildup was ten miles southwest of the airstrip; Arklin and his men would take a fairly direct trail through the jungle from the airstrip to the Communist camp. Leading a company plus two platoons and the four bazooka teams, each team augmented by a third man to help carry the

214

nine-pound rocket projectiles, he reached the airstrip before dark. There he conducted a quick inspection of the security, and then with Pay Dang beside him moved back into the jungle and started down the trail to the Communist camp.

The Meo company had the job of securing the route all the way from the airstrip to the Communist camp. Because of the necessity for close timing and speed on the return from the operation, the raiders would follow the same route both ways. As they headed down the trail in the darkness, Pay Dang and the Meo company commander dropped off men at intervals along the way. By the time they established a command post less than a mile from the Pathet Lao camp, an entire company of Meos was strung out along both sides of the trail all the way back to the airstrip. Arklin realized this was very thin security; still the Communists would be unable to ambush the trail without running into his flankers, and the ensuing fire-fight would warn him to take the more arduous alternate route back to the airstrip, cutting through the jungle and keeping off trails.

The two scouts who had remained at the Pathet Lao camp met Pay Dang, Arklin, the two platoons, and the bazooka teams at the Command Post. They reported that the Chinese and Viet Minh officers were still living in the bamboo long-house close to the east perimeter of the camp and that more Pathet Lao troops were coming into the camp all the time.

It was after midnight when Pay Dang and Arklin stationed the four rocket-launcher teams about 250 yards from the north perimeter of the Communist camp. One man on each team had a watch, and Arklin gave orders for them to commence firing at 0230. Leaving the bazooka men, Arklin and the Meos stealthily made their way around the Communist camp, being careful to stay beyond the Communist listening posts. It required almost two hours for them to crawl through the jungle to the positions they took up opposite the east perimeter.

The Communists were making no attempt to maintain noise or light discipline. Cooking fires burned all through the camp, which Arklin now estimated to be about one hundred yards square. When the Meo scouts told him they were exactly opposite the bamboo house of the Communist officers, Arklin hand-signaled a halt.

They rested in the dark jungle for half an hour, and at 0215 crept toward the edge of the camp. The perimeters of the

215

temporary camp were not clearly marked; there was no barbed wire, just a bamboo-stake fence more designed to keep the troops from wandering away from their officers than to prevent outsiders from penetrating. Ahead of Arklin's men the special-action squad slithered through the jungle. It would be their job to silently kill the sentries. Arklin wanted to get as close to camp as possible before the firing started. The raiding party suddenly halted as a guard, walking in haphazard fashion, wandered in their direction. They could clearly see him outlined in the faint glow from the bamboo longhouse. Suddenly the dark shadow that was the sentry seemed to loom larger—and then it disappeared completely. Arklin and his men started moving forward again. They came to the body of the sentry, its throat a bloody grin. Arklin and his men halted. Pay Dang would lead the actual assault on the officers' quarters and capture the Chinese Communists.

Arklin looked at his watch. It was 0227. He waited silently with his security squad as Pay Dang and the rest of the Meos crept almost into camp. Suddenly the whoosh of rockets roared from the north. The rockets exploded in the middle of the camp, lighting it up with the fiery white phosphorus. Confusion, screams of the burned, and aimless firing broke out throughout the Communist compound. Arklin and his squad with automatic rifles at the ready watched as Pay Dang and his men rushed to the bamboo longhouse and surrounded it. Four more rockets whammed into the camp, this time high-explosive rounds. In the densely occupied buildup area men were killed and wounded; terrified and shrieking Communists ran helplessly around in the flames. From the doors at both ends of the officers' quarters Communists desperately pulling on clothing and pistol belts emerged to rally their men. Coolly the Meos cut them down with automatic weapons. Pay Dang, holding his automatic carbine in front of him, rushed inside the longhouse followed closely by a squad. Another squad entered from the other side. Within moments the house was in flames from thermite grenades the Meos carried for the purpose.

Another salvo of rockets tore through the camp, like the others carefully aimed to avoid coming too close to the longhouse. Some Communist leaders succeeded in rallying demoralized troops and charged out of the camp to the north toward the rocket launchers. In the light of the blazing bamboo officers' quarters Arklin saw Pay Dang and his men emerge, dragging and beating two men in unfamiliar uniforms.

Arklin pulled a tin box out of his pocket. In moments Pay Dang and his triumphant Meos reached Arklin and thrust two badly mauled, unmistakably Chinese prisoners at him. Arklin plunged a thick-needled syringe into one Chinese Communist's bare arm and jammed the plunger down. The prisoner let out a scream that was stifled by the barrel of a rifle slapped across the side of his head. In seconds the other Chinese prisoner was subdued and also injected with heavy sedative. Already the Meos were tying the Chinese Communists by wrists and ankles to the heavy staffs they had cut, and as another volley of rocket fire shook the camp the Meos hefted the poles to their shoulders and set off with the limp prisoners into the jungle.

Arklin and Pay Dang followed, heading for the rallying point. There they would form and proceed along their secured trail back to the airstrip.

Communists were running about the edges of their half-destroyed camp, firing indiscriminately into the woods. A few of the officers who hadn't been killed by the Meos had managed to get groups of unwounded men to follow them into the jungle.

Arklin knew that they were a long way from safety. There must be well over 600 men in the camp, and it wouldn't take the hard-core Viet Minh officers and troops long to organize a pursuit. The Meo's hope was that the Communists wouldn't find their trail and come after them. Even though the flank security company would ambush a few of them, a determined pursuit by the Communists might catch the Meos. It was a chance Arklin had to take.

The ultimate success of the mission still depended upon the rocket-launcher teams. Arklin tried to picture their actions as he pushed through the jungle.

They would have dug pits and carefully camouflaged them. Then after they had fired four rockets each, they were to have hidden their rocket launchers and the remainder of their rockets in the pits. By now the bazooka teams would be scattered and hiding in the jungle as the Communists set out in pursuit. If they carried out the final stage of their mission, Arklin felt sure the main assault force, which had suffered no casualties yet, would safely make it to the airstrip with their two Chinese prisoners.

At the rallying point, a small clearing secured by three men with submachine guns, Arklin and Pay Dang allowed the minimum amount of time to regroup and then started off again. The men carrying the inert Chinese on the poles were relieved every five minutes in order to make maximum speed along the trail. The prisoners were carried in the center of the two platoons and Arklin walked right beside them.

They began passing their security stations. The men guarding the trail stayed in position after the column passed through. They would wait one hour to provide security for the rocket-launcher teams and then, proceeding up the trail, form a rear guard.

Sporadic shooting and shouting still could be heard in the jungle behind them. As they reached the trail the firing sounded closer and then the Meos heard unmistakable signs of pursuit. Once they were spotted, Arklin knew, half the camp would be after them.

He looked at the luminous-dial watch. It was 0300. By this time the Pathet Lao should have passed beyond the bazooka-men's hiding places, and the four teams should be climbing down from trees or digging themselves out of jungle bush and creeping back to their hidden weapons. Quietly and carefully, they would be pulling the cover from the pits and taking out the rocket launchers and rockets preparatory to firing another four salvos each.

The noise and shooting was getting closer, as the Meos hurried up the trail. Arklin dropped back to organize the rear-guard defense. There was no deviating from the trail now. They would have to make it to the airstrip on this route.

Suddenly the noise he had been straining to hear exploded from the jungle: the sounds of rockets being fired, followed by thundering blasts. Arklin cheered to himself. The Meo bazookamen had gone back to their weapons. The noise of the Communist pursuers lessened as they abandoned the chase and fought through the jungle to get back to their camp, which seemed to be under direct attack anew. About twenty seconds after the first salvo hit, the resounding blast of four more high-explosive rockets shook the air; twenty seconds later yet another thundering explosion rumbled through the jungle.

Arklin found himself mentally calling to the Meo men to get out while they could; they had done their job well. The diversion had succeeded. Pursuit had ceased.

Arklin's heart fell, his stomach tightened as he heard a sudden resurgence of firing in the jungle behind them. Had the Pathet found the Meos? The sharp rattle of small-arms fire kept up for several minutes. All three men on the rocket-launcher teams carried carbines, and it sounded to Arklin as though they were being forced to use them. He stayed at the rear of the column, hoping that as planned some of the bazookamen would catch up with them.

An hour up the trail Arklin began to give up hope. The security guard would already be forming behind them. If the brave Meo rocket-launcher teams weren't on the path now, they never would be. Arklin would have walked back, but his duty was to stay with the Chinese Communists until they were turned over to control.

The Meo were making record time up the trail. With the knowledge that their mission had been successful and that they had killed many Pathet Lao, the tribesmen strode along smartly. Even the men carrying the Chinese Communists were stepping out, to be relieved of their groaning, mumbling burdens before they could tire.

Pale false dawn was showing in the sky to the east when the forward platoon was challenged by the security guard at the airstrip. By the time the entire Meo contingent was gathered around the strip the sky was brightening. To Arklin's joy, three of the rocket teams had emerged unscathed after a jungle skirmish with the Pathet. One member of the fourth team was missing, and two wounded were carried along the trail. The security guards had saved them by waiting longer than the allotted hour. They had been at their positions when the two wounded Meos managed to stagger and stumble their way to the trail.

Just as the sun rose beyond the mountains, the distant purring of an airplane could be heard, and soon two small planes came into sight out of the west. Arklin pulled the pin on a yellow smoke grenade and the planes headed directly for the strip. First one, then the other gray and unmarked U-10 landed and braked to a stop. Frank Methuan jumped out of the first plane and strode across to Arklin, grasping his hand warmly and patting him on the back.

"You're slowing them down for us, Bernie," he cried happily. "The Communists are getting ready to hit poor old Kong Le and the other government battalions. The government troops are deserting in platoons."

Methuan looked around the airstrip and then back at Arklin. "Guess you couldn't snatch a Chicom for us, eh? We wanted one for propaganda. It would square whatever action we take if we could prove the gooks are here."

Arklin laughed. "Two Chicoms coming up." He yelled for Pay Dang, and the montagnard leader proudly led his men forward bearing the two Chinese Communists dangling from poles.

Methuan whistled. "Good work, Bernie." Then anxiously, "They're going to live, aren't they?"

"Sure. I knocked them out with Nembutol. They should be waking up about the time you get them back to base."

"Outstanding!"

"Thank Pay Dang and his Meos. They did the job, and incidentally they inflicted heavy damage on the Communist buildup. Pay Dang's boys killed a lot of the Viet Minh and Pathet officers when they picked up these two specimens. Where do you want them?"

"Put them in the other plane. I've got a guard in it."

"Any more orders?"

"Yeah. You get in this plane with me. You've done more than your job."

"But I just can't desert these people, Frank," Arklin protested.

"Tell them we'll get them evacuated by chopper and plane."

Arklin could barely conceal his anguish at the orders. "But they need me still."

"Bernie, there's a regiment of Pathet around this mountain. You've done your job. We don't want to lose you now. If the Commies get you they'll do very nasty things to you, boy."

"But my people couldn't organize themselves for evacuation. I've got to help them."

"Look—orders, chum."

"You could change them, Frank. I want to see these people safely out of here. We owe it to them. They've been magnificent."

220

"I promise you, we'll get them out before their village is overrun. And that could be pretty damned soon, now."

"Frank, we let them down once, remember. We just pulled out, took back the weapons and they were at the mercy of the Communists. If I desert them now they'll never trust us again. And they'll be hurt and lost. Please, Frank, try and understand. I couldn't live with myself if I didn't personally see them safely out of here. If we're attacked today they'll need me."

The CIA man regarded Arklin with a long, steady gaze. "You really are one of them, just like that old shit-kicker Williston said."

"Yeah. I guess my career is shot. At least let me finish this job. After that—what the hell. At least I'll be able to look myself in the eye."

"OK, Bernie," his control said decisively. "If that's what you want. We'll do our best to get you out. And by the way, don't worry about your career. After Williston blew his top about you some very influential people in the Agency decided he should be transferred to a desk down in the bowels of the Pentagon until his retirement. MAC is fighting it, of course. But don't you worry about your career. Oh, incidentally, I brought you something. I suspected you might not want to come right home like a good boy." He dug into the pocket of his coveralls and brought out a small cardboard box which he handed to Arklin.

"Congratulations, colonel, your silver leaves are in there."

Arklin looked down at the box and then gave Methuan a misty smile of thanks. "Frank, tell them I'll be on the last trip after you've taken my Meos and their dependents out of here."

The semi-conscious Chinese were dumped unceremoniously into the back of the second U-10 and it immediately took off. Methuan and Arklin shook hands.

"We can hold out for a while. The Pathet will have to send two battalions after us. They'll have to hit us before they can move on. Should give Kong Le and the government a few more days."

"We'll get everyone out, Bernie." Methuan grinned. "Williston said you were living with a naked montagnard girl. What are you going to do about her?"

Arklin's face fell. "That's one of the little tragedies in this kind of war. Nanette and I, we'll just have to say good-bye. She had a lot to do with my success on this job."

Methuan nodded and stepped into the plane. "You've got four or five days to say good-bye to her. See you in Vientiane—that's where we'll be taking you all."

He closed the door and the engine turned over, caught, and the propeller started whirling. Arklin stepped back and watched the U-10 turn into the wind and take off.

Arklin watched until the roar of the plane's engine had faded over the horizon. Then he said, "Let's go, Pay Dang. We've still got a lot of fighting ahead of us." He grinned at his montagnard friend. "Besides, Ha Ban must be wondering where we are."

7

FOURTEEN
VIET CONG POW'S

The hardest thing to do in Vietnam is to get yourself transported from one place to another. Almost always the last fifty miles are the hardest. It wasn't too hard to hop a milk run for Da Nang about four hundred miles north of Saigon, but I had to wait two and a half days for a flight across the fifty miles of mountainous jungle to the Special Forces camp at Lua Vuc.

The layover at the Special Forces B team in Da Nang was most interesting, thanks to Lieutenant Colonel Tex Quentin. A lean, white-haired veteran civic affairs administrator, Colonel Tex, as he was known to everyone, was in charge of the Special Forces civic action programs in I Corps.

Colonel Tex introduced me to Dr. Portland Francis, a medical missionary active in this part of Vietnam since his graduation from medical school ten years earlier. Special Forces had contributed engineering talent, materials and funds to help Dr. Francis and his mission build a leprosarium and an orphanage. When he heard I was heading out to Lua Vuc, Dr. Francis gave me a full briefing on the montagnard problems in this part of Vietnam, whose largest single tribe was the Bru.

Great animosity exists between the Vietnamese who inhabit the lowlands and the mountain tribesmen, he told me. The Vietnamese consider the montagnards a low and despised social order, calling them "mois," which means dirty savage. According to legend the mountain tribesmen once owned all of what is now central Vietnam, with their capital at the coastal city of Nha Trang. The beginning of the end came for the tribesmen when their king fell in love with and married a princess from the southern flatlands. She plotted his murder, and the now-leaderless montagnards were driven back into the mountains by the lowlanders and contained there ever since. The montagnards have never forgiven the Vietnamese for this incursion.

Doctor Francis and his mission were training Vietnamese missionaries to carry the Gospel to the mountain people. Because they were Vietnamese these missionaries had been able to make some progress toward mediating the disputes between montagnards and Vietnamese. But, Doctor Francis warned, I would still see many tragic examples of this unreasoning hatred. He looked at Colonel Tex to see if he had spoken out of turn.

"He'll find out for himself, anyway," the civic action officer said. "Wait till he sees the Vietnamese Air Force bomb a non-government-controlled montagnard hamlet."

"You can't mean that!" I exclaimed.

"I'm afraid I do. They've got a perfect excuse—if a montagnard refuses to live in a government-built and -patrolled village he must be Viet Cong."

"So why don't they stay in the government hamlets?" I asked. "The ones I've seen are well supplied and even offer good medical aid."

"They hate the regimentation of the Vietnamese who despise them; and besides, the ARVN troops aren't much protection against the Viet Cong. The Communists come in after dark, when the Vietnamese hate to fight, and kidnap the most intelligent montagnard leaders and send them north to be brainwashed. And what pitifully few supplies the tribesmen get from the government, USOM, and Americans like the Special Forces, are taken away by the VC."

"No matter what the poor tribesmen do, they lose," Doctor Francis said sadly. "The VC terrorize them because they're in government hamlets and not out helping the Communists. If they try to escape from both the Vietnamese and the VC and build villages on their own, the Air Force bombs them."

"Just because they're unsanctioned by the government?" I asked in disbelief.

"Ostensibly yes," Colonel Tex said. "All pilots returning

from missions with unexpended ordnance have standing orders from Vietnamese high command to pick non-government montagnard villages as targets of opportunity. And feeling the way they do about the mois, they go to it whenever they get the chance. Yes, I'm afraid you will be coming across a lot of newly made Communist montagnards out around Lua Vuc.''

"I understand you have missionaries out there with the tribes," I said. "They must be some help counteracting communism."

"They were." Doctor Francis shook his head. "But I had to call them back after the Taggerts' home was bombed by the Viet Cong. Reverend Taggert, his wife, and small daughter lived with the Bru people for almost two years. They did fine work bringing God to the tribesmen and keeping the Bru from Communist influence. Now, three months later, the Taggerts are still hospitalized back in the States."

I was taken to the leprosarium and the orphanage the missionary had built with the help of Special Forces engineering talent and, of course, funds. It was here I learned the shocking fact—to an American, at least—that what amounts to virtual child slavery was not uncommon in Vietnam. A Vietnamese or montagnard child who lost or became separated from his parents had no problem finding a new home. Many a foster parent would bind the child into a long period of near-slavery, even going so far as selling him to other parents for labor. As a result, the pleasant, airy orphan asylum on its beautiful beach was a source of particular pride to Doctor Francis and the Special Forces—many of whom chipped in for its upkeep out of their own monthly paychecks.

The constructive work of the missionaries and Special Forces civic action teams was a happy revelation in this war of unrelieved misery. I tried to see as much of it as possible before Colonel Tex saw me off for Lua Vuc on the workhorse Marine helicopter. It was loaded with supplies and personnel for several of the remote outposts and accompanied by two equally burdened H34's and two armed HU21b choppers flying escort.

In spite of the gun ships flying above us, three Viet Cong bullets tore through the chopper as it settled into the pad at Lua Vuc. I alternately sat on my flak jacket and wrapped the armored vest about me, trying to decide which way would give me the most protection.

Captain Vic Locke, in his third year of jungle warfare, was the American Commanding Officer at Lua Vuc. Locke had a formidable reputation as a Special Forces captain; he had no qualms when it came to getting an assignment accomplished. More than once he had boldly crossed the border into Laos to kill or capture a Viet Cong leader comfortably camped in privileged sanctuary.

Captain Locke and two of his sergeants were at the landing zone to meet the chopper. All during the time the green-bereted enlisted men unloaded their supplies, Locke was having an obviously heated argument with the pilot, who just as determinedly kept shaking his head. The moment the last of the supplies had been unloaded, the pilot shot the chopper into the air, the gun ships practically on the deck to discourage any more Viet Cong small-arms fire.

Captain Locke, wearing the thin montagnard brass bracelet on his left wrist that showed he'd been made an honorary tribesman, led me to the truck he had driven out to meet the flight. A squad of stumpy montagnards had just finished loading it. We all piled in and drove back to the camp. The montagnards kept their weapons at the ready, pointed out of the truck in all directions.

"Do the VC get in this close to the camp?" I asked.

"You never know where they are in this kind of territory," Locke answered. "They sneak up and plant a mine in this road once in a while."

The floor of the truck was heavily sandbagged. More than a few Special Forces men had saved their legs, if not their lives, by having their feet squarely over the sandbags when their truck hit a Communist mine.

The camp was a triangle of sandbags and mud walls, surrounded by barbed wire. At each of the three points was a large, high bunker. Several smaller machine-gun bunkers were built up along each of the walls.

The montagnard guards at the gate saluted and let us by the barricades. We pulled up in front of the teamhouse and Locke suggested we go in for some chow. Locke's Executive Officer, Lieutenant Grannum, stood when we walked in.

"Hey, Chopsticks!" he yelled toward the kitchen. "Bring the captain and his guest some chow. Hot goddamned chow," he added.

Grinning and bowing, the Chinese cook shuffled into the teamroom. "OK! OK! Chopstick bling. On dlubble!" The cook's eyes crinkled, apparently with pure joy at dispensing more of his food.

Locke watched him go. "We got to keep on old Chops' ass. He gets lazy and makes his girl, Tillie, do all the work. He's owned her for ten years."

A broad-faced, smiling girl, who looked to be a mixture of every ethnic culture that had ever passed through Vietnam, walked in gracefully and put a steaming bowl of rice and meat in front of us.

"She's nice, she's round, and she's all Chops'," one of the sergeants said and whistled. Tillie beamed at him, switched her long black hair and walked back to the kitchen.

"Where's the tea?" another sergeant roared.

"Tea come. Joe bring in tea," Chopsticks cried, and a short, incredibly walleyed little montagnard, dressed in a cutdown camouflage uniform, came in with the pitcher of iced tea. His wide smile looked as though it had been sewed on at birth. Turning his head sideways so he could keep one eye focused on where he was going, Joe filled all the glasses.

"Looks like Joe's got the ass," Locke remarked. "Chops must be making him do too much work. Joe doesn't speak much English. Watch: Hey, Joe, you a leg?"

Joe contorted with laughter at the old joke. "Joe no leg. Chopstick fucking leg." Everybody laughed, except a young, very preoccupied sergeant who hadn't said a word since we came in.

Locke's smile faded. "Sergeant Binney's our chief medic." He stood up and went over to the man.

"Still nothing you can do?"

"No, sir. You've got to get her to the hospital in Da Nang or she'll die. I can't mess with the thing. Manelli is with her now."

"Come on," Locke said to me, "might as well have a look at the kind of problems we have."

I followed Locke across the mud parade square and into another building. "This is our dispensary and field hospital," he explained.

To the right as we walked in was the pharmacy in which two LLDB medics were working. To the left was a waiting room, and seated on benches were a number of montagnard women, most of them holding babies. A dozen or so men in camouflage fatigues also were waiting to see a medic.

We walked in past examining rooms, through a ward in which a dozen men were lying, many in casts with arms or legs raised ceilingwards.

"Those are some of the casualties from our most recent patrol. We got hit hard by a company of VC that rushed us from across the border in Laos."

The last room was a small ward for female dependents of the strike force. An American sergeant was tending to an emaciated, feverish montagnard woman, who lay moaning on a cot, covered up to her shoulders with a white sheet. Her skin was yellowish and stretched tight over her face bones, the eyes deeply sunken in her head.

"No good, eh Manelli?" Locke asked.

The medic shook his head. "No, sir. You can't get her back to Da Nang?"

"No luck yet. Sorry." The captain leaned over the woman, who looked up at him with glazed eyes.

Locke took me aside. "Her baby died yesterday morning while she was giving birth. For some damned reason—maybe she's too small—it got stuck in some manner, and the medics don't have the facilities to get it free without risking an infection they can't take care of here. I've been trying to get a medical evacuation for her, but the Vietnamese Air Force have a rule in this corps area against evacuating civilians. Of course, she's a montagnard, and that makes it even worse, the way the Viets and the Brus get along. Her husband is in the strike force and knows she could be saved by a med evac. How are we supposed to win over these people for this government when its representatives treat them this way?"

"You couldn't have put her on the chopper that brought me in?"

"That's what I was arguing with the pilot about. But he had a tough schedule ahead of him, and besides, he didn't want to get his group's ass in a sling with their Vietnamese counterparts." Locke stared at the mortally suffering mother. "Some war. Is it like this all over Vietnam?"

"One way or another."

"I have a wife and three children on Okinawa," Locke

said. "I don't think this woman means any less to her Bru husband than my wife does to me. I know how I'd feel if the country I was fighting for wouldn't help my wife."

"How about the Vietnamese Special Forces camp commander? Can't he do something through Vietnamese channels?"

"Captain Nim?" Locke hooted. "He told me he'd be put in jail if he so much as *requested* evacuation for a sick montagnard civilian. I know he believes it. Of course, any time we pick up Viet Cong prisoners the Vietnam Air Force will get choppers out here practically on an emergency basis. They rush the POW's to Da Nang so that Vietnamese Intelligence can torture them—for information and recreation, as we say." Locke laughed bitterly. "But this poor woman—you'd never know it, she's only nineteen."

I let out a surprised gasp. "She must be thirty-five or forty!"

"You should see what she's been through the last couple of days. Come on, let's get out of here. I've got a man trying to locate a sampan to take her by river from here to Da Nang. I don't think she has much chance of living through the two-day boat trip, but it's better than letting her die here."

Outside the infirmary Locke led me back across the parade ground and into his operations room. A map covered with camouflage cloth dominated one wall. In red letters on the cloth was written KIN, the Vietnamese word for secret.

"OK," Locke said, "I'll give you a rundown on the situation and what we hope to accomplish on the patrol going out tomorrow." He pulled the cover cloth off the map and pointed to a red square. "Here's Lua Vuc, as you can see, only about five thousand meters from the Laos border."

His finger ran south from Lua Vuc about fifteen kilometers to a point that looked to be almost in Laos. "Here, there's a village with perhaps two hundred Bru men, women, and children. The VC are exploiting them, making them farm and work for them. Our Intelligence indicates that the Communists are planning to take the men across the border, train them, and send them back to attack this camp, along with a VC hard-core battalion.

"Our mission is to get down there, surround the village, and bring those montagnards back here. Later we'll help the Brus build their own village and give them pigs and supplies.

That way we get more Bru tribesmen for our own strike force and keep them from the Communists."

"What makes you think they'll come back with you?"

"Some of my Bru strikers have been to the village and spoken to the chief. He's agreed to come out himself and bring as many of his people as possible with him. We have guaranteed their safety in the new village. But it won't be easy. Some of the Brus in that village are strong Communist sympathizers. We'll try to neutralize them while the chief brings the willing ones in."

"Neutralize them?"

"Surround them with superior strength. Then we'll march them back here behind the others."

Locke dropped the cover over the map and sat down at a table. "We may have some real trouble, it's hard to tell. The only reason the Bru have agreed to come out is because they'll be living in an American camp. I've tried to convince our camp commander that it would be best if no LLDB were along on this mission. Just the sight of them giving orders or looking as though they were in command could blow the whole mission."

"Any luck?"

"Hell no. Captain Nim says he's going to lead this patrol personally. He's bringing two sergeants with him. Christ, why can't they learn in Saigon that the only way these montagnards will fight for the government is to let them have montagnard leaders as counterparts to us. There are plenty of good montagnard officers in the Army loyal to Saigon, in spite of the way they're discriminated against. If they make captain they're lucky, and they'll never see a field-grade commission." He sighed. "Well, enough of that. Let's get you fixed up with a weapon. We leave tomorrow at daybreak. If all goes well, we can surround the village before dawn."

Captain Locke, Sergeant Binney and the team sergeant, a big blond man whose name was Svenson, made up the American advisory team. Not surprisingly, the patrol didn't start until 9:00 in the morning. The LLDB captain wasn't ready until 8:00, and it took him another hour to get all the Bru platoon leaders and their men together and ready to move out.

We started south along the Laotian border with a company of about 130 montagnards. One American sergeant accompanied the point platoon, the other the third and last platoon. Captain Nim, Captain Locke and I walked at the head of the middle platoon, the two LLDB sergeants staying close to their commander.

It was difficult up-and-down terrain through the mountainous jungle region, but this was home territory for the wiry little tribesmen; they carried their weapons and packs with ease as they picked their way through dense foliage, slashing with machetes at the clinging thorn vines.

When finally Captain Locke, consulting his map frequently and taking compass bearings, advised Captain Nim that we were within four thousand meters of the montagnard village, I for one was on the verge of collapse. He advised Nim to put a watch on the village, and a squad of Brus munching on rice and dried fish set out. The rest of us, he said, should take a few hours sleep.

It was chilly when Locke roused me with a hand on my shoulder, a finger to his lips. Seeing silent activity all around me, I strapped on my pack and slung the folding-stock carbine. The luminous dial of my wrist watch told me it was 1:00 A.M. That meant we would have to travel only a thousand meters an hour to get in position around the village before sunrise.

Maintaining absolute silence, we picked our way slowly and carefully along the jungle path, partially illuminated by a pale sliver of new moon. Twice we waded through mountain streams, and after what seemed an eternity reached our objective. Responding to hand signals, the first and third platoons swept around the village, while the second platoon formed a skirmish line, ready to sweep through the village.

Nim and Locke surveyed the scene. Once again Locke advised him against letting his two sergeants open fire. While some of the more militant Bru tribesmen might take a few shots at the jungle, he said, if no answering fire was forthcoming the chief and his villagers would come along peacefully.

In the pale pre-dawn light Captain Nim made no effort to disguise his feelings. The first dirty mois that shot at him would be cut down. When Locke pushed groundward the submachine gun one of the two LLDB sergeants was carrying, Nim regarded the gesture contemptuously.

The two Bru tribesmen who had previously made contact

with the chief, and whose job it was to request that he gather his people before the Viet Cong came to take them away, made their final preparation. Then, the sky pink above the hills directly behind us, the two emissaries entered the village.

They came to the largest of the longhouses and one boosted the other up into the dark entrance. He disappeared and returned a moment later with the notched-log ladder, which he lowered to the ground. Both tribesmen went inside to reappear with the grizzled old Bru chief, wearing a loincloth and a black blanket over his shoulders.

It was cold at this time of the morning, and I wondered how these people could stand the mountain chill with so little clothing. The Bru chief led our two strikers to what looked like a small village square. He hugged his chest with both arms, trying to keep warm, and walked about the square to stimulate circulation. A few moments later the two young tribesmen climbed down the notched log from the chief's hut, each carrying what looked like a waterbuffalo horn.

The chief, noting that the sun was almost over the mountain-top, gave the signal to his men, and the village reverberated with the squawking bleats of the horns. Immediately heads poked out of the stilt houses, and notched logs were lowered to the ground. Montagnards in loincloths and with blankets covering their shoulders ambled to the parade grounds. Women with unconfined breasts appeared, carrying children.

The chief began talking loudly, and suddenly the people turned toward us and squinted into the sun. Some 20 or 30 men and women broke from the cluster of tribesmen and ran for their houses.

Captain Nim raised his carbine to his shoulder and shouted an order to his sergeants. His interpreter translated the order to the montagnard strikers who brought their weapons to the ready.

"You can't fire on those unarmed people!" Locke cried.

"They are not unarmed long," Nim retorted. "We kill now."

"Wait, Dai-uy!" Locke pleaded. "They can't see into the sun to shoot you, anyway."

From the houses toward which the montagnards were running, women handed out weapons to their men below, who took them, fell to the ground, and aimed toward the jungle.

The Bru chief shouted out, apparently ordering the militant tribesmen not to fire. But the VC sympathizers obviously had no intention of obeying.

A woman in one of the houses screamed something at the chief, then picked up a long French rifle and started firing in our direction.

"Hold fire, Nim!" Locke called.

Emboldened by her bravado, several VC sympathizers pumped bullets into the jungle.

The chief was shouting at the armed tribesmen to cease firing and Locke was trying to restrain Captain Nim from opening up on the village. It was a stalemate in our favor; because of our set positions, we could have disarmed the Viet Cong montagnards easily and taken the whole village back to Lua Vuc.

Then a round whistled so close to Captain Nim's ear that he jumped, and suddenly cut loose with his automatic carbine. Instantly, his two sergeants opened up with their submachine guns, and the strikers, though mostly Bru themselves, started raking the village.

Fire streaked back at us through the jungle. The fight was committed, and suddenly there were a lot more armed Brus shooting at us than had been anticipated.

Our two Bru emissaries tried to run for the jungle, but both were cut down from behind.

Nim and his two sergeants began lobbing hand grenades into the village, blowing the flimsy houses apart. The Brus fought back furiously and seemed on the point of charging us when our two reserve platoons, until now restrained by the American sergeants, turned on all their fire power. Realizing they were beaten, the Communist montagnards immediately slipped out of the village. The non-Communists who had been willing to go back to Lua Vuc ran off into the jungle, panic-stricken; but the strikers, seeing they were unarmed, did not shoot.

A tragic sight awaited us in the village. Eighteen dead montagnards lay about, blood running into the ground. Most of them had weapons near at hand and were indeed VC sympathizers, but others, including the old chief who had wanted nothing for his people but to live unmolested by either side in this war they couldn't understand and which offered them nothing no matter which side won, lay dead.

Cries, wails, and moans came from many of the houses, and squads were sent to investigate. Twenty minutes later, 15 wounded children ranging in age from about two to ten, were gently laid out in the village square.

We had 2 strikers dead besides the 2 shot in the back, and 7 wounded. After inspecting his casualties, Captain Nim stalked over to his American counterpart.

"Four die, 7 wounded," he said arrogantly. "Why you not let me shoot first? We kill all, no one die of us."

"If you had held your fire no one would have died on either side. We could have performed our mission and taken them back. They didn't really want a fight."

The children's wounds were heart-rending. Many had been badly burned when grenades set their houses afire. One little boy's left eye had been blown out. Almost every child had a bullet wound of some seriousness. They were dazed, fire-blackened, and strangely silent, as if afraid to call attention to themselves.

Sergeants Binney and Svenson were patching up the little Brus, stopping bleeding and trying to comfort the badly hurt and frightened children. When all had been bandaged, litters were fashioned.

Just an hour after the fire-fight ended we started back for Lua Vuc carrying the 15 wounded children.

We had to stop at frequent intervals so that Sergeant Binney could change dressings, administer shots of morphine, and keep checking for shock. We had no facilities for giving plasma, and one little girl, wounded in the spine, died on the way. We arrived at Lua Vuc just before dark, and Manelli and the tireless Binney took charge of the children. With plasma and more equipment, the two medics were confident they could keep the children alive overnight.

"You've got to get these kids to Da Nang, sir," Binney begged Locke. "I can't take bullets out of chest cavities. These kids need real medical attention, by tomorrow morning at the latest."

"They're civilians, Binney. You know the drill. By the way, did we ever get that woman on her way to Da Nang by sampan?"

Binney nodded grimly. "Yes, sir. The boat came back a couple of hours ago. She died on the river. Her husband has the body—the bodies, I guess I should say.'' He walked over to a softly whimpering little girl. ''Sir, isn't there any way we can get these kids to the hospital in Da Nang?''

Locke looked at the children who now filled the women's ward. ''I believe there is,'' he said decisively. ''I'll take care of it now. Just keep the kids alive until tomorrow.''

''Manelli and I can do that, sir.''

Locke was closeted in the American radio bunker all evening, and finally emerged late that night. Captain Nim was waiting for him in the teamroom. I listened, as he inquired about the children.

''When they well again,'' he said, ''maybe my wife, some friends take them our home.''

Locke looked hard at his Vietnamese counterpart. ''Thank you, Captain Nim. However, the Special Forces B team is supporting an orphan asylum in Da Nang and maybe that is where the children should go.''

''They better with family. Maybe in week, two week, they well. I have friend in Vietnam Air Force. Maybe he fly helicopter out here for children then. My wife, my friends meet children, take them home.''

''Why couldn't this friend help evacuate that woman whose baby died?''

''Take much planning.''

''Why can't this friend come tomorrow morning and take the children to hospital in Da Nang? Maybe they die they don't go to hospital.''

''No civilians go out with Air Force. Take much planning.''

''OK, Nim, we'll see what we can do. You know what he's trying to do?'' Locke asked when the Vietnamese officer had left. ''After aborting our mission by not holding fire, he wants those kids for slaves.'' Locke sighed. ''What a war! Anyway, those children will be safely out of camp first thing in the morning.''

''How did you manage that?'' I asked in surprise.

''Easy. I reported 14 wounded Viet Cong prisoners of war ready for immediate evacuation.''

He saw my eyebrows raise quizzically. ''What's the matter? They're wounded and they certainly are from VC-sympathizing families, or some are. They're sure not going anywhere, so I guess you'd call them prisoners.''

235

"They'll send a Vietnamese intelligence officer with the chopper, won't they?" I asked. "In fact, technically isn't this a mission for Vietnamese chopper pilots?"

"U.S. choppers are coming in," Locke said. "I reported frequent VC groundfire to the B team and they passed that on to the Vietnam Air Force. All of a sudden no VNAF choppers or pilots were available, and VNAF requested Army Aviation to make the run. But you can bet the Vietnamese intelligence officers will be waiting at the airstrip in Da Nang."

He laughed aloud. "Wait'll they see their 14 POW's. Right now they're probably drooling at the thought of a couple of days of torturing prisoners."

"What will happen to the kids when they arrive? I hope someone will be there to meet them."

"I sent a code message to Colonel Tex. He'll know what to do."

Early the next morning we were waiting at the chopper pad when we heard the chuffing of helicopters in the distant sky. A sergeant threw a smoke grenade onto the Landing Zone and then two Marine H34's started in. Flying cover above them, two armed Hueys darted and soared, keeping the area under careful surveillance, ready to blast with rockets and machine guns at the first sign of VC groundfire.

The A team had brought the children out on stretchers, and the medics made them ready for their trip to the hospital. Several Bru women who had sat up all night with the children were at the pad to see them off.

Captain Nim and his Executive Officer watched the children being taken to the Landing Zone with intense curiosity. "What you do with children here?"

Locke turned away from the boy with the shot-out eye and stared down at his counterpart. "I am worried about them. I call helicopters to take them to hospital in Da Nang."

"But it is not possible to move them by military airplane," Nim protested. "They are civilian."

"In about ten minutes you are going to see them lifted out of here, Captain."

"But I must say no. This against Vietnamese orders."

Locke didn't trust himself to argue further. Ignoring Nim, he went back to readying his brood of ex-Communist children. Nim, arguing vehemently, followed. Finally, the Special Forces officer could take no more.

"Nim, you people and Americans have big difference in what is right and wrong. For five months I've put up with it. But I have three kids of my own, and I and most Americans love all children. It makes me, and it makes the men on my team sick that we have to use tricks to save these children."

He gestured at the 14 tiny casualties who were being attended by all the available members of the A team. "Not only must we save them from dying out here, or being crippled for life because we cannot properly care for them— we must also save them from being consigned to a life of drudgery—and even being sold like slaves."

Nim was taken aback. He retreated before the silent, barely controlled fury of his counterpart. "You are American. Only adviser. I give the orders. Americans no good for Vietnam. Do not understand Vietnam."

Locke didn't bother to answer. The choppers began to hover and an American sergeant directed them down onto the pad. As soon as the big Marine helicopters had landed, the Americans motioned the strikers to carry the children aboard. Nim screamed orders, and the strikers placed the litters on the ground.

Locke took in the situation immediately. Gesturing at me, he ran to the nearest litter and grabbed one end. I took the other, and together we walked toward a big transport helicopter, its rotors still whirling for a speedy take-off. Immediately the rest of the team followed the Commanding Officer's example.

An officer stepped down from the helicopter cockpit and watched in astonishment as Locke and I handed up the litter to the door gunner and flight engineer. Gently they took it and placed it inside the helicopter.

"Captain Locke? I'm Captain Starret," the pilot introduced himself. "You have 14 VC POW's to go to Vietnamese Intelligence in Da Nang for interrogation."

"We're putting the POW's aboard, Captain. Most of them don't talk very well yet, so Intelligence may have trouble questioning them."

Starret looked at the children. "Are you sure, Captain, that we're supposed to be taking those children back? It's against regulations to evacuate civilians."

"I know that better than you, Starret," Locke replied.

"But these are VC POW's, captured from a VC village that fired on us."

Starret stood indecisively as the children were loaded aboard the two choppers. "Maybe," he said at last, "but I'd say they constitute a damned loose interpretation of the orders that came to Marine Aviation."

"If they don't have proper hospital care immediately, they'll die. Besides," he added, "in my report I have indicated that after preliminary interrogation, it is my opinion that every one of these Viet Cong prisoners, with proper guidance, can be won completely away from their Communist indoctrination."

Starret laughed loudly. "Goddamned, but you Special Forces types get to the grass roots of this war." He frowned slightly. "There'll be a mess of Vietnamese Intelligence types waiting at the pad in Da Nang. They're going to be damned surprised, and then damned, damned mad."

"Sorry about that, Starret," Locke answered cheerfully.

Starret watched the last of the children being loaded in spite of Nim's interference. "Who is that little dickhead?"

"That is my counterpart, the camp commander, Captain Nim. He violently disapproves of this maneuver. He says I've gone around regulations."

"There are plenty of others going to say the same thing," Starret affirmed with a smile. "Glad I was part of it. Good luck, Captain."

"Thanks, Starret." Locke told me to climb on. "Maybe you'll write it up our way if things get too tough."

I shook hands with Captain Locke and swung aboard, finding a bucket seat beside the crew chief. The children were silent, their eyes either closed or staring at the ceiling.

Just before we took off, I saw Locke's green beret pop in the door. "Just be sure that Colonel Tex gets to them first."

"No sweat," I shouted over the screaming engine. "And thanks for the hospitality."

Just under an hour later the H34 crossed the huge new jet airstrip in Da Nang, and settled down onto the Marine pad.

Outside stood two ambulances, two trucks, and two jeeps with Vietnamese markings. I was relieved to see Colonel Tex surrounded by a contingent of Special Forces personnel, and jumped down and pumped his hand.

Then, noticing a group of Vietnamese officers approaching

the helicopters with anticipatory smirks on their faces, followed by guards with levelled carbines, I asked him if the Viets knew what was in the helicopters.

The colonel gave orders, and immediately Vietnamese and American personnel from the B team began lifting out the children before the astonished eyes of the Vietnamese intelligence officers.

A Vietnamese major looked inside the first chopper, said something to an aide, and then in quick, short, jerky strides, went to the second helicopter and looked in. His rage was eloquent as he approached Colonel Tex.

A graduate of several American service schools, the Vietnamese spoke good English. "What means this, Colonel? Where are the Viet Cong prisoners we came for?"

"Those are the Viet Cong POW's," the colonel said, gesturing at the children being placed in the ambulances.

"That cannot be. It is impossible," the little major exploded. "Those are children."

The tall, lean, white-haired colonel gave him a languid glance. "Yes, you are right, Major. Fourteen children."

"The Americans at Lua Vuc have deceived us, then," he said ominously. "They conspired to break Vietnamese regulations. I will see the general. This will go all the way to Saigon. The American responsible for this must be immediately relieved of his command."

"Why, Major?" Colonel Tex asked softly.

"The signal said 14 wounded Viet Cong prisoners of war were waiting evacuation from Lua Vuc. Instead we find a bunch of dirty mois children."

Out of the corner of his eye Colonel Tex noted that the ambulances were loaded and the drivers were ready to move out. He turned back to the agitated Vietnamese. "Major, would you agree those 14 children were captured in Viet Cong-controlled territory?"

"Of course, Colonel."

"Would you say that they are Viet Cong?"

"Certainly. But, Colonel—"

Colonel Tex went on imperturbably. "They are certainly prisoners, are they not? And they are wounded, every one of them. To me, the Special Forces captain at Lua Vuc sent you just what the message described—14 wounded Viet Cong POW's."

"But they are children—" the major screamed.

"Major," Colonel Tex said slowly and distinctly, "if you have special requirements on what kind of wounded VC POW's you will accept, why didn't you fly out to Lua Vuc yourself this morning and make the decision on the spot?"

I didn't try to hide my grin as I regarded the sputtering Viet major.

"Maybe you have some explanation I can pass on to Vietnamese corps headquarters why not a single Vietnamese intelligence officer went on this official mission to Lua Vuc?

"I realize," the colonel went on, "that Lua Vuc was not secure this morning, with much Viet Cong groundfire reported over the past three days. But would that stop an intelligence officer from performing his duty?"

Angrily the little Viet major saluted Colonel Tex, who easily returned it. Followed by his retinue, the intelligence officer got into his jeep which, with a clanging of gears and jack-rabbit start, sped away from the helicopter ramp.

Colonel Tex watched them go. "Let's get out of this hot sun," he said to me. "I want to hear about the whole thing, and then we'll go over to see Doctor Francis. Civic Affairs has already given him the money to enlarge the facilities of the orphanage."

"Will they get good treatment at the hospital?"

"They're going to a USOM hospital. All personnel there are under American supervision."

In a dark, cool hangar, over a Coke, I asked whether any Americans would get into trouble over this.

His eyes were not placid now. "A flap like this, Special Forces men conspiring to deliberately circumvent Republic of Vietnam regulations is what a lot of straight-leg colonels and generals—" Colonel Tex smiled sheepishly. "Well, even if I never did get to be a jumper, I'm not a leg at heart."

He finished his Coke and put it in the rack. "Yes, a lot of conventional types who'd like to put Special Forces out of business would jump on this if they had the chance. We could all get relieved from the B-team commander down to the last sergeant on Locke's team.

"Fortunately," he said, "I don't think we have to worry this time. That Viet intelligence crew is scared of only

240

one thing more than physical danger, and that's loss of face.''

Colonel Tex started for the jeep. ''Let's get on over to the hospital and see how Doctor Francis is coming along. He promised to get our wounded Viet Cong POW's settled—for the next ten years or so.''

8

THE IMMODEST
MR. POMFRET

Skin ships are the number one morale factor to the Special Forces men who patrol the mountainous jungle terrain of Vietnam. These unarmed helicopters flown by United States Army Aviation pilots on medical evacuation missions have saved the lives of hundreds of Americans wounded in vicious jungle fighting.

I suppose no less than two dozen Special Forces men who were on A teams coordinated by the B detachment in Da Nang asked me to say hello to Mr. Pomfret for them when I visited I Corps, the northernmost military command of South Vietnam. The Special Forces professionals invariably said the same thing: "As long as Chief Warrant Officer Pomfret is flying his skin ship out of Da Nang, I'll go back to 'Eye' Corps for another tour."

When I met Chief Warrant Officer Pomfret in the Army Aviation ready room I was expecting to see a man just a little larger than life. It was much the same as when I met my first Special Forces man back from combat wearing his green beret; it took a while to realize he didn't stand nine feet tall and have the strength of ten men. He just studied and trained harder than most soldiers and happened to be a brave man. Mr. Pomfret just knew his machine better than most other helicopter pilots and was a very brave man.

Pomfret was lean, bright-eyed, had thick sandy hair and looked to be in his forties although he was actually younger. Lines caused by hours of agonizing concentration worked their way from the corners of his eyes to the corners of his mouth. Yet as he sat in the ready room he had the cheerful expression of a man doing what he knew best. A red-headed 1st lieutenant sat beside him. I introduced myself and mentioned a few names of friends Mr. Pomfret had hauled out of bad situations.

"Old Wop Pascelli?" Pomfret reminisced delightedly. "How is that tough little bastard? How's his gut?"

"Good as new," I answered. "He told me to tell you he's coming back just as quick as he can get his old lady on Okie to release him."

"Wop Pascelli." Pomfret shook his head. "Son of a bitch. The VC's got him with a round right in the gut," Pomfret told the young red-headed lieutenant who regarded him with undisguised worship. "The goddamned round hit his belt buckle, glanced into his web belt, opened up his belly, and jammed a hunk of belt right into the wound. And what did that little bastard do? He got on the radio and called in a med evac for himself, a wounded LLDB sergeant, and a couple of shot-up strikers. Holding his gut in with one hand he made the strikers cut out a Landing Zone, then he directed me in, helped the other wounded guys aboard, got on himself and that was it for him—he passed out cold. When I went to the hospital to see him a week later, he tried to steal his clothes and get me to smuggle him back to his A team."

"That was Pascelli," I agreed, and then got my first confirmation of the rumors that modesty was not one of Mr. Pomfret's failings.

"Those are the greatest guys in the world," Pomfret said. "I don't know what the hell would happen to them if it wasn't for me. There isn't another son of a bitch I really trust to go out there when it's really rough." He turned to the lieutenant. "Except maybe for you, sir."

The lieutenant—whom Pomfret introduced as Nichols—beamed at the praise. "The lieutenant here is the only skin-ship man I feel sure enough of so maybe I can go home to the States and sleep nights. Two consecutive tours, two years I put in because I don't want them Special Forces guys left out there when some dickhead is afraid to go get them. But now—" he grinned at Nichols. "My old lady is going to love you, sir."

A telephone rang and an Army Aviation captain answered. Pomfret was on his feet immediately and walked over, watching as the captain located on the huge map behind his desk the coordinates being given him over the phone.

"Major Sullivan," the captain said, "I can't ask a pilot to go out there. The ceiling's dropping fast, it's almost 1700 hours. Marine Aviation won't send in an H34 even with fighter escort. . . ."

The captain's voice trailed off and finally with a curt, "Yes sir, he's right here," handed the telephone to Mr. Pomfret.

The warrant officer listened to the commanding officer of the Special Forces B team for a few moments. "His only chance is to get out tonight?" he repeated quietly. Then: "OK, I'll try and get him, sir." Another pause, then: "Sorry sir, I can't wait for you to get over. I'll be in the air in five minutes."

"Lieutenant Nichols," Mr. Pomfret said as he hung up the phone, "do you want to go out near Kham Don with me? A captain hit bad on a patrol. Chest wound. The medic out there with him thinks he can pull through if he gets into an operating room in the next two hours."

"Let's go!"

"I can't get gun ships for you, Mr. Pomfret," the captain said. "Nothing should be flying into those mountains now. You get started up the wrong valley you'll never make it."

"Sir, I know every valley from here to Laos. Lieutenant Nichols and me will do OK. And as for gun ships? We can't afford to lose another Huey. Bad enough I'm going."

"Mind if I ride along?" I asked.

Mr. Pomfret gave me a hard look, quickly followed by a friendly smile. "Sure. The more the merrier."

Mr. Pomfret had the HU21b turbojet going in moments. His crew chief and door gunners were standing by. As the chopper began to lift into the air I glanced at my watch and was surprised to see that indeed only five minutes had elapsed from the time Pomfret had finished talking to Major Sullivan and marked the Landing Zone on his map until we were airborne.

Sitting in the middle of the long back seat I pulled a helmet over my head so I could hear the radio and intercom conversations. Pomfret and Nichols had slipped into their armored vests just before going aloft; now I did too.

"OK, Lieutenant, you take it," Pomfret said over the intercom. "I'll just watch." Nichols acknowledged and headed out toward the mountains. The late afternoon sun was low and the heavy dark-cloud cover looked ominous ahead. We bore right into the mountain range. "Follow the river, and where it splits off to the north, that's the valley we follow."

"I've got it."

Once in the mountain range the ceiling was so low that it was like flying through a tunnel. There was no chance to come up and see where we were. The two door gunners were alert, although there wasn't much they could have done to counter enemy fire from the Viet Cong infested mountainous jungle terrain below.

Mr. Pomfret and Lieutenant Nichols flew the skin ship through one valley after another, turning left and right almost as though we were driving along a road. And the ceiling continued to drop on us. Forty-five minutes out of Da Nang, Nichols said we should be sighting the Landing Zone any time if the coordinates were correct. Ten minutes later Mr. Pomfret, looking out at the terrain only a few hundred feet below us, called over the intercom, "There they are, Lieutenant. Jesus, what a Landing Zone! Looks like it's cut on the side of a hill."

Then, over the radio I heard the call from the Landing Zone.

"Pickup, Pickup, this is Jaybird. Do you read?"

Pomfret acknowledged as Nichols maneuvered the chopper for a landing. The door gunners held their heavy M-14 rifles ready for instant use on full automatic fire.

I heard Nichols calling now. "Jaybird, this is Pickup. Is the Landing Zone secured?"

"Now Lieutenant," I heard Pomfret's midwest twang cut in, "you know these here Landing Zones are never secure. Why make the guys lie to us?"

There must have been no more than six or seven hundred feet between the overcast and the ground below. We'd be in ground-fire range all the way back.

"Put her in, sir," Pomfret was saying. "You got it made now."

The Landing Zone looked impossible to me; there must have been at least a 25 degree slope. I couldn't see how Pomfret or Nichols could land. I could see an improvised litter with a man on it being held by a U.S. Special Forces man and a montagnard.

245

I watched, holding my breath, my stomach churning as Nichols gently lowered into the hillside Landing Zone, the front of the ship pointing at the top of the slope.

"Sir," Pomfret was saying, "last couple of these you did were number one, almost as good as I do myself."

Nichols didn't answer as we settled in. Then, over the radio, I heard a high-pitched ping of static and then another. If you knew what to listen for you could tell when a bullet hit the metal skin of a chopper.

"Don't pay any attention to them, sir," Pomfret was saying evenly. Another ping came over the earphones and I saw a small piece of the ship's skin open up above one of the door gunners as a round went through. The door gunners were firing now, although the noise of their shooting was muffled by the rotor blades. Lieutenant Nichols, looking out his side window, had lowered the Huey so that the front of its two runners, which served as landing gear, were resting on the ground; the rest of the ship hovered a foot and a half to two feet above the slanting Landing Zone. Instantly the litter to which the captain was securely tied was slipped onto the floor of the chopper. All the men I could see were firing everything they had at the Viet Cong, who had lain in wait for the helicopter they knew would come in. The door gunners hauled the litter safely into the interior of the plane, jammed new magazines into their rifles and put out heavy fire into the Viet Cong positions.

Instead of plopping up immediately, the HU21b took off skimming the trees running away from the Viet Cong fire. Then it slowly ascended until our rotors were cutting the soup above us and Nichols made it full speed out of the valley, both door gunners crouched, scanning the jungle now a mere five hundred feet below.

For forty minutes we made our way out of the maze of valleys. Looking ahead one would think the chopper was going to crash into what looked like a solid wall of jungle, but always another valley opened up. Finally we came to the big river and just as darkness closed in, we made out the lights of Da Nang.

Pomfret leaned back—I could almost hear him sigh over the interphones—and then he said the words that probably were the highest praise Lieutenant Nichols would ever hear in his life: "Yes, sir, Lieutenant, I'm ready to go home now, just as soon as they'll cut my orders."

246

2.

Back in Da Nang I heard the news that Captain Tom Harvey had made major. There is one thing we all love dearly around the Army and that is a pisswilliger of a promotion party. Like all promotions Tom's was way overdue.

Tom had an A detachment primarily engaged in surveillance on the Laotian border and for months I had been promising to visit him and go on a patrol with his strikers. A promotion party out on the border sounded unusual, so I stocked up on good bourbon whisky at the PX and requested transportation from the B team to Major Harvey's camp, Quam Duc.

An enthusiastic Australian captain, learning the adviser business from U.S. Army Special Forces, came along with me. There was a patrol scheduled, Captain Ian Frisbie told me, from Quam Duc north along the border to fix a site for a new Special Forces camp where he would be attached for several months. One day, the Aussie assured me, the Americans would be able to turn over a large part of the counterinsurgency work in Southeast Asia to the Australians.

Frisbie and I, combat packs on our backs, were deposited on the perforated steel-strip runway at Major Harvey's isolated montagnard strike-force camp. A truck drove up and Sergeant Milt Raskin, the team's chief medic, hopped down to greet us. He had a security group of eight montagnards in back, pointing their weapons out at all numbers of the clock. Frisbie and I threw our gear up with the yards and jumped in front.

Major Harvey greeted us in front of the headquarters bunker of Quam Duc, and as I shook his hand I noticed he was still wearing his captain's bars. Just then an LLDB lieutenant came up to him. "Dia-uy, the camp commander ask you come see him."

"What's this Dai-uy?" I started to say. "It's Major Harvey. . . ."

Harvey shook his head at me and raised a cautioning finger to his lips. Taking Frisbie and me aside, he said, "My counterpart, Captain Ling, does not know I'm a major. We

247

have worked so well together, one Dai-uy to another, that I don't want to change things. And I used to think *we* were rank conscious."

"No promotion party in the mountains," I said resignedly. "I brought in two full quarts of Jim Beam."

Harvey grinned broadly. "No sweat getting rid of that. We go out day after tomorrow. No reason we can't all do away with one bottle tonight. Captain Ling developed a hellofa taste for bourbon in the States."

"Don't tell me you are blessed with a good camp commander."

"The new LLDB colonel is the best thing that's happened in this war," Harvey asserted. "He's out kicking ass and taking names everywhere. He found Ling for me and that stud is a tiger."

Harvey eyed the bulge in my pack. "Now, you piker, how about a little of that celebration?"

On the second day of the patrol we were hit lightly. Major Harvey, Sergeant Raskin, Captain Frisbie and I were walking between the two platoons which made up the patrol. Lieutenant Duong, Executive Officer of the LLDB team, was walking near the point of the first platoon when the VC ambush was sprung on us. Instantly, Duong charged the Communists. All casualties were up front and the ambushers quickly beaten off.

One of our montagnard strikers was killed. That VC-sympathizing montagnards had staged the ambush was evident when we saw that the dead man had gotten it with a bamboo arrow launched from a crossbow. The arrow pierced a leather wallet, drove through the chest close to the heart, and the point came out our tribesman's back. Two other strikers suffered gunshot wounds, one seriously in the right side of the chest, the other, strangely, in the leg. Ordinarily montagnard Viet Cong shoot high. Major Harvey decided that somewhere in the vicinity there must be a hardcore North Vietnamese cadre training the montagnards they had persuaded or terrorized into fighting for them.

Now we had two wounded men who could not go on. The dead man was another problem. His brother and several close relatives were members of the strike force. It was imperative to them that the body get back to the village for burial; had the two wounded men been able to walk the rest of the patrol, the dead man's relatives would have carried the body the remaining five days to get it back to camp. Having been on patrols when this happened I did not relish the prospect of the stench of a corpse decomposing day by day.

Because Special Forces men are entirely conversant with tribal mores and superstitions, and because their respect for montagnard traditions enables them to command the loyalty of the tribesmen, Major Harvey knew there was only one course open to him now. The patrol searched for a partially clear piece of flat land that could be cleaned off quickly for a helicopter Landing Zone. Half a mile from the ambush such a site was found. While Raskin worked over the wounded, one platoon deployed itself around the Landing Zone and the other went to work cutting out all trees and obstacles. Harvey contacted his A-team Executive Officer by radio, gave him the map coordinates of the Landing Zone and requested immediate medical evacuation.

As we waited tensely for the helicopter to come in, Harvey gave the Aussie some pointers on our situation.

"This is about as tough a bind as you can get in out here," he said to the intent Frisbie. "By now the Viet Cong know we have wounded and must evacuate them—if we don't, we'll have one helluva time ever getting these yards to go out on patrol again."

Harvey studied the sky, heavy with clouds. "It's only 1300 hours and already the cloud cover is dropping. The choppers will have to follow valleys into us, staying under the overcast all the way from the eastern edge of the mountains."

He surveyed the terrain in our immediate vicinity. "The Viet Cong will be trying to sneak in on us as close as they can. The best we can do is hold them a hundred meters away from the Landing Zone. If the goddamned choppers get in here fast, we'll probably be OK. The VC might get in a lucky shot from outside our security, but it will take them a while to bring in heavy machine guns. That's why you have to get these med evac Landing Zones set up fast and get the choppers in and out before the VC can set up the heavy stuff and clobber them. That's what the Communists are really after when they hit us in a small ambush. Inflict casualties and the choppers will come in. Knock one down and it's a major VC victory."

"I suppose one helicopter costs more money than the

whole Viet Cong guerrilla Army spends in a month," Frisbie said.

Harvey nodded. "That's about right—if you can translate this war into money."

A montagnard striker, radio on his back, came up with Lieutenant Duong. "Sir," Duong said, "A team want talk you."

Harvey took the handset from the battery pack on the radioman's back. He heard his Executive Officer calling him. "Grant, Grant, this is Handy, Handy!"

"I read, Handy. This is Grant."

"Med evac on the way from Da Nang. It's an all-Vietnam Air Force operation."

Harvey threw a regretful, sympathetic glance at the two wounded men. "Handy, this is Grant. Understand an all-Vietnam Air Force med evac on the way."

"That is Roger, Grant. Sorry about that. I tried to get a U.S. med evac but no go anymore unless American wounded on the ground."

"Roger, Handy. Understand."

"Grant, this is Handy. I'll be standing by. If the usual happens maybe we can get U.S. evac tomorrow. Ceiling coming down fast here."

"Thanks, Handy. Grant out."

"Handy out—standing by."

Major Harvey looked serious as he put down the set. "Frisbie, in a few minutes you are apt to see one of the big sweats you'll be getting here."

"What's that, sir?"

"Just watch, you'll see."

He turned to Lieutenant Duong. "Maybe you'd better check security. Make sure everyone's at least one hundred meters out."

"Yes, Dai-uy." Duong, followed by a four-man security squad, started into the bush.

"How soon will the med evac be coming in, sir?" Frisbie asked.

Harvey pointed down the valley to the east where the cloud cover was now resting on the peaks of the mountains and falling. "Just keep looking that way, it shouldn't be long now. Da Nang is a fifty minutes chopper flight from here."

We all strained our eyes down the valley, and after about

ten minutes of staring into the dull-grey sky we heard the unmistakable sound of rotor blades and engines. Then, suddenly swooping down, we saw the Vietnam Air Force T-28 fighter planes with their yellow markings. The planes stayed as high as they could without disappearing into the overcast. "And that," Major Harvey said, "is the Vietnamese Air Force conception of flying cover security. Stay out of range of groundfire at all times."

We heard a groan from the strikers as the choppers came closer. The identifying yellow patch painted on the hump behind the pilot's seat of the H34 could be seen plainly now. The strikers had been through this before. Lieutenant Duong, who unlike most Vietnamese officers had taken the trouble to learn the montagnard language, began giving orders. We all took cover in the bush as the wounded were carried into the now open Landing Zone. The two helicopters were circling high above us. Sergeant Raskin pulled a second green-smoke grenade from his belt, activated it, and threw it beside the first, which was giving off the last of its smoke.

"The sons of bitches see us," Raskin growled. "Why the hell don't they come on in?"

The strikers watched hopefully as one of the yellow-backed helicopters began to descend uncertainly toward us. Lower and lower it settled toward the Landing Zone. When it was fifteen feet off the ground and still descending, its rotor blades fiercely slashing the air, blasting us with a tremendous downdraft, Major Harvey yelled, "By God, they're improving."

The two wounded men were being carried toward the chopper's open door, and the litter with the corpse had been lifted on sturdy montagnard shoulders preparatory to pushing it into the H34 when—pang! pang! pang!

Three bullets tore through the chopper's fuselage. The striker wounded in the leg had actually placed a hand on its doorstep when in a loud snarl of power the pilot reversed the rotor blades and the chopper leapt skywards. It shot up out of range, circled the Landing Zone once more, and headed back out of the valley for Da Nang.

Major Harvey silently watched the choppers disappear. Groans and curses came from the suddenly demoralized strikers.

"Fourteen hundred hours," Harvey said checking his watch. "Maybe we can get an American air evac." But his tone belied his words. "Duong, take a squad and find that sniper. Quick."

"Yes, Dai-uy."

"Sir, I'll go with Duong," Captain Frisbie volunteered. "We Aussies specialize in anti-sniper training."

Harvey nodded. "Right. Be careful." He looked at the menacing cloud cover. "In another hour or two nobody will be able to fly into this mess, not even Mr. Pomfret."

Harvey looked uneasily after Frisbie and Duong as they headed into the thickly wooded terrain. A squad of 12 montagnards followed them. "I hate to let the Aussie go out like that with no experience behind him."

"There's only one way he's going to get experience," Sergeant Raskin said. "The way we got it."

It took half an hour for Harvey, relaying through his A team, to put through another request for a med evac. This time he made it clear he wanted an American pilot. The reply finally came back that Vietnamese Air Force would not authorize an American pilot to evacuate non-American strikers. The following morning, if the Landing Zone was secure, an attempt would be made.

"By tomorrow morning," Harvey raged, "the VC's will be all over us. It will be impossible to provide the kind of security the Viets insist on."

"That chopper pilot could have made it easily," Raskin cursed. "Sonofabitch, one sniper and he's scared off."

"Nothing we can do but wait here and see how Duong and Frisbie make out." Harvey sat down, his back to a tree. We all sat in dejected silence, Raskin checking his wounded men every so often, waiting for the patrol to return.

"At least we're going out after the sniper," Harvey said at last. "Last time I was at the B team in Da Nang the MAAG advisers at 'Eye' Corps were having a hell of a time teaching one of the ARVN divisions how to cope with snipers. Every time a sniper opened up on a battalion, all three companies would fall back in confusion and the officers would abort the operation.

"Those poor guys advising the Vietnamese battalion commanders tried their damnedest to make them send out squad-size groups to track down and kill the snipers. Even if they didn't get them, the Viet Cong snipers would know that a

252

killer squad would always be after them and this might discourage them."

Harvey looked out in the direction his patrol had taken. "Finally, the senior American advisers convinced the Viets to send out an advisory on how to deal with snipers. I saw it and it was good, right out of advanced Infantry School at Benning. It explained how to organize and arm the killer squads—everything was there. In Da Nang all was happy at MAAG. No more VC snipers turning back a whole battalion."

Harvey pushed the jungle camouflage cap back on his head. "Well, hell, we're not going to change the Viets all that easily. Three weeks later the division commander put out the new directive, and we got a translation of it. It directed all battalion commanders to withdraw and set up ambushes in case the sniper attacks."

Bad as our situation was, Raskin and I both laughed heartily—then suddenly cut it off. Off to the west we heard small-arms fire followed by the sound of exploding grenades. Then silence. Twenty minutes later Duong reappeared; beside him was a montagnard, a broad smile on his face, brandishing a severed ear. The rest of the grinning montagnards followed Duong into the clearing, one carrying the sniper's weapon, a U.S. M-1 Garand with telescopic sight. To our shock, the last two were carrying Captain Frisbie, grimacing with pain.

One look at the Aussie, and Raskin ran across the Landing Zone to him, kit in hand. By the time Harvey and I reached Frisbie's side, Raskin had slit the leg of the Aussie's fatigue pants and was examining the messy puncture that went through the shin and out the calf.

"Pungi-stake wound," Raskin growled. "A mean sonofabitch." He took a morphine surette and gave Frisbie a shot in the arm.

"That was damned stupid of me, sir," Frisbie said between clenched teeth. "I'm sorry."

"They're hard to see," Harvey said. "We get a lot of guys with pungi stakes in their legs."

The morphine began to take effect and Frisbie lay back. Silently Raskin handed Harvey three pungi stakes. "One of the yards pulled this one out of the captain. He picked up a few others that were in the bush, just as I taught them."

Harvey looked at the sword-sharp bamboo stakes, which are placed in heavy grass at about a 45-degree angle to the expected direction of enemy approach. Frowning deeply he handed one to me. As we all feared the points were smeared with an evil-smelling brown-black coating—human excrement the VC use to poison the stakes.

"We've got to get him out fast, sir." Raskin turned the Aussie over, slit the rear of his pants, and jabbed a long needle into the exposed buttocks. Harvey nodded. Perhaps the leg could be saved if Frisbie got to the military hospital in Nha Trang fast enough. I'd seen horrifying infections boil up in a few hours from such wounds.

The two wounded montagnards tried unsuccessfully to conceal their relief at the sight of the wounded Australian. Now there was a chance of an American-piloted medical evacuation.

Harvey motioned to the radio operator to follow him out of Frisbie's hearing.

"Handy, Handy, this is Grant, Grant. Come in."

"Grant, this is Handy."

"Handy. The Aussie got a pungi stake in the leg. A shit-dipped one. If we can't get him out today he may lose the leg. See if you can get the B team to call direct to Army Aviation. Mr. Pomfret will come in. We got the sniper. That doesn't mean the VC's won't try to move up more snipers and maybe even heavy machine guns. But if Mr. Pomfret knows the whole situation he's one man that will make a try for us."

"Roger, Grant. I will try to contact Army Aviation immediately. Will call you back as soon as I make contact. Handy out."

Harvey breathed deeply. "I knew I shouldn't have let Frisbie go out. There's an art to steering clear of pungi stakes. We should have given him a week of training first." He walked back to where Frisbie lay. "Feel any better?"

"Thank you, sir. The morphine's working quite well now."

"I've requested an American med evac, Frisbie. There's one man that might come in for you, Mr. Pomfret. He's the finest skin-ship man in the whole world. He should have gone home six months ago, but he says he couldn't sleep at night knowing there's nobody out here that can get Special Forces guys out of the jungle the way he can."

The details of my flight with Mr. Pomfret came back clearly as I stood at the Landing Zone—this time on the other side of a med evac operation. It was almost the same time of day, the ceiling was dropping fast, and we had no idea how well the Landing Zone was secured. I wondered if Mr. Pomfret really would come in himself. Now that he had decided he could go home, it didn't make sense for him to go on taking chances.

The radio operator called to Major Harvey to take a call from the A team. He returned a few moments later. "A single skin ship is going to try and get through. They can't risk a gunship escort." Harvey looked around for Lieutenant Duong and asked him to make a thorough security inspection. "And maybe we send two squads beyond the security perimeter to knock out any snipers that might start shooting."

I bent over Raskin, who was trying to get Frisbie's wound as clean as possible. Already the skin was puffed and purple.

"How's the leg, sir?" he asked. "Do you feel it through the morphine?"

The Aussie nodded, gritting back his pain.

Raskin shook his head. "This is a mean sonofabitch," he said to me. "I'd rather take a round any day."

It was nearly 5:00 in the afternoon when the distant chuffing of a helicopter echoed down the valley. Raskin, who had done all he could for Captain Frisbie, stepped into the Landing Zone and when he saw the Huey coming in just under the cloud cover he pulled the pin on a smoke grenade. The chopper headed directly towards us, dropping as it came.

"Those are brave sons of bitches," said Harvey. "Right in range of any VC's. No gunships."

The chopper was directly over the Landing Zone, ten feet up, when to our horror we heard the unmistakable deep staccato bursts of a .50-caliber machine gun about five hundred yards west of us. This heavy machine gun is the most effective anti-aircraft weapon the Communists have in Vietnam. With an accurate range of six hundred yards or better, it has been responsible for many of our aircraft losses.

We saw rents tear the side of the ship, and the door gunners open up futilely with their M-14's. Still the skin ship settled down until, six feet off the ground, another machinegun burst caught it. The chopper listed and then plummeted, the whirling rotors digging into the ground, windmilling the fuselage onto its nose and then down on its left side. All of us ran to the wreck, the turbojet engine steaming and screaming. Then the engine noise died. Both door gunners climbed out the skyward door, miraculously uninjured. They slid open the door to the co-pilot on the right and helped him out. He seemed uninjured also. Pulling the pilot out was more difficult. The crew chief climbed back inside the plane. We could hear groans from inside. Raskin jumped up on the side of the fuselage and helped the crew chief extricate his pilot. The pilot's helmet had been knocked or torn off his head in the crash. I recognized Pomfret instantly. So did Major Harvey.

Gently, Raskin and the crew chief laid the warrant officer on the ground. The medic knelt beside him, opening up the front of his flying fatigues. Pomfret's eyes fluttered. He seemed conscious.

"He isn't wounded," Raskin said. "I can't find any broken bones." Gently, he explored for damage and then his face tensed as his fingers felt under the helicopter pilot's neck.

"Get a litter out of the chopper," he commanded.

The door gunner jumped up on the fuselage, and reaching inside pulled out a stretcher. Unfolding it, he locked it into shape and laid it beside his pilot. The co-pilot, a young 2nd lieutenant, looked down anxiously. "Is he all right?"

Pomfret's eyes opened and he looked up. Hoarsely, he rasped, "I can't move. Can't hardly feel anything."

"Help me get him on the litter," Raskin ordered.

Tenderly, as Raskin steadied his head and neck, the crew and Major Harvey lifted Mr. Pomfret off the ground and placed him on the stretcher. They carried him off the Landing Zone.

Pomfret looked up anxiously at Raskin.

"It's your neck, sir. Seems a vertebra got cracked out of place."

"You mean I got a broken neck?" Pomfret closed his eyes, his voice dying. "I can't feel anything. Can't move."

Harvey looked at his watch. It was 4:45. "Do you think we could get another skin ship in, Mr. Pomfret?"

Pomfret struggled with each word. "Maybe," he said faintly. "Can you knock out that fifty?"

"I'll take two squads out myself," Harvey said harshly. "We'll get it—at least we'll harass them so they can't shoot straight."

Pomfret swallowed. The lines of his face knotted together. "Tell the B team to send Nichols. Tell Nichols I'm down."

He mustered his strength, then: "Nichols will get in. But get that fifty. . . ." Pomfret's voice was gone now, his breathing fitful.

"We've got to get him out, sir," Raskin said. "With a broken neck he'll die out here overnight. Maybe they can do something for him in Da Nang, but he really should get to Nha Trang."

"Right." Harvey ran over to the handset and told his A-team Executive Officer to get through to Lieutenant Nichols personally and tell him what happened.

"Raskin," Harvey said after signing off, "you're in command here. If Lieutenant Duong comes back tell him to go out again and look for the .50-caliber machine gun. Tell him for Christ's sake to get out five or six hundred meters. We've only got another hour and a half of daylight, not even that with the cloud cover so damned heavy. If the chopper comes in and gets out safely I want you to move everyone up onto that hill for the night. I'll join you up there. The code for tonight is nine."

I was careful to remember that—and glad I could count to ten in Vietnamese. If anyone challenged with a number, identification was the number that added to nine.

Harvey stooped beside Captain Frisbie. "See you later. They'll have you out with us again in a couple of weeks."

"Thank you, sir," he said weakly. "At least I shan't go walking into another pungi."

"Good man." Harvey dropped to one knee alongside Mr. Pomfret's stretcher. "Radio message went through, Mr. Pomfret. I'm taking two of my best squads out after that gun now."

Pomfret tried to answer but his voice failed him. Major Harvey patted his shoulder, stood up and signaled the montagnard company commander.

"Need another American on this mission, Major?" I volunteered.

Harvey grinned and shook his head. "You stay here. I want you alive to remember all this."

The squad fell into place and marched out behind him into the jungle.

Harvey had been out half an hour when Sergeant Raskin rose from Mr. Pomfret's side. "I'm going to walk the security perimeter. If the chopper comes in before I get back here's a smoke grenade.'' He pursed his lips grimly. "You can wave them off if the ground fire is too heavy.''

"Roger.''

I stood at the edge of the Landing Zone, smoke bomb in hand, staring out toward the hills in the west where the Viet Cong .50-caliber machine gun had been an hour ago. I wondered how Harvey was doing.

I stopped by Captain Frisbie's stretcher. The second shot of morphine had put him partially to sleep. Mr. Pomfret's eyes were closed—Raskin had given him some medication also.

Nichols would be coming in under worse light and ceiling conditions than he had experienced on the med evac I had flown with him and Mr. Pomfret. Also, there was the heavy machine gun to menace him.

Sergeant Raskin returned to the Landing Zone and I handed him the grenade. Just then we heard the welcome sound of a helicopter flying down "Destruction Alley,'' or so the place seemed to me by now. Tensely we waited, and then the black bulb hanging under the wide rotor blades showed up against the dirty-gray clouds.

Raskin pulled the pin and threw the smoke bomb into the Landing Zone. Several montagnards helped the two wounded strikers toward the edge of the Landing Zone. The dead montagnard was also carried out. It would be quite a chopper load.

The Huey spotted our smoke and started to slant directly into the Landing Zone. There was a sudden, not unexpected, burst of heavy machine-gun fire. We couldn't tell whether any rounds actually hit the helicopter, but it continued to slant in.

The burst of .50-caliber fire had hardly died away before a tremendous series of blasts rang out from the hills to the west. Grenades exploded in rapid succession over what seemed to be a wide area. Then came the sharp rattle of small-arms fire. No return .50-caliber fire could be heard in what sounded to be a brutal fire-fight.

Raskin directed the skin ship to the ground, and he and I picked up Mr. Pomfret's litter, ran to the chopper, and shoved it aboard. We loaded Captain Frisbie; the corpse was tucked under the back seat, and the two wounded strikers were lifted aboard. It looked like a full load already but Lieutenant Nichols motioned Mr. Pomfret's three crew members aboard, and then with a down-blast that almost blew us off the Landing Zone the doughty little skin ship popped up into the air and skittered back down the valley towards Da Nang.

Raskin and I each breathed a quick sigh of relief—but our work had hardly begun. Hastily, we organized the montagnards amd made a fast forced march for the hilltop Major Harvey had picked out to beat off the expected Viet Cong attack.

3.

One week later, back at home base in Nha Trang, I headed for the hospital. The nurses and doctors were getting to know me by now, so many of my friends were in their care.

"How's Mr. Pomfret?" I asked the chief surgeon, a lieutenant colonel.

The surgeon shook his head. "Paralyzed."

I felt a cold chill in my stomach, and for lack of anything intelligent to say asked if he would ever recover.

"It is very hard to be optimistic now," the surgeon replied. "Why don't you go in and see him? There's a whole A team from 'Eye' Corps in there now. They leave tomorrow to go home to Okinawa."

I walked along the boardwalk laid over the sandy soil—the beach was just a short distance away. There were rows of tents and temporary wooden structures, screened-in but open to the breeze blowing off the sea. Mr. Pomfret was in an officers' ward and I saw Captain Locke and his entire team around the skin-ship pilot's bed. As I approached I saw a little informal ceremony was taking place. Captain Locke took the green beret off his head and placed it on the bed beside Mr. Pomfret's rigid form. I couldn't hear exactly what he said; I did not want to interrupt. Then the presentation was over and the team was saying loud good-byes.

"They'll have you back in this war in six months, sir!"

"We aren't coming back until we know you're flying again."

"Hey, sir! That goof-off spec four, Krofault, remember? He's still at Clark Field Hospital. He said to thank you for his leg."

I waited until Captain Locke and his men had finished, then walked down the narrow passage between the beds until Mr. Pomfret could see me.

"Hiya!" he greeted me.

"How you feeling?"

"I'll make it." Then his eyes brightened. "What happened after I left? Major Harvey got the fifty, huh?"

"I should hope to tell you. He had his strikers spread out all over the place. The minute the Viet Cong opened up, there were at least four yards in grenade range of it. They had a hell of a fight and damned if they didn't all get back."

"Good. Well, Nichols did all right."

"He sure did."

I picked up the green beret Captain Locke had put on the bed.

Pomfret's eyes followed me. "Hey, how about that?" he said, pleased. His voice began to trail off: "They made me an honorary green beret."

"They couldn't have given it to a better man." It was just the kind of remark he would have made himself. Mr. Pomfret was never one for false modesty.

Too bad he couldn't hear me. He was fast asleep.

9

HIT 'EM WHERE
THEY LIVE

My diminutive, brown-skinned intellectual friend from Fort Bragg was surprised to see me step off the Army Aviation Caribou onto the airstrip of his top-secret base. In fact as Captain Jesse DePorta stared at me from under his beret he looked as though he were wondering whether to shake hands or throw me in some detention chamber for the duration of the Vietnam war. The pilot of the ship, knowing that no unauthorized people—and a civilian writer was about as unauthorized as you could get—were allowed to even know about the existence of this base, much less set foot on it, hastily explained our presence. It shouldn't have been necessary. An ugly series of frayed holes down the side of the plane, and oil leaking from the shot-up engine onto the cement apron of the runway told the story.

I had started out on a routine supply mission that morning, and coming out of the northernmost Special Forces camp in South Vietnam a Viet Cong machine-gun battery had opened up on us. The pilot did not dare throw the faltering plane into a banking turn at our low altitude. He pushed on and landed at this secret base, thirty miles on a straight course from where we picked up the rounds.

"Don't even carry your camera off the plane," the pilot told me. "And forget anything you see here."

The first thing I saw was Captain DePorta in the front seat of a jeep, a machine gunner behind him covering us.

"Hiya, Jesse," I said with a sheepish grin. "I was wondering if I'd see you this trip."

"I wish you hadn't." Then, to the pilot: "How long will it take you to get your plane in shape to fly out of here?"

"I don't know, sir. Could be a couple of days."

"We'll arrange a chopper evacuation for the civilian," DePorta said.

"Thanks," I acknowledged.

"It will take a couple of hours or more to get one to come over from Da Nang." DePorta studied the Caribou a few moments and I was relieved to see a white-toothed smile split his mahogany-colored face.

"Looks like you had a hairy one," DePorta said, his Philippine accent noticeable.

"The groundfire gets worse every month," said the pilot.

"Let's go have a cup of coffee."

"The civilian too?" I asked.

"Come on."

The pilot shook his head. "I'd better stay with the ship. When you send for the chopper ask them to sneak a mechanic in here too, will you?"

"Will do," DePorta agreed.

I hopped into the back seat of the jeep and we were off. As we drove along a dirt road through scrub trees and bush I heard staccato bursts of machine-gun fire and single shots that sounded like high-power riflefire. A few minutes later we passed a firing range where I saw men in green berets and Vietnamese in the red LLDB berets. I could see some of the weapons they were firing.

"Looks like the School," I remarked. "Not an American weapon on the line." I craned my neck and looked back as the jeep sped on.

"You shouldn't be seeing all this."

A few minutes later we reached a cluster of low wooden buildings and pulled up in front of a teamhouse. Inside, DePorta asked if I wanted coffee or iced tea. I chose the latter.

"Been a long time, Jesse," I said sipping the cold drink. "I heard you were doing something like this but no one seemed to know where you were."

"What do you mean, something like this?"

"After you've been over here a while things begin to add up. Inadvertently one of the guys, forgetting I'm an unauthorized civilian, showed me the sterile warehouse in Saigon.

You know, where all the weapons, clothes and equipment have been bought from either Communist bloc or neutral countries. If infiltrators using them get caught where they aren't supposed to be, the United States can't be implicated."

DePorta nodded soberly, but didn't answer.

"I suppose the men on that line we passed could fire and fieldstrip any weapon made in the world."

DePorta shrugged.

"What is this place, Jesse? The SFOB for some action against the Viet Cong in their own territory?"

A montagnard came in and asked DePorta something in a guttural language. DePorta answered in kind.

"I'd forgotten what a linguist you are, Jesse. Was that Bru you were talking?"

"Yes. I get along in Bru, Vietnamese, and one or two other montagnard dialects."

"Can I go with you, Jesse?"

"Go where?" he asked innocently.

"Where you people here are getting ready to go."

"We have no plans. Besides, I'm afraid the kind of missions we're planning would be restricted to"—he grinned at me—"unauthorized civilians."

"Can you show me any more of this place?" I asked. "Tell you what—the only people I'll blab it to will be VC's."

DePorta laughed loudly. "OK," he said, "we'll take a little drive."

This story is about a full A team, a joint U.S. Special Forces-LLDB detachment, in its guerrilla role. The mission described shows how all the skills on an A team are blended to achieve a single objective.

I wasn't on the operation, obviously, since it was top secret and one amateur, or even one less-than-outstanding professional, could cause the mission to fail.

I had my first inkling that a mission such as DePorta and his men were planning might be in operation when I read of the tragic crash in early December of an unmarked transport ship just outside Da Nang. Vietnamese pilots had been flying the ship and in it were 30 Veitnamese and 2 United States Special Forces men on a top-secret mission. They were all

263

wearing jump gear. Understandably, Vietnamese and United States authorities refused to divulge any information on the plane or its destination.

Later, through information from various sources, I was able to project the story which follows.

1.

Captain Jesse DePorta sat in the briefing room of the Special Forces Operating Base listening to Colonel Volkstaad up from the J-3 Special Warfare Board in Saigon.

Beside DePorta sat the Commanding Officer and the staff officers of the Special Forces Operating Base. A select group of 20 Special Forces men, wearing jungle fatigues, occupied benches behind the Philippine-American Special Forces captain. They were an unusual-looking crew; they seemed to be Asiatics dressed in American uniforms.

The Nordic-looking colonel's blue eyes snapped with excitement as he addressed his audience. "Men, you have necessarily been isolated here in the briefing center for the past two weeks, so I'll bring you up to date on the political situation that forces us to activate your operation sooner than we had expected."

The men leaned closer.

"As of now, the political situation in Saigon is, to be frank, a shambles." Colonel Volkstaad smiled wryly. "The civilian government of Premier Huong cannot last much longer. The Buddhists are rioting in the streets, the students are being inflamed by Communist agitators, and Intelligence reports that the Viet Cong are getting ready to launch their largest offensives since the war began. We suffered a tremendous loss of prestige in the eyes of the world when a few Viet Cong guerrillas destroyed our jet bombers at Bien Hoa with mortar fire and killed or wounded so many Americans."

The colonel paused, catching the eye of first one, then another of the men listening to him so intently. "After taking too many defeats here in Vietnam lying down, we're going to do something about it. We're going to hit 'em where they live!"

There was a buzz in the room. The colonel held up his

264

hand. "There have been too many unsuccessful attempts to set up guerrilla operations against the Communists. We mean no offense to our Vietnamese allies, but to date their efforts have achieved negative results and most of the men who went out have either been killed or captured. Now we're forced to try something new: a joint U.S. and South Vietnamese operation, led and commanded by Americans."

The colonel walked to the large map. "We have picked a solid Communist area, industrialized and alert to possible infiltration. You have been studying assessments of the area for months and you must know how important it is to the Communists. The electric plants are good, the factories in the north of your area are turning out military equipment, and even Chinese copies of Russian and American weapons. There have been no less than three Vietnamese attempts to infiltrate this area. All failed. Your area is one of the most important staging centers for the Viet Cong guerrillas slipping into South Vietnam. If your mission is successful it will do more to shake up Hanoi than even air strikes, because for the first time we will be spreading dissension and carrying out frequent, unexpected, and damaging guerrilla raids in a Communist heartland."

Colonel Volkstaad pointed to the center of the area outlined in red. "Here is Hang Mang, the most important city within a radius of one hundred miles. It controls the entire area. The electric plant there, installed by a combined Russian and Red Chinese team, supplies power to the province. Cripple Hang Mang, and you will prove that our guerrilla ground forces can do the same to any Communist city, including Hanoi.

"Someday, we don't know when, but it could be soon, there will be new negotiations. We want to negotiate from strength with a shaken, fearful Hanoi. Your job is to show Ho Chi Minh just how we can cripple his industry and supply lines, and assassinate his leaders. Your mission—officially known as 'Falling Rain'—will prepare the way for infiltrating 50, maybe 100, guerrilla teams into Communist strongholds in North Vietnam, and we will erode Hanoi's will to keep up the guerrilla warfare against its neighbors."

Colonel Volkstaad silently surveyed the group of dark-skinned "Asiatics." "The Communists will never be able to prove the United States is behind this operation. No man here could be picked out of a crowd as a Caucasian. You will be

265

supplied completely with sterile equipment. Oh, Hanoi will know who is behind this operation. But Hanoi will be cautious about charging America with a land invasion of a major Communist stronghold. It would show up their weakness."

The colonel paused. "That is all I have to say. We all wish Acbat the very best of luck. Operation Falling Rain depends on you!"

"Thank you, sir," DePorta said. "Acbat will do its job!"

Colonel Volkstaad took a front seat beside Colonel Langston, commanding officer of the Special Forces Operating Base. A sober-faced, gray-haired major took Volkstaad's place.

Major Fraley, scarred and grizzled from a lifetime of combat, was the S-3 or operations officer of the Special Forces Operating Base. Everything pertaining to the actual workings of the mission was his immediate responsibility.

"Right!" he began, acknowledging all Colonel Volkstaad had said. "This will be the read-back briefing on Operation Falling Rain."

Fraley stepped to the large relief map of Indo-China facing the room, and placed his hand on a mountain range above a large valley. "Here is the Guerrilla Warfare Operating Area Acbat will open up. DePorta, you start."

DePorta walked to the map. "Acbat infiltrates the GWOA at 2300 hours at this point," he began indicating the spot on the map. "The reception party on the Drop Zone will be led by Major Luc of G-2 this SFOB, who has been working for a month with the Tai tribesmen we will live with. Every member of Acbat knows Major Luc by sight.

"Our mission is to open up the GWOA, which runs eighty miles from north to south and from twenty to thirty miles east to west." DePorta traced the area on the map.

"As soon as we have established our base in the center of the GWOA we will contact the underground in Hang Mang, about fifteen miles from infiltration point.

"We will send patrols out to locate operational sites for A detachments Artie and Alton. As soon as we have sites and potential indigenous guerrillas for them, we will call in Artie and Alton." DePorta nodded to Captain Sampson Buckingham, a burly, short Negro in the second row, commander of Alton. Then his glance shifted to Captain Victor Locke, commander of Artie. Locke was of pure Anglo-Saxon extraction but his darkstained skin and brown eyes made him blend with the rest of the non-Caucasians in the room.

"When we are ready for Alton and Artie to infiltrate the GWOA Acbat becomes Batcat, the B detachment for Operation Falling Rain. We activate the operation when Artie and Alton are ready to hit their targets. Then, sir, we make Uncle Ho cry 'Uncle.' "

Major Fraley, standing beside DePorta, said, "Right. That's the overall mission. Now, for the Special Operations readback. Captain Smith."

The Executive Officer of Acbat, Brickley Smith, stood up. Though pure Caucasian his eyes and skin were dark and his black hair was worn in unmilitary bangs. DePorta had handpicked Smith, not only for his skills but because he sensed Smith neither planned nor wanted to return from the mission alive.

"Our first operation will to be exfiltrate Major Luc. We will clear a U-10 Landing Zone and advise the SFOB. Our second special operation is to kidnap the province political chief in Hang Mang, one Pham Son Ti.

"Ti is the most powerful man in the GWOA and all the other chiefs, while in theory equal to him, are in fact taking orders from him. He is an old line revolutionary who commanded a Viet Minh regiment against the French, not as a nationalist fighting colonialism but as a hard-core Communist. He makes all the decisions on policy in our GWOA and reports directly to Hanoi. Taking him from the Communists will deprive them of one of their best and most vigorous men."

Smith paused, reached down onto his seat, and held up a sketch of a surly, shock-haired Oriental. "This is Pham Son Ti. As soon as Acbat has infiltrated our asset, Ton"—Smith gestured at a Vietnamese in the second row—"will immediately start planning with the underground the abduction of Mr. Ti. As soon as we grab him we'll send him back to the SFOB for interrogation on how they direct and control the population in the Communist North, and how they guard against infiltrators moving around the countryside—the biggest problem facing us."

Smith continued matter-of-factly. "Our third special assignment is to plan assassination of Communist political officers throughout our area of operations."

Fraley nodded and Smith sat down. "Lieutenant Vo," Fraley said, "you and Sergeant Ossidian are in charge of intelligence. Will you read back your part of the operation?"

"Mr. Ton," the Vietnamese officer said, "is a native of Hang Mang who defected from the Viet Cong to us the first chance he had. I also have connections in Hang Mang. Ton's family are Catholics who lost most of their property and money when the Communists took over. They were merchants. Ton has a female cousin, one Quand, who is in the opium trade in Hang Mang. We hear that she is close to Ti."

Lieutenant Vo spoke good English and was proud of his ability to talk to the Americans. "Quand has a brother, Pham. He also hates the Communists. They will both help us."

Major Fraley nodded. "Ossidian?"

"Our intelligence on the Tai people we will be working with is short," the swarthy Syrian said. "The chief, Muk Thon, was a sergeant with the French Army for three or four years. My asset here, Krak"—Ossidian pointed at the montagnard seated next to him—"was in the army with Muk Thon. Krak is a Tai tribesman who came to us a year ago to tell us his people would help fight the Communist lowland Viet Cong. Thon's village, like most of them, grows opium poppy and we hope to use this to penetrate the corrupt elements in the city and use them against the Communists." Ossidian described the area and the target analyses he would make on site.

Then Fraley asked each of the other members of Acbat to describe his assignments on the operation.

When the briefing was complete Major Fraley introduced Major Copitz, the G-4 or supply officer who would help Acbat draw and check equipment.

As the men stood up and stretched, Captain Buckingham and Captain Locke walked over to DePorta. "Jesse," Buckingham said, "don't you forget us. We gotta stay right here in isolation in the briefing center until we infiltrate. We're all professionals but you can keep men on ice just so long."

"Don't worry, Sam," DePorta promised. "I'll get Alton and Artie out where you can get zapped just as fast as I can."

Major Copitz came up to DePorta. "Ready to go into the sterile supply center, Captain?"

"Let's go."

Followed by his team they left the briefing room, walked

through the solarium where the light-skinned men had lain in the sun, constantly rubbing a greasy liquid into their skin which stained it dark brown, and on past the operations situation room, intelligence, and personnel into the barnlike logistical building.

DePorta's men spent the remainder of the day drawing their sterile equipment. Not one item of equipment from boots, socks, and underwear to radios, weapons, and medical kits could be traced to American manufacture.

Sergeant Rodriguez, a dark-skinned Latin, and Captain Smith had spent three weeks preparing sterile demolition equipment. Sergeant Frenchy Pierrot, the chief medic, had made up the surgical packs he and his Vietnamese assistant, Sergeant Lin, would carry, from medical supplies brought in from all over the Communist and neutral world. Certain American-manufactured drugs were transferred to foreign-made containers. Ashton Everett, the Negro communications expert, had likewise assembled all his radio equipment from foreign components. Master Sergeant Earlington Mattrick, the Negro team sergeant, supervised all phases of equipment withdrawal, taking care to see that Krak and their Bru tribesman, Manong, both of whom found it difficult to communicate, were completely outfitted.

The weapons were also "international." Only four U.S. weapons were issued—the M-1 and M-2 carbine and the 60- and 81-mm. mortars. So many had been captured or sold around the world that they were considered sterile for this operation.

It was dark by the time Acbat was issued East German-made parachutes. They had a few hours to rest and then loaded up in the unmarked C-46.

2.

Airman 1st Class Kunitski held up both hands, fingers outstretched. Ten minutes. Captain DePorta nodded and felt his stomach churn as he looked out the open door into blackness. The engines of the C-46 pounded their way back into his consciousness as he was torn back from momentary reverie. He knew fear but he was in complete control of himself and his men.

DePorta looked down the stick of six men, hands folded over their emergency 'chutes, staring ahead or at the steel cable running the length of the plane above them. Very soon they'd stand up and hook the static lines of their parachutes onto it.

From across the aisle Captain Brick Smith caught his Commanding Officer's eye. He nodded. A slight smile touched his lips. The cold lump in DePorta's stomach was slightly warmed by the feeling of confidence he felt in his Executive Officer.

Acbat was a good team, DePorta knew. For six months he had trained them in everything he had learned about guerrilla warfare while fighting the Japanese in his native Philippine Islands from 1942 to 1945. And DePorta's men had trained him also. Sergeant Rodriguez was a devastatingly clever demolitions man, as was Smith. Master Sergeant Mattrick was one of the finest hand-to-hand combat men in Special Forces, and he had taught his small commander how to kill an attacker twice his weight without a weapon. The Negro team sergeant was the fine administrative man DePorta also needed.

Frenchy Pierrot had a well-deserved reputation as a combat medic, more than once having operated on wounded men while tossing grenades and firing at an oncoming enemy. And there could be no more sophisticated a man with radio equipment than Sergeant Everett.

Yes, DePorta knew he had a good team. And on this mission he, the American commander, was in complete operational control of the team. Although for years it had been apparent to the men in combat against the Communist Viet Cong guerrillas that it was better if the Vietnamese did not have final control of military operations, the United States continued to support this policy, to prove Americans were merely acting as advisers.

But in the case of an operation as delicate as this one, which would be constantly on the verge of disaster, U.S. Military Assistance Command had politely but firmly insisted in talks with Vietnamese high command that if the U.S. were to be part of an unconventional warfare mission into Communist heartland, Americans must exercise command at all levels.

Sergeant "Ski" swung up to the cockpit door, opened it, and stepped inside. The U.S. Air Commando pilot flying the airship was regularly changing course in banking turns, right and left, as he flew a tactical course toward the Drop Zone.

Enemy radar thus would be unable to plot the plane's course as it flew at twelve thousand feet. Below, there was a ground station operated by a small detachment of Special Forces communications men in a montagnard-fortified village. The plane would home on this station and then, after flying over it, track out on the beam at 95 degrees. Twelve minutes later the plane would be over the Drop Zone prepared by Major Luc and the Tai tribesmen.

The most dangerous part of the mission, the time when the team members had no control over what might happen to them, was coming up. Everything depended upon the men on the ground. This jump had been simulated several times, but the real thing was never the same.

The men of Acbat suddenly felt the plane descending rapidly. Drop altitude was one thousand feet. The pilots had barely time to descend and slow up for the drop before they would be over the Drop Zone. DePorta, with only the glow of red lights to see by, kept his eyes on Ski in the dark cabin. The crew chief, with earphones and a microphone harnessed to his head, conversed with the pilots. He held up one hand. Five minutes.

Brick Smith stared into the cold blackness crowding the door at his commanding officer's right. Even on practice jumps there was something about the minutes before throwing himself out of an airplane that made his blood tingle and the tips of his fingers itch. With more than seventy jumps behind him he still knew the clutch of apprehension before a jump. Three hundred jumps could not stop the feeling that was, no matter how you disguised it in your mind, fear. Man just wasn't psychologically constructed to throw himself out of airplanes. But this time he wasn't afraid. This time he just didn't care what happened to him.

Smith patted the Czech-made submachine gun hanging under his left arm. If the Viet Cong were waiting on the Drop Zone he'd have an honorable death fighting them to the end. If they only wounded him so he could no longer fight there was the poison pill disguised as a wart cemented on the back of his left wrist.

He'd tried to convince himself that his wife wasn't the only one who'd taken another man while her husband was on the other side of the world. But it hurt.

Smith almost felt sorry for the rest of Acbat. They were

normal men doing a job they wanted to live through. Jesse DePorta had a devoted wife, a Mexican girl, who had no idea what he was doing. But DePorta knew he was an American uniquely qualified for the job ahead and had volunteered for it.

All the men of Acbat stood an excellent chance of being dead in a few minutes—or worse, beginning a living death, lost and hurt in the Viet Cong-infested jungle. Smith felt a sense of exhilaration. No matter what happened, it was highly unlikely he would come back alive. He ached for the moment he would plunge into the black prop blast and be lost in the vicious jungle war that had become his life.

He had loved Kathy. She had been his life, his anchor. And then on his last tour in Vietnam it had happened. His wife had betrayed him with a captain—a straight-leg captain at that—and did not even bother to deny it when he faced her with the truth.

Smith was aware of DePorta standing and of Ski giving them three fingers. The plane had levelled out at one thousand feet. Time to get the bundles in the door. He reached both hands for the bundle to the rear of the door, wrestling it to the kick-out position.

DePorta hooked his static line into the cable. The rest of Acbat did the same. Captain Smith and Sergeant Pierrot at the right door and DePorta and Sergeant Mattrick at the other balanced the heavy bundles containing their equipment. The red light came on beside the doors. DePorta stuck his head out the door. The blast of rushing air distorted the flesh on his face. Less than two minutes from the Drop Zone, on correct heading and altitude at exactly the correct time. If all was well below he should see the lights. He strained his eyes, trying to pick out the inverted L on the ground.

"One minute!" Ski shouted. Suddenly the lights winked from the blackness of the ground ahead. There was the L—the long side running the length of the Drop Zone. Just as they came over the light forming the small leg of the L they would push the bundles out and jump. Ski was checking equipment. DePorta felt himself slapped in the rear as Mattrick cried "Two, OK."

"One, OK!" DePorta shouted back, ready to jump. They were almost over the L now. The red light changed to green beside the door. DePorta threw his weight at the bundles, which toppled into the night, and made a vigorous exit after them. Holding a tight body position—his chin tightly in his chest, arms pressed to his sides, hands clutching the emergency chute—he was blown back in the tearing prop blast. He looked down at his legs, straight out and pressed together. Then came the slight opening shock of the 'chute and immediately DePorta looked up to make sure his canopy was open. It was. He found he was facing the rear of the disappearing plane. He watched the other 'chutes open against the sky.

There was absolute silence now. The lights were off again below. Even the roar of the plane's engines had ceased. The transport plane would fly for another five minutes on the same track so as not to give away the Drop Zone location in case enemy radar was following its course. So far so good. Now it was all up to the reception committee. The recognition code number was seven. Not that it would do them much good, DePorta thought grimly, if there weren't friendlies waiting for them.

The ground came up. Knees bent, toes extended, DePorta relaxed his legs and body to the point where he could still maintain control. He hit, rolled into some bush, and jumped to his feet. He had hardly started to gather in his parachute when three montagnards were on him. DePorta held up four fingers. The lead tribesman held up three. DePorta breathed a sigh of relief. He heard muffled thumps as the rest of Acbat hit.

The guides led DePorta off the Drop Zone to a slight knoll rising above the open area. Standing on top of it was a Vietnamese in black pajamas taller by a few inches than DePorta.

"We are glad you are here, Captain DePorta," the Vietnamese said.

"I am glad to see you again, Major Luc. Very good Drop Zone you marked for us."

"The Tai people will bring all your men and bundles to this spot," Luc said. "Then you will have a hard march ahead of you. We have many, many Tai carriers so you and your men will not have to carry your packs." This rarely occurred except in behind-the-lines missions.

"We're all in shape for anything, Major." DePorta's enthusiasm pleased Major Luc.

"This is a very great day."

"We'll do our best." DePorta saw Captain Smith come up beside him. Luc welcomed the Executive Officer. When Acbat was completely assembled on the knoll and the four bundles broken down and distributed among the Tai tribesmen, along with the men's personal packs, Major Luc ordered them to get started.

"I will stay here with some of the Tai people," he explained to DePorta. "At first light of dawn I will personally inspect to be sure the Drop Zone is sterilized. Remember the teaching at Fort Bragg? The smallest thing left on the ground could compromise our whole mission."

Krak, the Tai asset, after conversing in low tones with his people and Major Luc, took his place beside Captain DePorta as the montagnards and Acbat started to penetrate the jungle. Acbat had hit the Drop Zone at midnight as planned. They now had a four-hour hike to their first operating base.

As the file of montagnard bearers wound through the jungle trails DePorta and Smith checked their direction frequently by compass. Landmarks were non-existent in the jungle. They were proceeding in roughly a southeasterly direction from the Drop Zone. After the first hour the march was entirely uphill. At the end of two hours they had walked, by DePorta's estimate, six thousand meters, and a rest was called. They must have been well up in the mountains, DePorta felt, as the air was cool, almost cold. The montagnards stood and the men of Acbat followed. Although all of DePorta's men were in top physical condition for this mission they were glad that this once the Tai men were carrying the equipment.

Finally, the long, exhausting march terminated in a flat area close to the top of a mountain. In the faint glow of false dawn DePorta could make out the outline of a typical montagnard village. The longhouses were on stilts, and clusters of storage cribs, also on stilts, stood near the houses. As they entered the village Krak left his commander's side and supervised the stockpiling of the supplies under one of the long raised houses.

In the red glow from a dying fire in front of one of the houses, DePorta saw a gnarled old man in a loincloth, holding his arms to his body under a shawl to combat the cold of dawn, rise and walk toward them. Krak suddenly appeared at the tribesman's side and escorted him to where DePorta and Smith, the rest of Acbat around them, were standing.

Krak, in French, introduced the chief of this Tai village to DePorta. Muk Thon, also speaking in French, welcomed DePorta and his team to the village. Proudly, Muk Thon told them that he had fought with the French in 1952. In fact, he said, in their village, a small team of French soldiers had lived for many, many months.

Krak supplied the information that some Tais like Muk Thon's group had frequently moved their villages in the past ten years to avoid the Communist government troops. Nevertheless, the Democratic Republic of Vietnam (North Vietnam) still tried to track down the wandering Tai tribes and put them under some form of direct government supervision.

Muk Thon gestured at the bamboo house on stilts under which the supplies had been placed. "This will be the house for your men," he said.

DePorta thanked the chief and told Smith to get the men settled in the longhouse. Smith and Sergeant Mattrick led the tired men of Acbat to their new quarters.

At Krak's suggestion DePorta accompanied Muk Thon back to his hut. There they sat before the fire, the chief reaching out to its warmth with his hands.

Although the Vietnamese, in common with most Orientals, usually avoided coming to the point in important matters, the montagnards are blunt people who mistrust talking around subjects. Therefore DePorta immediately began a partial briefing of Acbat's mission in slow French.

"We will train and arm all your men to fight the Viet Cong lowlanders," DePorta began.

"We hate the Viet Cong," Muk Thon said vigorously. "They steal our poppy, they try to make our young men join their Army, and they make us pay taxes."

"We will change all that," DePorta declared. "But first we must be strong. We will find a training ground far from this village and begin to make soldiers of your men."

Muk Thon shook his head. "No. The men know how to fight. They get guns, they fight. They have no time to train. They must work in the fields, grow our rice, manioc, and care for the poppy."

"But they must be trained."

"I was in the French Army. I know how to fight. My men will follow me. You give us guns."

"But the men have to learn how to use them."

"In one day, here, without leaving the village, they learn," Muk Thon insisted. "Men must work in fields."

DePorta employed the tactic he had been saving. Shifting from French to the Tai language he said, "I and my men came up here to help you fight the Viet Cong lowlanders. We will give you guns, equipment, and money to pay the fighting men. But your men must be trained well by my men."

The squatting chief stopped rocking, motionless with surprise at hearing this newcomer speak his language. After several moments of silence he said, "You speak the language of the Tai. Good. But what of the crops?"

"While half the men train, the other half work the fields."

Muk Thon puffed his pipe impassively. "This is the time we get the poppy juice."

"We pay you and your men. You do not need to tend the poppies."

"No!" Muk Thon exclaimed defiantly. "Poppy die if we do not care for it. Then when you go away we have no poppy to sell."

"Half your men work fields, the other half train," DePorta went on doggedly. "We will pay better than the Viet Cong Army. And if a man has a wife he is paid extra, and for children, extra still. We pay in local money."

Thon closed his eyes and rocked back and forth on his haunches, puffing on his pipe. "When will come the first payday?" Muk Thon asked practically.

"When we have enlisted the men and assigned them rank."

"It will soon be daylight," Muk Thon said, a trace of enthusiasm in his tone. "We can start then."

"Are all your men loyal? If one betrays us the whole mission is lost."

"No Tai man, woman or child would betray this village," Thon said, his eyes flashing.

Feeling he was making progress, DePorta pushed on. "Now, Muk Thon, you, as chief, will become a colonel in the Tai Army we will form. And we will pay you more than the Communists pay their colonels."

DePorta reached into his pocket and drew out the three silver buttons that designate the rank of colonel in the Vietnamese Army. He handed them to Thon. "As soon as we open the bundles you will be issued a uniform."

Thon took the insignia and stared at the gleaming silver in

his brown hand. "As your adviser I too carry the rank of colonel," DePorta went on. "After a week of training we will evaluate the men of your village and create the ranks for our force."

For the moment, at least, Muk Thon seemed placated. DePorta knew it would be a mistake to push the Tai chief any further at this time.

The smell of cooking wafted across the village as the women prepared the morning meals.

"Colonel," DePorta said, "we have brought some rations with us but we will have to buy all our food from your village soon."

Thon was smugly pleased at being addressed by his new rank. "I will send women to your house to make fires and cook for your men. My wife and daughter will cook breakfast for you and me here."

"Thank you, Colonel." DePorta glanced toward the longhouse assigned to Acbat. "I will see how my men are and return."

Sergeant Mattrick was sitting in the door, his Swedish K submachine gun across his knees. Captain Smith was examining the bundles.

"There'll be some Tai women along to cook for you," DePorta told them.

"No thanks. I'll eat my own rations for a couple of days," Mattrick said. "It's going to take a while to get used to Tai food."

"Right," DePorta agreed. "Brick, come over and risk the state of your stomach having hot chow with me and Colonel Muk Thon."

DePorta and Smith walked to Muk Thon's longhouse. Krak was there, squatting on his haunches beside the chief.

"Colonel Thon," DePorta said as they approached the fire, "this is my Executive Officer, Lieutenant Colonel Smith."

Soberly Smith snapped a salute at the squatting chief, who was instantly on his feet at attention, returning the salute in a military manner. In French, Smith said, "It is an honor, Colonel."

"The honor is mine."

Thon's wife and daughter bustled among them. The older woman, though leathery and wrinkled, exuded dignity. She

277

was slender and taller than most montagnard women—as tall as DePorta.

Muk Thon's daughter, Luy, was a handsome, graceful girl in her mid-twenties, with long black hair carefully combed, and skin lighter than that of the montagnards from the south. Her breasts protruded from the shawl she wore around her shoulders. In her thin face and ample eyes DePorta saw a deep sadness. What tragedies had she experienced in this tragedy-ridden land? he wondered.

"You will have breakfast?" she asked in French. Both officers accepted.

Luy soon returned with two bowls of steaming broth, large chunks of meat floating in it, and laid them in front of Smith and DePorta. There was a gourd dipped in each bowl and Muk Thon's wife placed a bowl of boiled rice before them.

The soup was strong and gamy but it tasted nourishing and the two Americans were hungry. "This soup has great authority," Smith said chewing on a piece of meat. "Meat's tender too."

DePorta agreed. "They believe in natural tenderizing," he said between mouthfuls. "They take as long as twenty minutes to beat an animal to death before cooking it."

Luy knelt before Smith. "Aimez-vous?" she said.

"Very good. What kind of meat is it?"

"Monkey," Luy said proudly. "We were going to eat dog but when Major Luc said Americans were coming I prepared the monkeys."

Luy looked steadily at DePorta. "You are American, Colonel?"

"Yes, American by nationality—but like you, I am born Asiatic. Have you heard of the Philippine Islands?"

"Oh, yes. My husband had many maps." Her face clouded. "He was French. He and three other soldiers lived with us for a year."

Smith looked at DePorta.

"Her husband must have been a member of the Groupement de Commando Mixtes Aeroportes. They tried to do the same thing we're here to do. The Communists hated them." DePorta asked Luy, "Your husband was Groupement de Commando Mixtes Aeroportes?"

Her eyes brightened and she nodded vigorously.

"I don't think more than a fraction of them ever left

Vietnam alive." DePorta nudged Smith and went on. "But we will not worry, we have much better support."

"What happened to her husband, Krak?" Smith asked.

Luy's eyes dropped to the ground. Krak shrugged uncomfortably.

In English, DePorta said to Smith, "The tribe forced Muk Thon to give him and the other Frenchmen to the Communists after the war was over in return for complete pardon and peace for this Tai village."

"How did you know?"

"One of the little pieces of information they came out with in the commander's briefing."

"What makes you so sure they won't double-cross us?"

"Much has happened in the past ten years. Our Area Specialist team at the SFOB believe the Tais will stick solidly behind us." DePorta stood up and looked off into the eastern sky at the ruddy sunrise. "We have much work ahead of us in the next few days. I suggest we get a few hours sleep. This afternoon we can start officially signing up recruits and getting them on the payroll."

The heat of late morning and the sun steaming into the hut woke DePorta. Lieutenant Vo was on guard at the door; the rest of the team was just waking. DePorta stood up, pulled off his sweater and walked to the door.

In English, Vo said, "Major Luc is just back. He is with the chief."

At Muk Thon's house, DePorta found Major Luc and Krak. Thon had pinned his colonel's insignia on a ragged black pajama shirt.

"It was a good thing I stayed," Luc said in English when he saw DePorta. "Much evidence on the Drop Zone. But we cleaned it up so the Viet Cong suspect nothing."

"We'll have to exfiltrate you, Major Luc. They'll need you back at the SFOB," DePorta said. "Did you have time while you were here to look for U-10 Landing Zones?"

"I made the time," Luc said. "Always I was thinking I would have to get out of here."

"We'll get you out as soon as we can," DePorta promised. "Now, let's get this show on the road."

By the end of the afternoon one side of the longhouse had been partitioned off for the dispensary. Sergeant Pierrot and his Vietnamese assistant medic, Sergeant Lin, had arranged their limited medical supplies and equipment, cut a new door in the end of the bamboo structure, and built steps up from the ground so the sick could more easily enter. Colonel Muk Thon, who had been issued his camouflage uniform, had ordered a medical check for all men who would be joining the guerrilla force. This would be every able-bodied man in the village; they would train in two alternating companies.

Luy was the first to arrive at Frenchy Pierrot's dispensary. She led a ten-year-old boy whose body was covered with open red sores which almost closed his eyes. Frenchy examined the boy. Then he gave Luy a bar of strong medicated soap. "Take him to the river and wash him with this," he instructed Luy in French. "Then bring him back to me."

"Merci, monsieur," the boy said.

"You speak French?"

"Oui, monsieur."

"My husband was French," Luy explained. "We try to teach the boy his father's language."

"What is his name?" Frenchy asked.

"Muk Lon. His French name is Pierre. His father gave him that name before the Viet Minh killed him."

"Pierre," Frenchy said with mock sternness, "three times every day I want you to take the soap I gave your mother and wash yourself with it in the river. Then you will come to me. Do you understand?"

Pierre nodded solemnly.

"Do the people of the tribe have soap?" Frenchy asked.

"We cannot buy it," Luy replied.

"Then we will make it," Frenchy replied. "I will teach you and you will teach the village women."

"They will be happy to learn."

At the other end of the longhouse, Sergeant Ossidian's operations and intelligence room had been set up with maps on the walls and acetate overlays on which information about the area and targets was being steadily grease-penciled.

Manong, the Bru tribesman ethnically close to the Tai and able to speak their language, had located several other men who had fought with the French and was already indoctrinating them in the use of the foreign weapons that would be distributed to the recruits the next day.

Sergeant Ashton Everett, the Negro communications chief,

and his assistant, Sergeant Trung, had their radio assembled and ready to start transmitting and receiving. Communications would be the most difficult part of this operation. It was known that the North Vietnamese had acquired from Russia via Red China the latest technical skills and sophisticated equipment for detecting possible anti-government radio signals or messages from bases outside North Vietnam to agents operating on the border or inside.

Ordinarily, for Acbat to transmit without fear of their base being discovered, the communications men would have to carry their equipment many miles. However, one ingenious officer had developed a ruse which would work for a while, and postpone the time when more intricate methods of anti-direction-finding transmission must be used.

At exactly 1800 hours DePorta, Smith, the two commo sergeants, and Major Luc gathered on the hill above the village.

The antenna had been stretched between two trees, oriented by compass so that it would be precisely broadside to the radio station at the SFOB two hundred miles to the south. Sergeant Trung sat by the transmitter ready to tap out DePorta's message. The signal would inform the SFOB that all personnel were safe and the operation ready to proceed. It also gave a preliminary request for a U-10 evacuation of Major Luc and the time, two days later, that next radio contact would be made and full Landing Zone details transmitted.

Smith turned to DePorta as a Tai tribesman, sitting on the seat of the generator, began grinding the cranks that produced the electric current to power the transmitter. "I hope this brilliant idea works or we'll be up to our ass in Communist troops before morning."

DePorta grinned confidently. "It will work, if we don't overdo it."

Sergeant Everett, staring at his watch, nudged Trung as the minute hand hit 6:00 P.M. Sergeant Trung began to tap out the message. On the official Thailand Army radio frequency, carefully monitored in Hanoi, Trung began sending the message which when analyzed by the Communists would sound like the usual series of Thai code words emanating from Bangkok and other military bases in Thailand every day. There would be no need to make a direction-finding check on such routine traffic.

In five minutes Trung had tapped out his message and the radio equipment was packed up and they were on their way back to the village.

The SFOB would acknowledge the message the next day at a predetermined hour.

For the next three days Acbat worked almost around the clock. The medics, between physical checks of the men, helped the women with many disorders. Fifty per cent of the Tai babies had been dying because the mothers had no milk in their breasts to nurse them. Pierrot added to his list of medical supplies fifty pounds of a dehydrated milk formula for expectant Tai women. Skin disease was prevalent and a complete dermatological unit was put on the list for the first airdrop.

Bad teeth by the dozens were pulled, relieving toothaches, and water purification methods were introduced.

A patrol commanded by Sergeant Mattrick went out to assess the surrounding area and check out the Landing Zone for evacuating Major Luc.

3.

Acbat had been in the Tai village four days when a party of tribesmen along with Smith and Mattrick went out to Landing Zone Hairy to exfiltrate Major Luc. The same day Ton left camp to slip into Hang Mang and make contact with the underground.

When both missions had left the village DePorta went to Muk Thon's house on stilts for a private meeting. "Colonel," DePorta said to the Tai chief sitting on the floor of his house, "tomorrow I want to move to the new location we found eight kilometers west of here. We will make it our headquarters. We will take the training company with us and leave the field workers here."

Muk Thon slowly took his pipe from his mouth, his eyes never leaving DePorta. "No! This is our home. The Tai people will not leave it."

"Colonel"—DePorta talked in French now, adding urgency to his words—"we must keep our company together. It is important that we become established in a new location."

"We Tai people do not leave our village," Muk Thon insisted.

Hearing Muk Thon's vehement tones, his wife and daughter entered from outside.

"The American says we must leave our village!" Muk Thon cried.

"Must we all go?" Luy asked.

DePorta shook his head. "Just my men and the company of Tai men we are training."

"I say none of us go." Muk Thon said decisively.

"Suppose Nguyen That Ton gets caught?" DePorta asked. "How long do you think it would take before he told everything?"

Muk Thon sat silently for a few minutes, puffing at his pipe. "My men do not move without their colonel," he said stubbornly.

"And there is always a chance that Major Luc and my deputy, Lieutenant Colonel Smith, might be picked up and tortured."

Luy gasped. DePorta glanced briefly at her. Then he said to Muk Thon, "Colonel, our mission here against the Viet Cong depends on training these men and not getting caught. I am requesting that you move with the training company to the new camp." He turned slightly towards Luy. "Lieutenant Colonel Smith will be in charge of training. He is proud to work with such an experienced warrior as you, Colonel."

Luy blushed slightly and turned away. The flattery hit its mark and Muk Thon finally said, "If my wife and daughter will leave this home I will go."

Five days later, after the successful U-10 exfiltration of Major Luc, it was necessary for Acbat to send a long communication to the SFOB.

DePorta summed up Acbat's first ten days in its operational area and then read his message to Smith before giving it to Everett for encoding and transmitting. He reported that Nguyen That Ton had been successful in joining up with the Hang Mang underground. Good progress was being made on planning the abduction of the province official officer, Ti. All targets were under surveillance. An outlet for selling the gold leaf for local currency had been established. A meeting was scheduled two days hence between Acbat Intelligence and underground representatives. Acbat was looking for a third base of operations and would send coordinates when the base was established. Two platoons of Tais were undergoing accelerated guerrilla training. Krak had led a small party to a Tai village where a base of operations for Alton was being set up. Krak and the assistant medic, Lin, stayed to provide badly needed medical aid and prepare the Tai people to the north for the arrival of Alton. Much leprosy was reported. Extra supplies would be required by Alton. Manong had successfully made contact with his Bru tribesmen to the south. He reported his area would be ready for Artie soon. He also reported heavy Viet Cong military traffic building up.

DePorta finished his message with a list of coordinates of Drop Zones and another emergency Landing Zone in the area, giving their altitudes, the obstructions around them, and the compass heading of the long axis of the Landing Zone.

"This better go by balloon, sir," Everett said when he saw the length of the communiqué.

"Right," DePorta agreed.

Everett reached for the specially ruled code pad and made a swift, accurate encoding of the long message. It took the commo sergeant about fifteen minutes to finish. Then he unlocked a metal box and took out a small transistorized transmitter. Everett grinned up at his Commanding Officer. "I should get hazardous-duty pay every time I use one of these, sir."

"That you should, Everett."

Everett plugged a battery power-pack into the small transmitter, and began tapping out the message with the telegraph key. A magnetic tape whirred through the transmitter, recording the dots and dashes. Everett worked the key for close to ten minutes before he completed the message. Then he touched a switch on the tiny transmitter and the tape rewound.

"Ready to go, sir. This sends on the channel monitored twenty-four hours a day at the SFOB."

"Send it, Everett."

From the metal box Everett drew out a large deflated balloon and a helium bottle. He carried them out of the thatched-roof commo center, the small transmitter in his other hand.

"Let me help you, Everett," Smith offered. He took the balloon and inflated it with helium, holding the wire thread attached to the balloon through a vulcanized loop. He clipped the inflating valve shut and let the balloon rise, handing the wire to Everett.

"Sir, you'd better stand back," Everett said. "No sense us all getting it if this thing misfires."

DePorta and Smith retreated to a safe distance. Everett pulled a long, thin antenna wire from the transistor as he attached it to the balloon. The last thing he did before releasing the device was to pull the safety wire from a red button protruding from the transmitter. Closing his eyes and grimacing, he pressed the red button and let go.

The balloon popped upward, carrying the radio high into the sky. The wind caught it and blew it eastward toward Hang Mang and the sea. The three men watched it float lazily away. Sky-colored, the balloon was soon invisible.

Everett shook his head. "I know the charge isn't supposed to blow it up for an hour or unless it touches the ground but I sweat those damned things every time."

"I don't blame you, Everett," DePorta said. "But think of the Communists trying to use their radio-direction-finding sets on a balloon. Must be pretty frustrating."

Everett grinned. "Yes sir. That message will keep repeating for an hour, from a different location every minute."

"And we'll be moving to still another new location pretty quick too," DePorta said. "So don't get too comfortable here."

DePorta and Smith left the commo center and walked back to the sleeping platform the Tai men had built for the American commander. "Brick," DePorta said, "we've got to find another new base. Ossidian and Vo will be going in to meet Ton near Hang Mang in two days. I don't want any of us in this camp after they leave. If they are picked up and fail to bite the pill, the Communists would get everything out of them . . . even Ossidian."

"You want me to look for a new camp?" Smith asked.

"Let's talk to Muk Thon."

As they approached the Tai colonel, his daughter, and Pierre—whose skin sores were now almost cured—Luy looked up from the manioc she was pounding in a hollowed-out log. She caught Smith's eye and smiled broadly. Smith grinned back.

Smith spread his map on the ground and asked Muk Thon

for directions to the high plateau the Tai chief had described to the Americans.

"I hope this place is as good as they say," DePorta said. "There should be a good Drop Zone close by and water and strong natural fortifications, if everything Muk Thon says is true."

As they studied the map, Luy placed her wooden grinding club on the ground. "I know the way. It was my husband and I who found it. He was going to build a fort there. I will take you there."

"You must stay here, Luy," Smith said. "It will be a long, hard jungle march."

"She does know this place," Muk Thon confirmed, standing up abruptly. "She can lead you." And satisfied that no more mental effort on such abstractions as maps was required of him, Muk Thon left.

DePorta grinned at his Executive Officer and clapped him on the shoulder. "You've got a guide!"

"But, Jesse, this will be one rough stroll."

DePorta shrugged. "Your mission is to find a B-team headquarters that can be at least semi-permanent. She can take you there. Frenchy will mind the boy.

"You take half the team and send back guides for the rest of us. Ossidian and Vo go to Hang Mang to make their first contact tomorrow night and I want this camp cleared before daybreak the next day."

In French, DePorta asked Luy, "Can you take him to the place in time to send guides back by tomorrow night?"

"But of course . . . if Colonel Smith does not get too fatigued."

DePorta's brown face split in a white-toothed grin. "Take plenty of salt tablets, Brick."

In an hour Smith, Mattrick, and Rodriguez, with one platoon of Tai guerrillas, were on their way to the new campsite, Luy in the lead setting a brisk pace, her basket seeming to float on her back.

As the day wore on and they plunged deeply into the heavily wooded mountainous jungle, Luy signaled one of the Tai men to walk in front of her and cut away the tangled thorny vines and scrub that slowed their passage and scratched their skin. Smith had issued his platoon sets of jungle fatigues and pairs of Communist Chinese-manufactured jungle boots, which made it easier for them to penetrate the thick foliage. Luy had allowed Smith to put a jacket over her but refused to wear the pants and boots, preferring her long black skirt and buffalo-hide moccasins.

Smith was amazed at her endurance. He had been in training for such a mission over a year, yet he could feel the strain of this constant uphill climbing.

It was late in the afternoon when the jungle began to thin out, and soon they were in high, open country. It was cool. Smith judged the altitude must be five thousand feet. Higher mountains ranged to the west.

"We are here," Luy announced.

Ahead of them, beyond the open space, was a rocky knoll another two hundred feet high. A stream ran past the craggy head of rock.

Smith looked about him, greatly pleased. The place could easily be defended long enough to allow most of the B team to exfiltrate through the jungle. Tired though he was, Smith climbed the rocky knoll. It provided an excellent view of the land area for fifty miles to the north, east and south. He could see the lowlands lying in the haze. With a telescope it would be possible to observe traffic along the roads and into and out of the city on any reasonably clear day. For radio transmissions and reception this rock was ideal, and their headquarters could be easily camouflaged from observation by the Communists' sparse air force.

Mattrick and Rodriguez also climbed the rock summit. "Just what we need," the team sergeant said admiringly.

Leaving the rocky crown the Americans scrambled down to the stream. The montagnards were already dragging bamboo poles and saplings from the tree line and constructing sleeping platforms. Luy, Smith noticed, had commandeered two Tai men to build hers. His pack had been carried over to where she was standing, supervising the construction of her quarters.

With the help of several tribesmen Mattrick and Rodriguez began to build their own shelters. Smith strolled over to Luy. Anxiously she watched as he surveyed the work—it would be a king-size sleeping platform. Already, he noticed, his poncho had been stretched across the top of the frame to keep the dew off the platform, which was covered with Luy's poncho.

When Smith made no comment Luy gave him a saucy

smile. "I thought it would be best if we shared our blankets. It will be very cold up here."

"We must not let you get sick from the cold," Smith replied with a grin. He reached into his pack for a piece of soap. "Shall we scrub off the dirt?"

Luy nodded and she and Smith made for the stream, walking downstream from the others until they found a wide spot. They stripped off their hot, sweat-soaked clothes and splashed into the cold water, soaping each other and laughing. Clean and refreshed, Luy washed their clothes and hung them up in the afternoon sun to dry. Then, still naked, they sat on a rock and let the sun dry them. It seemed natural; the montagnard men and women always bathed together.

Later Smith slipped on his underpants, which had dried enough to wear, and Luy wrapped a cloth about her, sari-like, and they walked back to the camp.

Refreshed and revitalized, Smith and Luy made a further inspection of the area. "We must get your people to work immediately on clearing fields," Smith said as they walked about. "We'll have to grow enough crops here to feed 100 people, many more than that if we decide to hold the place after the Communists know we're here."

"Yams and manioc will grow anyplace," said Luy, "and during the rainy season these montainsides are flooded, so we can grow as much rice in a hectare as they can in the lowlands. Very rich for growing poppy, too," she added.

"Money we don't worry about, food is the problem," Smith replied severely. "There is no reason to raise opium until we finish this war."

Luy shrugged her bare shoulders. "Poppy comes naturally to us."

Mattrick, Rodriguez, and a group of the Tai men had finished their shelters and were splashing around naked in the stream. Luy's presence inhibited none of them.

A Tai tribesman came up to Luy and talked rapidly to her a few moments. She turned to Smith. "The men ask if they can go hunting now. It is the good time."

"What will they hunt for?"

"They say there are plenty of gibbons in the trees."

"Tell them to go ahead."

Curious, Smith followed the Tai hunting party. "In the early morning and just before dark is the best time for monkeys," Luy explained. "Have you ever seen the mountain people hunt monkeys?"

Smith shook his head. He watched as the tribesmen looked up into the trees alertly. Then he heard a shrill chattering and tried to locate the monkey. One of the Tai men spotted the animal peering down from a tree. From the quiver on his back he took out a long, thin, sharpened bamboo arrow with three woven fins. He had a square of white cloth in his hand through which he pushed the arrow. Then he dipped the arrow tip in a brown paste, laid the arrow in the groove, and pulled back the fiber bowspring until it caught on a peg.

Everyone stood still as the crossbowman took aim and pushed on the peg. The arrow twanged into the air and impaled the monkey through his stomach. The shocked animal looked down at his belly and stared at the piece of white cloth partially protruding from it. Then, with his right index finger he industriously began to poke the piece of white cloth back into the wound.

"The poison on the arrow does not work for a little while," Luy explained. "The monkey could swing away from us before he died and we would not find him. But he thinks the little rag came out of his stomach and he will sit there trying to push it back in until he dies."

"Doesn't the poison spoil the meat?"

"We have been hunting like this for many generations. We never had any trouble."

The monkey's motions became slower and slower, and in three minutes it toppled from the tree at the hunters' feet.

Four gibbons were killed this way, and brought back to the Tai camp. Cooking would begin at 8:00. Smith and Luy supervised the digging of the cooking pits and the placing of poncho screens around them to contain the glow of the fires. The pots the men had carried on their backs were filled with water and put on to boil.

Much later, Luy brought Smith a pot of rice and monkey meat. They ate together at their sleeping platform, silently. Far below them the dim lights of Hang Mang gave off a faint brownish glow.

Mattrick and Rodriguez had constructed their own sleeping platforms nearby so that the three Americans would be close in the very unlikely case of a raid. Half the platoon would be on the alert all night.

The Tai platoon leader came over to Luy and talked urgently with her for several minutes. Luy looked up into the sky, shuddered, and said to Smith, "The Tai say bad sign in the sky, maybe new Yang, maybe bad new Yang, come. Star doesn't work." Luy pointed skyward and Smith looked up. A bright round star was visibly moving across the heavens.

"Haven't they seen that before?" Smith asked. "America put it there."

"Why did your country put it there?" Luy asked.

For twenty minutes, until the star was out of sight and the tribesmen lost interest in it, Smith tried to tell them about bouncing radio waves off Telstar. As Luy translated his words, the Tais only scoffed. But they finally did believe that the United States owned its own star, and were impressed further with the powerful Americans who had come to help them.

Smith was bone-tired. Rodriguez was already asleep, and Mattrick was on watch. They had divided the night into three three-hour stretches, and Smith had taken the 3:00 to 6:00 A.M. watch. He was a little uneasy about sharing a sleeping platform with Luy in front of his two sergeants, but since she was the chief's daughter and the idea had been hers, everyone realized it would be impolite and bad form for him to have refused. Besides, he liked her.

Smith and Luy lay down next to each other between their blankets, both wearing the standard peasant garb, black pajamas. Smith had hardly laid his hand across Luy's thighs, in answer to her intimate caress, before he felt himself falling off into a deep sleep.

"0300 hours, sir," Rodriguez whispered, what seemed a moment later.

"Right," said Smith, instantly awake.

As he sat up on the platform, he muttered, "Must be freezing." Luy stirred but remained asleep. Looking around the dark silent camp, he suddenly thought of Kathy. He thought of the leg captain and let out a soft groan.

Luy was sitting up beside him in an instant, her arms holding him tight.

"Sorry to wake you," he said.

"You are sick?"

Smith did not answer.

"You think of other woman?"

Still Smith remained silent.

290

"When my people gave my husband to the Communists I tried to kill myself," Luy said matter-of-factly. "They said he would not be hurt but the Viet Minh killed him even though the war was over."

"They'll do the same to us if they get us," Smith said, "though they can't prove we are Americans."

Luy's presence was quietly comforting. He felt rested now. He just wished he could stop seeing Kathy in his mind: her beautiful tanned face and blonde hair falling loosely about it.

Luy drew him to her and then whispered, "Come, lie down. I'll stay awake with you."

Luy shivered and rolled close to him. Her hands were loosening the waist band of his pajamas and he realized that she had already removed hers. He let her slide his pants off and open his jacket.

Now, as her thighs and stomach drew close to his, Kathy was gone. Luy placed one of her thighs between his. He could feel her strong firm muscles quiver against him. His own involuntary reactions stirred Luy further and she pressed her full breasts to him. The coldness he had felt since losing Kathy began to melt. He wanted very much to take Luy's taut body and lose himself in her. He pulled her under him. Luy gasped, and cried slightly. The bamboo slats of the sleeping platform squeaked, and the understructure creaked like an ancient door.

Brick remained motionless. Mattrick and Rodriguez could hardly help hearing, he thought. Slowly he allowed himself to part slightly from Luy and settle onto his back. But Luy gently pulled herself closer and they kissed. It was a firm, full kiss. As they lay together—waiting, anxious—the first shrill hooting came from the jungle. Soon it was answered and then the early morning shrieks and twittering of the gibbons resounded from every side of the jungle. A regiment could overrun the camp before it could be heard above the noise of a thousand simians screaming at each other.

Luy and Brick looked at each other in the pale dawn. They smiled, laughed, and in one smooth motion Luy slid under him, and he gently let himself deeply into her. Luy's delighted cries, the protestations of the sleeping platform, and the muted body-sounds were drowned out by the shrill siren-like cries raised by the thoughtful gibbon community.

Just after Smith had left for the mountaintop, Ton had contacted Acbat by radio and requested the earliest possible meeting, giving details for finding the rendezvous outside the Viet Cong check points ringing the city. DePorta held Ossidian and Vo from leaving camp until the guides reported that Smith had approved the new headquarters site.

"Not that I think you or Vo would allow yourselves to be captured alive, Ossidian," DePorta said as the intelligence men started off. "But it is impossible to be too careful."

Ossidian nodded. "You never know what's going to happen, sir."

"You really think you need to go, sergeant?"

"Sir, I've got to get the feel of these underground agents Ton has recruited if I'm going to run intelligence. I've got to see a couple of them, talk to them, put them on the spot, maybe make them sweat a little. Then I know what I'm working with."

"We'd be in trouble losing both you and Vo."

"I'll do whatever you say, sir." Ossidian looked his commander in the eye. "But I've worked with agents all over the world and I know—"

"Right, Ossidian. Do what you have to do."

The small commander of Acbat watched Ossidian, Vo, and two Tai guides, all dressed identically in black pants and blouses, with black and red bands tied about their heads, and wearing Tai thong-sandals, start out for Hang Mang.

Four hours later they saw the main north-south road into Hang Mang running down the low, flat land below them. Ossidian called a halt.

"This is no Boy Scout hike," he panted to Vo. "But Jesus Christ, going back is going to be a bastard."

Vo breathed heavily and sipped some water. "I think I stay down. Ton say he have good identification and cover for me. I make my own contacts and check his out too."

Ossidian nodded. "If it looks OK you stay." He stared down the valley at the cluster of buildings, two and three stories high, that made up the city of Hang Mang, about two square miles in size, with a population of 40,000. A thin layer of smoke, from the industrial complex the Communists had built up, lay over the city.

"We got three jobs to do down there, Vo. First we have to get the province political chief, Ti."

"OK."

"Second we got to keep close watch on our targets: the power plant, Ti, and the bridge to the north."

"Right," Vo said. "And third we start setting up the rescue nets for pilots."

Ossidian grinned. "Let's go!"

Once they reached the main road and started south toward Hang Mang, Ossidian felt a constant clutch in his stomach. Neither he nor Vo had any identification papers. They were absolutely vulnerable. He frequently glanced at the wart on the back of his left wrist and the clutch tightened. He didn't want to die—certainly not before he'd seen his mission through successfully.

They had been walking south on the road for half an hour when Ossidian began to recognize some of the landmarks Ton had described in the radio message. He looked for the large farmhouse on their right, set back about fifty meters from the road. Ton had called the rendezvous for 6:00 P.M. since there was a 10:00 curfew in the city, and without a special pass, anyone on the city streets or roads leading into Hang Mang was subject to severe interrogation.

Ossidian was for once in his life thankful for his coarse features and swarthy complexion. "Coarse"—that was how a blonde, thin and trim, a girl he had once wanted badly when he was younger, had described him. As he swung down the road, montagnard style, he did not worry about standing out from other people. He was burly, but so were many of the montagnards, and he was only a little taller than the average tribesman. The Tai men were the tallest montagnards in Indo-China.

Ossidian's eyes wandered in all directions. Every landmark, the signs, the few motor vehicles that passed, all were carefully marked.

Suddenly a stench assaulted him. It nearly knocked him off his feet, and made him want to run to escape it. Conquering the nausea that threatened to overcome him he saw a nearby oxcart moving toward the country. Lieutenant Vo coughed,

293

and exclaimed, "Those mois! They fertilize their crops from the city's public toilets."

As Vo was talking, a grinding of gears sounded from behind them and Ossidian turned. An open military-personnel carrier, which had been driving slowly down the road, the Viet Cong soldiers inside looking at everyone walking toward the city, suddenly sped up to get away from the insufferable oxcart.

Ossidian watched the surveillance patrol racing down the crumbling macadam highway. He knew that the people were strictly controlled in all sectors of their GWOA. But the SFOB could get little information from the area. One of Ossidian's most important tasks was to provide a complete study on exactly how the population was controlled by the Communists in their heartlands. Since Pham Son Ti was the chief political officer in the GWOA and in charge of population control, kidnapping him was all important.

It was 5:30, almost dusk, when suddenly a sharp command was shouted from behind. They turned. Ossidian's heart stopped. His stomach chilled. Two khaki-clad civilian police officers wearing stiff-billed caps were approaching them on bicycles. Both had submachine guns slung over their shoulders.

Vo and Ossidian exchanged helpless glances. "Let me talk," Vo said. "We're both Tai tribesmen but you do not speak Vietnamese. Have the package ready when I tell you."

The policemen braked to a stop and one of them—perhaps an officer by the decorations on his shoulder strap, Ossidian thought—started questioning them. Vo answered in halting Vietnamese.

The conversation went on and the police made many threatening gestures with their weapons as Vo slapped empty pockets, apparently in response to demands for identification papers. Finally, the tone of the interrogator softened and a crafty smile spread over his face as he looked at Ossidian. Vo snapped his fingers and Ossidian reached back into his basket, pulled out a coarse brown-paper envelope, and handed it to Vo. The officer snatched it from him, opened it, and took out a pinch of brownish powder, which he sniffed.

Now Vo and the policeman conversed in low tones and the gesturing with the submachine guns ceased. Ossidian's heart began to return to normal speed, his breathing became more controlled.

The policeman abruptly stuck the envelope into his pocket and he and his companion rode off. Vo and Ossidian starting walking on toward Hang Mang.

"That was close," Vo said.

"What happened?"

"I convinced them you were the chief of a poppy-growing tribe on the border and you worked directly with the province political chief, Ti, selling raw opium."

"I caught it when you said his name."

"The people here know the political chief buys opium from the mountain people. Some he sells for his own profit, some he turns over to the government to be sold for gold on the international market. The police did not want to take a chance on having trouble with Ti so they took a bribe of that envelope of dried poppy juice for themselves. They'll sell it for six months' wages to the Chinese black-market buyers."

Ossidian breathed deeply. "It's a good thing they're as corrupt here as anywhere else."

"Corrupt?" Vo asked teasingly. "We have a way of life which not the Communists nor anyone will stop."

Thirty minutes after their narrow escape Ossidian could tell from the landmarks Ton had described that they were close to their destination.

It was exactly 6:00 in the evening when up ahead, beyond a dry rice paddy, Ossidian saw the patch of coconut trees set out in straight rows with banana trees growing below them. As he came closer the intelligence sergeant made out the discolored cement house set back from the road. The sun had set by the time they turned into the path from the main road to the farmhouse.

Ton had used the right word, *déclassé*, Ossidian thought, approaching the building. Once it must have been the comfortable farmhouse of relatively wealthy people. Now it looked beyond repair.

Ossidian motioned Vo to go past him down the path toward the rear of the house. Trees and foliage grew uncultivated around the place like an invading jungle. The two Tai tribesmen brought up the rear. A door stood half open and Vo looked from it to Ossidian and back into the dark room. Ossidian gestured Vo in.

"Chow ow," came a soft female voice from inside.

"It is Quand," Vo said to Ossidian, as the woman continued in Vietnamese. "Everything OK."

A smiling Nguyen That Ton stepped to the doorway and beckoned them in. "You will like very much, Quand," he said. "She is number one woman."

Ossidian did not return Ton's cheerful smile. "This big deal, Ton," he said. "Business only."

"Important to keep close to all contacts," Ton said. "I learn this from American school."

When Ossidian was introduced to Quand, who lighted a candle so he could see her plainly just as he entered the back door, he realized Ton had not exaggerated. She wore a black au dai and a strand of pearls around her neck encased in the high collar of the Vietnamese-style dress. Ossidian's assignments in certain French-speaking parts of the Middle East stood him well.

"Enchanté, mademoiselle," he said, brushing the back of Quand's hand with his thick lips. In French, he went on, "I have been looking forward to meeting you. I am told that your beauty is only exceeded by your ability as a businesswoman."

Quand bought his little speech. "Monsieur, je suis enchanté aussi." Then, a shrewd look came into her eye which Ossidian did not miss. "I hope you will be pleased at the price I was able to get from the Chinamen for your gold leaf Mr. Ton asked me to sell to obtain local currency."

"What did you get?" Ossidian asked.

"Translated into your money, $38 an ounce. That's a little more than you'd get in America. I kept my regular 15 per cent commission for handling this dangerous negotiation."

Ossidian was surprised at Quand's knowledge. "How do you know what we get in the United States?"

Quand smiled enigmatically. "I and my brother here"—she gracefully indicated a smiling, heavy-set, middle-aged Vietnamese—"have been in business for many years, since my father was murdered." Her eyes became hard. "Mr. Ton tells me you have bought for resale all of Muk Thon's poppy."

Ossidian nodded. He knew he was in the presence of a woman with class and wished his French was better than adequate or that he could speak Vietnamese.

"Perhaps we can also do business. I fear you have spoiled

a rich supply for me by paying him too much. But then I'm sure that you will sell it back to me for what I would have paid Muk Thon, since your mission in Hang Mang is not business and I and my brother can help you."

Ossidian began to feel on solid footing. His career had been occupied in using corruption and greed in foreign countries to further the national objectives of his own.

"We'll have no trouble doing business," he said smoothly. "I have much gold and poppy to dispose of and, as you suggest, I look for profit in much different currency than you."

"Good. Now, what do you want of us?"

Ossidian shot a look at Ton. "Can we trust her?" he asked in English.

"Certainly, as long as you do not cheat her in money matters. She is a distant cousin of Ti, but she hates the Communists. They executed her father in 1956 when the political officer in Hang Mang denounced him as being counter-revolutionary. Her father refused to give up his land to be divided among the peasants after the land reform act was passed."

"How about her brother?" Ossidian asked.

"Pham? He hates Ti and the Communists." Ton turned to Pham and said in French, "The American is worried you might be with the Communists."

Pham spat on the floor and turned to Ossidian. In careful French he said, "My father was executed because he owned all the land around this house. Now we only own the house with no land to support it. I was put in their dirty, rat- and snake-infested jail for a year for being his son. There were many hundreds of executions and I was waiting my turn when all the way from Hanoi orders reached here that errors were being committed in the name of land reform. I was released with hundreds of the wealthy class from jail. And what does our political chief in Hang Mang tell us when we come home? He says he and the People's Democratic Government hope that those who were sent to jail in error and whose fathers and brothers were executed in error would understand the problems of forming a new government and forgive those who erred and go back to work for the people in peace."

"We have no wish to help the Communists," said Quand. "But we are trapped here in Hang Mang. We would be shot if we tried to leave and were caught. It takes much money to buy your way out."

"What do you want?" Ossidian asked.

"If we can hide enough gold and currency my brother and I would like to go to Saigon or—" She paused, her eyes bright. "Maybe we could go to Hong Kong."

"You want to go to Hong Kong?" Ossidian asked, as though it was the easiest request to grant he had ever heard.

Quand and Pham nodded vigorously.

"You work with me, and Ton and Vo and you two will get to Hong Kong with enough gold leaf and poppy to put you in big business." For a clincher, Ossidian reached into his pack, pulled out a brown package, and tossed it to Quand.

"Muk Thon cultivates the best poppy I've ever seen," Ossidian said. "Now it's my job to sell it."

Quand examined the brownish powder at length. "You want me to sell this for you?" She crushed it between thumb and forefinger, sniffing it. "Not the best, but I will get you what I can."

Ossidian shook his head. "It's a down payment—you understand? A down payment for what we are buying from you."

"What do you want from me?"

Ossidian glanced at Ton. "Have you told her what we want?" he asked in English.

"You want me to help you get Pham Son Ti," Quand stated. "No, I do not speak English, but I know what you really are after. My brother and I can help you do this. Ti is our cousin but that does not stop him from many bad things." She lowered her gaze from Ossidian to her hands folded in her lap.

Ossidian took in the pose for a moment and turned to Ton. "Her cousin does not treat her as a sister?"

Ton smiled lewdly. "No. But she does not treat him as a brother in business dealings. As political chief he is in charge of disposing of all the poppy in this province. In this as in other things she is his unwilling partner."

"OK!" Ossidian pronounced the universal English expression. Then, in French: "We have talked enough. The first thing I want is Ti. Quand—I want you somehow to make him come to this place . . . and soon."

"But how?"

298

"He wants more poppy, doesn't he?"

"Yes."

"Tell him you have a new tribesman with a high grade of poppy that will bring more gold in Hong Kong than the old poppy."

Quand thought a few minutes. "That might work," she said. "He sometimes likes to watch me make the first contacts so he knows how much I really pay. Then he takes it from me at almost no profit to me." Her mouth turned down. "He takes me too."

"You'll get paid for all the times he takes you until we take him," Ossidian said harshly. "Just get him here. I'll handle it after that."

Quand stared back at Ossidian as though he were an enemy. After several moments she said, "I will bring him here. But you must have the poppy."

"I will supply a Tai chief for him to bargain with, and five kilos of poppy. That ought to bring him out. In New York City that much raw heroin would be worth over $1,000,000."

"Five kilos!" Quand cried.

"That's how much I bought from Muk Thon since I've been with him," Ossidian answered.

"I will bring Ti out." She nodded to herself. "And after you take him I will sell it, and you and I will share the profit." Quand gave Ossidian a smile that almost made him forget he was an intelligence sergeant in the United States Army Special Forces.

"Something like that, chérie. You get Ti out here, I'll have the poppy."

Pham grasped Ossidian's hand. "It is a privilege to work with a man of honor such as yourself," he said.

Ossidian's shoulders twitched and he suppressed a smile. "And for me, the same," he replied in formal French. "Now, since Lieutenant Vo is going to stay with you, he and I will have a little talk outside before I go back." Ossidian bowed to Quand and Pham.

"Ton," he said, "you and Vo will see that what I need is here and tell me by radio when I can come for Ti."

Ton assured the intelligence sergeant that all would be ready and then Ossidian led Vo outside the farmhouse, an arm around the Vietnamese lieutenant's shoulder, for a last strategy meeting.

They talked in hushed tones for a few minutes and then Ossidian and the two Tai tribesmen headed back for the mountains. It would be an all-night trek across the fields, avoiding the roads and the Communist security system around Hang Mang.

5.

DePorta received three messages from the SFOB stressing the importance of capturing the province political chief in Hang Mang. In fact, until Ti or someone like him could be kidnapped and brought back to the SFOB for interrogation it was considered highly inadvisable to attempt infiltrating another guerrilla team into the meticulously policed areas of the GWOA. The abduction of Ti was DePorta's chief objective now. It was constantly on his mind.

Five nights after Ossidian's meeting with Ton, Sergeant Everett announced he was getting a signal on Lieutenant Vo's frequency. Ossidian, an anxious DePorta, and Smith crowded around the set.

In two nights, Vo radioed, they should be prepared to receive a poppy-hungry province chief at the old farmhouse. Ti would arrive at approximately 1800 hours.

Captain DePorta personally commanded the operation to kidnap the province political officer. Captain Smith would take over Acbat if DePorta was lost and Mattrick would become Executive Officer and intelligence officer.

DePorta, Ossidian, and two of the Tai tribesmen who had excelled in the assault-group training Rodriguez and Smith had been giving, gained the main road into Hang Mang about the middle of the afternoon of the day set for the abduction of Ti. Wearing the loose black garb of the tribesmen, the black and red cloth tied about their heads and the Tai sandals, they walked single file and unevenly spaced along the narrow road. All carried woven baskets on their backs. Occasionally, ancient trucks and square military vehicles passed from both directions, the khaki-clad soldiers in cloth caps paying no attention to the dusty, ragged montagnards.

Ossidian led the way. The sun was hanging close to the tops of the mountains in the west when he spotted the small coconut grove beyond the rice paddy on his right. He reached the path to the house, turned in, and strode nonchalantly toward the back of the building. There was a two-wheeled buffalo cart standing there, loaded with pungent fertilizer—manure and human excrement mixed. Hideous as the smell was, Ossidian sniffed in satisfaction and then found a tree and sat down, leaning his basket against it. A few minutes later DePorta rounded the back of the farmhouse, smelled the load, and sat windward of it. The two tribesmen, who arrived a few moments later, seemed unconcerned and squatted near the cart. The water buffalo stood still between the shafts; a rope attached to the ring through his nose was tied to a post.

DePorta looked around for the driver of the buffalo cart but could see no one.

He watched Ossidian reach into his basket and draw out a long-barreled black pistol. Into a carefully oiled light-leather holster hanging down inside his left pajama leg, the sergeant thrust the weapon.

At dusk, a Vietnamese dressed in the manner of the political-officer class, khaki shirt and slacks, entered the grounds. As he came behind the farmhouse DePorta recognized Lieutenant Vo but remained motionless until Vo approached him.

"You came yourself?" Vo asked.

"Ossidian says we need an authentic Tai chief to negotiate the sale of some poppy."

Vo nodded. "This may be a very tight thing. I am dressed exactly as Ti was when he went to his office this morning, except for a pistol. You have the real poppy?"

DePorta nodded. "In my basket. Five kilos."

"Good. Ti is a big man and he may not come alone. We may really have to sell the poppy to get out without being caught."

"No!" Ossidian growled. "We'll get him if he comes here."

"Be careful," Vo warned. "Right here we could ruin the whole mission."

"We'll be careful," said DePorta.

Vo nodded and looked at the manure cart, wrinkling his nose. "I see my auxiliaries are doing their jobs well. Can you drive a water buffalo?"

"I grew up with water buffalo in the Philippines."

"Good. Who will make the shot?"

Ossidian patted the holster inside his pants. "That's my job."

"Be sure Ti is out of sight of the road when you shoot," Vo cautioned. "Ti does not like coming out here. He wants the poppy badly, but if Quand weren't giving him more than raw opium he wouldn't come. Ti thinks Quand wants him out here so she can 'persuade' him to restore these lands to her family. He isn't thinking of danger to himself."

DePorta examined the oxcart. It was built like a large, tightly woven basket, almost waterproof, holding the rich load of fertilizer. "Inspired, Ossidian, truly inspired," DePorta complimented his intelligence sergeant. "But won't he smother if we stick him in this?"

Vo heard his commander's words and approached the cart. At the rear he located a hook and pulled it. As a square trap door opened, DePorta jumped backward, expecting a load of manure to be released.

"Do not worry," Vo said proudly, "this is not my first" —he grinned at Ossidian—"what do you Americans say? Caper?"

Ossidian nodded.

"This is not my first caper," Vo repeated.

Neatly imbedded in the cart's offensive load was a wood shaft running all the way from one end to the other. The door was loosely woven so fresh air could circulate through it.

"Very, very number one, Vo," said Ossidian.

Vo smiled, pleased, and then, looking at the reddish glow beyond the mountain, became serious. "They will drive up to the front of the house and get out of the car. We must be ready. I go inside until I am needed."

Ossidian slowly walked from the back to the front of the house and found a position in the overgrown jungle that once had been a decorative hedgerow. He left DePorta standing near the malodorous oxcart.

Suddenly Ossidian tensed as he heard the churning of engines and rattling of vehicles coming up the road. Two square French army-personnel carriers pulled up on the main highway beside the driveway into the farmhouse. Instantly, a squad of khaki-clad troops armed with rifles and submachine guns leaped to the ground and took up positions along the road, blocking the entrance into and out of the farmhouse.

Ossidian's heart pounded. He well knew the vulnerability

of guerrillas forced to come into town. How many had been betrayed into *his* hands by agents they had trusted?

A few moments later a small, dirty, gray sedan pulled into the property. It proceeded along the rough drive. Immediately following it was an open jeeplike vehicle. A military officer sat beside the driver, and in the back two more armed soldiers held submachine guns ready for business.

Ossidian shrank into the thick foliage. From there he could see DePorta, looking like a defiant Muk Thon, with two Tais flanking him and a few steps to his rear. Whether soldier or montagnard, DePorta was a redoubtable chief.

The sedan kept going, bouncing and swaying until it hit bottom and stopped. Instantly, the slim, oval-faced girl with long black hair, wearing an au dai of the same color, opened her door and stepped out.

The driver's door opened and a man in pressed khakis, wearing a pistol in a leather holster on his belt and an officer's cap, reluctantly eased himself out of the car. He walked around the car, and as he reached Quand the officer and two armed men from the jeep came up behind him.

Quand pointed to DePorta, and her companion—it was Ti, Ossidian recognized him from pictures and sketches supplied by the underground—started to stride toward him purposefully. Had Quand betrayed them? Somehow he would kill her and Ti before he was killed if this were the case. As Ti came abreast of Ossidian's position and clearly saw the Tai chief and his two tribesmen he halted. Turning to the three men behind him, Ti motioned them to stay where they were and then he and Quand moved on toward DePorta. Ossidian crept through the thick growth, always directly opposite Ti.

Ti reached DePorta and stood looking down at the small "Tai chief," hardly bothering to conceal an expression of disgust at having to deal with this mois.

They began to converse, Quand arguing shrilly, Ti apparently trying to restrain her. The price was obviously being discussed. As Ossidian had hoped would be the case, a new supply of opium—the first deal for five kilos, almost twelve pounds—was too important to be lost by antagonizing the source.

Skillfully DePorta maneuvered Ti, Quand subtly helping, until they were directly behind the decrepit farmhouse. DePorta pointed at his basket on the ground against the yellowed, crumbling back wall. Ti and he started walking toward it. Ti pointed down at the montagnard pack and DePorta bent over, pulled out a large packet, and handed it to Ti who, in his eagerness, almost snatched it. Ti began to examine it at once.

Stealthily Ossidian crept through the thick bush surrounding the farmhouse and finally he reached a position less than fifteen feet from where Ti, DePorta, and Quand were standing. He made sure the security guard could see none of them. Ti was so excited with the five kilos of dried poppy juice he was caressing, pinching between thumb and forefinger and sniffing, that he seemed hardly aware of the loud haggling going on between Quand and DePorta.

Slowly Ossidian slid the pistol, which fired tiny hollow needles of nerve-paralyzing serum, from its holster, raised it, took careful aim, and steadied his right wrist with his left hand. He held his breath. The target, Ti's exposed neck, was small. Ossidian squeezed the trigger. There was a slight recoil and an almost inaudible hiss.

Ti slapped at the back of his neck and cursed. Quand slapped her own cheek and shouted at DePorta, pointing at the oxcart. Three more times Ossidian fired.

Ti was just reaching into his pocket, presumably for money to complete the transaction, when he quietly collapsed against the outer wall of the farmhouse and slid to the ground. Seconds later, with Quand still keeping up her loud bargaining, Vo stepped out the door, grabbed Ti's hat, and slapped it on his head. While he was going through Ti's pockets, taking everything in them, DePorta unbuckled the pistol belt, slipped it off the unconscious province political chief, and handed it to Vo, who strapped it around his own waist. In a moment Vo had walked beyond the rear of the house where he could be observed by Ti's security squad. He and Quand appeared to be having a private discussion.

DePorta and his two Tais scooped up the limp form of the political chief and shoved the body into the open shaft of the fertilizer cart, shutting and hooking the trap door. As soon as Ti was safely stowed away, DePorta picked up a stick he had previously cut, untied the ox, and jabbed him into motion. Responding to furious gesturing by Vo, DePorta halted the oxcart in sight of the security patrol and approached him.

From his pocket, the intelligence officer impersonating Ti

brought out a roll of currency. This he handed to DePorta, who in turn passed over the large package of poppy.

Then Vo, allowing Quand to urge him toward the rear of the property, gingerly moved past the oxcart and they walked as far as they could. Vo was still in sight of the security guards as Quand pointed over what had been her father's lands and Vo nodded and pointed also.

Ossidian had unobtrusively slid from the tangled vines and fallen in with the two Tai guides. Jabbing the ox, DePorta drove the cart past the security squad, who yelled curses at the dirty mois, retreating from the nauseating stench. DePorta kept going up the rutted drive and finally reached the main road. The officer of the guard approached the Tai contingent. But as he neared them, he suddenly thought better of the idea and fell back, allowing them to gain the road.

The overpowering stench never left them as they walked. The cart grated slowly along the highway. Every vehicle that passed them from the direction of town was a nerve-wracking torment. If Vo's plan to continue impersonating Ti did not work the police and Army would be thundering after them. It was dark now, yet there were still too many people on the road for them to pull Ti out of the oxcart, abandon it, and carry the prisoner on foot.

Two hours after they had left the farmhouse they came to the road which turned from the highway into the mountains. But they continued on. The masses of oxcarts and people travelling in both directions, trying to get to their destinations before the curfew hour, made the transfer of Ti from the cart impossible.

Up ahead, coming at them from the north, two headlights bounced up and down in the rutted road. DePorta went on driving his water buffalo impassively until the light approached him and the vehicle stopped, blocking the animal's way. It was the usual square French military car, open, carrying two officers in the back and two soldiers in the front. One of the soldiers jumped out of the heavy car, its dim headlights on DePorta.

DePorta prayed that Smith had followed his suggestion and set up still another camp and an escape route to it that none of the four on this operation could know about. He glanced at the wart on the back of his right wrist. Ossidian stood motionless, out of the direct beams from the personnel carrier's light. He had a basketful of local currency from the black market sale of the gold which Ton had given him, just before slipping off to go back to town. The money would be impossible to explain.

In Vietnamese, the soldier, a noncom, asked DePorta why he was out on the road so late. DePorta answered in a torrent of Tai, gesturing at the hills. He heard the noncom ask the officer what to do with this mois who would certainly still be on the road after curfew hour. DePorta thrust his stick into the putrefying mess in the cart, and chattering in Tai began to stir it sharply, pointing at the rice paddies and then the mountains.

Waves of effluvium forced the noncom back as though he had been slammed in the chest. The two officers screamed curses at the soldiers. The noncom who had stopped DePorta leapt back into the car and in a screech of rubber on gravel the Army car jumped forward and streaked down the road.

DePorta and Ossidian breathed deeply for many moments and then proceeded on north. It was another hour before one of the tribesmen triumphantly pointed out the turnoff they wanted.

With his stick, DePorta headed the buffalo off the road and along the rutted path, the tribesmen leading the way. The starlit sky gave off enough light for them to see, and three hours later the path came to an abrupt end in the foothills of montagnard country. DePorta unhitched the buffalo and turned it loose. Then he pulled down the cart's rear gate and hauled a faintly moaning Ti out of the shaft.

Four Tai tribesmen and Sergeant Pierrot materialized out of the darkness. Pierrot, cursing the ghastly odor, flashed a light into Ti's eyes, pulling the lids back and examining them. He took Ti's pulse, listened to his breathing and stood up. "He looks OK, sir. I guess we can give him another shot."

"Go ahead," DePorta commanded.

The medic took a prepared needle from the case in his pocket and slid it into Ti's arm. "He's good until morning. Then we've got to let him come around, get a little exercise, and eat something."

Ti was strapped to the stretcher and the enlarged party continued their march into the mountains. Every hour they had to take a good rest. As the trails became steeper the Tai men took more frequent turns carrying the stretcher.

By morning they were deep in the mountains, about fifteen

miles north of their headquarters. As the sun burned down on them, Ti, his legs hobbled so he couldn't run, began to moan and stir. DePorta kept pushing the group onward until Ti suddenly let out a yell and with a violent flop almost twisted the stretcher to which he was tied out of the hands of the two carriers.

DePorta came back in the file to see the groggy but now awake Communist official. "How do you feel?" DePorta asked cheerfully in Vietnamese.

Ti stared up, struggled against his bonds, and then subsided. "You will all die," he rasped.

Then the smell of the fertilizer in which he had been carried suddenly assailed him and he choked and gagged, trying to turn on his side. "Let him off the litter," DePorta ordered.

The restraining ropes were untied and Ti was dumped to the ground. Slowly he stood up, his legs shaking. DePorta offered him a piece of concentrated chocolate. With his two hands, which were tied together, Ti batted it to the ground. DePorta shrugged.

"Sir," Ossidian spoke up. "We don't exfiltrate him until tomorrow. It's only another six hours to where we're going. Let Frenchy and me have him for the day. There's a lot I'd like to find out."

DePorta considered Ossidian's request. "That wasn't part of the operation originally. At the SFOB they'll have much more advanced methods of interrogating him. They will get a complete report to us on what they get out of him. Your means of interrogation, Ossidian, might spoil him for the professionals. We should send him back virgin, so to speak. I'm sure he's never been on the wrong side of an interrogation before."

Ti, hardly believing his ears that these mois were speaking what he knew to be English, began to look seriously worried. Realizing that the discussion was probably about his own disposition he ceased crying defiant threats.

Reluctantly, Ossidian bowed to his commander's decision. DePorta walked over to his captive. "Now, Ti," he began in Vietnamese, "we have a long way to go. You may either walk or we will carry you on that—" he indicated the stretcher. "It is not our intention to hurt you in any way. But if we have to carry you, you will be rendered unconscious with drugs. Take your choice. If you decide to walk, and it seems that you are holding us up, you will also be immediately knocked out.''

Ti stared sullenly at DePorta, Ossidian, and Pierrot. DePorta, looking up at the rising sun, grew impatient. ''Frenchy . . .''

The medic immediately opened his kit and took out a hypodermic needle. Ti saw it and blanched.

''I will walk.''

''Then pick up that ration and eat it,'' DePorta snapped, ''you will need strength.''

Ti looked into DePorta's hard, black eyes. He stooped, picked up the chocolate bar, and ate it. DePorta nodded and turned to his men. ''Let's all eat and keep going. I want to reach location Snatch before dark.''

Except for a two-hour rest at noon they pushed steadily through the mountainous jungle. It was 4:00 in the afternoon when they met their first challenge from the advanced security guard that had been posted around their objective. Twenty minutes later they were in a large clearing on a plateau high up in the mountains. Rodriguez and a squad of Tai tribesmen were waiting, three large, square canvas bags sitting on the ground in front of them.

''Madre Dios, I could smell you coming half an hour ago!'' Rodriguez exclaimed. Ossidian walked toward the demolitions sergeant, who hastily backed away. ''We can talk from a distance.''

''You'll get used to it,'' said Frenchy. ''Wait'll you get a whiff of the prisoner.''

Ti was led forward and Rodriguez moved even further away. DePorta said something to the tribesmen and they quickly tied the Communist captive to a tree, seated so that his face was against the trunk, his arms and legs tied around it.

''While it's still light let's get the stuff unpacked,'' DePorta advised. Rodriguez, Pierrot, and Ossidian each took a bag and unstrapped it, dumping the contents on the ground. Rodriguez held up a heavy fatigue suit with a built-in harness. ''You want to put him in it tonight, sir?'' he asked.

''Yes, let's make sure he's in it properly. We don't want an accident after all this.'' The team commander walked over to Ti and ordered him freed from the tree. ''Now, Mr. Ti,'' he began, ''it gets very cold up in these mountains. We do not want you to get sick so we will put a nice warm suit on you tonight.''

Two tribesmen led Ti into the field. The Communist looked at the equipment dubiously. "Into that suit!" DePorta commanded. Ti hesitated. "Do you want us to put you into it?" DePorta asked sharply.

Slowly Ti, with the help of Rodriguez and Ossidian, climbed into the coveralls, thrust his arms into the sleeves, and stood in the suit. Rodriguez gave the rig a thorough inspection. Ossidian held an olive-drab crash helmet. "Let's make sure this fits him."

The intelligence sergeant adjusted the straps until the helmet fitted tightly on the prisoner's head. "He's all set, sir."

"Good. We can do the rest before sunrise. Now, the four Americans are going to watch our man two hours each all night. Pick your own hours. I'll take 4:00 to 6:00. Snatch is set for 0630."

At 5:30 in the morning DePorta, never taking his eyes off the fitfully dozing prisoner, wakened his three sergeants. "Set up Sky Hook," he commanded.

Using flashlights with white filters to dim the beam, the sergeants opened the other two canvas bags. They laid out on the ground a mass of plastic sheeting, a large coil of braided nylon rope, and a heavy metal helium bottle. The bottle was attached to a hose and the plastic bag began to inflate, slowly taking on the shape of a dirigible with four stabilizing fins.

At a sign from DePorta, Frenchy went to his kit, took out a small syringe, and holding it concealed in his palm approached the dozing Communist. DePorta unzipped the coveralls in one fast motion, and Frenchy grabbed one of Ti's shoulders, ripping the prisoner's shirt open as he reached and jabbed the needle into the first bare piece of flesh he saw.

Ti howled obscenities at DePorta when he realized what had been done to him. DePorta cracked the Communist across the cheek with the back of his hand and momentarily silenced him.

"You won't really sleep, you'll see it all," DePorta said in Ti's language. "We just want to be sure you do not feel like moving around for the next two hours. You can relax, we will do all the work."

Before DePorta had finished talking, the Communist's eyelids began to droop. Ossidian walked over to DePorta and the doped Ti. "We're all ready, sir. The balloon is almost set to go up."

DePorta and Ossidian helped a dazed Ti to his feet and half led, half carried him out into the middle of the field. The indistinct light of first dawn revealed Rodriguez working with the equipment. They set Ti down in the field and Rodriguez made the nylon rope fast to the harness built into the stout coveralls. DePorta zipped the suit up tight, locked it, and Ossidian clapped the crash helmet on Ti's head and fastened it. They watched the balloon slowly ascend into the pinkening sky. Five hundred feet above them the balloon snapped taut the rope attached to the harness, and rested motionless in the still air. Two red pennants flew from the rope, marking off a fifty-foot section just below the balloon.

"What's the time?" DePorta asked.

"Snatch minus fifteen," Pierrot answered.

The montagnards, having no idea what to expect, watched the proceedings with great curiosity, pointing at the balloon and then at Ti.

"Jesus!" Rodriguez exclaimed. "Wait until those nice clean Air Force types get a smell of Ti. They'll eject him."

"They'd better damn well not," said Ossidian.

The four Americans waited tensely. Ti flopped over on his side, but Ossidian and Rodriguez, holding him, sat him upright. Then, in the distance, they heard the buzz of plane engines. The sun was rising, painting the white balloon gold. The red pennants hung down in the stillness. Suddenly, on a north-south course, they saw the drab-brown, unmarked Army Caribou coming at them just above the tree tops. Every man held his breath. It was a tough catch to make. A yoke protruded from the front of the plane, which headed straight into the fifty-foot target section of the rope. The yoke hit the stretchable nylon rope and the catch in the center sprang shut on it.

Ti was gently raised a foot and then two feet above the ground from between Ossidian and Rodriguez. And suddenly the Communist was snatched high into the sky so abruptly that he seemed to disappear. The Tai tribesmen shouted in awe, slapping themselves all over; then they laughed and cried out to each other until the plane was out of sight behind the mountains and the sound of its engines no longer vibrated in the sky.

310

"OK," DePorta ordered. "Let's police up and get out of here. We've got a tough march ahead of us if we're going to make it home before dark."

It was just before sunset when the four exhausted Americans and their Tai tribesmen made contact with the outer-security listening posts of the camp. Captain Smith, alerted to their approach by the short-range radio, was at the edge of the woods to welcome them back.

"Congratulations, Major," he said, reaching for DePorta's hand. "My God! You all stink—sir."

"You should smell the other guy."

Smith grinned. "So that's what they meant at the SFOB?"

"What did you get from them?"

"We are now Batcat, the B detachment of this GWOA. You have been promoted—in the U.S. Army that is—to major. Alton and Artie are ready to go when you call for them. And S-2 says the prisoner is one of the toughest Communists he's ever worked over—his stinking so bad doesn't make it any easier for them either. But he'll break. They're sure of it."

DePorta and Ossidian grinned at each other and kept on walking, followed by Pierrot and Rodriguez, directly to the stream. There they stripped off all their clothes and sat in the water splashing themselves. "Man, get some GI soap," Ossidian called to Smith.

While the four Americans scrubbed, Smith continued bringing them up to date. "Things are really going to hell in Saigon. The SFOB said we must activate Falling Rain before the end of the month."

"That's pretty short notice," DePorta snapped.

"Right. But we've been lucky so far, we're ahead of schedule. Krak's all ready in the north. He says our medical program is winning over the whole village, and other villages too. Alton can recruit a minimum of 100 healthy Tai guerrillas right away."

"Good," DePorta said.

"Manong is ready for Artie. They need medical help badly. He's spending most of his time trying to help the sick and reports that a good medic can get the entire Bru population with us. The Viet Cong are walking south through the Bru country every day, sometimes in company and even battalion strength."

"Batcat's making progress," DePorta said. He stood up, naked, and walked toward Smith. "Do I still smell?"

"Well . . . nothing we can't live with. Here's a clean set of pajamas."

Two evenings later Batcat received a serious setback. Ossidian, haunting Everett's communication shack, was on hand for Vo's first radio check-in since the kidnapping.

Quand had been picked up for interrogation, Vo reported. Although she had an unshakable alibi, he was worried.

On his safe channel, far out of range of the nearest Communist radio-directional-finding equipment in Hanoi, Vo described what had happened after DePorta had left.

When it was dark, Vo and Quand walked toward Ti's car, waving the security squad to go on ahead. Vo followed the jeep out the driveway and into town, the security squads behind the sedan.

Quand, who had many times driven with Ti, showed Vo how to drive into the electricity-starved dimly lit compound. The car and the girl were familiar and Vo, dressed like Ti, was his same stature, so that they had no trouble once inside the compound getting into Ti's office.

Using the keys he had taken from Ti, Vo searched the office for two hours. Prepared for this foray, he had brought along the materials to make wax impressions of all the official stamps. He collected every type of blank identification document he could find and then he and Quand locked up, left the office, re-entered Ti's sedan, and drove out of the compound.

It was midnight, two hours after curfew, but Ti's car was well known and they were not stopped. Vo drove up in front of the house Quand shared with her brother Pham and her mother. Across the street from Quand's home lived the block captain, a minor Communist functionary charged with checking and reporting on every man, woman, and child in the block to the area chief, who in turn reported to higher Communist authorities all the way up to Ti himself.

They remained parked, the car's headlights on, until the block captain came to his door to check on the flagrant violation of curfew in his block. Seeing the political chief's vehicle, the old party hack came to attention, saluted, and went back inside after watching Quand step out of the car and enter her home.

312

Vo also reported that he had set up two new underground cells entirely independent of Ton, Quand, and Pham. These groups were recruiting auxiliaries. He had given both unit leaders radios so they could communicate with him. Now, Vo reported, it was time for him to get out of Hang Mang. At any hour he might be compromised.

Ossidian agreed and told Vo to come back to the Tai village, where he would be met and escorted to Batcat headquarters.

"Here it comes, as it had to," DePorta said when Ossidian gave him the report. "These province officials will probably let Quand go, but when the new political officer comes in, he'll put her through an interrogation that will break her."

"We've probably got a few more days, sir," Ossidian said.

"Why don't we tell Vo to bring her out with him?" Smith suggested. "When you think what they'll do to her!"

DePorta shook his head. "They'll be watching her. Anyone who talks to her now will be compromised. Vo's right. He's got to get out. I'm afraid we can do nothing for her."

Batcat's commander walked to the communications center. The Negro sergeant was screening the airwaves. "On your next report to the SFOB give them Request Bravo. Ask for earliest possible Drop Zone."

"Right, sir. 2200 hours is next normal contact," said Everett.

"That's good enough."

6.

Drop Zone Bravo was confirmed for 0200 hours on the day of the infiltration. Since DZ Bravo was the open area in front of the outcropping of rock around and on top of which Batcat was set up, it would be an easy reception. The biggest problem was to judge the wind so that none of the jumpers landed on the rocks.

Vo had arrived at Batcat headquarters the afternoon of the Drop Zone with all the blank identification documents he had taken from Ti's office.

"They let Quand go, as I thought they would," he reported. "I kept away from her, although by radio I talked to Pham. Quand's story held up. She and her brother think they are safe now. Ton knows better. He has already headed north and will keep in touch with us. I told him his most important mission was to get the escape and evasion net set up. Soon many pilots will be down in the north." Vo smiled. "Pham asks for more gold to sell and poppy too."

"Pham and Quand could be real number one black market operators if they lived long enough," Ossidian remarked grimly.

Vo stared at the ground. " A new province political chief is coming down from Hanoi today. Tomorrow they'll surely take Quand again. Maybe she'll hold out a day, perhaps even two days. No more."

"Lieutenant Vo," DePorta said. "We have two A teams coming in at 0200 tomorrow. By 0300 we'll begin briefing. I want you and Ossidian ready to help brief them on your experiences setting up the underground. They in turn will have all the information extracted from Ti at the SFOB to pass back to you. Time will be short. Their guides will start leading them to their operational areas at 0700. I want them on site before Quand talks."

"Yes, sir," Vo replied. "I confess my failure in not killing her before I left but I would have compromised myself. Also, there was Pham. I would have had to kill him too. The risk of compromise was too great."

"You did well, Vo. I'll report your professional intelligence work."

"Thank you, sir."

"The identification documents you got from the political chief's office and his capture have been the two biggest victories of our mission."

The drop had taken much planning. Since the day of Acbat's arrival at the permanent headquarters, the prevailing wind for every hour of the day and night had been studied. Direction and velocity were carefully plotted. At 2:00 in the morning it had been found that the air was invariably still, with the breeze picking up on this high mountain plateau just before sunrise. It would be a two-door jump from 800 feet, and with little or no wind the 24 men and six bundles would land in a tight pattern about 850 yards in length. The open area was 900 yards long, so the wind drift had to be calculated closely.

The operations area had been enlarged, and benches made to seat the two A teams for the briefing. A high bamboo fence, the poles split down the middle and placed gripping each other so not the faintest glimmer of light could get through, had been built around the briefing area.

Thirty minutes before the drop, five of the trained Tai tribesmen, holding flashlights, formed a T at the north end of the field. The plane would fly directly down the leg of the T from north to south and the first man would jump directly on the cross. DePorta stood 50 yards east of the T and precisely lined up on the crossbar. Thus the pilot looking out his left window would easily be able to line up and know when to press the button changing the red light above the door to green for jump.

The positive identification for the plane was time, altitude, and course. If it was not on exactly a 360 degree heading, at 800 feet altitude, and arriving within two minutes of 0200, DePorta would not turn on his flashlight, the signal for the others to light theirs. Sergeant Pierrot and ten tribesmen were stationed in the trees at the south end of the Drop Zone in case any jumpers overshot and landed in them. As much as a one second delay in getting out of the plane could cause the last men in the stick to land in the trees.

The quiet of the night was broken precisely on time by the sound of airplane engines. At 0158 DePorta flashed his light skyward. The five tribesmen followed his example. The large, dark plane loomed against the sky and exactly over DePorta the parachute canopies began to blossom in the air. First came the bundles, then the 24 men.

It had been a precision drop and the last two men out of the plane landed 20 yards short of the trees. Twenty-four disciplined Tais, lined down the field, dashed out as the infiltrators landed, to help carry in parachutes and harnesses, and the packs each man wore hanging below the emergency chute clipped to his chest. Recognition codes were answered with numbers of fingers held up and less than ten minutes after the first man hit the ground the two A teams were grouped around their commanders at the west side of the field. The montagnards carried the six bundles to the operations area as the two A teams followed DePorta. All 24 men were dressed identically in sterile camouflage fatigues.

Luy and some of the women were in the briefing area serving soup, hot rice, and monkey meat. As soon as the two teams were seated, the members of Batcat standing opposite them, DePorta began the briefing.

"We have little time," DePorta began abruptly. "One of our female underground agents may be picked up for interrogation at any time. Alton and Artie will start out at 0700 hours today for their objective areas. We have good guides for you. You will not consult maps or compasses. Ten minutes out of here you would never be able to find your way back. If you are ambushed and you know you can't make it, shoot your guides. Only they could lead the Communists to us."

The grim briefing went on for an hour. Lieutenant Vo was introduced and he, Ossidian, and the intelligence sergeants for Artie and Alton withdrew for a specialized briefing. Other specialists met in separate groups.

"Jesse," Captain Sampson Buckingham said. "S-2 told me to tell you that getting Ti has put this program ahead three or four months."

DePorta nodded. "Let's go over your missions. Vic, you are taking Artie down with the Bru tribe to the south of the GWOA. What did they tell you to do at the final briefing?"

"Train guerrillas," Locke answered, "and set up escape and evasion nets for pilots. The Navy and the Air Force will start hitting targets in this GWOA first and then work up until they start hitting Hanoi."

"It's about time," DePorta said. "What else?"

"We'll work on intelligence and set up ambushes and assassination squads. Ti gave us a list of every political officer both civilian and military. We know their names, where they live, and how to hit them. My main job is to build up a G force and kill as many VC on their way to the south as possible. The FOB figures that if Artie is successful it will take ten men from the Regular Army divisions chasing us for every one guerrilla they can send south. And that ain't economical for them. When I'm organized I'll split the detachment and set up an SFOB with some of my old Meo buddies across the border in Laos."

DePorta nodded. "Buck?"

316

Captain Buckingham approached the map of his area. "Like Vic said, thanks to that fellow Ti, who finally cracked and spilled buckets, we got names and locations of the three political officers we assassinate. Our big job, though, is the industrial plants in the north of the GWOA. My team's strong in demo men, we have four. We've got the lightweight plastic mortars and we'll have that road so lined with electronically detonated mines that patrols won't dare use it for a week."

"What about psychological warfare?" DePorta asked.

"I've got ten balloons. Each one will float a radio transmitting easy-to-decode messages. My radios are set to blow themselves up after six hours of transmissions. In Hanoi's radio-monitoring center it will sound like a hundred different guerrilla groups are taking over in this GWOA. The Vietnamese Air Force will stage flyovers and dummy parachute drops." Buckingham let out a basso laugh. "The Viet Cong will be running every way at once."

"Yes," DePorta said gravely, "and the police will start picking up and jailing civilians all over the GWOA. There'll be a thousand false confessions tortured out of innocent people who will implicate 10,000 more. The way the Army and political police will go after the citizens will stir up plenty of dissension for our psy warriors to work on. But we'll have a hellofa time not getting caught when we form underground organizations and E and E nets."

"The theory is," said Buckingham, "that Hanoi will be so shaken when it sees what we're doing it will start wanting to negotiate. Uncle Ho doesn't want the Chinese to come down to North Vietnam and help him any more than we do. The Viets had the Chinks for two thousand five hundred years and hated every day of it."

DePorta looked at his watch. "Let's get over to intelligence. Lieutenant Vo will manufacture identification documents for you. But don't trust them too long. Vo's little larceny will be discovered sometime. Most of what he got were identification papers for politically stable montagnards. I guess that means yards that turn their poppy over to the government. When they find out that one hundred blank documents are missing they'll be arresting and interrogating half the loyal Communist montagnards in the GWOA. And if I know my Meos and Tais and Tays and Muongs we're going to have a lot of montagnards who suddenly hate Communists."

It took four days before Artie arrived at its operational area and made contact with Manong. Alton radioed into Batcat five days later that it had joined up with Krak. Both teams admired the amount of preparation before their arrival.

The evening of the day Buckingham's team reported reaching its operational area, Muk Thon brought DePorta the most disturbing news yet. The village had been surrounded and searched by a company of soldiers. It was the first time that soldiers had been up into the mountains that high. Although Muk Thon declared not one person in the village had told about the Americans, the soldiers had been suspicious. They had dragged Muk Thon's deputy chief away with them for further questioning.

DePorta called a meeting of Batcat. "We've been lucky so far but now we must be doubly cautious. We may have to run at any time. We have another base secured and everyone should know how to find it in case we get separated during a breakout."

"Rodriguez?" DePorta called.

"Sir."

"Tomorrow I want to inspect this area with you for defenses. If we are attacked we might as well kill as many Viet Cong as we can before we break out."

"Yes, sir. Captain Smith and I have rigged up a lot of good stuff around this B team. We could kill two companies with our mines before we had to start shooting."

Sergeant Everett called out for Lieutenant Vo. Signals were coming in on the frequencies assigned the underground recruits. Vo, Ossidian, and DePorta clustered around the four radio receivers in front of Everett. "Two transmitters are sending simultaneously from Hang Mang," he said.

"One is my new agent," said Vo. "The other is Pham." He listened, frowning deeply and shaking his head. DePorta who had also been listening, sighed and walked away from the commo center.

"What is it, sir?" Ossidian asked.

"Pham said that Quand was released again and is entirely clear. They are no longer suspicious of her, and she and Pham would like to meet with Lieutenant Vo and myself at the farmhouse tomorrow evening. They have important information to pass to us."

Batcat's commanding officer looked to the lowlands in the east. The sun was setting in the mountains behind them. "Vo's agent, who Pham and Quand don't know, was reporting that Quand, Pham, and their mother have been missing several days. You see what's happening?"

Ossidian nodded grimly. "The Commies have them and are trying to bring us in."

Vo joined DePorta and Ossidian. "I transmitted to my new agent, Toc, and told him to call us every morning and evening at 6:00." Seeing the frown come to Ossidian's face, Vo went on quickly, "There is no way they can pick up other agents' signals with Pham's radio. I gave Pham a radio made in Communist Germany. Toc has a Czech-made transmitter operating on a much higher frequency band."

"Is Toc reliable?" Ossidian asked.

"I have faith in him. Like my family, his was Catholic but they had too much property and business to leave. They lost it anyway."

A long series of dots and dashes came from the communications room. DePorta hurried back, standing over Everett as he took the letters down on his decoding pad. The transmission stopped and Everett handed the message to DePorta, who read it quickly. "Well, this is it. The SFOB asks us to pick the date for Operation Falling Rain. It must come before the last day of the month. That gives us fourteen days maximum."

"Batcat is about ready now," Smith said.

DePorta shook his head. "Negative. I was a guerrilla three years in the Philippines. I'll leave the date to Buckingham." DePorta wrote out a message for the commander of Alton and gave it to Everett for transmitting. "It is too soon," he said. "But we will do our best."

Captain Buckingham chose to take every one of the allotted fourteen days. Captain Locke was ready in less time than that. Meanwhile, Batcat had set up a new headquarters location for an emergency. Viet Cong troops from Hang Mang had twice more returned to Muk Thon's village but failed to find any evidence of the guerrillas that had infiltrated from the south.

By monitoring Army channels and through Toc, Lieutenant Vo learned there was much unrest in Hang Mang. The curfew was strictly enforced. Many more soldiers were on the street now and the new chief political officer was questioning citizens day and night.

Batcat trained and rehearsed for its part in Operation Falling Rain. Luy could sense Smith's mounting tension as the days passed. Their sleeping platform was removed from those of the other members of Batcat, and Luy had personally rebuilt it so firmly that they did not need to rely on the gibbons to insure their sound security.

Lying beside him, Luy sensed this was a momentous night. "It is tomorrow?" she asked.

Smith stared up at the thatched roof of the sleeping platform. He was aware of a profound change since he had come here. He was not afraid to die, but now he did not want to die. He said quietly: "We go tomorrow, we hit the next night."

"I will go too."

"No. There will be too much killing. You must stay with Pierre."

"We should go together . . ."

"I cannot let you come, Luy."

". . . then if you die I will bring you back to the village and you will be waiting for me when I die. I could not live if you died and they did not bring you home."

Smith turned on his side and reached for her. "Let's stop all this 'dying' talk. We're here, now, right now, aren't we?"

Luy grasped him hard.

"So let's do something about it."

7.

DePorta glanced at his Czech-manufactured wrist watch uneasily and then locked eyes with Muk Thon. "We are late already, Colonel." DePorta tried to keep the irritation from his voice.

"Then let us go," Muk Thon answered. The Tai chief was dressed for the mission, his pack basket containing an automatic rifle and five hundred rounds of ammunition.

"Colonel, we need you to stay here. If we are killed only you can help the Americans who will take our places to train the Tais to fight the lowland Viet Minh."

"I am the colonel," Muk Thon boomed in French. "I must lead my men." He pulled his pipe from some recess in his black pants and savagely thrust it between his teeth.

"What do you think, sir?" Smith asked DePorta in English. "Maybe we'd better take him along."

"He hasn't trained with the others. He's old. I don't think he'd make it. If he held the others back we'd be in trouble. Besides, I really want him here. When he wants to, he can be a big help in recruiting and training."

Smith shrugged. "If you can make him stay, my beret is off to you, sir."

"There's one thing I haven't tried," DePorta said. He reached into his pocket and pulled out the silver star of a general and pinned it on the front of the black shirt he was wearing.

"I did not tell you, Colonel, but I just received orders making me a general before starting out on this mission."

Muk Thon looked intently at the star. Then he took the pipe out of his mouth, gave a military salute, and said in French, "At your orders, my general."

"Tell me, Colonel," DePorta said, "have I been right in the orders and advice I've given since I came to you?"

"Certainly, General."

"Have I always seen the men are paid on time, that they are properly uniformed and supplied?"

"Yes, General."

"Has your village profited from our stay? Have we given you a better price for your poppy than the Viet Cong?"

"Always, General."

"Was I not right to get my men and those of yours we are training out of your village before the Viet Cong came and searched it?"

"Yes, General."

DePorta paused and went on in softer tones. "We are two experienced military men, are we not, Colonel? We have learned to work together well."

"I am happy to say yes, General."

"Then you will understand if I give you a direct command, Colonel. Your orders are to stay and help guard the headquarters and be prepared to work with the American who takes my place if I do not come back."

Muk Thon stared at DePorta, his eyes dropping to the star.

He nodded slightly. "I must obey the orders of a general. I will stay."

"You are a fine officer, Colonel," DePorta said, clapping the Tai chief on both shoulders with his hands. "We all feel safe going off because you are here."

Muk Thon saluted smartly and DePorta returned it, watching the Tai chief walk back toward the headquarters area.

"Now let's get started," said DePorta.

Following the frequently rehearsed plan, DePorta, Smith, Rodriguez, Pierrot, and Lieutenant Vo left the camp at noon, thirty-six hours before Falling Rain would be activated. Master Sergeant Mattrick was in command of the B team. Sergeant Everett would coordinate all communications and Ossidian would keep a complete intelligence file on all activities of the two A teams and Batcat so that if a new B-team commander and Executive Officer had to be jumped in they could carry on. Sergeant Lin would be able to take care of the medical facilities of the expanding Batcat-Tai community and treat the wounded who made it back from Falling Rain. Sergeant Trung would be the commo man on the operation.

Spaced out over two miles the best Tai warriors led the way down from the mountains toward the lowlands and the targets in and around Hang Mang. Keeping clear of all trails and paths they made their way toward the first objective, the secondary Mission Support Site.

The Tai tribesmen and all the members of Batcat wore the usual montagnard dress. Some were in black pajamas, some in nondescript slacks and short-sleeve shirts; a few wore the traditional loincloth. Every man had on his back a Tai basket in which he carried his weapon, grenades, and food covered over with a Tai blanket.

The Americans were spread out throughout the file, DePorta at the front and Smith in the rear. Though it had been argued among the members of Batcat that it was unwise for both the Commanding Officer and Executive Officer to go out on a mission from which neither stood more than a fifty-fifty chance of returning, both were so qualified for their particular jobs that nobody else could have replaced them.

It was late in the afternoon when Smith became aware that the Tai man behind him was "stealing his ass." He turned to tell the tribesman to keep back six feet and saw it was Luy, striding along, a basket on her shoulders.

"OK, you asked for it," he scolded softly, keeping up the pace. The Tai tribesmen near them were grinning broadly. Smith knew that with Luy watching not one of the Tai men would fail in his assignment. Muk Thon would have kept them in line too.

It was after dark when the point of the long column was challenged by the secondary Mission Support Site security squad and identified itself. Here a small camp within sight of the main north-south road had been prepared so everyone could rest the remainder of the night. Food had been stored and a radio transmitter and receiver already installed. At any time on the march from Batcat Headquarters to this point, the column could have dispersed, shed their burdens if necessary, and made their way one by one to this point, where a second supply of everything except the heavy TNT was stored.

The morning of the day of Falling Rain, Batcat began to fan out. Lieutenant Vo and Major DePorta, now dressed as petty merchants, in slacks and sports shirts, mounted two waiting bicycles, each with a bundle of effects tied over the rear fenders. They carried well-worn plastic briefcases. Soon they reached the main road into Hang Mang and became lost in the heavy traffic.

At noontime a buffalo cart half full of wood came to a halt on the main road, five hundred yards in front of the secondary Mission Support Site. The peasant driving it was having difficulty with his faltering beast. Rodriguez and four of the Tai tribesmen immediately made their way down a path toward the road. They reached the buffalo cart and offered assistance, unobtrusively placing their baskets on top of the load. Soon the water buffalo, shaking his massive horns, started forward. The montagnards followed along.

Brick Smith and Frenchy Pierrot waited until it was dark. At 6:00 they set out. Luy insisted on following her man through it all, and rather than argue fruitlessly he agreed.

Frenchy, medical kit over his shoulder, commanded two platoons of heavily armed Tai tribesmen. Smith's job was to demolish the only bridge over which rail and truck traffic could pass to reach Hang Mang and points south; Frenchy would set up two ambushes on the road north of the bridge. The closest Viet Cong garrison to the bridge was two miles north of it. A battalion was quartered here. As soon as the

323

ambush was sprung, Frenchy would make it back to the operation's rally point in the foothills and set up a medical aid station. A series of such stations led halfway up to the mountain headquarters of Batcat.

Brick Smith, Luy, and their three assault squads of 12 Tai tribesmen each, reached their primary Mission Support Site just before the 10:00 curfew. Two agents of Lieutenant Vo's burgeoning underground had purchased three of the numerous small fishing shacks on the mud flats below the bridge ten days earlier and had been going downriver toward the sampans every day. The bridge was well lit, the electric plant in Hang Mang feeding juice out to this most important structure on a priority basis. The lights of the underpowered town itself gave off at best a brown glow at night.

A locomotive dragged ten to fifteen and sometimes twenty freight cars across the bridge twice a day, Vo's watchers had reported. Smith's objective was to drop the bridge into the river, thus destroying both rail and road communications into Hang Mang and south to the Ho Chi Minh trail over which guerrillas and their supplies moved into South Vietnam.

Luy and Smith, followed by the first Tai assault squad, entered one of the fishing shacks. The second and third squads occupied the other two shacks. His men were ready. When Rodriguez destroyed the electric generator in town, the bridge would be plunged into darkness and they would blow it.

Jesse DePorta was slated for the first Batcat mission of the night: assassinating the new political officer. DePorta and Vo had casually cycled up to the checkpoint outside of town and flashed their identification documents. They were passed on, and proceeded into the middle of a meagre market. Leaving their bicycles in the municipal rack, and taking their packages and briefcases, they walked to the rooms Vo's agents had rented for their primary Mission Support Site. The surveillance of block chiefs was minimal during the day and the two strangers walked into the building and opened the unlocked first-floor room. It was possible to see a corner of the building housing the province political officer and his staff. Vo had learned that the new chief, sent from Hanoi, trusted none of the provincial officials. So suspicious of everyone was he, that he would not even allow anyone else to drive or touch the car he had inherited from Ti.

The great value of assassinating political chiefs, DePorta had stressed, was that you hurt the central government without alienating the population. In Hang Mang the people still knew one another and shared their own regional problems and sense of humor. The outside political chiefs remained outsiders. Even when a local boy had been sent as far as Hanoi for training, as in Ti's case, and then returned to his native province, he could no longer communicate comfortably with his townsfolk. He was a bureaucrat with arbitrary power over them.

While Vo moved about Hang Mang, personally visiting his underground recruits and giving them gold leaf and currency, DePorta remained in their safe house until 9:00 in the evening. One hour before curfew he walked out onto the street. He carried a neat plastic briefcase as he strolled past the corner building of the province political officer. In the yard, beyond a guarded gate, stood the familiar drab little sedan. DePorta's special pass with his picture on it would allow him to visit the province political offices. It was the one issued to the montagnard tribesmen who were loyal Hanoi political appointees. There was no way of telling whether by now the card was compromised. Still, DePorta chose a bold course of action. Just before 10:00, a wide smile on his face, he approached the guard at the gate and presented his identification. The guard looked at it, and up at DePorta, and let him walk through.

DePorta had studied sketches and drawings supplied by Vo of the courtyard of the chief political officer's compound. Outside steps led from the courtyard to a balcony that surrounded the second floor and faced into the center of the compound. The security had been tightened, DePorta noticed, with two khaki-clad guards at each of the staircases leading up to the second-floor balcony. With the mysterious disappearance of Ti, which was probably no longer so mysterious after the interrogation of Quand and Pham, the new political chief trained in Peking and Hanoi, Le Xuan Dung, was understandably security-conscious.

Casually, as he approached the two guards at the center steps that led directly to the political chief's office, DePorta slipped the large official government envelope from his briefcase. It was marked KIN (secret) and was addressed to Le Xuan Dung to be hand delivered and opened personally. The envelope had been one of Vo's masterpieces—the contents one of Rodriguez's.

The charge inside the envelope had been molded into the shape of a sheaf of papers from what the Special Forces men fondly called the "Pride of DuPont"—a plastic explosive, several times as powerful as TNT. It had even been bound into an official government-document binder, fastened together with a red top-secret seal to be broken only by the person to whom the document was addressed. There was always the possibility that one of Dung's aides might open the envelope for him, but nobody else would dare break the seal—which would detonate the charge.

Boldly, DePorta started to mount the steps, but was instantly halted by the guards. Smiling, he showed them the official envelope. Unconvinced, one of the guards escorted DePorta up the stairs to Dung's office.

From this point on, DePorta knew his own chances of coming out alive were slim. But even if he had to detonate the charge himself, he'd get Dung. It wouldn't be necessary to be close to the province political chief with this device: it would kill through the wall of a room. At the door to Dung's outer office the guard politely knocked. The door opened. An Army officer, a major, stared at DePorta and his escort. There was conversation between the guard and the major, who turned to DePorta and asked him to identify himself. DePorta held out the envelope in one hand. The major looked at it suspiciously, saw it was official, and took it brusquely. DePorta took out the document identifying him as an official political representative of the Tai tribe.

The Communist major nodded, and DePorta, with a valid excuse for his accent, explained that he had been in Hanoi at a meeting of montagnard chiefs and had been asked to deliver this envelope personally to Le Xuan Dung.

The major assured DePorta that the envelope would be passed on to Dung and curtly dismissed the man he thought to be a montagnard courier.

"It is most important that the political chief reads the contents tonight," DePorta said before turning away. The major did not answer.

DePort outstrode the guard to the staircase and was at the

bottom and heading out the gate before his escort had resumed his post at the bottom of the steps. DePorta's only job now was to get himself back to Batcat headquarters. It was close to the curfew hour but his pass had held up. He mounted his bicycle and had just started peddling out of Hang Mang when the tremendous blast knocked him off his bicycle. The concussion was stunning. In a triumphant daze he slowly picked himself up from the street. Looking back, he saw a thick cloud of smoke and debris sifting down from the dark sky. Other people were now trying to stand, staring about them in shock.

DePorta picked up his bicycle and, staying in the shadows of the barely lighted street, unobtrusively worked his way toward the outskirts of the city.

Rodriguez, hidden in the storage shack across from the electric plant, smiled grimly. The shattering explosion from the center of town signaled the unmistakable success of his handiwork. Peering out over the rutted street and railroad tracks to the most important source of power in the GWOA, Rodriguez watched the confusion within the heavily guarded plant. The armed guards at the gate looked nervously about. A personnel carrier, used by the guards, stool outside the barracks. Moments after the blast the guards, led by a sergeant and an officer, tumbled out of their quarters. Rodriguez had added enough thermite to his plastic explosive to start intense fires burning throughout the compound. The center of Hang Mang was streaking flames in all directions and the smell of smoke and explosive permeated the air.

Rodriguez watched the guards pile haphazardly into the truck. The officer screamed orders to the two guards on the gate. The guards swung the gate inward and the personnel carrier raced toward it. Instantly, Rodriguez and his little squad went into action. As the troop-filled vehicle tore out of the gate and turned right into the rutted street, four hand grenades arched toward it. They burst almost simultaneously in a violent, ripping explosion. The vehicle, suddenly awash in shredded bodies, rocked wildly and fell back on its torn-up wheels.

Before the two gate guards could get their rifles off their shoulders they were cut down by one of the Tais with a Schmeisser submachine gun, and Rodriguez and his men rushed inside the electric plant. Two of the Tais took the guards' positions, holding levelled submachine guns, their belts hanging with grenades whose pins had been straightened for instant pulling.

More guards fell out of the barracks to see what was happening and were instantly ripped apart with submachine-gun rounds. A Tai tribesman ran to the barracks, pulled two grenades and tossed them into the building. Moments later the guardhouse erupted. Rodriguez made for the large generators in the main plant, his two Tais beside him. They burst into the huge generator room. They saw no one. Rodriguez went to work. Packing charges around the shafts of motors and generators, and inside the generators against the electric wind-ings, he tied the explosive circuit together with detonating cord. In five minutes Rodriguez had all three generators ready to blow. Unreeling det cord as he went, he ran from the generator barn. He set a minute-delay time fuse into the explosive cord and then sprinted for the gate.

The Tais followed Rodriguez as he crossed the road and railroad tracks and fell into the ditch on the other side. Moments later the deafening explosion shook the plant, the concussion waves rocking the five men in the ditch, knocking their wind out.

The town of Hang Mang went black. Not an electric light burned in the province. It would be weeks before standby power could be generated, and a year before the minimal power supplied by the plant could be restored. The five saboteurs shoved fresh magazines into their submachine guns and headed for the rally point.

Brick Smith, Luy, and a 12-man assault squad were crowded into one of three shacks that made up their primary Mission Support Site. The other two squads had a shack each. It was almost 10:00. Although this was the first time Smith had seen the bridge, every one of his men had walked across it and studied it during the past month. All knew every move they would make during the operation and had rehearsed it on mock-ups of the bridge and terrain over and over again. The brightly illuminated structure with its six guards—two at each end and two in the middle—must have seemed to the company in charge of its security an absurdly safe installation.

The guard company barracks was situated only fifty yards

from the north end of the bridge. It always housed a complement of 40 soldiers and a lieutenant. To insure maximum alertness the guards on the bridge were relieved every four hours.

Smith's biggest worry was a successful demolition job. It was an old-style steel and concrete T-beam bridge supported in the middle of the river by a heavy concrete piling. The only way to blow it quickly and produce maximum damage was by use of pressure charges. A line of TNT blocks across the center width of the two spans, which reached from the piling to the two banks, would cut and tilt them into the river. To insure this maximum damage Smith had planned to stretch a third line of TNT blocks across the middle of the bridge above the piling. This would weaken the span at the center so that when the bridge was cut the broken spans would tear off from the pilings and slide into the river. Thus the heavy coastal boat traffic dependent on the river to get to the sea would also be blocked. With the lack of heavy construction facilities the river, as well as the main route south, would be blocked indefinitely and it would take months to even get a road-traffic bridge rebuilt.

Smith and Rodriguez had discussed the plan for over a month and Rodriguez had once risked going down and walking across the bridge. The use of pressure charges was the quickest way they could figure out to do the job. But the job would require more than six hundred pounds of TNT, a prohibitive load for guerrillas to carry in. Therefore tamping was a necessity. Enough tamping piled on top of and around TNT directs and concentrates the full explosive force of the charge straight down. None of the destructive force is dissipated into the air in concussion or shock waves. With tamping the amount of TNT required to cut the reinforced concrete of the bridge into Hang Mang would be reduced by 50 per cent. But how could they prepare and carry sandbags to the bridge?

Smith had quickly come up with the answer. Now, as he grimly thought over what he had to do, the sudden dull explosion in the distance roused him. Just a few more moments. His tribesmen were grinning in anticipation. Smith got to his feet. Four of his men, carrying heavy tripod-mounted German Solothurn MG-34 machine guns with maximum range of two thousand yards, were ready to pick up their

329

thirty-five pounds of weapons and ammunition and rush for their positions. Another four men in the next fishing shack, armed with Russian 7.62 RPD heavy machine guns, were also ready. These guns had been transported part by part to the fishing shacks and silently reassembled in the dark. The assault force with Schmeissers, Russian AK's, Swedish K's and other foreign makes of submachine guns were also set to go. Smith, his pack heavy with explosives, and six of his men similarly burdened were ready to rush onto the bridge as soon as it was clear. He had been practicing for three weeks and had cut down the time from twenty-nine minutes on his first attempt on the mock-up to the required eleven minutes.

They waited tensely, minute by minute. Suddenly all the lights on the bridge went out and moments later another detonation vibrated in the air.

The eight heavy-machine-gun crews charged into the darkness for their positions. There was just enough light coming from the starlit sky to make out the single-story guard company headquarters. As Smith and his explosive carriers ran out of the shack, the assault force was already rushing the bridge. Submachine-gun fire crackled as the trained Tai tribesmen gained the bridge and began gunning down the guards. The guards at the far end of the bridge began firing back and a brief sharp firefight ensued. One montagnard twisted to the ground, dropping his weapon.

Then the deep-throated roaring of eight heavy machine guns blasted the night. The guards running from their barracks were instantly cut down and the machine gunners continued to pour their heavy fire through the flimsy barracks walls. With the last of the bridge guards disposed of, Smith began setting out his explosive squares, lacing detonation cord through them and binding them tightly together. First a solid line of TNT was placed across the southernmost span. Then the tribesmen dragged the bodies of the six guards to it and tamped them over the TNT. Meanwhile the heavy-machine-gun firing had ceased and only an occasional pistol or rifle shot marred the stillness of the night.

As Smith exactingly placed his charges along the center of the bridge, his Tais came up behind him, dragging bloody, tattered bodies and laying them across the explosive blocks. Soon the first line of explosive blocks was buried under a heavy heap of corpses. As Smith moved back to place the final line of charges, the center charges were quickly tamped with the bodies of the slaughtered guard company.

Massive firing suddenly broke out north of the bridge, about a mile up the road. Unruffled, Smith worked methodically. Finally the last of the charges was set. He stretched the detonating cord along the road to the north for fifty yards until he was opposite the bullet-frayed guard barracks.

The Tais continued to pile the torn corpses on the final line of explosives. When the tribesmen ran out of dead guards Smith made a last hurried inspection of the tamped charges. There were one hundred and ten pounds of TNT blocks across each of the three widths of the bridge that had to be cut, or a total of three hundred and thirty pounds in all. A twisted grin spread across his face as he estimated there must be more than one thousand pounds of bodies for each hundred pounds of TNT. A comfortable margin. The best tamped demolition job he'd ever performed.

The firing to the north was still resounding through the night, illumination flares lighting up the sky. Smith yelled an order to his tribesmen and instantly they left the bridge, carrying their dead comrade and helping two tribesmen who had been wounded.

Frenchy and his ambush should have pulled back already, Smith thought worriedly as the firing up the road continued. At least a full battalion was available to move down the road and Frenchy's two platoons would be no match for them.

Luy was close to Smith as he spliced a two-minute time fuse into the end of the det cord. He pulled the pin, placed an arm around Luy, and hurried her away.

The montagnards led the way along the path leading westwards from the road. They were heading straight for the mountains. Smith counted the seconds as they trotted, and turned in time to witness the flash of the tremendous explosion he had set.

While the concussion of three hundred and thirty pounds of TNT detonating should have been enough to blow them all off their feet, the Communist guard company had done their final job well. Only a dull shock wave could be felt through the ground. Smith was confident that the tremendous shattering power of the TNT had been driven through the entire bridge.

"Hey, Luy, you want to go back and see how we did?"

She shook her head vehemently, a shocked look on her face.

As the firefight to the north waned, Smith's expression became set.

"OK, keep moving fast," he ordered, and the Tai tribesmen resumed pushing for the hills.

By the luminous dial of Smith's wrist watch it was thirty minutes after midnight when the point man of the first squad was challenged and identified himself. They filed into the rally point and immediately saw that Frenchy's ambush platoon had not been as lucky as they. By flashlight Frenchy was working on gunshot wounds. Smith saw several still bodies laid out and other men, on litters, lying quietly.

Frenchy looked up from his work. "Did the bridge go OK, sir?"

"Sounded that way to me. Thanks for the time—we needed it."

"My two platoons hit a reinforced company. They did a hellofa job. We must have killed 20 enemy on our mines alone. Pinned them down and shot the shit out of them. Grenades—the works. My problem was to get the Tais out of there while we still had the advantage. They wanted to go in for an all-out massacre."

"How many casualties did you take?"

"We only lost three dead. A couple more may die, I'm afraid. I've got seven wounded. Those Commies were really hitting us. They must have something like our M-79, 'cause we were getting damned accurate incoming grenades."

"See anything of the others?"

Frenchy shook his head. "Sergeant Trung here has been getting a hellofa lot of interesting radio traffic."

Smith hunted up Trung. The Vietnamese communications man was ecstatic.

"Dai-uy! All over, they don't know what's hitting them. Only battery sets working now because no electricity. I pick up many calls. What you Americans say? The Communists all fuck up!"

While Trung was monitoring his radio set he kept an eye on the electronic device in front of him whose green scope showed an unbroken white line across the middle of it. Frenchy frequently looked up from his work to stare at the glowing tube. Smith never took his eyes from it.

Every few moments Trung threw a switch on the box that caused the line to dance and then settle back to a constant horizontal. Smith and his three squads had been at the rally point for half an hour when, at one of Trung's switchovers, the white line became an oscillating vertical series of peaks and valleys.

"Dai-uy!" Trung exclaimed. "Station two!"

Frenchy and Smith stared at the scope. "Lots of metal," Smith commented.

"Looks like a platoon or larger, sir," said Frenchy. "Coming through the north pass we used two hours ago to get here."

"They know we're up here by now."

They studied the glowing pattern in the dark. "I'd say they're right in the killing zone now, sir," the medic said.

"Let 'em have it, Trung!"

Trung pressed a button on the side of the set. Instantly a tearing explosion ripped through the air two miles to the northeast. Frenchy, Smith, and Trung stared at the scope. Even peaks and valleys appeared.

"All that metal is lying pretty quiet now, sir," said Frenchy.

"Should be. Two and a half feet of solid shrapnel from two feet to four and a half feet above the ground for a distance of one hundred meters. That would cut down anything."

A few pips moved in the otherwise stable pattern. "Looks like a few of them might be alive to wonder what happened," said Frenchy. "Trung, switch back to the main route."

Trung toggled the switch and the unbroken white line again cut across the green glow of the face of the tube.

It was another hour before Rodriguez and his montagnards arrived at the rally point from the southeast. The team now lacked only DePorta and Vo.

"At least we know Major DePorta's mission was a success," said Rodriguez. Everyone was silent. The orders were to pull out of the rally point by 4:00 A.M. in order to have two full hours of darkness to reach the mountainous jungle of Tai territory.

"Dai-uy! Dai-uy!"

Smith turned to see the green glow almost obscured by the vertically oscillating white line. "Christ! Armor!"

Rodriguez chuckled. "We got ten three-and-a-half-inch

armor-piercing rockets ready to slice up the road." The demolition sergeant studied the active green and white tube. He looked at the second hand of his watch and back to the tube. "Let's give them about two minutes and then we'll let go. Between the rockets and our high-power claymore mines we ought to knock off half the column."

The guerrilla warfare experts stared from the scope to their watches and back. At the end of two minutes, with the white agitations still filling the screen, Rodriguez said, "What do you think, sir?"

"Hit!" Smith rasped.

Trung touched the button. The night opened up with white flame to the north. Sharp explosions pierced the silence. The rumbling detonations continued and the glow from the electronically ambushed column became more brilliant as gas tanks and ammunition exploded. Batcat's men at the Rally Point stared at the brightly lit sky to the north, shaking their heads in awe. This was the biggest ambush of its kind ever tried. Its success looked to be phenomenal.

"Madre Dios!" Rodriguez gasped.

After a few moments they looked back at the scope. It glowed a dull green with no white line at all. "We blew up our detector with the column," Smith said.

They were still staring at the glow in the sky when Major DePorta and Lieutenant Vo finally arrived. They had found it wise after their rendezvous to leave their bicycles and walk cross-country.

DePorta allowed a few moments for boisterous greetings. Then, in commanding tones, he said, "OK, no critiques now. Let's get back to headquarters. We've got less than two hours before daylight. And we don't want to be anywhere around when the Viet Cong come out of shock."

The Tai tribesmen took turns carrying their dead and wounded as they trudged back into the hills, intoxicated with their victory. The Americans constantly had to quiet them down.

By daylight they were in dense mountainous jungle. As Luy and Brick walked together up to Batcat's headquarters the Tai girl occasionally smiled happily at him, and clutched his hand.

Just at dusk the guerrilla party reached the outer defenses and were escorted back to the camp.

DePorta, Smith, Rodriguez, and Vo headed for Sergeant

Everett's radio center. Pierrot remained with the wounded. Ossidian and the assistant medic, Sergeant Lin, were standing by the radios waiting for them.

"How are the results coming in?" Smith asked.

"Just monitored a broadcast from Hanoi, sir," Everett replied. "Lin says they're accusing the United States and South Vietnam of bombing Hang Mang and the industrial complex."

"Have you heard from Alton or Artie?" DePorta asked.

"Captain Buckingham reports they carried out all their missions but lost one American demo sergeant killed in action," Everett answered. "Captain Locke carried out all his assignments. Four assassinations successful. Considerable destruction of Viet Cong equipment. Locke estimates 30 enemy KIA in ambushes they set. Not bad, sir!"

"Hanoi is paralyzed with fear," Lin went on.

"Any news from Hang Mang?"

"Toc says we were successful, sir," Lin replied. "Four people were killed with the political chief and the building is destroyed. There is no electricity and no communications. The police and Army have been arresting everyone on the streets, even dragging them from their houses."

"Anything on the bridge?" Smith asked.

"Toc heard rumors that it was destroyed. There are also rumors that the bridge guard company deserted to a man."

"Well," DePorta said to the men of Batcat, "now we are like in a submarine. We have shot our torpedoes and we go to the bottom and hide quietly. We will wait at least a month before thinking about another operation. Everybody just rest and stay hidden. We will see much enemy air surveillance. Everett and Trung will monitor all radio stations."

DePorta clasped and unclasped his hands. "We have now given the Communists just a little preview of what they're in for. If they want to keep a war going we will give them one right where they live."

DePorta broke his exuberance with a cautioning frown. "Our first victory was not costly. Do not expect us to be so lucky again. But we needed the victory. It gives us strength for recruiting new guerrillas, new underground, and new auxiliaries.

"Hanoi is now warned. Careful as we've been, we must be doubly careful." The small, brown-skinned commander pursed

335

his lips. "I hope no man here forgets that he volunteered for a mission which still he may not live through.

"Now we must keep pressure on the Communists. Next thing they know there'll be A teams around Hanoi and Uncle Ho will be asking for a new peace conference. Only we'll be talking from strength.

"It's a new kind of war we fight today, yes? No such thing as win or lose. Just which side has the muscle to make the other side agree when the bargaining starts."

DePorta winked at Smith. "What are you waiting for? Get onto that sleeping platform while you have a chance. Before you know it we'll be on the move."

"NEVER GIVE UP"

The green berets—the Captain Kornies, the Major DePortas, the Sergeant Hankses, the Captain Lockes, the Bernie Arklins, yes, and the Sergeant Ossidians—are serving the cause of freedom around the world.

Green berets are currently operating in France, Germany, and other European countries. Special Forces men can be found, if you know where to look for them, in the Congo and Ethiopia. They are active in Iran, winning the Kurd tribesmen from Communism. In Asia, besides Vietnam, Special Forces men are in Korea, Formosa, Thailand, and Malaya on more or less overt missions. Their covert operations in Asia are even more widespread. In many Latin American countries the green berets are performing important missions, both in the civic action and combat training fields.

Wherever they are, Special Forces men have the rare ability to adapt quickly to existing conditions. As such, they can be considered a potent new weapon against the Communist "war of liberation"—a new type of warfare. Foremost in the Special Forces' code is "never give up," and never has that been more important to remember than now. For the sad truth is that many influential Army generals would be far from unhappy to see the unconventional, self-confident wearers of the jaunty green beret absorbed into standard units—the fate of an elite predecessor, the Rangers.

But strong support of Special Forces came with the national recognition it received when President Lyndon B. Johnson awarded the Congressional Medal of Honor to Special Forces

Captain Roger Hugh Donlon for extraordinary heroism in South Vietnam.

There is far more to be said about Special Forces than can be packed into any one book. It may interest readers of these stories of the green berets to know that many of the problems described here are already being resolved. No longer, for instance, do planes on orders from Vietnamese high command indiscriminately loose unexpended ordnance on montagnard villages not under government control. An American Special Forces major, a B-team commander, put his career on the line to stop this inhuman harassment of the simple mountain people caught in the squeeze between Viet Cong terrorism and traditional Vietnamese hatred.

An attempt is being made by the Vietnamese government to train montagnard leaders and commission them in the Army of the Republic of Vietnam so they can lead their own people against the Viet Cong terrorists. The Luc-Luong Dac-Biet is steadily improving the quality of its officers, which makes their American counterparts' advice more effective in fighting the Viet Cong.

As was the case with Mr. Pomfret, the proudest possession I own is the green beret given to me by an A team in a heavy combat zone. The detachment was commanded by Captain Hugh Fisher and its camp stood about five miles west of Tay Ninh City. The dread Black Virgin Mountain, headquarters of the Viet Cong in that part of Vietnam, loomed to the north of the camp. I spent ten days with Captain Fisher and his men sweating out Viet Cong attacks, setting out ambushes, learning much about intelligence work from Sergeant First Class Tucci, and watching Sergeant First Class Baer take care of critically wounded civilians when a hamlet was overrun by the Viet Cong near us. I celebrated the victory when a Luc-Luong Dac-Biet officer came through in the clutch and charged an ambush.

Before I left Tay Ninh, Lieutenant (now Captain) Robert Blair, the Executive Officer, and Master Sergeant "Jo" Johanssen (last heard from in Thailand on the Red China border) canvassed the team to find out who had an extra green beret. Finally, red-headed Staff Sergeant Thurmond Ramsey produced one. At a ceremony solemnized with Jim Beam bourbon the beret, which still has Ramsey's name tag sewed into it, was given me by the entire team.

As this goes to press the intensity of the war in Vietnam has been stepped up and more Americans are being killed and wounded every day. What the outcome in Vietnam will be is anybody's guess, but whatever happens, Special Forces men will continue to fight Communism and make friends for America in the underdeveloped nations that are the targets of Communist expansion.

ABOUT THE AUTHOR

For two years Robin Moore lived with the U.S. Army Special Forces at Fort Bragg, North Carolina, and in South Vietnam before completing his novel THE GREEN BERETS. He co-composed the famous "Ballad of the Green Berets" with Sgt. Barry Sadler. Mr. Moore fought for the survival of the elite unit, when conventional Pentagon brass attempted to eliminate the Green Berets from the U.S. Army. Every year he participates in Green Beret training missions. Mr. Moore, who is also the author of THE FRENCH CONNECTION, is currently living in Connecticut.